To my wife, **Betty,** and my children, **William,**
    Lori, and **Scott,** whose love,
        encouragement, advice, and support
        have given me the continued inner strength
        required to complete my second book.

William C. Wester, II

Contributors

Charles P. Colosimo, Ph.D.
Clinical and Health Psychologist
Affiliated Psychological Service
Dayton, Ohio

Ann M. Damsbo, Ph.D.
Private Practice
Consultant to FBI, ATF, and NIS
Escondido, California
Naval Hospital, San Diego

Gary R. Elkins, Ph.D.
Psychologist, Department of
Psychiatry
Scott and White Clinic
Assistant Professor of Psychiatry
and Behavioral Sciences
Texas A & M University College
of Medicine
Temple, Texas

Thomas L. Feher, M.D.
Medical Director, Pain Control
Center
Providence Hospital
Everett, Washington

Richard B. Garver, Ed.D., ABPH
Clinical Professor of Psychiatry
University of Texas Health Science
Center
San Antonio, Texas
Consultant Hypnotherapy Clinic,
Department of Mental Health,
Wilford Hall
USAF Medical Center
Consultant to FBI
Private Practice

Harold P. Golan, D.M.D.
Tufts University School of Dental
Medicine
Boston City Hospital
Boston, Massachusetts
Past President, American Society
of Clinical Hypnosis

D. Corydon Hammond, Ph.D.
Associate Professor and
Co-Director,
Sex and Marital Therapy Clinic
University of Utah School of
Medicine
Salt Lake City, Utah

Marlene E. Hunter, M.D., CFPC(C)
Assistant Clinical Professor
University of British Columbia,
Department of Family Practice
West Vancouver, British Columbia
Past President, Canadian Society of
Clinical Hypnosis (B.C. Division)

Carolyn Kowatsch, Ph.D.
Vice President
Behavioral Science Center, Inc.
Private Practice
Cincinnati, Ohio

Alexander A. Levitan,
M.D., M.P.H.
Clinical Associate Professor
University of Minnesota
Minneapolis, Minnesota

Herbert Mann, M.D.
Private Practice
Psychosomatic Medicine and
Hypnotherapy
San Jose, California
Past President, American Society of
Clinical Hypnosis

Charles B. Mutter, M.D., ABMH
Clinical Assistant Professor of
Psychiatry and Family Medicine
University of Miami School of
Medicine
Assistant Professor
Southeastern College of
Osteopathic Medicine
Private Practice in Psychiatry
Miami, Florida
President-Elect, American Society
of Clinical Hypnosis

Karen Olness, M.D.
University of Minnesota
Department of Pediatrics
Department of Family Practice and
Community Medicine
Minneapolis, Minnesota
Past President, American Society of
Clinical Hypnosis

Victor Rausch, D.D.S.
Private Practice
Waterloo, Ontario

William Russ, Ed.D.
Associate Director, Psychological
Services
Cincinnati Public Schools
Private Practice
Cincinnati, Ohio

Shirley Sanders, Ph.D., ABPH
Private Practice
Clinical Psychology Services
Chapel Hill, North Carolina
Past President, American Society
of Clinical Hypnosis

Dennis E. Sies, J.D., Ph.D.
Admitted to the Ohio Bar
Assistant Professor of Political
Science
Northern Kentucky University
Highland Heights, Kentucky.

Aruna Thakur, M.B., F.R.C.P.(C)
Clinical Assistant Professor
Department of Psychiatry,
University of Saskatchewan
Private Practice
Saskatoon, Saskatchewan

Kripa S. Thakur, M.B., F.R.C.P.(C)
Clinical Assistant Professor
Department of Psychiatry,
University of Saskatchewan
Private Practice
Saskatoon, Saskatchewan

Moshe S. Torem, M.D.
Chairman, Department of
Psychiatry and Behavioral Sciences
Akron General Medical Center
Professor of Psychiatry
North Eastern Ohio University
College of Medicine
Akron, Ohio

William C. Wester, II,
Ed.D., ABPH
President
Behavioral Science Center, Inc.
Clinical Professor, Wright State
University School of Professional
Psychology
Consultant to FBI and ATF
Private Practice
Cincinnati, Ohio

J. Adrian Williams, Ph.D.
Psychotherapeutic Systems
Institute, LTD.
Private Practice
Charleston, Illinois

David N. Zahm, Ph.D.
Community Mental Health Center,
Inc.
Lawrenceburg, Indiana

Foreword

THIS is as thorough a tome as the first volume edited by Drs. Wester and Smith and published by Lippincott in 1984, already in its second printing. Between the two volumes, some 50 experts in the field of clinical hypnosis, including seven past presidents of the American Society of Clinical Hypnosis, are gathered in a unique written symposium. The second volume comprises rather new areas, such as Tourette syndrome, and up-to-date information in other areas discussed earlier in hypnosis publications. Expertly guided by the editor, the authors present the latest findings in a consistent and clear chapter outline, making it easy for the busy practitioner to find what they are interested in.

Even though the five chapters of Unit One give us a "general introduction to hypnosis," this is not an introductory text. Unit Two, "General applications," is already highly specialized and the last nine chapters comprising Unit Three deal with particularly difficult areas, providing a highly practical encyclopedic treatise in each chapter.

Throughout the book the refreshing trend of modern clinical hypnosis is evident. This is the moving away from rigid techniques, inductions, scores and rituals, and into the hypnotic methods which can be called *new* hypnosis. Naturalistic approaches, permissive maneuvers, open-ended techniques, more attention to the clinical *process* and less emphasis on laboratory methods are all part of it. The new hypnosis makes a special effort at utilizing whatever patients offer, consciously or not, verbally or somatically, in order to help them move from problem or symptom to solution or cure. A sense of genuine respect for the individual appears nowadays, as the 24 chapters show. The clinician is not the all-knowing and powerful authority, as in traditional hypnosis, but rather a clinical researcher looking for what is present in the hypnotic interaction in order to use it for the patient's benefit.

Out of the 24 chapters a human technology emerges: the method by which the powerful tool for change called hypnosis becomes effective *can* be learned. There are definite patterns in this human technology.

This human technology, in my view, employs five basic or master techniques which appear in different forms for the treatment of different conditions but are essentially and consistently uniform. They are genuine hypnotic techniques, if by technique we understand a "complex move, prescription or suggestion made by the therapist in order to convert ideas into practical use," as Sherman and Fredman (1986) explain. Or again, "carefully designed plans of action founded on theory and observation of behavior" (Sherman, Fredman, 1986) leading to improvement, better functioning and greater sense of freedom and self-control on the part of the patient. "But they are also *master* techniques in that they have been found useful with a wide variety of difficult situations," as de Shazer (1985) puts it in his search for therapeutic interventions to get to the heart of change and optimal functioning.

The first of these master techniques is a form of *activation of personality parts* by which patients are put in touch with more positive, healthier and stronger aspects of themselves than those on which their symptoms or problems make them focus and are helped, by this contrast, to perceive the personality "part" tied up to the problem differently. Very close to the ego state therapy of the Watkins (1979), this activation of personality parts is adapted effectively for many conditions.

The second master technique is the concern with *goal attainment:* index what patients believe they can accomplish or become, keep that goal clearly in their mind's eye and their energy will not be wasted on "the problem." The goal becomes so attractive that patients cannot not strive towards it.

But to make the goal more attainable there is another master technique used in many different ways. This is *mental* rehearsal or a getting used to "the process" of change, becoming familiar with new perceptions, reactions and conduct conducive to the goal to be attained. By mentally practicing the steps leading to the goal the future becomes the present.

The fourth master technique is a positive outlook on one's world. This is what family therapists call *reframing:* the bottle is half empty or half full. Though both statements are true, probably one has greater energizing power than the other depending on the situation. This hypnotic technique appears in many ways and forms, indicating that it is applicable to innumerable human situations since perception is essential to the manner in which we construct our reality.

The final master technique is a way of tapping patients' inner resources on the precedent of true *past accomplishments,* even though these successes might have been in areas unrelated to the current problem. It is a method of "potentiating," as Rossi (1980) calls it, inner strengths, personal experience, effective beliefs, acquired knowledge and life wisdom in order to apply them to the solution of the present difficulty.

At the time when clinical hypnosis is leaving behind what is purely experimental and developing unique approaches concerned with the individual rather than with averages and uncontaminated variables, this book is a serious example of the new hypnosis, unenmeshed from experimental elements. It shows clinical hypnosis as scientific in its own right, independently of experimental hypnosis.

In an era of superspecialization this volume offers the invaluable service of not letting us forget the larger field in which hypnosis works.

It is my privilege to present this excellent book to the professional reader. Together with the first volume, it will become one of the important modern sources of information for all clinicians using hypnosis in their professional work and a treasured addition to university, clinics and hospital libraries.

Daniel L. Araoz, Ed.D., ABPP, ABPH
Professor, Long Island University

References

de Shazer S: Keys To Solution in Brief Therapy. New York, W. W. Norton and Co., 1985

Rossi EL: The Collected Papers of M. H. Erickson (4 volumes). New York, Irvington Press, 1980

Sherman R, Fredman N: Handbook of Structured Techniques in Marriage and Family Therapy. New York, Brunner/Mazel, 1986

Watkins J, Watkins H: The theory and practice of ego-state therapy. Grayson H (ed): Short-Term Approaches to Psychotherapy. New York, National Institute for the Psychotherapies and Human Sciences Press, 1979

PREFACE

CLINICAL Hypnosis: A Case Management Approach has been written as a comparison volume to *Clinical Hypnosis: A Multidisciplinary Approach* (Lippincott, 1984). At the first American Society of Clinical Hypnosis Annual Meeting following the publication of *Clinical Hypnosis: A Multidisciplinary Approach,* a good friend and colleague (Dr. Kripa Thakur) suggested that I needed to assemble a second book with topics not covered in the first book, with a complimentary group of authors in the area of clinical hypnosis, and with an emphasis on case management. I accepted Dr. Thakur's suggestion and began work immediately.

Once again, I reached out to my many colleagues who had not written a chapter for the first book. The response and acceptance were excellent. The contributors to *Clinical Hypnosis: A Case Management Approach* include some of the major experts in the area of clinical hypnosis with several Past Presidents of the American Society of Clinical Hypnosis.

Each contributor was provided with a chapter guideline. I asked for six segments including:

1. **Foundations**
   A review of the experimental and clinical literature which serve as a foundation for the practice of hypnosis in the discussed area.

2. **Assessment**
   A discussion of the means of assessing the patient for hypnosis in the area discussed.

3. **Intervention Process**
   A description of the specific treatment plan for the patient in terms of overall case management. A description of the methods used to bring about trance, and of the subsequent interventions in the area, i.e. suggestions, deepening techniques, and the manner in which the hypnosis is used to carry out the particular procedure.

4. **Assessment of Effectiveness**
   A discussion of the means of determining effectiveness of your system of assessment and intervention.

5. **Future Trends**
   A discussion of the future developments of hypnosis in your area.

6. **Excerpt of Session**
   Narrative with commentary.

As will be seen in the Table of Contents, most of the chapters follow this pattern. Because of the fact that this format did not lend itself to all topic areas those contributors used their own judgment as to format when writing their chapters. The two books together include more than fifty different experts in the field of clinical hypnosis.

It is hoped that the reader will find this volume as beneficial as the first. My personal thanks goes out to the contributors who have made this laborious job a most enjoyable experience.

William C. Wester, II, Ed.D.

Acknowledgements

I have many people to thank for their efforts in helping this work become possible. Certainly, my wife and family deserve special thanks for their patience and endurance, frustrations, and discouragements, when I found myself questioning my need to publish a companion volume to my first hypnosis book. I owe a sincere thanks to my Manuscript Editor, Patricia T. Overbeck, Ph.D.; my typist, Norma Malecki, and my proof reader Kathy Kessler. The Office Manager of BSC, Inc. Publications, Deane Zurenko, deserves credit for coordination of activities necessary for the publication of this work.

William C. Wester, II, Ed.D.

Contents

19 Hypnosis in Assertiveness and Social Skills Training
CAROLYN KOWATSCH, Ph.D.

20 Hypnosis in the Treatment of Depression
MOSHE S. TOREM, M.D.

21 Hypnosis in Sexual Dysfunction
HERBERT MANN, M.D.

UNIT ONE
INTRODUCTION TO HYPNOSIS

1 A BRIEF HISTORY OF HYPNOSIS

WILLIAM C. WESTER, II, Ed.D.

Hypnosis under various names has been used for as long as records have been kept. Suggestive therapy is probably the oldest of the therapeutic methods (Wester, 1982). Gravitz (1984) describes the fact that temples were founded in ancient Egypt some 4000 years ago and in ancient Greece and Rome about 2000 years ago. Individuals would come to the "sleep temples" for relaxation and forms of healing.

For a brief overview of the history of hypnosis, a chronological approach will be used to highlight major events and influential historical people.

Early History—The Influence of Magnets and Stars

The early history of hypnosis was strongly influenced by belief in the stars, magnetic fields and exorcism. A Swiss physician, Paracelsus (1493-1541), believed that the stars influence human behavior. Paracelsus felt that the influence of the stars came from their magnetic nature and that magnets had an influence on the human body (Udolf, 1981).

Gravitz (1984) describes the work of Robert Fudd (1574-1637) and Johann Baptist Van Helmont (1577-1644). These two men believed that individuals possessed a magnetic force and that when two people met a magnetic field would develop. Magnets could therefore be used to effect cures.

One of the more colorful early figures was Valentine Greatrakes (1629-1683), who became known as a healer because he treated patients by simply stroking them (Gravitz, 1984). Greatrakes was noted for his successes and became known as the great Irish Stroker. This title was not unusual because for many centuries kings and princes were said to have the power of healing through the "Royal Touch" (Kroger, 1977).

The influence of magnets continued. Kroger (1977) reports that Father Maximilian Hell (1720-1792), a Viennese Jesuit, became famous for his magnetic cures which were obtained by applying steel plates to the naked body.

About the same time, a Catholic priest, Johann Gassner (1727-1779), believed that many diseases were caused by evil spritis and could be exorcised by prayer (Kroger, 1977). We continue today to see the power of suggestion and prayer in a variety of healing services.

Mesmerism

The 18th century Austrian physician, Franz Anton Mesmer (1734-1815), had a significant impact on the history of hypnosis. Gravitz (1984) describes Mesmer as being universally considered the "father" of modern hypnosis. Mesmer believed that the body responded to various gravitational forces which he termed "animal magnetism." He believed that rearrangements of these magnetic forces would restore a person to good health. Mesmer's medical practice flourished until two royal commissions mandated that the practice of mesmerism be considered unscientific charlatanism.

Hypnosis and Sleep

Marquis de Puysegur (1751-1828) was the first to suggest a similarity between sleep and hypnosis. He also felt that hypnosis was associated with clairvoyance (Crasilneck, 1985).

"Hypnosis"

The term "hypnosis," first used in 1841 by an English physician, James Braid (1785-1860), was derived from the Greek *hypnos* meaning sleep. Braid rejected the magnetic theories and placed emphasis on the importance of suggestion as the prime treatment modality.

Crasilneck (1984) describes John Elliotson (1781-1868) as an English surgeon who conducted experiments using mesmerism and who accepted Mesmer's theories of a physical force that could be transmitted from the living operator or from objects previously charged. Elliotson also published the *Zoist*, a journal dealing with cerebral physiology and mesmerism. The first copy of the journal was published in 1843 and continued for a total of 13 volumes.

Hypnosis for Surgery

James Esdaile (1808-1859), a Scottish physician and surgeon, performed a number of operations in India using hypnosis as the sole anesthesia. Kroger (1977) states that the first recorded uses of hypnoanesthesia were in 1821 by Recamier, who performed surgery on patients under mesmeric coma.

Magnetism Idea Changes

Abbe Faria, who came to Paris from India and gave public demonstrations of hypnosis between 1814-1815, stated that cures were not due to magnetism but to the expectancy and cooperation of the patient (Kroger, 1977).

Crasilneck (1985) states that Jean Marie Charcot (1825-1893) believed that hypnosis was similar to hysteria and that both were the products of a diseased nervous system.

Ambroise-Auguste Liebeault (1823-1904), a country doctor, and Hippolyte Bernheim (1827-1919), a prominent neurologist, stressed the role of suggestibility in hypnosis. This approach became more widely accepted than the pathological theories of Charcot. Liebeault and Bernheim collaborated and jointly treated over 12,000 patients (Crasilneck, 1985).

Influence of Freud

Sigmund Freud (1856-1939) had studied with Charcot in 1885 and in 1895 co-authored with Joseph Breuer (1842-1925) *Studien Uber Hysterie,* which emphasized the use of hypnosis to recover original memories in order to release stored-up emotions from the unconscious (Crasilneck, 1985).

Mesmerism in America

The strong influence of mesmerism was seen in the United States as late as 1861. The Phreno-Magnetic Society of Cincinnati, Ohio, was organized on June 14, 1842 to actively seek out subjects and to embrace every opportunity for making practical phreno-magnetic experiments. These experiments were made in order to establish whether the "magnetizer" had power over the "magnetizee" as compared with bodies of metal, the magnet, and the galvonic battery. Dr. John Elliotson was an honorary member of the Society. Between 1845-1861, a well-organized and active Mesmer Society flourished in New Orleans. Historical records also indicate the existence of a Mesmer Society in Philadelphia (Wester, 1976).

Rejection of Hypnosis by Freud

Morton Prince (1854-1929) became noted for using hypnosis in the treatment of multiple personalities (Crasilneck, 1985). About this time, Freud began to reject hypnosis as his psychoanalysis began to receive greater and important recognition. Many other noted individuals had an influence on the continued development of hypnosis. Alfred Binet (1857-1911), most noted for the development of the first modern I.Q. test in 1904, published a book with Fere on animal magnetism. Pierre Janet (1859-1947) continued the investigation of hypnosis even though Freud was rejecting the idea of hypnosis (Udolf, 1981).

Hypnosis Becomes Scientific and Accepted

Clark L. Hull's (1884-1952) classic work, *Hypnosis and Suggestibility: An Experimental Approach,* described his attempts at controlled experiments covering a wide range of hypnotic phenomena. More recently, Ernest R. Hilgard has become a leader in the area of hypnotic research. His work at Stanford University's Laboratory of Hypnotic Research has been well received. Dr. Hilgard's original book, *Hypnotic Susceptibility,* was republished under the title of *The Experience of Hypnosis* in 1965 (Udolf, 1981).

Professional organizations began to emerge with the establishment of the Society for Clinical and Experimental Hypnosis in 1949. SCEH was expanded into an International Society in 1959. The American Society of Clinical Hypnosis was formed in 1957, with membership restricted to professionals in medicine, psychology and dentistry. The British Medical Association reported its approval of hypnosis in 1955 for the treatment of psychoneurosis and hypnoanesthesia for pain control in childbirth and surgery. The Council on Mental Health of the American Medical Association in 1958 recognized hypnosis as a legitimate treatment method. Lankton (1983) states that even prior to the AMA's official recognition they dedicated a journal (1956) to the medical uses of hypnosis.

The Influence of Erickson

The last 30 years have been a tremendous growth period for hypnosis. Books too numerous to list have been published on hypnosis, and many scholarly researchers and clinicians will be listed in books to come as their works withstand the test of time. One man, however, stands out as having had the greatest impact on modern hypnosis. Milton H. Erickson (1901-1980) was the founder of the American Society of Clinical Hypnosis and editor of the first *ASCH Journal.* Erickson is noted for the development of utilization and indirect suggestions.

In 1980, the First International Congress on Ericksonian Approaches to Hypnosis and Psychotherapy was held. This was recorded as the largest gathering of clinicians to honor and study the work of a single therapist (Lankton, 1983).

Beyond 1986/87, one can only speculate. The Ericksonian influence will be seen for many years to come. The increasing acceptance of incorporating modern hypnosis into treatment procedures will increase.

This author has been personally influenced by many great authors in the field, such as Erika Fromm, Harold Crasilneck, James Hall, William Kroger, Karen Olness, Daniel Araoz, Fredericka Freytag, Stephen and Carol Lankton, Edgar Barnett, David Cheek, Irving Secter, Joseph Barber, Theodore Barber and Roy Udolf. Their writings will continue to have a significant impact on the field of hypnosis.

As research on the human mind, its capabilities and powers, continues, hypnosis research will also increase and continue on a parallel track. We have only begun to tap the potential of the human mind.

References

Crasilneck HB, Hall JA: Clinical Hypnosis: Principles and Applications, 2nd ed. New York, Grune & Stratton, 1985.

Gravitz MA: Hypnosis in the historical development of psychoanalytic psychotherapy. In Wester WC, Smith AH: Clinical Hypnosis: A Multidisciplinary Approach. Philadelphia, JB Lippincott, 1984

Kroger WS: Clinical and Experimental Hypnosis, 2nd ed. Philadelphia, JB Lippincott, 1984

Lankton SR, Lankton CH: The Answer Within: A Clinical Framework of Ericksonian Hypnotherapy. New York, Brunner/Mazel, 1983

Udolf R: Handbook of Hypnosis for Professionals. New York, Van Nostrand Reinhold Co., 1981

Wester WC: Questions and Answers about Clinical Hypnosis. Columbus, OH, Ohio Psychology Publishing, Inc., 1982

Wester WC: The Phreno-Magnetic Society of Cincinnati—1842. Am J Clin Hypn 18:277-281, 1976

2 INDUCTION AND DEEPENING TECHNIQUES

D. CORYDON HAMMOND, Ph.D.

Hypnosis is a state of concentration and selective attention that occurs naturally. In everyday life we become absorbed inwardly in thought, remembrance, fantasy, or in reading a novel. Our thoughts and attention may become so deeply fixated that we drive a car extended distances without conscious awareness, guided by some other level of consciousness. Perhaps this focused state is not unlike focusing the rays of the sun through a magnifying glass. The sun's rays are powerful, like our mind. But when focused and concentrated, they become exceptionally powerful and can burn a hole through sheet metal. Hypnosis is a focused mental state wherein we use more of our potential, and in which imagery and ideas to which we are receptive can have greater impact. Hypnotic induction and deepening consists of facilitating an inward focusing of attention preparatory to the presentation of thera-peutic ideas and images or a request that the patient engage in self-exploration.

In this chapter, we will briefly review the process of induction and then elaborate the basic principles of induction and suggestion. Finally, a variety of methods for inducing and deepening involvement in a hypnotic state will be described.

The Process of Induction

1. *Assessment and Establishing Rapport.* Hypnosis is a cooperative venture, rather than something we do *to* a patient. The therapist is simply a facilitator. There-fore, prior to induction, we must establish a relationship wherein we are per-ceived as warm, empathic, respectful, trustworthy, competent and caring. Furthermore, because we are not "hypnotists" who use hypnosis as our only method of therapy, we must diagnostically determine the nature of a problem and our tentative treatment plan. Learning about patient personality, interests and hobbies is also invaluable preparation for the later individualization of the hypnotic experience.

2. *Orienting the Patient.* Much resistance to hypnosis can be avoided if the ther-apist takes 10 minutes to educate the patient about common misconceptions. This author defines hypnosis, talks about examples of the everyday trance, and counters myths about loss of consciousness and amnesia, fear of loss of control, and the

fear of betraying secrets. The concept of "hypnotic talents" is also introduced, with the explanation that we each experience hypnosis in individual ways. A few individuals can experience all the hypnotic phenomena, but most of us are excellent at some phenomena, mediocre at some, and perhaps unable to experience one or two. Such a conceptualization counteracts discouragement if patients do not experience everything that is suggested. Patients' feedback is encouraged so that hypnosis may be tailored to them.

In preparing the patient for induction, check for contact lenses. Unless contact lenses are soft and can be left in to sleep, they will distract the patient. Patients are also encouraged to rest their hands and feet apart so that they do not touch. This position seems to more easily allow dissociation to occur. Finally, if the patient is ill with a cold, the first induction is postponed.

3. *Fixation of Attention and Deepening Involvement.* Hypnotic induction and deepening are not distinct steps, but simply component parts of the process of narrowing attention and facilitating an inward absorption. Deep relaxation is not necessary, but is usually part of this process (Edmonston, 1986). Various induction or deepening techniques are simply tools or formal rituals for encouraging the process, rituals that often meet patient and therapist expectations and needs for structure. However, induction and deepening may also occur more informally through "conversational inductions" similar to those Erickson (1980) sometimes used.

4. *Facilitating Unconscious Response.* After focusing attention, the therapist can create positive expectancies and offer acceptable imagery and suggestions to the patient. However, hypnosis is not merely the act of a therapist externally offering ideas to a passive patient. Truly, hypnosis is a sophisticated method of communicating ideas in a receptive state. It is also commonly an evocative process of stimulating inner associations, memories and resources. The therapist can be valuable in creatively offering new frames of reference for consideration. But the therapist is like an incubator that creates a favorable environment, the actual hatching deriving from processes within the egg itself.

Erickson and Rossi (1979) described the importance of "depotentiating habitual frames of reference" and mental sets, which creates a new openness to ideas and allows more autonomous unconscious processes to occur. This technique may be achieved with distraction, confusion, relaxation, dissociation, surprise, presenting binds and double binds, etc. In hypnosis, we seek to bypass consciously learned limitations and facilitate unconscious search and the use of latent potentials.

5. *Trance Ratification.* As part of a hypnotic experience and prior to the conclusion of the experience, it is important to provide the client with a convincer, ratifying the power of his or her mind to assist in accomplishing goals. This is an

often overlooked, yet vital hypnotic principle that has been found to enhance the effectiveness of treatment.

For example, the author often facilitates glove anesthesia, testing it with a pin or needle. Subsequently, the suggestion may be given: "You have now seen the incredible power of your unconscious mind, to control your body and your feelings. You have more potentials than you realize. And when your unconscious mind is *so* powerful that it can even control something as fundamental and basic as pain, you know that it can control anything having to do with your feelings or your body. And because of that tremendous power of your unconscious mind, your (pain, appetite, depression, etc.) can and will come under your control."

6. *Re-alerting the Patient.* The final step in hypnotic induction is to ask the patient to reawaken or return to a normal state of consciousness. This may be done in a structured manner ("In a moment, I will count from 10 to 1, and as I do so you will gradually awaken, feeling alert, refreshed, and clear-headed") or more permissively ("Now, at your own pace and speed, take several refreshing, energizing breaths, and come fully alert and awake"). It is quite rare to have difficulty in "awakening" a patient. When the difficulty is encountered, patients may simply be asked to verbalize the reason for not wishing to awaken. Sometimes the trance feels so peaceful in contrast to the turmoil of their lives that they hate to awaken and face life again.

Principles of Induction and Suggestion

Law of Reversed Effect. The principle that the harder one consciously endeavors to do something, the more difficult it becomes to succeed is of particular importance in bringing about physiological effects. Have you ever gone to bed too late and tried to help yourself fall asleep only to find yourself more wide awake? How successful are we in trying to will an erection, orgasm, perspiration or salivation? In your hypnotic work, use imagination and imagery rather than an appeal to the will. For example, instead of merely suggesting, "Your hand is getting lighter and lighter," add descriptive imagery of helium balloons attached to the wrist and fingers.

Law of Concentrated Attention. This is the principle of repetition. When we concentrate attention repeatedly on a goal or idea, it tends to be realized. In formulating important hypnotic suggestions, repeat them, for example, three times. You may use somewhat synonymous words and phrases. However, one of Milton Erickson's (1980) contributions was in giving *both* direct verbal suggestions and using metaphoric examples as an indirect way of repeating suggestions. Thus, Erickson often told a metaphor or two to "seed" an idea, then made a bridging association that directly pointed out the relevance of the stories to the patient's problem, and finally gave a direct suggestion or two.

Principle of Successive Approximations. In regard to the concept of repetition, we should not expect our patients to immediately produce various hypnotic phenomena. As therapists we too often have one of the same problems as our patients: we harbor magical expectations about hypnosis, that it will produce instant change. We want immediate gratification. But people seldom leap tall buildings in a single bound. Another unique aspect of Erickson's masterful technique was his patience in facilitating phenomena, breaking tasks down into steps, and taking time to do "trance training" with patients.

In like manner, avoid the authoritarian suggestions that lay hypnotists thrive on: "You will immediately. . . ," or "In five minutes you will . . . ," or "By the time you awaken your pain will be completely gone." As individuals, patients will require varying amounts of time to respond to suggestions. Therefore, in phrasing suggestions, it is often desirable to be permissive regarding time (Erickson and Rossi, 1979).

Law of Dominant Effect. Stronger emotions tend to take precedence over weaker ones. Therefore, rather than appealing to the conscious will, enhance the effectiveness of suggestions by associating them with a strong emotion. In like manner, the therapist can arouse internal states of tension and anticipation in the patient that can only be resolved by the production of a desired hypnotic response.

Create Positive Expectancy. Experienced hypnotherapists may be more effective because they act utterly expectant and confident that suggestions will occur. Their attitude inspires confidence in patients.

The Carrot Principle. Therapists often, in effect, seek to get behind their patients and push them toward goals. But some patients dig in their heels and resist. Instead of pushing people from behind, motivate them from in front, toward something. During induction, deepening, and along with suggestions, intersperse comments about the patient's goals. With patients who give precedence to logic and reasoning (rather than emotion), provide logical reasons for them to accept your suggestions.

Principle of Positive Suggestion. Rather than seeking to override existing motives or attitudes, create positive motivation and attitudes. Whenever possible, change negative suggestions to positive ones. In the treatment of a migraine patient, for instance, it will be ineffective to suggest, "You will feel nothing in your head." Instead, focus on creating positive imagery and suggestions: "And as you enjoy warming your hands in front of that fire, you rest more and more deeply, simply aware of the comfort."

Principle of Positive Reinforcement. Reinforce the patient both in and out of trance: "You're doing that very nicely" and "You've done some very good work today, and I hope that your unconscious mind will take a real pride in how hypnotically talented you are."

Principle of Trance Ratification. Use hypnotic phenomena to convince patients about the power of their unconscious minds. Create a positive expectancy, sense of self-efficacy and belief in their ability to change. Trance ratification methods may include: limb catalepsy, time distortion, glove anesthesia or analgesia, limb heaviness, levitation, ideomotor signaling, amnesia, recall of forgotten memories, ideosensory phenomena, and response to posthypnotic suggestions.

Principle of Interspersing Suggestions. Suggestions may be subtly interspersed within stories, anecdotes, or "deepening" techniques. Words or phrases, set apart by very brief pauses or changes in voice tone, that convey additional meanings and suggestions may be included.

   For instance, the author was working with a woman for both obesity and marital problems. She had an annoying habit of interrupting rather than listening. Therefore, the following suggestions were given (and recorded on cassette tape for use in self-hypnosis). Notice the commas that indicate very brief pauses. "It will be interesting for you to learn to listen, to your body. And as you listen, to your body, you can notice how you feel satisfied. And rather than interrupting, the natural balance of things, you can listen respectfully to feelings, and sensations of your body, noticing how soon you feel comfortably full and contented." Two problems were being addressed at once. The reader is referred to Erickson (1980) for masterful examples of this technique.

Erickson's Principle of Utilization and Individualization. Milton Erickson emphasized the need to individualize hypnotic procedures. But many lay hypnotists and even some professionals assume that hypnotic response is merely a trait and individualization is unnecessary. Thus, they mass produce popularized self-hypnosis tapes, presenting everyone with the same induction and suggestions. But hypnosis appears most effective when it is individualized (Nuland and Field, 1970; Holroyd, 1980), and takes into account each patient's unique personality, interests and preferences. Therefore, the author (Hammond, 1985) has patients complete a take-home paper and pencil checklist of life experiences, interests and values. This list provides quick information for use in individualizing induction, metaphors and suggestions.

   As an example of individualization, we can determine by brief questioning which sensory modalities a patient is primarily able to imagine (visual, auditory, kinesthetic, olfactory), and then tailor the imagery we suggest accordingly. We recommend questioning your patients after initial hypnotic experiences and encouraging their feedback on how to make their experiences more effective.

In individualizing hypnosis, Erickson could be either highly directive and authoritarian or very permissive and indirect, depending on the patient (Hammond, 1984). When you have an excellent relationship with a highly-motivated patient, who is dependent, used to taking orders, and a good hypnotic subject, you can be highly forceful and direct in your suggestions. With a rebellious, independent person, who is not as hypnotically talented and is more resistant or ambivalent in motivation, you will want to become more permissive and indirect. In individualizing hypnosis, you may also take into account personality type and needs. In a highly competitive patient, for example, one might choose as an induction a dual levitation of both arms, suggesting a curiosity about which hand will reach the face first.

Another facet of individualization is Erickson's principle of utilization. The therapist accepts utterly whatever occurs with the patient and then seeks to use, displace, and transform it. In hypnosis, this technique is essentially the parallel of using empathy and respect to establish rapport in psychotherapy. Thus, if a patient yawns in a tired way, one may comment, "Have you ever noticed, how after a yawn, your whole body relaxes more deeply?" If a patient has some muscles jerk slightly in one leg during the process of induction, the therapist may say, "And you notice the little muscles jerk in your leg, which is a good sign that the tension is really flowing out of you, as your muscles relax." Patient behavior, even if it might be interpreted as problematic, is thus accepted and suggestions may be connected to it.

A new patient complained that in hypnotic attempts with a previous therapist he could only enter a light hypnotic state because his mind kept wandering. Therefore, the following suggestions were offered during the induction: "And as we continue, undoubtedly your mind will begin to wander, to think about other things. And different images may run through your mind. And that's perfectly all right, because for a little while, your conscious mind doesn't have to do anything of importance. Just allow your unconscious mind to wander in whatever way it wants, because the only thing that matters, is the activity of your unconscious mind." The patient went into a profound, deep trance and experienced spontaneous amnesia for almost the entire process.

Hammond's Law of Parsimony. Finally, it is suggested that you use the most parsimonious method to accomplish the therapeutic task. Today, many individuals seem to be making hypnosis much more complicated and difficult than it needs to be. Such methods often stem from misinterpretations of Erickson's work (Hammond, 1984). Esoteric, multiple-embedded metaphor and confusional techniques are seldom necessary and usually meet the therapist's needs far more than the patient's.

Hypnotic Induction Techniques

Now that we have reviewed basic principles, we will turn our attention to some specific induction techniques. It should be pointed out, however, that induction-deepening is an ongoing (rather than two-stage) process that often involves several techniques. Thus, almost any induction technique may also be used as a deepening technique, and many deepening techniques may also be used for induction.

Eye Fixation Induction. This procedure is a traditional technique, occasionally complicated by the fact that some patients do not easily develop eyelid heaviness, even though they may be quite hypnotically talented in other ways. Therefore, it is best to phrase suggestions permissively, in a more fail-safe manner:

> I'd like you to concentrate on one spot on the ceiling, and keep your eyes focused on that spot. And as you do so, just breathe easily, comfortably and deeply, allowing your body to begin to relax. Before long you may notice that your field of vision may gradually begin to change. Perhaps things away from that spot may begin to get hazy or fuzzy, and some people notice their eyes begin to water. And now I notice [utilizing what the therapist will presumably observe at some point] that your eyes are beginning to blink. And as they focus on that spot, the muscles around your eyes will begin to relax, along with the rest of your body. And your eyelids will begin to feel heavier, and heavier. And as they feel heavier, they begin to blink more frequently. That's right. And after a time, you may begin to notice that the blinks begin to get longer, and slower, as your eyes begin to feel more and more tired, and your eyelids feel heavier and heavier. And whenever your eyes feel so heavy, and so tired, that they feel like they just want to close, you can allow them to close, and stay closed.

The therapist's pattern may need to continue for a time. However, some patients can stare at a spot indefinitely without responding. For these patients, it is helpful to being using another induction technique simultaneously so that they are not as aware of not having done well with one approach. For instance, the therapist may begin using progressive relaxation, and upon reaching the face ask the patient to close his/her eyes.

Progressive Relaxation Induction. This procedure is a gentle, easily mastered induction/deepening technique that a vast majority of patients find very pleasant:

> I'd like you to concentrate on your feet, and to allow them to become very deeply relaxed. In fact, you may even want to imagine in your mind's eye, what it would look like, if you could see all those little muscles becoming soft, and limp, and relaxed. And as you imagine that process, some level of your mind knows how to use those images, to bring about the very thing you're imagining. Now I want you to pretend, that the relaxation is beginning to flow and spread, like a gentle river, upward through your ankles and into your calves, as you let go, of all the tension in your calves. (pause) And allow that comfort to continue to flow upward, into your knees, and behind your knees, and through your knees, into your thighs. Perhaps

once again imagining what it would look like, if you could see all those large muscles relaxing, and becoming limp, and soft, and relaxed. Maybe already noticing a gentle heaviness in your legs, as they just sink limply and deeply relaxed, into the chair, and into the floor. And pretend that this comfort continues to flow and spread upward, into the middle part of your body. Flowing into your pelvis and abdomen and stomach (pause), flowing into your hips and lower back. Deep, soothing relaxation, that's gradually inching its way up through your body, from muscle group to muscle group. Flowing into your chest (pause), into your back (pause), between your shoulder blades, and into your shoulders. As though, somehow, just the act of breathing were increasing your comfort. As if somehow, with every breath you take, it were just draining tension out of your body, allowing you to sink deeper, and deeper [timed to exhalations and lowering voice] relaxed, with every breath you take. And imagine that comfort flowing into your neck and throat. Maybe once again, imagining what it would look like, if you could see all those little fibers and muscles becoming soft, and limp, and deeply relaxed. (pause) And that comfort can flow up your neck, into your scalp (pause), and out across your scalp, just bathing your head in comfort, and relaxation. And that relaxation can flow down into your forehead and temples, and like a gentle wave of relaxation, down across your face, into your eyes, into your cheeks, into your mouth and jaw. Just let go of all the tension, in your face, and mouth, and jaw, allowing all those muscles, and the skin, to just droop and sag, limply and comfortably. And that relaxation can flow back down your neck, and across your shoulders, and down your arms. Down through your elbows (pause), down through your wrists (pause), down through your fingers, all the way down to your fingertips.

When not familiar with the subject, the therapist may have the patient nod his/her head when the relaxation reaches certain places in order to better individualize the pace.

Arm Levitation. This is a very useful technique that is often trance ratifying and assists in facilitating dissociation and glove anesthesia:

As you rest back, I'd like you to hold your arms straight out in front of you [therapist models], so that the fingertips are very lightly touching your slacks, just behind your knees. Good. And I'd like you to close your eyes [this is optional], and simply concentrate on the sensations, noticing the feeling and texture of your slacks, in the tips of your fingers. And as your fingers touch very lightly, just barely touching, I want you to take three or four very deep breaths. And as you do so, just notice what happens. (pause) Notice how as you breathe in, your hands just naturally lift, and float up. And as you continue noticing that sensation, you can wonder, which of your hands is going to begin getting even lighter, and lighter, [timed to inhalations] and begin floating up. Notice the curious, interesting sensations, as one of those hands begins getting lighter, and lighter, lifting, lifting [timed to inhalations, elevating the pitch of your voice, and lifting your locus of voice direction], and it begins to float up.

If the hand is not yet lifting, suggestions may be added: "And I really don't know which finger is going to begin getting lighter and float up first.

Will it be your index finger, or your middle finger, or your little finger? First one finger, and then another." Continuing:

Almost as if, helium balloons were attached with strings to each fingertip, and around that wrist. Floating up, lighter, and lighter. And the wrist begins to lift, and the elbow begins to bend, and up it comes. And with each movement, and with each little jerky motion of that hand up, toward your face, you sink into a deeper, and deeper hypnotic state. Lighter, and lighter, lifting, lifting. Almost as if it were magnetically attracted toward your face. That's right. [As the hand gets close to their face], but I don't want your unconscious mind to allow that hand to touch your face, until you're in a very deep hypnotic state.

When a levitation is progressing slowly, the therapist may assist the patient, gently lifting the fingers or upwardly stroking the underside of the forearm and hand. After the hand reaches the face or a reasonable height, suggestions for an increasing heaviness may be given and the downward movement used for deepening.

Catalepsy Induction. Using the thumb and middle finger, gently grasp the patient's wrist and lift his/her arm in front of the chest. Then, very gradually break contact as you increasingly sense that the arm will remain suspended in mid-air. In the process of gradually letting go of the wrist, it is helpful to use your index, right and little fingers to make very slight, distracting touches so that it is much more difficult for the patient to determine precisely when you completely break contact. As the arm is lifted, some of the following kinds of suggestions help facilitate the catalepsy: "I'm going to lift your hand and arm up, and I'm just going to leave it, right there;" "And as I just leave your hand right here, can you focus your attention on one spot on that hand?" [This suggestion combines catalepsy with eye fixation. Arm heaviness may then be suggested as the hand moves downward, the eyes closed]; "How comfortably can it rest there?"; "Does that arm become fixed, right there?"; "And it can remain there, all by itself." Once catalepsy has been produced, levitation to the face or heaviness and sinking to the lap may be used along with accompanying suggestions for deepening. For further details about this technique, refer to Erickson and Rossi (1981).

Internal Fixation Inductions. Imagery may be used to internally fixate attention for induction. The imagery may involve favorite settings or activities, or it may be stimulated through the telling of metaphoric stories.

Induction by Posthypnotic Suggestion. After an initial trance experience, it is helpful to give the patient posthypnotic suggestions that establish a conditioned cue for rapid induction. This technique helps shorten the time required for future induction. For example: "In the future, whenever you want me to work with you hypnotically, you will be able to rapidly enter an even deeper hypnotic state than the one you're now in. Whenever you want me to work with you, all that I'll have to do is simply to touch you on the shoulder, like this [demonstrating], and that will be the signal to your unconscious mind, to rapidly take you into a very deep and tranquil hypnotic state." Variations of this suggestion may then be repeated two or three times.

Confusional and Surprise Inductions. Surprise was sometimes used by Erickson (1980) for facilitating rapid induction or reinduction, for instance, by saying to the patient who just awakened from trance: "Are you really awake? Are you sure? Or do your eyelids begin to get heavy again, and your eyes begin to close?" The reader is referred to Erickson (1980) for an explanation of how confusion may be used for overcoming resistance by overloading the patient's conscious, intellectual mind. These advanced methods clearly have their place with resistant patients. However, confusional techniques can be overused by narcissistic therapists who enjoy feeling superior and impressing people with their fancy verbal work.

Children's Inductions. Children are often excellent hypnotic subjects. Gardner and Olness (1981) present a wide range of hypnotic inductions for children of varying ages.

There are numerous other induction techniques (for example, eye opening and closing, dual induction, nonverbal induction) that are essentially limited only by the therapist's creativity. Edmonston (1986) provides a comprehensive and historical perspective on the wide variety of induction methods available, and Crasilneck and Hall (1985) model a large number of techniques.

Techniques for Deepening Hypnotic Involvement

Controversy exists concerning whether "depth" of trance has any relationships to therapeutic response. Erickson (1980) suggested that depth was unimportant and yet at other times emphasized that he rarely presented significant suggestions until after 20 minutes of deepening. And, in fact, Erickson very often utilized lengthy hypnotic sessions. Others suggest that therapeutic response is more a matter of native talent level than of depth of trance. It does appear, however, that in order to produce certain hypnotic phenoma (for example, time distortion, hallucinations, revivification), greater depth is required.

Fractionation. This procedure consists of awakening and fairly rapidly rehypnotizing the patient several times. It is widely believed to be one of the best deepening techniques, although recent research suggests the possibility that response may be very individual (Hammond, Bartsch, McGhenn, and Grant, 1986).

Silence. Quiet periods are an underutilized deepening method. Suggest that the patient dream about a favorite place or activity. "And as you do so, I'm just going to give you some quiet time, to enjoy your dream, and to drift deeper and deeper with every breath you take. And by the time I speak to you again, you will be in a much, much deeper hypnotic state." A silent period of one to five or more minutes may then be given, which simultaneously provides the therapist with planning or case note time.

Downward Movement. Downward movement (for example, walking down a staircase, moving down an escalator) is often facilitative. Barber (1977) beautifully models the use of a staircase in deepening.

Interspersing Patient Motivation and Needs. "And you're going deeper because you want to get rid of this excess weight and live a long life, so that you can raise your children."

Contingent Suggestions. Going deeper may be made contingent on a behavior that is inevitable or already in progress; "And with every sound of my voice, you can drift deeper;" "With every breath you take, your comfort increases more and more;" "And as your [cataleptic] arm gradually moves down, with each little movement, you can drift into a deeper and more comfortable state."

Breathing and Counting. Hartland (1971) originated a technique that the author has found popular and effective with patients:

> In a moment, I'm going to gradually count from one to five, and as I count each number, I'd like you to take five very deep breaths. And as you let each breath out, you can enjoy becoming more and more deeply relaxed, and drifting deeper and deeper into a hypnotic state. One, take a very deep breath [as patient exhales and while exhaling yourself], and let yourself sink deeper and deeper [relaxes]. Two, a very deep breath [exhaling], letting go further and further. Three, another very deep breath, letting go of all the tension and tightness. Four, a very, very deep breath, drifting further and further into comfort. And, five, take a very deep breath indeed, and sink very, very deep now.
>
> Now in a moment, I want you to take another very deep breath, and fill your chest, and hold it until I say, "Let go." And when I say, "Let go," let that breath out as quickly as possible. And as you do so, you'll feel yourself sagging limply back into the chair, and you'll become much more deeply relaxed, and much, much deeper in a hypnotic state. Okay, take that very deep breath, fill your chest, and hold it. (10 second pause) Hold it. (10 second pause) Hold it. (10-15 second pause, carefully monitoring if the patient can hold his/her breath this long) Now let go! And go very, very deep into trance.

Miscellaneous Techniques. Counting from one to 10, timed to patient exhalations, may be used with contingent suggestions for deepening. Double tasks, for example, imagining listening to favorite music while an arm levitates, tend to overload, occupy and distract the conscious mind and may be useful with patients who become spectators of the hypnotic process. Previously mentioned induction techniques (progressive relaxation, catalepsy, levitation) are likewise effective for deepening. Utilizing a series of graduated tasks and automatic movements may deepen a trance (Hartland, 1971). And, finally, a deepening technique may be as simple as instructing patients that as you gently push down on their shoulders they will feel themselves drifting deeper.

Therapists are well advised to master a variety of induction/deepening techniques so that hypnosis may be individualized to the talents and preferences of patients. Furthermore, diversity of technique makes life much more interesting for the therapist and encourages continued use of hypnosis. As you become secure with many of these existing methods, your hypnotic technique can become increasingly innovative, spontaneous and creative (Hammond, 1985).

References

Barber J: Rapid induction analgesia: A clinical report. Amer J Clin Hypn 19(3):138-147, 1977

Crasilneck HB, Hall JA: Clinical Hypnosis: Principles and Applications. Orlando, Grune and Stratton, 1985

Edmonston WE: The Induction of Hypnosis. New York, John Wiley & Sons, 1986

Erickson MH: The Collected Papers of Milton H. Erickson, M.D. Edited by EL Rossi. New York, Irvington, 1980

Erickson MH, Rossi EL: Hypnotherapy: An Exploratory Casebook. New York, Irvington, 1979

Erickson MH, Rossi EL: Experiencing Hypnosis. New York, Irvington, 1981

Gardner G, Olness K: Hypnosis & Hypnotheraphy With Children. New York, Grune and Stratton, 1981

Hammond DC: Myths about Erickson and Ericksonian hypnosis. Amer J Clin Hypn 26:236-245, 1984

Hammond DC: An instrument for utilizing client interests and individualizing hypnosis. In Lankton S (ed): Elements & Dimensions of an Ericksonian Approach. Ericksonian Monograph 1. New York, Brunner/Mazel, 1985

Hammond DC, Bartsch C, McGhee M, Grant CW: The use of fractionation in self-hypnosis. Submitted to the Amer J Clin Hypn, 1986

Hartland J: Medical and Dental Hypnosis and Its Clinical Applications. London, Bailliere, 1971

Holroyd J: Hypnosis treatment for smoking: An evaluative review. Int J Clin Exp Hypn 28:341-357, 1980

Nuland W, Field PB: Smoking and hypnosis: A systematic clinical approach. Int J Clin Exp Hypn 18:290-306, 1970

3 IDEOMOTOR SIGNALING

ANN M. DAMSBO, Ph.D.

Ideomotor activity is an intrinsic part of hypnosis. For this reason, a comprehensive review of the literature is impossible since virtually all hypnotherapists utilize or observe ideomotor activity, but few have selected it for commentary.

The author's experience with ideomotor techniques started with David Cheek, M.D. in 1960. Cheek has been the primary resource in this area, and the reader wishing more in depth information regarding the uses of ideomotor activities is referred to his book, *Clinical Hypnotherapy* (Cheek and LeCron, 1968).

The earliest recognition of the phenomenon of ideomotor activity, according to Weitzenhoffer (1957), was made by Chevreul, who in 1812 related it to dowsing (water divination) and the Ouija board. Chevreul (1854) published a description of the Chevreul pendulum. Weitzenhoffer (1957) illustrates the use of the pendulum with detailed description.

T. X. Barber (1972) credits Schultz (1932), Hull (1933), Arnold (1946) and Mordey (1960) with explaining ideomotor activity as tiny muscular contractions which are produced when a subject imagines a movement. These tensions may increase to observable movements. Meares (1961) also explains ideomotor activity as a slight tension produced in the muscles with the thought of a movement. Barber (1972) notes that the movement occurs only in the limb that is being imagined as moving.

Hull (1933) was probably the first to demonstrate that it made no difference whether the initiating action was from thoughts or heterosuggestion. Erickson (1968), a student of Hull's noted that ideomotor activity can take place in the waking state as well as in hypnosis. Kroger (1977) supports the concept of waking ideomotor movements occurring without heterosuggestion in such occurrences as a mother opening her own mouth while feeding a baby or a passenger in an automobile applying pressure to an imaginary brake when danger threatens. Erickson (1961) dates his own use of ideomotor activity to his work with Hull in 1923.

Delprato (1977) explores the role of Pavlovian conditioning via the Chevreul pendulum in relation to hypnotic behavior. His research supported the hypnothesis that Pavlovian factors contribute to Chevreul movement.

Hilgard and Hilgard (1975) discovered the Hidden Observer through ideomotor response. While conducting a demonstration of hypnotic deafness with a blind volunteer, E. R. Hilgard asked the hypnotically deaf student for an ideomotor finger response if some part of the individual could hear him. The student responded by raising a finger, and after coming out of hypnosis asked why his finger had lifted.

Pratt, Wood and Alman (1984) note that a true ideomotor response will be slow and trembly or quick and jerky, while a voluntary movement will be more rapid and smooth.

Meares (1961) suggests that the elaboration of ideomotor movement may be an explanation of hypnosis. Hilgard (1965) notes that ideomotor action, including suggested eye closure, arm movement, joint stiffness and catalypsy, are the most familiar manifestations of suggestions responded to in hypnosis. Kroger (1963) argues that ideomotor activity as an inhibition theory of hypnosis fails to explain the complicated psychological reactions elicited during hypnosis. Haley (1958) identified levitation as an involuntary trance phenomenon. He further states that ideas that lead to "ideoid" (ideo-like) actions are interpreted as reality and the resultant convictions lead to hypnosis. Haley cites Arnold's opinion that ideomotor activity involves the limbic system connecting the premotor and motor cortexes.

Schneck (1953), August (1961), and Brownfair (1967) include among ideomotor movements pendulum, finger movements, other levitation, Ouija board, eye catalypsy, dowsing and automatic writing. Hilgard (1965) includes hypnotic inability to move as ideomotor behavior.

Clinical Uses of Ideomotor Techniques

Ideomotor movements are frequently incorporated in inductions. Stein (1968) often started an induction by asking the patient or volunteer to clench the dominant fist for confidence and positive feelings and progressed to involving the entire upper extremity along with other deepening techniques. He set up the non-dominant fist for uncovering techniques, especially for threatening material, reserving the dominant fist as a refuge after dealing with painful material. Crasilneck and Hall (1975) also describe using ideomotor techniques for hypnotic induction—especially finger levitation progressing to hand arm levitation.

LeBaron (1964) found ideomotor movements useful in establishing rapport with patients with severe mental disturbances. Gardner and Olness found that the visible sign of a pendulum or finger twitch helped establish rapport and convince children that hypnosis had been achieved.

Cheek and LeCron (1968) describe in detail the use of uncovering techniques. They suggest seven keys to psychogenic illness: conflict, motivation, identification, masochism, imprinting, organ language, and past experience. Using ideomotor signals, the patients indicate which of these apply to them. Cheek (1969) notes that ideomotor signals contradict conscious responses at times and are usually more reliable.

Anderson (1977), Kroger (1977), Barnett (1984), and Murray-Jobsis (1984) utilize ideomotor techniques to access unconscious emotional tensions and bring them into conscious awareness in order to encourage more appropriate behavior patterns.

Cheek (1975) notes ideomotor head and shoulder movements when regressing patients to birth memories. Cheek (1974) treated as adults some of the babies he had delivered and was able to verify the ideomotor movements as corresponding to their presentation at birth. If the birth memories contributed to adult feelings of rejection, Cheek often suggested in teaching sessions ways that one could re-interpret the birth experience and feel loved and accepted.

Jencks and Krenz (1984) describe their use of ideomotor signaling in self-analysis. Erickson (1980) described his personal use of the techniques for pain relief and correcting his polio handicaps.

Cheek (1969) found the techniques useful in emergency situations with his obstetrical patients and could work with them over the telephone until more defini-tive help could be arranged. Kroger (1977) discusses his use of the techniques in obstetrical and gynecological problems.

Gardner and Olness (1981) and Cheek and LeCron (1968) assessed and cor-rected habit disorders with the aid of ideomotor techniques.

Implementation of Ideomotor Techniques

With either the Chevreul pendulum or ideomotor finger signals, the patient and the therapist can set up the basic four responses used for ideomotor questioning. Any ideomotor movement can be used, and if the patient is physically unable to use the suggested movements the therapist can establish something the patient can do.

The four basic responses are: "yes," "no," "I don't know," and "I don't want to answer." If needed, different responses can be set up. Although a different finger can be used for each response, it is easier to monitor if all the fingers are on the same hand. Often the response is so minimal that the therapist can merely see the tendon tension, and frequently the patient is unaware of minimal movement. The therapist can report the response to the patient. The pendulum can move side to side, back and forth, in a clockwise or counterclockwise circle. To set up the responses, it is best to ask concrete questions and avoid ambiguity. Usually only the "yes" and "no" responses need be set up, with the suggestion that a different response will be "I don't know" or "I don't want to answer."

Typically, one might ask the patient to think "yes" and ask a question with a "yes" answer, such as "Are you sitting in a chair right now?" For a "no" response, "Are you eating an ice cream cone right now?" will set up the appropriate signal.

If painful or sensitive material is likely to be uncovered, it is comforting to have a safe haven set up such as the Stein clenched fist—the dominant one. Since the therapist does not always know when an abreaction will be triggered, routinely setting up the haven or incorporating it in the induction assures patient access if needed. Patients frequently demonstrate resistance when asked to close the dominant fist, maintaining that they are ambidextrous. To forestall the response, simply ask the patient to close the hand he writes with. The non-dominant hand is used to displace negative or uncomfortable feelings or tension.

The signals can be set up prior to induction with some patients and used to determine whether or not it is all right to go into hypnosis. Once the subject is in hypnosis, one can obtain permission for uncovering through ideomotor signals.

When one gets a negative response to such a request, one can ask if further investigation can take place in the future. If the patient is agreeable, he is then asked to see calendar pages slip away the way the movies use them to denote passage of time. The date exposed when the daily pages stop falling off is the date on which the patient agrees to learn more about himself. If one gets dates too far in the future or continues to get negative responses or the patient starts switching the signals, then it is time to stop and deal with the resistance.

Cheek and LeCron (1968) outline cookbook-like techniques in the progression of questions for various conditions. The areas which are particularly meaningful are those where the conscious answer is at variance with the ideomotor response. The author experienced such a response when reviewing Cheek's questions on obesity. On the question, "Do you tend to dislike yourself as to your body image?" in contrast to the conscious "yes" response the ideomotor response was clearly "no." Dr. Cheek worked further and uncovered a past experience when the patient was ill and underweight. The physician treating her illness stated in a very authoritarian manner, "You will be healthier if you are heavier. Don't ever go on a diet. If you do you will wind up back in the hospital." Neither the physician nor the author had had any experience with hypnosis at that time. Years later, when using the uncovering techniques with Dr. Cheek, the author realized that she had been in an hypnoidal state when the above statements were made. Cheek suggested that perhaps the author viewed the extra adipose tissue as an insurance against further illness.

Each response can serve as further uncovering and a therapeutic lead. Cheek and LeCron's book is excellent for the novice in step by step ideomotor questioning; once the student feels comfortable with the technique, he can proceed on his own.

The author typically uses the following verbalization to elicit ideomotor responses.

> Imagine you can see the arteries that nourish right index finger. These arteries have muscles in the walls and when these muscles relax the diameter of the arteries is larger, permitting the blood to flow more freely and causing the finger to get warmer. When the finger gets warmer, it can signal the change in temperature by lifting up, seemingly all by itself, actually as an internal biofeedback signal from your unconscious mind. If we had a sensitive thermometer we could actually measure the change in temperature.
>
> By saying "change in temperature" instead of "rise in temperature," one can elicit the signal for the decrease in temperature which sometimes occurs. Sometimes the finger presses down instead of rising. Congratulate the patient on any response and remind him that it is his finger and he can use it any way he likes to demonstrate

his ability to alter the temperature of his finger. When minor resistances occur, it is usually helpful to remind the patient that locus of control rests with him.

Once the patient has been able to alter finger temperature, remind him that he can alter circulation anywhere in his body, and the finger can signal such a change. This skill can be used to alter the course of tension and migraine headaches. With tension headaches, the author has the patient displace the tension and pain to the non-dominant hand and drop it on the floor (Damsbo, 1979).

Children can be told that they have a magic finger. The magic finger can stop a nose bleed, turn off pain, keep time to music in a fantasy cartoon during dental procedures, and provide a fascinating distraction.

When an ulcer patient gave a "yes" response to indicate his ulcer was bleeding, he was asked to let his "no" finger rise when he had turned off the bleeding. Soon, the desired response ensued. A guaiac test was positive for the day following the interview and negative the next.

A gynecologist was able to get her own menstrual cycle under control while waiting for a more convenient time for a hysterectomy.

During the author's first month as a pre-doctoral intern, a patient was referred to her for hypnosis to treat his suffering from periodic dissociative states. The patient carried on normal activity during the blackouts but had no memory for the activity.

After preliminary evaluation, finger symbols were set up, and the patient was asked if hypnosis would be all right. Three separate and distinct signals were elicited one after the other—"yes," "no," and "I don't know." Further questioning revealed the same phenomenon. Although multiple personalities were not discovered as frequently then as they are now, acting on a hunch the author asked if more than one personality was responding. A "yes" response prompted further questions leading to the discovery of three personalities. The intern excitedly reported her findings to the referring and supervising physician, who gently reminded her that multiples were rarely discovered (true at that time) and that the likelihood of a student psychologist discovering one in her first month of training was extremely remote. A different personality reported for the next visit in order to explain to the therapist what the initial presenting personality had been unable to explain. The patient was presented to the supervising physician, who subsequently admitted the patient and took over his therapy.

Many physical conditions (if not all) are affected by emotions. Most patients are familiar with adrenalin and its effect on the autonomic nervous system during periods of fear and anger. Many other chemicals, including endorphins, respond to emotional changes, and probably many such have yet to be discovered. There is an ideal homeostatic level for all body chemicals, one that is fluid, changing with changing needs and conditions. An ideomotor response can signal when the patient's body has achieved this homeostasis for his needs at that moment. The hypnotized subject, with the repression of the critical factors, will accept such suggestions without detailed proof. The author has discovered, however, that the suggestions are more acceptable if she believes them herself, at least in theory.

Ideomotor signals can indicate blood pressure changes, check internal bleeding, change circulation, increase or decrease digestive output, gastro-intestinal functioning, heart rate and muscle tone, to name a few uses. Incidentally, patients given assignment in hypnosis can use finger signals to indicate completion of various phases of the assignment.

Nailbiting and other nervous habits respond well to age progression. The patient is regressed to birth and asked to give a finger signal, then progresses to the first incident of nailbiting or other habit. Even if no clear memory evolves, the patient can experience the feeling, displace it to the non-dominant fist, and drop it on the floor. This portion of the treatment can be repeated several times—progressing to other incidents until a new pattern of clenching the fist is set up instead of nail-biting. One teen-age girl, after only one session, grew such long nails that she no longer felt she could do housework for fear of ruining them.

Tension and stress are the roots of many problems. It is helpful to explain that some tension is desirable—that one needs it for survival. One can tolerate a little water sloshing in the bottom of a boat, but when it starts lapping around the ankles it is a good idea to start bailing. So it is with tension. The non-dominant hand is useful in bailing out tension by the handful.

Forensic use of hypnosis with victims and witnesses of crimes should be video-taped. With one camera on the subject and another in a close-up showing the hand doing the finger signals, the viewer can compare verbal and ideomotor responses. While ideomotor signals are not absolute indicates of truth, they tend to be more accurate than verbal responses.

Hypnotic Questioning

A woman in her late thirties was referred by the ob-gyn oncologist for protracted pain following pelvic cancer surgery. Using Cheek and LeCron's (1968) seven keys, the hypnotic questioning took the following form:

Ideomotor response

Is there some psychological reason why you still suffer from pain?	Yes
Would it be all right to learn what this reason is?	Yes
Are you identifying with someone else who has had similar pain?	No

Are you using this pain to punish someone?	No
Are you using it to punish yourself in some way?	Yes
Haven't you punished yourself enough after all you have gone through?	No
Would it be all right to know why you are punishing yourself?	Yes
On the count of three, squeeze your left (non-dominant) fist and something can pop into your mind that will have something to do with the reason you are punishing yourself.	Patient clenches left fist on the count of three.
Did something pop into your mind?	Yes
Would it be all right to tell me about it?	Yes
You can talk in hypnosis.	Verbally: This probably doesn't have anything to do with it, but when I had the first surgery for cancer in Hawaii I was in the same ward, the same room, and the very same bed I was in when I had an abortion (tearful abreaction).
Is it all right to talk about this pregnancy?	Yes (ideomotor)
Had you thought about the child in terms of sex—possibly a name?	Yes, I think of her as a girl named Sylvia.
Let the tears flow. Tears are good medicine. Is there anything else about Sylvia you want to tell me?	I remember that the day I was to have the abortion as I was leaving the house I saw a picture of my father, who had died shortly before, and I looked at the picture and asked him to take care of my baby.
That is very sad and you have punished yourself severely. Could you stop punishing yourself soon?	Yes

Imagine seeing a daily calendar. Watch the pages drop off one day at a time and let your "yes" finger rise when you see the date you can stop punishing yourself.	Pause followed by a "yes" response.
What is the date?	April 24th
This year? Two months from now?	Yes

On the date specified the patient slipped into a coma and died a few days later in spite of the fact that the surgeon had expected a full recovery.

 A patient in her early forties had had several episodes of sudden onset of numbness and paralysis in her left upper extremity. The condition had cleared spontaneously on several occasions and had cleared with sodium amyton on two other occasions. She was referred for hypnotherapy. No paralysis was noted on arrival.

Ideomotor response

Is there some psychological reason for this symptom?	Yes
Is it all right to learn what this reason is?	Yes
Is this symptom due to some inner conflict?	No
Are you identifying with someone who may have had a similar condition?	No
Are you punishing someone with this symptom?	Yes
Do you know whom?	Verbal: My husband
Do you know why?	Verbal "no"
	Ideomotor "yes"
Please go back in time to the first time you suffered this condition and when you are there let your "yes" finger rise.	Pause, then "yes"
Now do you know why you have the symptom?	Verbal "no"
	Ideomotor "yes"

Squeeze your left fist on the count of three and something can pop into your mind that will help you know what this symptom means to you.	Squeezes fist on the count of three.
What did you think of?	I had just learned that my husband was cheating on me.
When your arm is paralyzed, who does the housework?	My husband (big smile). He waits on me, too.
It seems a shame to put an end to all of that.	Right!
Isn't it inconvenient to have your arm paralyzed—especially when he isn't around?	Yes—it's hard to diaper the baby with one hand.
Would you like to learn how to turn the symptom on and off at will?	Verbal "yes!" (eyes gleaming).

Teaching patients voluntary control of a symptom used to manipulate others seems to be questionable ethically, but once a patient knows he can control a symptom his sense of fairness and guilt usually prevents deliberate malingering. If it does not, the patient would have found some other way to manipulate the situation had he given up the symptom. More probably, he would not learn how to control the symptom. The above patient was able to reproduce her symptom in hypnosis and then clear it up as she regained full control of her arm with a given signal.

Cheek (1969) reported the use of ideomotor signals to communicate with critically ill patients, including unconscious patients. Since the sense of hearing is often intact when a patient shows no other signs of comprehension, an ideomotor response can sometimes be a means of communication with a patient who can respond in no other way.

When a pain no longer serves a useful purpose, a finger signal can trigger a substitute response such as warmth or tingling instead of pain. It is easier for the patient to alter the response than to eliminate it.

The author, after minor foot surgery, set up a response for the "yes" finger to rise should there be any discomfort. A month after the surgery, while she was on grand rounds, someone accidentally stepped on the operated foot. Immediately, the ideomotor response took place, and the substitution of warmth for pain was almost instantaneous.

Ideomotor movements are automatic and sometimes occur naturally. Stein (1969) notes that the clenched fist is often present at birth. It is a sign of defiance and/or independence and certainly of strength. Therapists have learned to utilize such a natural tendency to enhance their use of hypnosis in uncovering techniques, unconscious responses, triggering mechanisms and forensic uses. Ideomotor movements can be used for inductions, post-hypnotic suggestions and to signal changes in physiology. These tiny, at times, almost imperceptible twitches serve many valuable purposes.

References

Anderson, JW: Defensive maneuvers in two incidents involving the Chevreul pendulum—a clinical note. Int J Clin Hypn 25:1, 1977

Arnold MB: On the mechanism of suggestion and hypnosis. J Abn Soc Psychol 41:107-128, 1946

August R: Hypnosis in Obstetrics. New York, McGraw-Hill, 1961

Barber TX: Suggested ('hypnotic') behavior: the trance paradigm versus an alternative paradigm. In Fromm E, Shor RE (eds): Hypnosis: Research Developments and Perspectives. Chicago, Aldine Publishing, 1972

Barnett EA: Hypnosis in the treatment of anxiety and chronic stress. In Wester WC, Smith AH (eds): Clinical Hypnosis: A Multidisciplinary Approach. New York, JB Lippincott, 1984

Brownfair JJ: Hypnodiagnosis. In Gordon JE (ed): Handbook of Clinical and Experimental Hypnosis. New York, MacMillan, 1967

Cheek DB, LeCron M: Clinical Hypnotherapy. New York, Grune & Stratton, 1968

Cheek DB: Dreams and premature labor. Am J Clin Hyp 12:1, 1969

Cheek DB: Communication with the critically ill. Am J Clin Hypn 12:2, 1969

Cheek DB: Sequential head and shoulder movement appearing with age regression in hypnosis to birth. Am J Clin Hypn 16:4, 1974

Cheek DB: Maladjustment pattern apparently related to imprinting at birth. Am J Clin Hypn 18:2, 1975

Chevreul: De la Bafuette Divinatoire, du Pendule dit Explorateur et dea Tables Tournantes au Point de Vue de l'Histoire de la Critique et de la Methode Experimentale, Parie: Mallet-Richelieu, 1854

Crasilneck HB, Hall JA: Clinical Hypnosis: Principles and Application. New York, Grune & Stratton, 1975

Damsbo AM: Tension headache treated with hypnosis. In Burrows GD, Collison DR, Dennerstein L (eds): Hypnosis 1979.

Delprato DJ: Pavlovian conditioning of Chevreul's movement. Am J Clin Hypn 20:2, 1977

Erickson MH: Historical note on the hand levitation and other ideomotor techniques. Am J Clin Hypn 3, 1961

Erickson MH: Deep hypnosis and its induction. In LeCron LM (ed): Experimental Hypnosis. Citadel, 1968

Erickson, MH: The Collected Papers of Milton H. Erickson, Rossi E (ed). 1:121, 3:31, Irvington, 1980

Gardner G, Olness K: Hypnosis and Hypnotherapy With Children. New York, Grune & Stratton, 1981

Haley J: An interactional explanation of hypnosis. Am J Clin Hypn 1:2, 1958

Hilgard ER: The Experience of Hypnosis. Harbinger, 1965

Hilgard ER, Hilgard, J: Hypnosis in the Relief of Pain. New York, Wm Kaufmann, Inc., 1975

Hull CL: Hypnosis and Suggestibility, An Experimental Approach. New York, Appleton-Century Co., 1933

Jenks B, Krenz E: Clinical application of hypnosis in sports. In Wester WC, Smith AH (eds): Clinical Hypnosis: A Multidisciplinary Approach. New York, JB Lippincott, 1984

Kroger WS: Clinical and Experimental Hypnosis. New York, JB Lippincott, 1963

Kroger WS: Clinical and Experimental Hypnosis, 2nd ed. New York, JB Lippincott, 1977

LeBaron G: Ideomotor communication in confusional states and schizophrenia. Am J Clin Hypn 7:1, 1964

Meares A: A System of Medical Hypnosis. New York, WB Saunders Co., 1961

Mellor NH: Hypnosis in juvenile delinquency. GP, 1960

Mordey TR: The Relationship Between Certain Motives and Suggestibility. Unpublished Master's Thesis, Roosevelt University, 1960

Murray-Jobsis J: Hypnosis with severely disturbed patients. In Wester WC, Smith AH (eds): Clinical Hypnosis: A Multidisciplinary Approach. New York, JB Lippincott, 1984

Pratt GJ, Wood DP, Alman BM: A Clinical Hypnosis Primer. Psychology and Consulting Associates Press, 1984

Schneck JN: Hypnosis in Modern Medicine. New York, Charles C. Thomas, 1953

Schultz JH: Das Autogene Training. Stuttgart: George Thieme Verlay, 1932

Stein C: Practical Psychotherapeutic Techniques. Charles C. Thomas, 1968

Stein C: Practical Psychotherapy in Nonpsychiatric Specialities. Charles C. Thomas, 1969

Weitzenhoffer AM: General Techniques of Hypnotism. New York, Grune & Stratton, 1957

4 STYLES OF CLINICAL SELF-HYPNOSIS

SHIRLEY SANDERS, Ph.D.

This chapter classifies four orientations to the use of clinical self-hypnosis. In addition it provides brief descriptions of the orientations, extent of their use, the perceived role of the therapists, the goals and types of problems for which the orientations can be used. Finally, a clinical example of an eclectic approach to self-hypnosis is presented.

Self-hypnosis has been given much attention over the years. As far back as records have been kept, there are descriptions of temple sleep, meditation and dream therapy which mirror descriptions of self-hypnosis as we know it today (Crasilneck and Hall, 1985). Nonetheless, only in the last few years has self-hypnosis been a critical object for study (Fromm et al., 1981). Yet little has been specifically described about the diversity of ways in which self-hypnosis is put to use in the clinical situation. The purpose of this chapter is two-fold: 1) to classify the different orientations in relation to the use of self-hypnosis; and 2) to provide brief descriptions of orientation, extent of use, role of the hypnotherapist, types of problems, goals of treatment, interaction of orientation with self-hypnosis, timing of teaching self-hypnosis, and frequency of practice. Clinical examples illustrating eclectic techniques will be provided so that the clinician can compare different orientations to self-hypnosis to better determine which orientations correspond to the clinician's style and the patient's problems

What is Self-Hypnosis?

Self-hypnosis is an altered state of consciousness that is self-induced. This altered state of consciousness is similar in many ways to hetero-hypnosis, and most people learn self-hypnosis by first experiencing hetero-hypnosis (Sacerdote, 1981). Many theorists believe that all hypnosis is self-hypnosis; that is, the patient chooses to enter the hypnotic state using the hypnotherapist's instructions. Others believe that self-hypnosis, although similar in some ways to hetero-hypnosis, has its own unique qualities.

Indications of Self-Hypnotic Experience

Therapists report the following indications of hypnotic experience:

1. *Slowing of respiration.* This phenomenon is also characteristic of hetero-hypnosis and reflects a relaxation response as described by Bensen and Flipper (1975). In addition, slow, deep breathing may have been suggested as part of the induction.
2. *Slowing of verbalization.* When the patient enters self-hypnosis in the office and is asked to describe imagery or experience, the verbalizations are slower. Again this phenomenon parallels the expected response in hetero-hypnosis.
3. *Facial muscles relax.* As the patient enters self-hypnosis, the characteristic loosening of muscles is exhibited, particularly when the patient uses a relaxation self-induction.
4. *Apparent increase of comfort.* The patient reports less tension, less pain, more positive emotion.
5. *Self-report.* The patient reports to the therapist that he or she is in or has been in self-hypnosis.
6. *Eye-lid flutter.* An early sign of self-hypnosis is the eye-lid flutter, again paralleling hetero-hypnosis.
7. *Hallucinations or images.* The patient reports experiences of positive and negative hallucinations. Imagery is heightened and tends to be more free-floating unless limited by therapeutic suggestion.
8. *Increase in inner awareness of body, emotion, self.* This response appears to be the essence of the alteration of consciousness as reflected by modification of cognition, affect and perception.

The indications of self-hypnosis are very similar to those of hetero-hypnosis. More frequently, however, patients report having difficulty achieving the same level of depth or comfort on their own as compared to sessions where the therapist is present. This difficulty may be related to dependency needs of the patient, resistance to treatment, or ego deficits. In the case of ego deficits, it is important to limit the free-flowing imagery to build the patient's confidence. Resistance needs to be discussed and as well as the role of practice in developing skill in self-hypnosis.

Self-Hypnosis Induction Techniques

The range of individual self-hypnosis induction techniques is impressive. Most therapists simply describe a specific induction technique rather than a classification. Nonetheless, most of the induction techniques reported here can be classified as follows:

1. *Physiological:* relaxation, breathing, Jacobson's Autogenic, eye roll, eye fixation.

2. *Ideo-motor:* clenched fist, on signal, counting backwards.
3. *Imagery:* apple, stairs, comfortable place.
4. *Kinesthetic:* reversed levitation, blowing out cheeks, levitation.

While this list is not exhaustive, it does suggest that there is a wide variety of individual self-hypnosis.

Orientation to Self-Hypnosis

Sanders (1986) conducted a survey on the use of self-hypnosis by therapists in the American Society of Clinical Hypnosis. Based on 233 replies to the survey, a 22 percent response, she classified clinical self-hypnosis orientations into five categories. See Table 4.1

Table 4-1. Clinical Orientation

Type	N	%
Behavioral	65	28.6
Eclectic	79	34.8
Analytic	16	7.0
Physiological	52	22.9
Other	15	6.6

Behavioral use of self-hypnosis is widespread. Both psychiatrists and psychologists subscribe to the use of behavioral techniques and view themselves either as teachers or prescribers. See Table 4-2.

Table 4-2. Role of Therapist

Role	Mean	MD	Ph.D.
Teacher	5.4	.83%	.87%
Prescriber	3.8	.45%	.32%
Guide	3.5	.41%	.56%
Healer	3.1	.31%	.21%

Goals. Behavior modification techniques are designed to change behavior by 1) eliminating deviant behavior, and 2) building up new adaptive behavior in small progressive steps. These goals are well suited for integration with self-hypnosis.

Interaction of behavior modification and self-hypnosis. Because it leads to an alteration of consciousness that reflects ego receptivity (Fromm et al., 1981) absorption (Tellegan and Atkinson, 1974), and increased imagery (Singer and Pope, 1981), self-hypnosis facilitates the strengthening of contingencies and behavior rehearsal in imagery. In addition, by the suggestion of adaptive dissociation, a copy mechanism which maintains, temporarily, selected ideas out of consciousness, deviant behavior can gradually be extinguished and replaced by new, healthier behaviors (Sanders, 1986).

Timing and practice. The behavioral use of self-hypnosis requires that the patient be taught self-hypnosis early in treatment with frequent home practice assigned. This use of frequent but spaced intervals of practice clearly differentiates behavioral self-hypnosis from a more psychoanalytic approach, to be discussed later.

Types of problems. Long-standing habit problems are frequently approached with behavioral techniques in conjunction with self-hypnosis, for example, smoking, weight control, performance anxiety, pain, phobias, trichotillomania, eneuresis and pain, among others (Crasilneck and Hall, 1985).

Eclectic Orientation

Therapists of an eclectic orientation use techniques from a wide variety of theories, combining behavioral, psychoanalytically oriented, physiological, and naturalistic techniques where appropriate. These therapists are "not orthodox" but tend to creatively combine techniques that "work" with specific patients. While such therapists are flexible, they are also well informed and can relate rationale and theory to the patient's problem. In Sanders' survey, the majority of therapists were eclectic and evenly divided between psychiatrists and psychologists. The role of the therapist is perceived as teacher, guide or prescriber.

Goals. The goals of eclectic therapy are mixed in that behavior change and insight as well as support of adaptive functioning may all be relevant. Thus, the eclectic therapist using self-hypnosis may intermittently shift focus from one goal to another, depending on the patient's needs and the situational context.

Interaction of eclectic therapy with self-hypnosis. The broad range of induction techniques serves eclectic therapy well. Particularly, imagery and deep breathing provide a non-directive approach to self-hypnosis, although when more direction is necessary any of the induction techniques are appropriate. Eclectic therapy permits free association, guided imagery, partly unguided imagery, dream interpretation and problem solving techniques to be used. Self-hypnosis is well-suited to the inclusion of these tasks.

Timing and practice. The eclectic therapist may teach the patient self-hypnosis during the first two weeks of therapy. Practice may be spaced as in more behavioral approaches or massed, that is, several brief practice sessions a day as opposed to one 30-minute practice session a day as seen in hypnoanalysis. The frequency of practice depends not only on goals and strategies used, but also upon the integrity of the patient, the ability to tolerate long periods of imagery without outside contact. Although patients without significant ego dysfunction can do well, the more vulnerable patient may panic under prolonged massed practice.

Types of problems. Generally, eclectic self-hypnosis is a combination approach which counter-balances behavioral, physiological and uncovering techniques where appropriate. A wide variety of problems can be approached since the permutations of possibility are so great. Thus, diverse problems such as anxiety reactions, identity crises, certain types of narcissistic disorders, phobias, pain, habits, and severe disturbances can be treated with an eclectic approach.

Psychoanalytic Self-Hypnosis

These hypnotherapists using self-hypnosis within a psychoanalytic approach tend to see themselves as non-directive, benign guides. They monitor and move in to redirect if the patient feels overwhelmed, but generally maintain a non-directive position vis-a-vis the patient.

Extent of use. Psychoanalytic use of self-hypnosis is not widespread, and relatively few therapists endorse this orientation. The ban imposed on hypnosis by Freud in 1903 still influences limiting the use of hypnosis. Interestingly, both psychiatrists and psychologists appear to use a psychoanalytic approach to self-hypnosis about equally. Table 4-3.

Table 4-3. Orientation to Service

Type	Behav	Ecl	Anal	Phys
M.D.	14	38	29	18
Ph.D.	36	37	23	4

Goals. The goals of hypnoanalytic self-hypnosis are primarily to uncover cognitions, feelings, and memories. Psychoanalytically-oriented techniques such as age regressions, hypnotic dreams, imagery of the ideal self and integration are used to accomplish these goals. As in psychoanalysis, the patient is an active participant, generating free-floating imagery leading to mind expansion and insight to be shared with the therapist.

Interaction of self-hypnosis and psychoanalysis. The interaction of psychoanalytic technique with self-hypnosis is compatible. The altered state of consciousness and decrease of the censor foster free association, imagery and regression. The therapist can interpret on a variety of levels, for example, interpret transference, content, affect, self-perception, social interaction. The patient can employ self-hypnosis at home to further work-through affect, content and situation. The nature of the transference is of crucial importance, and the patient can experience the full range of transference reactions within a relatively long-term hypnoanalysis utilizing self-hypnosis which minimizes dependency.

Timing and practice. Self-hypnosis is taught sometimes within the first month of hypnotherapy. The patient is instructed to practice self-hypnosis once a day for 30 minutes to allow mind expansion and intense imagery to develop. This focus on massed practice at regular but infrequent intervals is necessary for the full development of inner experience.

Types of problems. Psychoanalysis self-hypnosis requires ego-integrity. Self-growth experiences, personality reconstruction, neuroses and narcissistic personality are some of the problems addressed.

Eisen and Fromm (1983) present an interesting method interweaving hetero-hypnotic psychotherapy, psychoanalytic technique and self-hypnosis. The hypnotherapist acts as a dependable parent figure, who is supportive and available when that is desirable, and who also encourages and fosters the patient's efforts to develop his/her own inner resources and ability to function autonomously. In this author's view, the interaction between therapists and patient is critical.

Physiological Self-Hypnosis

A physiological orientation to self-hypnosis is based on the assumption that mind and body interact and that self-hypnosis is a way of accessing that interaction. Current research in pain and in psychoneuroimmunology reflects the growing conviction that self-hypnosis will serve a useful purpose in the wholistic treatment of disease. The basic techniques require the patient to image certain organs and or metaphoric ideas which represent organs or to achieve a deep hypnotic state that will impact on the physiological functioning of the body. It is hypothesized that imagery will trigger physiological reactions, much like the image of eating a lemon triggers saliva. Relatively few therapists in the survey identified themselves as holding a physiological orientation, and of those who did the majority were psychiatrists. The role of the therapist in this orientation is that of a healer or prescriber.

Goals. The goals of physiological self-hypnosis are to access the physiological level of functioning, thus reducing physical tension, lowering blood pressure, decreasing heart rate, decreasing digestive juices, increasing the production of certain natural pain reducing substances and increasing the effectiveness of the immune system. Certainly, some of these responses are easily monitored, for example, relaxation, heart rate, blood pressure. Others are more difficult to track, and still others are in a hypothetical format needing more controlled research. Nonetheless, impressive anecdotal studies are reported (Crasilneck and Hall, 1985).

Interaction of physiological concepts with self-hypnosis. Hypnosis and imagery interact significantly. Imagery of a comfortable scene induces relaxation and a lessening of body tension. Physiological metaphors such as rubber bands which represent headache pain can be loosened in imagination and the patient feels more comfortable. Deep breathing seems to lead to more parsympathetic system activity and to reduce sympathetic activity. The mind-body interface cannot be denied.

Physiological therapists may teach the patient self-hypnosis within the first few weeks of therapy. They may ask for frequent but brief practice sessions, such as Luthe and Schultz's (1969) Autogenic Training and use of guided imagery exercises. There is relevant work with cancer patients (Margolis, 1982-83); work in pediatrics (Gardner and Olness, 1981); work in neurology (Sarbin and Slagle, 1980); see also Meszaros, Banyai and Greguss (1982).

Types of problems. Psychophysiological disorders, neurological problems, especially those involving loss of motivation, pain, anxiety secondary to illness, management problems, control of emotion related to illness as well as psychophysiological disorders are all relevant to a physiological orientation. It is surprising that more therapists do not follow a more frankly physiological model.

Model for Teaching Self-Hypnosis:
An Eclectic Approach

The two cases presented here are viewed as eclectic in orientation in that both contain techniques from behavioral, physiological and psychoanalytically-oriented approaches. Behavioral techniques are used for covert conditioning of imagery and relaxation. Physiological techniques are used to monitor thermal response to relaxation imagery, and physiological metaphors are used. Psychoanalytically-oriented techniques are used in hypnotic dreams, age regression and free association. The approach begins with body language and tension reduction (physiological) and moves towards a more psychoanalytically-oriented insight model. However, the model makes use of behavioral contingencies and cognitive techniques to implement behavioral change.

Thermal biofeedback readings are taken by the therapist during the session, and the patient is asked to monitor these readings as part of home practice. The purpose of thermal biofeedback readings is to monitor the direction and the degree to which the temperature changes. In the office, the therapist monitors the temperature and works with the patient as in any hetero-hypnotic situation, reinforcing relaxation and imagery, asking for input and amplifying helpful imagery. While the patient is instructed to create helpful warming imagery, the patient is not left alone with the biofeedback monitor in the office. The feedback given is provided in an interactive manner by the therapist, who observes the monitor and reports back to the patient. The focus is more on the images, thoughts, feelings that trigger temperature changes rather than on the amount of temperature change itself. Cognitive awareness of the trigger for change leads to the beginning of self-control. The process of imaging the trigger and receiving feedback validates the patient's ability to affect his/her physiology. The therapist asks the patient to practice at home inducing the effective trigger.

The practice of self-hypnosis, utilizing thermal biofeedback monitoring, appears to create an intermediary space where age regression, age progression, hypno-anesthesia and perceptual distortion can be experienced in a soothing, safe manner, for example, a holding environment (Winnicott, 1959). The rich imagery can be useful in gaining control of physical symptoms and success in developing a feeling of self-control, out of the office, at home, and at work.

The first hetero-hypnotic induction is the template that the patient follows in practicing self-hypnosis. Before terminating the hypnotic experience, the therapist gives a post-hypnotic suggestion that the patient practice the relaxation or deep breathing induction at home at least three times per days so that it becomes easier and easier to enter hypnosis.

The therapy hour is divided into three parts: 1) non-hypnotic review (15 minute); 2) practice of self-hypnosis, reinforced and guided by therapist (15 minutes); and 3) non-hypnotic debriefing (10 minutes). The therapist can adjust the time requirements to his or her own time frame; for example, a 45-minute session requires some reduction of each part. By a division of the session into three parts, both conscious and unconscious reactions can be activated and indirectly monitored by the therapist. In this way, the therapist can interpret whether the patient is receptive, resistant or overwhelmed at both the conscious, non-hypnotic level and the hypnotic-unconscious level. This model presumes that change can best be accomplished by a combination of conscious-unconscious motivations and that the personality functions best when both conscious and unconscious processes are activated, much like a finely-tuned car which runs on eight cylinders, rather than an untuned car which runs poorly when one or more of the cylinders are deactivated.

Case Examples

The following case examples illustrate the training in and use of eclectic self-hypnosis with two patients. Both patients with psychosomatic disorders were referred by a physician for hypnotherapy. Neither patient wanted traditional psychotherapy. Because of their psychosomatic problems, the use of an eclectic approach was indicated since they were uncomfortable with their spontaneous thought and felt out of control of their bodies. In this therapeutic model, the patient could learn self-hypnosis so as to be more in control of the symptom. The use of monitoring the imagery and hand warming was useful in motivating the patient to use effective imagery. In addition, the temperature readings were helpful in determining the degree of mastery the patient had gained over reducing tension and fostering relaxation. As the patients became more confident, more free association and psychoanalytically-oriented insight techniques could be used.

Case Example One

Cindy, a 35-year-old white female had migraines which occurred on a weekly basis. While she was in ongoing insight therapy, she wanted help in reducing the discomfort and frequency of the migraines. She was referred for hypnotherapy by her therapist. During the initial interview, she presented herself as intellectual, logical, but not psychologically minded. Her history revealed that her mother had migraines as did her grandmother. Cindy believed that her migraines were unrelated to stress. This patient appeared physically tense, sitting up in a rigid manner, with a strained expression on her face.

After a discussion of relaxation and hand warming, an electrode from the Cyborg J-42 Biofeedback Monitor was fastened to her right index finger. She was instructed to close her eyes, sit back in the chair and describe a comfortable scene. As she described her comfortable scene, her breathing rate decreased, her musculature relaxed and her temperature decreased. Her imagery was of a comfortable place. As he described the relief of comfort, her temperature began to rise. The therapist reinforced the comfort described and the enjoyment of it.

The therapist suggested to the patient that she could practice the comfortable, relaxing imagery exercise at home. She was to note her temperature only before practice and after practice and to report on her practice at the next session. Warming was to be monitored by a Biotic Band.

Home practice revealed an average temperature change of two degrees warming per practice session. Within four?regular migraines. Follow-up at six months and one year reflected continued relief.

Case Example Two

Ed, a 34-year-old white male with a diagnosis of adult asthma, was referred for hypnotherapy to reduce his anxiety about his response to asthma and to learn ways of reducing his attacks through relaxation. This patient experienced great fear and impatience during stress—fear that he would not be able to breathe and impatient at having to wait his turn in line, when driving and in many other life situations.

After discussion of relaxation and hand warming as a way of monitoring, the patient was instructed to close his eyes and to describe a warm, comfortable scene. After he described the scene, he was asked how he felt. He described himself as relaxing, more quiet and breathing easily. In addition, his temperature rose.

The therapist reinforced the comfortable images and suggested that the patient practice at home, thinking of the comfortable scene and monitoring the temperature before and after the practice.

The patient reported fewer asthmatic attacks and less need for medication after six sessions. We continued to work on increasing his confidence and sense of self-control over four months. Follow-up at six months and one year indicate that the patient continued to remain in control and to have fewer asthmatic attacks.

Discussion of Cases

Initially, both patients did not want to talk about life stress. Rather, they wanted to learn a technique that would reduce the reaction to stress. After one week's practice, Cindy was able reliably and predictably to increase her peripheral temperature by at least two degrees. She spontaneously described the feeling of warmth as being very relaxing. She felt that the home practice was not as dramatic as self-hypnosis in the office, but she believed that she was successful both in warming and in relaxing.

Ed responded to the sessions by very vivid self-directive imagery. He eloquently described the comfort of his chair. He was able to shift spontaneously to his breathing and to imagery that would help him master his fears of losing control of his breathing. The therapist served to amplify his imagery of more flexible breathing and to suggest that he begin to use this imagery whenever he became frightened or impatient. He liked the notion of the images functioning as a prevention of attacks. Clearly, the patient provided the necessary imagery and meaning, while the therapist served to reinforce them.

Occasionally, patients will have initial difficulty warming. No matter what warm images they use, the temperature goes on a downward spiral. This phenomenon appears related to conflict about the effects of warming as well as to reflect a struggle with the therapist over who is in control. Discussion of these concerns and home practice lead to successful hand warming.

While traditional relaxation procedures were not used, the induction consisted of imagery described by the patient and reinforced by the therapist. This technique is a utilization technique as described by Erickson (1958). Given the appropriate environment, patients can use imagery and reverie as a way of entering a hypnotic state.

The physical appearance of the patients suggested that they were in a hypnotic state. Their muscles seemed more flaccid and relaxed; their reaction time was slower; they seemed more receptive to their own imagery and to suggestions by the therapist than before the procedure was initiated.

The imagery of the patients was concrete but detailed and quite vivid. They talked as though they were at their imagined places rather than in my office. According to Bensen (1981), such involvement is characteristic of hypnosis.

Both patients began to feel more in control of their imagery and of their bodies. Their symptoms decreased as they continued to practice self-hypnosis. During home practice, the average increase in temperature was two degrees. A change of one degree or more is considered significant. While more change was obtained in the office, more sensitive electronic biofeedback equipment was used in contrast to the Biotic Band. Nonetheless, the important factor appears to be direction of change rather than absolute amount of change. During their home practice, their imagery became more detailed and more elaborated. At times, they created even more comfortable images which they reported.

These case examples, although positive, are not intended as generalizations for other patients. Rather, the intention in this chapter is to highlight the importance of matching a treatment to a patient's needs and requirements. These patients needed to learn control of their bodies. The use of imagery generated by the patient, which triggers relaxation and warmth and which is reinforced by the therapist and specifically prescribed for home practice, is an example of matching a specific imagery technique to a patient's needs.

This model should be effective with other types of patients, such as panic disorders, where the patient feels extreme anxiety and feels out of control. Simple phobias, too, would be receptive to this approach. It would be useful to try the method with a variety of disorders where the patient is interested in learning self-hypnosis but fears more unstructured experience.

In summary, this chapter has included a discussion of styles of clinical self-hypnosis. Four orientations were presented and compared as to goals, times of practice, role of therapist. Finally, two clinical examples of an eclectic self-hypnosis therapy were described.

References

Banyai EI, Meszaros I, Gregussi AC: Alteration of activity level: The essence of hypnosis of a by-product of the type of induction. In Proceedings of the 28th International Congress of the Physiological Society. Budapest, London, Pergammon Press, 1980
Benson H, Flipper MZ: The Relaxation Response. New York, Morrow, 1975
Crasilneck HB, Hall JA: Clinical Hypnosis: Principles and Applications, 2nd ed. New York, Grune & Stratton, 1985

Eisen MR, Fromm E: The clinical use of self-hypnosis in hypnotherapy tapping the functions and imagery and adaptive regression. Int J Clin Exp Hypn 31:243-245, 1983

Erickson ME: Naturalistic techniques of hypnosis. Am J Clin Hypn 1:3-8, 1958

Fromm E, Brown DP, Hurt SW, Oberlander JZ, Bower AM, Pfeifer G: The phenomena and characteristics of self-hypnosis. Int. J Clin Exp Hypn 29:189-246, 1981

Gardner GG, Olness K: Hypnosis and Hypnotherapy With Children. New York, Grune & Stratton, 1981

J-42 Feedback Thermometer (Reg. TM) Cyborg Corp. Boston, 1977

Luthe W, Schultz JH: Autogenic Methods. New York, Grune & Stratton, 1969

Margolis CG: Hypnotic imagery with cancer patients. Am J Clin Hypn 25:128-134, 1982-83

Sacerdote PP: Teaching self-hypnosis to adults. Int J Clin Exp Hypn 29:282-299, 1981

Sanders S: Styles of clinical self-hypnosis. Presented at the 26th annual meeting of the American Society of Clinical Hypnosis, November 1983

Sanders S: Survey of ASCH members' use of self-hypnosis. Presented at the annual meeting of the American Society of Clinical Hypnosis, March 1986

Sanders S: Prescriptive self-hypnosis. Presented at the annual meeting of the American Society of Clinical Hypnosis, November 1983

Sarbin TR, Slagle R: Psychophysiological outcomes of hypnosis. In Burrows GD, Dennerstein L (eds): Handbook of Hypnosis and Psychosomatic Medicine. Amsterdam, Elsevier/North Holland Biomedical Press, 1984

Singer JL, Pope KS: Daydreaming and imagery skills as predisposing capacities for self-hypnosis. Int J Clin Exp Hypn 29:271-281, 1981

Tellegan A, Atkinson G: Openness to absorbing and self-altering experiences ("absorption"); a trait related to hypnotic susceptibility. J Abn Psychol 83:268-277, 1974

The Biotic Band (Reg. TM), Biotemp Products, Inc., 1950 W 86th Street, Indianapolis, Indiana

Winnicott DW: Transitional objects and transitional phenomena: A study of the first not-me possession. Int J Psychoanalysis 34:89-98, 1953

5 INDIRECT HYPNOTIC APPROACHES

J. ADRIAN WILLIAMS,Ph.D.

The indirect hypnotic approaches were devised to circumvent the resistance to hypnosis and therapy frequently exhibited by patients in the clinical setting. These approaches have proved useful in both the induction of hypnosis and its utilization for psychotherapeutic and medical purposes.

While indirect methods may take a different route to the induction of hypnosis and to its clinical application, the actual hypnotic *state* induced is the same as that produced by other induction techniques. It has been noted (Erickson, Rossi and Rossi, 1976; Erickson and Rossi, 1979), however, that indirect approaches to hypnosis frequently yield deeper and more cooperative trance states. Such techniques presumably achieve their effects as a result of the capacity of the individual patient to both perceive and respond to stimuli outside the awareness of his or her conscious mind (Erickson, 1964a, 1980, 1983; Erickson, Rossi and Rossi, 1976; Erickson and Rossi, 1979, 1981; Williams, 1982a, 1982b; Zeig, 1980). The patient's ability to perceive and respond to various minimal cue stimuli at an unconscious level allows the hypnotist to facilitate therapeutic change in a manner which bypasses the rigid limitations of the patient's conscious sets and stereotyped frames of reference. It has been typical of the indirect approach to therapy that the changes initially introduced by the therapist may seem small (Haley, 1973), yet they tend to be incorporated as a fundamental component of the patient's behavior so that the change tends to be naturally escalated by the patient to deal with large areas of his or her behavior, affect, and cognition.

A further advantage of indirect hypnotic techniques is that the patient treated by these methods tends to respond to the various suggestions and instructions in an individualized manner consistent with his or her own personality. Specifically, the patient will generally assimilate and implement the indirect communications in such a manner that he or she goes into a trance and/or carries out therapeutic suggestions in his or her own idiosyncratic and personalized style. This situation allows hypnosis and therapy to be provided in a highly individualized format that utilizes the patient's own particular strengths and weaknesses as an integral part of the therapy, thereby maximizing the therapeutic results.

The original impetus for indirect hypnotic approaches was derived from the work of the late Milton H. Erickson, M.D. Erickson's career spanned some 50 years, **41** and his findings were presented in some 150 scientific articles and several books. A major problem associated with this work that was Erickson's creative and brilliant intervention techniques were not presented in a general paradigm that would allow other therapists to readily formulate similar interventions. This problem has been addressed in recent years in the works cited above. This author has elaborated a "key concepts" view of the indirect approach to hypnotic psychotherapy that attempts to provide a more general paradigm for formulating clinical interventions while avoiding the excessive rigidity of a purely theoretical formulation.

Six Key Concepts

There are six key concepts in the author's formulation (Williams, 1982b, in press) of the indirect hypnotic approach: 1) observation; 2) speaking the patient's language; 3) patient rigidity; 4) the utilization approach; 5) hypnosis; and 6) multiple level communication. We may briefly consider each of these concepts. The application of observational skills is of critical importance in the use of the indirect approach to hypnosis. Careful clinical observation allows the therapist to acquire much of the operational information necessary for effective intervention with a patient. The therapist attempts to "speak the patient's language" in the course of his or her interactions with the patient. Speaking the patient's language refers to the therapist's ability, through observations, to identify essential characteristics of the patient's personality, cognitive structure, affective structure, and patterns of behavior, personality, cognitive structure, affective structure, and patterns of behavior, and then to utilize those characteristics to communicate both verbally and nonverbally with the patient, to devise a treatment strategy in accord with those characteristics, and to effect a resolution of the patient's problems in a manner acceptable to the patient's personality as a whole (Williams, 1982b). Patient rigidity, which refers to functioning that is stiff, unyielding, and devoid of flexibility, may frequently be observed in a patient's behavior, internal frames of reference, attitudes, beliefs, or cognitive associations. Rigidity is considered, in this approach, to play a significant role in the formation and maintenance of psychotherapy. The utilization approach is quite complex, but can be summarized as a means of approaching the patient which utilizes the patient's presenting behaviors, attitudes, reactions, and symptomatology to actually resolve the patient's symptoms. Hypnosis is considered an integral component or the indirect hypnotic approach. A thorough working knowledge of the various hypnotic phenomena, the chaining of behaviors, and altered states of awareness is critical. Finally, multiple level communication is also critical to the effective application of indirect hypnotic approaches, since it provides the basis on which the therapist may present a variety of therapeutic ideas and suggestions outside the patient's conscious awareness.

The listing of key concepts above serves only to identify them superficially. Clearer understanding will require their examination in detail. Further development of indirect hypnotic approaches has been receiving increasing attention (DeShazer, 1979; Gindhart, 1981; O'Hanlon, 1982; Rossi, 1982; Williams, 1982a, 1983, 1985a; Zeig, 1983, 1985), and these developments will affect the clinical practice of hypnosis and hypnotic techniques for years to come.

Assessment

One of the primary applications of the indirect approaches to hypnosis has been in the treatment of patients resistant to other, more traditional forms of hypnosis and therapy. The assessment of such patients for possible application of hypnosis has typically followed an observational, naturalistic format rather than an assessment process of formal tests and measurements. This observational assessment, as employed by the author for hypnotic induction, focuses on the degree of the individual subject's "response attentiveness," a term coined by Erickson to describe the tendency of the good hypnotic subject to develop a focused, attentive state relative to others in interpersonal interaction and to be unconsciously responsive to the minimal cues inherent in the interpersonal communication by the therapist. Those utilizing the indirect hypnotic approaches make the general assumption that the patient is likely to be hypnotizable; clinically, the question is simply what approach will be required from the operator to induce and utilize hypnosis most effectively with the subject at hand.

The decision as to what induction and treatment approach will be employed with a given patient is based on the results of the therapist's observations of the patient. Variables such as topic areas which stimulate the patient's attention and interest, the patient's patterns of associations, the patient's internal frame of reference, his or her primary modes of sensory perception, and the constellation of symptoms presented are commonly evaluated to provide avenues of inducing and utilizing hypnosis. The goal of this form of assessment is to acquire information that can be used to direct the subject's attention and to gradually focus it on matters of inner relevance and importance to the therapeutic tasks.

A clinical example may help to clarify the comments above. In mid-1983, the author saw a 25-year-old, college educated, white female who was referred by her psychiatrist for treatment of severe choking during eating. No medical basis for the choking had been discovered despite examinations by numerous specialists and a thorough diagnostic workup at the hospital. The psychiatrist had attempted to utilize a traditional hypnotic approach, with no results. He referred the patient, Val, to the author as a last option before long-term analytic treatment. Val presented herself in a highly controlled, precise way. She related her pertinent history in a precise manner, which corresponded well with the information provided by the referring physician. Val reported herself to be a shy, withdrawn individual who easily became nervous. She described her choking condition as one which tended to come on suddenly, with little forewarning, and over which she had no voluntary control. She explained that she had lost between 10 and 15 pounds in the preceding two months and that it took her some 60 minutes to eat a soft sandwich.

Inquiry regarding the circumstances surrounding the first occurrence of the problem in eating elicited only vague statements indicating that she had choked initially while at a get-together with her husband and some friends. Her vague comments were viewed with interest, as they were in striking contrast to her previous overly precise mode of presentation. The food at the party was unremarkable. The primary point of clinical interest was a casual observation by the patient that she had gone to the party only because her husband had pressured her, even though the gathering was with some of her friends.

A general history was taken, which revealed that the patient had suffered from spells of hyperventilation five years earlier. Val reported that the hyperventilation had been successfully treated through administration of diazepam. She also reported that she was currently in her second marriage and that she had one child from the previous marriage. She denied any other medical or psychological problems and claimed that everything was going exceptionally well in her current marriage. Her husband was extremely supportive of her, and they related well in *all* areas—the emphasis was hers. She mentioned that the author, "being a shrink," would probably want to know about her sex life, that everything was fine there, and that there was no need to discuss that subject any further. As she made the comments regarding her sexual adjustment, Val began to shift about in her seat, crossed her legs, and folded her arms across her lap. Her comments were made in a rather defensive, final tone of voice. The author asked no further questions regarding her marriage or sexual adjustment, but went on to other areas of a general history, getting the clear impression that Val did not like and would not cooperate with "being told what to do."

Her verbal emphasis throughout the interview was on negative aspects of experience, that is, what she could *not* do, and on numerous instances in which she had said "no" to people in her interpersonal environment. Val followed the comments and observations the author made during the initial interview in an absorbed manner, showing response attentiveness. She appeared to be particularly responsive to those comments which utilized words emphasizing sensory and emotional components of experience.

The information gathered above suggested to the author that despite her negativism Val would be a good hypnotic subject. Her style of interaction indicated that she would respond to an induction approach that emphasized the sensory and emotional components of her experience, that was presented in a precise, controlled fashion, and that did not lead her to perceive herself as being given orders. The subsequent initial induction of hypnosis proceeded by the author having Val focus in a rather precise, stepwise fashion on alterations in her respiration, her heart rate, and sensations of lightness or heaviness in her limbs. Hand levitation was induced nonverbally through an extremely light, hesitant suggestion of lifting her wrist. This lifting was spontaneously continued by the patient in a series of small upward jerks reminiscent of the ratcheting of a cogwheel. Induction of a deeper trance was achieved by the chaining of each new suggestion onto the successful completion of a previous suggestion. In this manner, the author was able in the first session of hypnosis to elicit hyperamnesia, anesthesia, time distortion, amnesia, and negative auditory and visual hallucinations. These varied hypnotic phenomena were employed with the goals of 1) training the patient to respond comfortably from an unconscious level in the hypnotic state, and 2) increasing the options available to the therapist during the intervention phase of treatment to follow.

Intervention Process

The intervention process is generally structured to take advantage of the information secured during the assessment phase. Indirect suggestions are offered in a manner which fits within the overall context of associations, behaviors, interests, and modes of sensory perception exhibited by the hypnotic subject. The author sees the intervention process as one which flows quite naturally from the assessment phase, and often may be initiated during the course of the assessment procedure. Indirect suggestions may be presented in the form of interspersed comments (Erickson, 1966), binds, double binds, metaphors, jokes, plays on words, anecdotes, paradoxical instructions, and permissive directions.

The author generally considers intervention to consist of two components, the overall treatment strategy and the specific intervention techniques. The overall treatment strategy is the general plan of approach to the clinical problem presented by the patient, that is, *what* the therapist considers necessary to successfully accomplish the therapeutic goals. For instance, with the patient who presents in a resistant, highly rebellious, dichotomizing manner, the author might decide to utilize a treatment strategy based on paradoxical directives and assignments. This paradoxical strategy would be selected to fit the idiosyncratic behavior, attitudes, affective response, and associative structure of the particular patient.

The technique component of the intervention process represents the *how* of accomplishing the strategic goals on a moment by moment basis in the therapeutic interaction. The techniques are thus the actual procedures and interactions between therapist and patient that are implemented to initiate therapeutic change. Paradoxical techniques include specific direct commands, authoritarian statements, predictions, etc. that tend to superficially convey a message directing action contrary to how the therapist might actually prefer the patient to respond. These techniques, while perhaps forceful, are actually indirect in that they are employed with the strategic goal of motivating the patient to cooperate with therapy through resisting the actual directions being given.

The case of Val offers points of interest for a study of indirect intervention procedures. After securing the information outlined above (Assessment), the author hypothesized that Val's eating problem was a conversion-type reaction, a condition that has been described as *globus hystericus*. The available evidence, while incomplete, suggested to the author that Val had significant sexual conflicts, that she had significant conflicts with perceived authority figures, and that she apparently had combined these two conflicts and projected them onto the marital and sexual relationship with her husband. The result was the formation of symptoms, that is, the tendency to choke when eating. Since Val had so specifically and vigorously rejected at a conscious level the notion of any sexual problems, the author concluded that efforts at symptom resolution based on insight would probably fail. The author's clinical experience led him to the opinion that Val would be unlikely to respond to paradoxical techniques, that she might simply leave therapy. Further, the original referral had been for hypnotic therapy, and that was what Val indicated that she was expecting and willing to accept.

Thus, the author developed an intervention strategy aimed at resolving Val's symptomatic behavior within the parameters of what would be acceptable to her individual personality. Val's problem was hypothesized to be primarily sexual in nature, yet her conscious level rejection of the possibility of a sexual etiology militated against an overt exploration of this area. Further, since the actual physical behaviors involved in choking were involuntary in nature, the author decided to direct part of the therapy toward reestablishing a more normal pattern of eating and swallowing, a strategy which would be expected by the patient. Recollecting experiences with patients who experienced similar rigidities and resistances (Erickson, personal communication, 1978; Williams, 1982a, 1982b, 1983, 1985a, 1985b), the author utilized an extremely indirect approach that would deal with the hypothesized sexual and authority conflicts completely outside the conscious awareness of the patient. Work by Erickson (Erickson, Rossi and Rossi, 1976; Erickson and Rossi, 1979) and the author's own clinical experience assured him that should his hypothesis prove inaccurate the patient would simply not respond to this line of suggestion. The initial interview had demonstrated that Val was, in fact, quite capable of going into a hypnotic state and developing many of the classical hypnotic phenomena. Thus, the author evaluated the therapeutic task as primarily one of developing a suitable set of techniques to implement the strategy outlined above.

A hypnotic state was induced by recapitulation (Erickson, Rossi and Rossi, 1976) and was deepened by negatively worded suggestions. The patient was told that she did *not* have to pay any attention to the author, that she did *not* have to listen to the author's comments, that she did *not* have to attend to an increasing relaxation, etc. In this manner, a satisfactory medium to deep trance state was induced. Subsequent therapeutic suggestions were associated with the patient's kinesthetic response in such a manner that the execution of the physical response (inhalation, exhalation, body movements, etc.) tended to establish a momentum of response that facilitated acceptance of the therapeutic suggestion. An anecdote of the treatment of a previous patient suffering from a post-traumatic stress disorder resulting from a sexual assault was related to Val in order to introduce the idea of a problem having a sexual etiology. Interspersed throughout this anecdote were various suggestions (Erickson, 1966; Williams, 1982a, 1982b, 1983) that served to activate amnesic processes for trance events. Subsequent to this anecdote, the author spoke at some length to the patient, gradually and progressively interspersing a set of suggestions that associated eating with comfort and appetite with pleasurable emotional and physical sensations. Further interspersed suggestions focused on feelings of comfort being associated with sexuality and sexual behaviors. Through the use of a confusion technique (Erickson, 1964b), the patient was reoriented to an earlier period in her own history. Various anecdotes were then presented which provided her with the opportunity to view her own sexuality and sexual behavior in general in a more positive light. The concept of comfort in sexual areas was also systematically introduced as having occurred over a period of time in the patient's own personal history, while the author was apparently training the patient in the hypnotic phenomenon of hypermnesia. The response of comfort with sexual matters was subtly linked with pleasant associations in all sensory and affective modalities. Finally, a distraction technique was employed, with the author giving the patient very detailed instructions in the trance state as to how to develop a self-hypnotic state. These instructions and the hypnotic session were terminated with directions to the patient on how to awaken herself from the trance state. This distraction technique was employed with the aim of diverting the patient's conscious attention away from the therapeutic implications of the work, which could then proceed to be elaborated behaviorally from an unconscious level.

The nature of the indirect hypnotic work described above is such that suggestions are often given by virtue of tonal emphasis, by allusion to ideas previously (though perhaps casually) presented, by implication, through use of symobolism, etc. A brief excerpt is presented to give the reader some of the flavor of this approach. The excerpt is from the session described immediately above, and focuses on a portion of the confusion approach utilized to reorient Val to an earlier period in her life. Rather than directing Val to develop an age regression, the method employed made use of a series of statements engaging in a train of associations that became increasingly absorbing and elicited a response of age regression. The comments below were made utilizing a deliberate rate of speech, with vocal emphases implying that each idea was a matter of considerable significance and should be closely attended to. The excerpt presented is taken from just past the half-way point of the hypnotic session, with the patient already in a medium depth of hypnosis. The session was in fact conducted on a Monday, not a Tuesday. Perhaps one of the first things that is noticed about the transcript is that there is a tendency for the reader to become caught up in the ideas being presented. In an actual hypnotherapeutic session, the patient's response is generally to wonder what the point is and where the speaker is leading; this reaction typically results in an increasing absorption in what is being said. Various grammatical errors were intentionally made by the author in his remarks to Val in order to further confuse the time sense of the communication. The general trend of the author's communications led the patient backward in time while subtly encouraging that regression to be experienced as occurring in the present. Comments on the microdynamics (Erickson and Rossi, 1976b) of the hypnotic communications are presented in the righthand column.

Excerpt from Hypnotherapeutic Session

. . .I may point out what we both know that today is Tuesday, and yet we've all had the experience of going all day Saturday, and having it feel like a Sunday. Or going all day Tuesday, and having it feel like it ought to be Wednesday. And so in fact we are able to think of one day as a completely different day.

This statement demands agreement, yet is false (it was in fact Monday).

A series of true statements that she could identify with experientially.

Now we all know that Tuesday follows Monday, that Wednesday follows Tuesday, that Thursday follows Wednesday, and so on. And that it will do that this week just as it did last week, and the week before that. And in fact (pause) it is sometimes difficult to remember whether we did such and such *this* week, or was it *last* week? And we might do something several weeks ago and not really specifically recall whether it was two weeks ago or three weeks ago.

Truisms that tend to facilitate acceptance of subsequent statements. Val was likely to be so confused regarding the initial statement above that she would find it easier to accept it rather than try to figure it out, particularly when the tonal emphases reflected complete confliction on the part of the author.
    Indirect amnesia; further confusion regarding the identification of time.

Just as there are four weeks in most months. Four weeks in this month, so there is four weeks in last month.

Truism, facilitating acceptance.

Grammatical error which served to shift tense (i.e. experience) to present.

    And dates are a very interesting thing because they follow one another, so that a month ago Tuesday followed Monday, two months ago Sunday followed Saturday, and it's really nothing to cause anyone to gulp in disbelief to recognize that one day

Play on multiple meanings of the word "dates."

Indirect cue referring to original symptom, which alerts the unconscious to use of multiple level communication.

follows another now just as it did a month ago, two months ago, a year ago (pause) ten years ago (spoken softly). Now (pause) at one time your birthday as a little girl fell on a Tuesday. And still other times it fell on a Wednesday, or a Saturday.

Preliminary for age regression to childhood.

And one of the nice things about birthday parties is that there is always something pleasant to do. Might have soft drinks and games, and little girls enjoy having games at their birthday parties. Pin the tail on the donkey. And some of the games that little girls enjoy change as the little girls grow older. So that every young lady, at some point, discovers that spin the bottle is much more interesting than pin the tail on the donkey.

Reorients to little girl age, and is integrated into previous pattern of days of the week, which focused her on the days, thus allowing indirect suggestion of age regression.

Present tense ratifying regression.

This includes Val, and implies her response can be similar.

Val appeared for her next session reporting considerable improvement. She described herself as feeling much more emotionally and physically comfortable at meals. She now was able to eat even sticky foods, as opposed to just soft sandwiches. Further, she was able to eat a full meal in approximately half the time that she had previously required for just a soft sandwich. Val also demonstrated a comprehensive amnesia for the events of the trance state. The author saw her for the remainder of this session and for a follow-up session, at which time her progress was maintained.

The use of an indirect hypnotic approach provides several points of interest in this case. Since the case was a purely clinical one, and not a research project, many of the controls and measures available in the experimental situation were not applicable. Further, the very nature of the indirect approach does not easily lend itself to standardized, replicable experimental control, since extensive use is made of the patient's individual personality structure, his or her unique idiosyncracies, and the situational variables in the treatment session. Thus, the effectiveness of this approach is generally measured in terms of clinical response to the original problem. Val has remained symptom free, both according to her family physician and as confirmed by telephone follow-up with Val some three years later. In terms of effectiveness, the clinical results have been satisfactory as determined by the patient's subsequent adjustment. There has been no further choking while eating, and Val remains able to eat any food she desires. Regarding the proposed etiology of the original symptom, Val reported that she and her husband are much closer and even happier now, and she demonstrated a much more relaxed, casual attitude regarding her sexual adjustment. She spontaneously comments that things have improved considerably in the sexual relationship with her husband and that perhaps she "used to be a little uncomfortable about sex." Val remarked that she still did not recall what had been done in her hypnotherapy sessions, but that she was glad she had been referred for hypnosis.

Future Trends

The author anticipates increasing utilization of the indirect hypnotic approaches in the future. Interest in and study of these approaches continues to increase. A large number of clinicians are now employing indirect hypnotic techniques on a daily basis; the author frequently receives questions and/or comments from other psychotherapists relating to new applications of the indirect approach in clinical practice. This increasing clinical activity has spurred an interest in innovative approaches to hypnosis and psychotherapy and has done much to restore the credibility of and interest in the anecdotal case report. Many workers are attempting to develop and refine naturalistic methods of research, which will increase the scientific rigor of study and will ultimately open many doors to areas of the clinical practice of psychotherapy not currently amenable to organized scientific investigation.

References

DeShazer S: On transforming symptoms: An approach to an Erickson procedure. Am J Clin Hypn 22:17-28, 1979

Erickson MH: The "surprise" and "my friend John" techniques of hypnosis: Minimal cues and natural field experimentation. Am J Clin Hypn 6:293-307, 1964

Erickson MH: The confusion technique in hypnosis. Am J Clin Hypn 6:183-207, 1964

Erickson MH: The interspersal hypnotic technique for symptom correction and pain control. Am J Clin Hypn 8:198-209, 1966

Erickson MH: The Nature of Hypnosis and Suggestion. New York, Irvington Publishers, Inc., 1980

Erickson MH: Healing in Hypnosis. New York, Irvington Publishers, Inc., 1983

Erickson MH, Rossi EL, Rossi SS: Hypnotic Realities. New York, Irvington Publishers, Inc., 1976

Erickson MH, Rossi EL: Two level communication and the microdynamics of trance and suggestion. Am J Clin Hypn 18:153-171, 1976

Erickson MH, Rossi EL: Hypnotherapy: An Exploratory Casebook. New York, Irvington Publishers, Inc., 1979

Erickson MH, Rossi EL: Experiencing Hypnosis: Therapeutic Approaches to Altered States. New York, Irvington Publishers, Inc., 1981

Gindhart LR: The use of a metaphoric story in therapy: A case report. Am J Clin Hypn 23:202-206, 1981

Haley J: Uncommon Therapy. New York, Ballantine Books, 1973

O'Hanlon W: Strategic pattern intervention. J Strategic and Systematic Therapies 1:26-33, 1982

Rossi EL: Hypnosis and ultradian cycles: A new state(s) theory of hypnosis? Am J Clin Hypn 25:21-32, 1982

Williams JA: Indirect hypnotic therapy of compulsive stealing. Swedish J Clin Hypn 9:41-44, 1982

Williams JA: An analysis of an atheoretical system of psychotherapy: Ericksonian approaches to psychotherapy. Dissertation Abstracts International 43:740A, 1982

Williams JA: Indirect hypnotic therapy of nyctophobia: A case report. Am J Clin Hypn 28:10-15, 1985

Williams JA: Erickson's use of psychological implication. In Zeig J (ed): Ericksonian Psychotherapy: Clinical Applications. New York, Brunner/Mazel, 1985

Williams JA: Key concepts of an atheoretical approach to psychotherapy. In Yapko MD (ed): Strategic and Hypnotic Interventions: Practices and Principles. New York, Irvington Publishers, Inc. (In press)

Zeig J: A Teaching Seminar with Milton H. Erickson, M.D. New York, Brunner/Mazel, 1980

Zeig J: Ericksonian Approaches to Hypnosis and Psychotherapy. New York, Brunner/Mazel, 1982

Zeig J (ed): Ericksonian Psychotherapy: Volumes I and II. New York, Brunner/Mazel, 1985

UNIT TWO
GENERAL APPLICATIONS
OF HYPNOSIS

6 HYPNOSIS IN PSYCHOTHERAPY
Part I: Hypnosis in Psychiatry

CHARLES B. MUTTER, M.D.

Hypnosis in one form or another is used by all health care providers; any patient who uncritically accepts suggestion, either direct or indirect, is accessing input from the therapist. Any suggestion, whether verbal or nonverbal, given with or without ceremonial trance induction, that alters the mind set of the patient is, in fact, hypnotic in nature. The psychiatrist should be sensitive to this concept since his verbalizations are readily grasped by the patient, and his language and therapeutic approaches should be designed to produce healthier changes in the patient's functioning.

Table 7-1 lists the general uses of hypnosis in psychiatry. Since each chapter in this text addresses a specific disorder that is encountered in psychiatric practice, this chapter will provide a broader overview of hypnosis as a technique, factors influencing effectiveness, hypnoanalytic techniques, the mind-body relationship, and clinical applications.

Hypnosis as a Technique

Hypnosis is not a treatment form but a technique that can be implemented for symptom alleviation, mobilizing transference, and analytic purposes (Fromm, 1984). All these uses help the patient gain greater mastery of his mind and body. Ego strengthening occurs through the reduction of anxiety and fear, with the patient developing a more rational understanding of his problem and a more positive attitude about his ability to solve it.

Factors Influencing Effectiveness

Certain factors influence the effectiveness of any psycho-therapeutic intervention (Table 7-2). The initial step in the treatment process is the establishment of rapport with the patient. The assessment of the patient's personality structure, formulation of a diagnosis, and determination of motivation for change are the bases for understanding the patient and his problem and provide the foundation of hypnotic inter- 55 vention. Clear and honest explanations about the patient's problem, the role of hypnosis, and misconceptions can eliminate unrealistic expectations and enable the patient to develop trust in the therapist. It is essential to know what the symptoms mean to the patient and under what conditions they were formed.

Table 7-1. Use of Hypnosis in Psychiatry

1. Analytic Investigation

2. Habit Disorders
   - A. Smoking
   - B. Obesity
   - C. Tics, thumb sucking, nail biting
   - D. Enuresis

3. Psychoneuroses
   - A. Anxiety and depression
   - B. Obsessive and compulsive reactions
   - C. Dissocation and fugue states
   - D. Conversion reaction
   - E. Phobias

4. Personality and Character Disorders
   - A. Substance abuse
   - B. Exhibitionism

5. Psychophysiologic (Psychosomatic) Disorders

6. Organic Disorders
   - A. Acute and chronic pain
   - B. Neurologic disorders
   - C. Head trauma
   - D. Cancer and terminal illness

7. Psychosis and Borderline States

8. Forensic Investigation

9. Sexual Dysfunction

10. Crisis Intervention and Stress Management

11. Multiple Personality Disorder

12. Post-Traumatic Stress Disorder

Table 7-2. Factors Influencing Effective Treatment

1. Rapport

2. Assessment of patient's personality structure

3. Motivation for change

4. Transference

5. Hypnotizability

6. Patient's expectations

7. Secondary gain

8. Therapist's traits

The phenomena of transference and countertransference are concepts basic to psychiatry. In hypnosis, one may see a heightening of transference and counter-transference reactions (Crasilneck, 1985; Fromm, 1984; Wolberg, 1975). A therapeutic alliance must be formed before hypnotherapy ensues. Some individuals have difficulty developing interpersonal relationships, and hypnosis may serve as a catalyst. Fisher (1954) demonstrated the long-term value of even a single hypnotic induction with these types of patients. The uncritical acceptance of suggestion by the subject usually negates any form of transference resistance.

Although hypnotizability varies with each patient, it is the author's experience that almost all patients respond favorably to the hypnotic experience. Occasionally, as in the example which follows an exception may arise.

A 62-year-old male was referred by his family physician because of herpes zoster (shingles) affecting his seventh left intercostal space. He had cutaneous lesions along that nerve segment which did not respond to steroids, nerve blocks or analgesics. He was a conscientious, work-oriented individual who took great pride in his business skills. Having retired five months prior to the onset of his symptoms, he was spending a great deal of time at home. He described his wife as a good homemaker and mother but admitted to having developed numerous conflicts with her following his retirement.

The patient expressed the hope that hypnosis would allevitae his suffering since all else had failed. He was a good hypnotic subject, and he developed hypnoanalgesia during trance. Post-hypnotic analgesic suggestions were utilized, and a follow-up appointment was scheduled for reinforcement of these suggestions. He cancelled his appointment two days later, claiming that he had not experienced any relief. At a later date, an informant advised me that the patient seemed much improved, although he still complained of pain to his wife. It was further discovered that, prior to his retirement, he had received very little attention from his wife. His illness and pain brought him greater attention. Psychodynamically, the second gain influenced his reluctance to give up his symptoms. This case illustrates the importance of an indepth evaluation not only of the symptom but also of the meaning of that symptom, that is, the function it serves.

Perhaps the most critical factor which influences the effectiveness of hypnosis is the personality of the therapist because he serves as a role model who must be free of anxiety while working with his patient. He must be clear in his appraisal and set realistic goals that will serve the patient's needs. He should be aware of any bias that could interfere with the treatment process. Finally, he should see himself as a facilitator, attributing any success to the patient.

Symptom Alleviation

Perhaps the most common use of hypnosis in psychotherapy is symptom alleviation (Kroger and Fezler, 1976). Direct symptom control is often practiced in emergency procedures, hysterical reactions, hyperventilation and acute generalized anxiety states (Wolberg, 1975). The anxiolytic effect of hypnosis increases the patient's capacity for adaptive control by allowing him to explore and develop his inner resources. More detailed examples of direct hypnotic intervention may be found in other chapters in this book which focus on specific conditions.

Hypnoanalytic Techniques

One of Freud's great contributions was the concept of psychic determinism, that our present behavior is a product of earlier life experiences. The analyst attempts to find the source of the patient's problem, allow abreaction and, eventually, resolve the problem through personality structural change (Fromm, 1984). Common resistances may be encountered as a result of repressed unconscious drives, impulses, and traumatic memories (Wolberg, 1964; Hartland, 1971).

The effect of hypnotic regression and suggested hypermnesia can uncover the traumatic event more rapidly than usual psychoanalytic techniques, thus shortening the course of treatment (Barnett, 1981; Pratt, Wood and Alman, 1984). Various regressive and uncovering techniques have been designed to find the source of the problem (Hartland, 1971; Barnett, 1981).

Generally, two methods may be utilized. The first is age regression during which the patient relives the experience. He is given the suggestion that he is back in time and able to see, hear, and feel the experience. The second method is a dissociation technique wherein the patient is asked to visualize himself on a television screen as an actor in a script, back in time when significant events occurred. The latter method is more often utilized when an event is too traumatic for the patient to re-experience. At times, hypnotic relaxation alone can produce spontaneous memory recall (Mutter, 1984).

Another investigative technique is the use of dreams (Sacerdote, 1967, 1977; Hall, 1977). The patient is placed in trance, and suggestion is given that he have a dream for the purpose of retrieving repressed memories. Certain patients have difficulty recalling traumatic events. A posthypnotic suggestion may be given that they experience and record those dreams which are related to the source of the problem (Mutter, 1981; Sacerdote, 1977), dreams which may help to explain the meaning of the symptoms or function as a process in working through the problem.

The analyst often is taught that the patient must have conscious awareness of the source of his problem before resolution occurs. Erickson (1978) maintained, however, that the unconscious already knows the source of conflict and needs only to be stimulated to resolve it (Erickson, Rossi and Rossi, 1976). Erickson recommended short-term treatment and attempted to facilitate rapid movement in therapy with the following hypnotic suggestions:

> The unconscious part of your mind knows the source of your problem and knows what it needs to solve it. And I do not know how long that will take (metaphor for time distortion is used here)....and I don't know if your unconscious mind will share with your conscious mind that source or just solve the problem without your conscious knowing how it was solved (Erickson, 1978).

The above dialogue illustrates how Erickson used direct suggestion in an indirect manner to stimulate unconscious search and problem resolution. His therapeutic strategy enabled the patient to see his problem in a different way than before (Erickson, 1978).

The Mind-Body Relationship and Psychosomatics

Psychiatric literature stresses the use of hypnosis in the treatment of psychosomatic disorders (Sachs, 1982; Frankel, 1975). It is difficult to separate functional from organic illness, and it is doubtful that any condition exists entirely in one form (Chiasson, 1984). A number of problems may arise when one is treating patients with psychosomatic illness. By the time the patient has been referred to the psychiatrist, he has usually been seen by multiple specialists, who have performed extensive examinations and suspect that there may be some emotional connection which aggravates or triggers the symptoms.

The patient may have some idea about his illness, but it is essential to find out what he truly understands. Quite often, he has limited insight and will tell you that the problem is not in his head because he really feels his symptoms. A great deal of time is spent in the presenting symptoms; a detailed history is obtained regarding onset, factors which aggravate or diminish intensity, and medications and their effects. As the diagnostic interview progresses, there is a gradual shifting to consideration of the psychosocial stressors which may influence the symptoms. The therapist should be attuned to the patient's semantics, slips of the tongue, and body language. The unconscious mind knows the source of the problem, and the therapist needs to look beyond the patient's verbalizations in order to gain clues into his dynamics.

Whether or not hypnosis is to be utilized, the patient should be guided in psychotherapy to the point where he is able to understand the mind-body connection—at least on an intellectual basis. During the waking state, I begin to help the patient develop this intellectual insight, using the following dialogue:

> There is no action that can exist unless a thought comes first. You cannot drive a car unless you think about getting somewhere. You cannot eat unless a feeling of hunger is present. You cannot build a building or any structure unless there is a series of thoughts in the form of a blueprint. Does that make sense?
>
> Now, there are some things you do automatically without full conscious awareness, such as eating. You do not think about how you are going to hold your fork, move it in a coordinated manner into the food, and lift it up to your mouth. Your mind memorized how to do that a long time ago; and you do it automatically, almost without thinking about it. Is that not so?
>
> How many times have you driven a car to a given place and not remembered exactly the time sequence from leaving to arriving—or how many lights you have passed? Does this make sense to you? (When the answer is yes, proceed with the following.)
>
> Now, if you are able to see that a thought precedes an action, can you also see that the way you think about something will influence that action or outcome? For example, suppose you awaken in the morning and say to yourself, "My God, not another day to get through!" How do you think you are going to feel? (Usually, the patient responds, "bad" or "terrible." That's right.
>
> The next question that needs to be explained is how can a single, fleeting thought that enters and leaves your mind cause such a profound reaction on your body. *If* I were to ask you to do this...but please *do not* do it...to think of the worst or more terrifying experience in your life, you would begin to notice one or more symptoms developing—your mouth getting dry, a lump in your throat, tightness in your chest, feeling your heartbeat (palpitation) or more rapid breathing (hyperventilation), a tightness in your chest, a knot or twisting in the pit of your stomach, shakiness, sweating, or an urge to run to the bathroom. All these symptoms are real because you *feel* them, and they are triggered by a thought.

Once the patient recognizes the concept that a thought precedes an action or outcome, you can then introduce the idea that how he thinks or how he reacts to a stressor can have a profound influence on his body and his symptoms. While the therapist knows that feelings are internalized and involve organ systems, the patient may not have this awareness; the patient needs to establish this link, if only intellectually, before further work in trance can be effective. The dialogue continues:

> Perhaps you can see that somewhere in your experience you have developed a habit of thinking the worst about certain situations that you face; and, perhaps, you can now

see how this can make you feel tense or uneasy or give you certain uncomfortable symptoms that certainly make you suffer. How well are you able to relax? (Usually, the patient states that he cannot—or not readily.) Are you willing to let that happen? (If the patient nods or demonstrates body language that indicates that he is receptive, an induction technique is then utilized.)

The above strategy serves three purposes. First, it helps in the establishment of rapport with the patient by enabling him to see that you understand him and accept his belief that he truly has pain and suffers. Secondly, this technique helps him to develop a link between how he thinks and under what conditions his symptoms may arise. Such intellectual insight will eventually make the patient more amenable to treatment strategies. Finally, this dialogue and the use of a series of truisms help to come down the patient's attention, thus facilitating trance induction.

A variation of this technique can be used with patients who have chronic pain with anxiety and/or depression. Patients with chronic pain become depressed because they feel they have lost executive control (Mutter and Karnilow, 1983). The same linkage of thoughts with symptoms is developed prehypnotically as follows:

> You know that when you feel tense or under stress your body can get very tight. Your muscles tighten and the weakest parts of your body will feel that the most. You also know that you become more irritable, short tempered, and more quick to say things because you are annoyed and later regret having said them. Your mind also knows that when you become more calm and relaxed you can tolerate discomfort to a greater extent, and things that would usually bother you seem to be less bothersome.

The therapist may also facilitate trance by modeling behavior and allowing the body to become more relaxed as he speaks to his patient, nodding his head affirmatively where affirmative respones are appropriate, and closing his eyes slightly as he carefully observes cueing by the patient that he is responding. As the patient begins to mimic these behaviors, the therapist can assume that it is now time to proceed with ceremonial induction and therapeutic strategies.

Clinical Applications

Table I lists some of the common problems encountered by the psychiatrist. Unit II in this book covers these topics in greater detail. In my clinical experience, many psychiatric conditions are produced by the patient's earlier misconceptions of an event which subsequently result in psychic and physiologic symptoms. One psychotherapeutic approach is to enable the patient to understand the source of his problem so that he is able to restructure his thinking and thereby gain greater adaptive control. An alternate method is direct symptoms removal with repetitive reinforcement so that the patient can re-establish a homeostatic level. Two case histories illustrate hypnotherapeutic strategies.

Case I

A 53-year-old male was seen for psychiatric evaluation because of a chronic post-laminectomy pain syndrome with severe depression. Three years prior he had worked as a hospital maintenance engineer, and while lifting an air conditioner he experienced sharp pain in his back radiating down his right leg. A complete orthopedic workup, including myelogram and CAT scan, revealed a ruptured intervertebral disc in his lower back. He underwent a laminectomy and progressed well for approximately two months, but the pain recurred and persisted despite physical therapy and flexion exercises. Further evaluation revealed a second ruptured disc. Shortly thereafter, he underwent a spinal fusion, and improvement was noted for approximately six months. The pain again worsened, and his doctor told him that, in all probability, scar tissue had formed and he had to live with his pain because further surgical intervention was not recommended.

The patient had been very work-oriented and in good physical health prior to his accident. Now, for the first time in his life, he felt that he had no control of his fate, and he became severely depressed. He lost his self-esteem, his libido diminished, and he was fearful of taking too much pain medication lest he become addicted. His depression deepened, and he took an overdose of sleeping pills. Fortunately, he was found and was admitted to the hospital where he underwent a series of nine electroshock treatments. He had temporary improvement but again became more depressed and withdrawn, with marked difficulty in interpersonal relationships. Antidepressants and analgesics seemed to give him minimal benefit, and he was subsequently referred to me for hypnotherapy.

The anamnesis revealed that the patient was a former football player who was highly respected for his physical skills. He had suffered two fractures during college but was able to tolerate the pain, even playing while in a cast. The grandson who lived with him also demonstrated considerable athletic prowess, but the patient had great difficulty relating to him. Part of the therapeutic intervention was directed toward getting the patient to recall some of his prior skills and share them with his grandson to aid his grandson in enhancing his skills.

The patient could not, however, bypass his pain which became a chronic reminder of his inability to function as before. A hypnotherapeutic strategy was devised to help him reinterpret his pain as a protective message rather than an ominous one. Following induction and deepening, this verbalization ensued:

> You know that when you drive a car, there are lights on your dashboard. When a red light goes on, indicating that the car is running hot, you know that you must pull the car over to the side of the road, check the radiator, the water pump, the thermostat and the hoses so that you can find the problem and allow the car to cool down. It is good that your car has a functioning red light signal to protect it, because if you drove the car and ignored the red light you could burn out the bearings or do other damage to the car. Allow your mind to think of your body as your car that gets you

through life, and when you feel discomfort it is your red light signal telling you to stop and pull over to the side of the road and cool it.

Although this metaphor was useful to the patient, he needed to be protected further so that he would not move beyond his physical capacity as he began to feel relief. A second suggestion was given to reinforce the first, as follows:

> The inner part of your mind, known as your unconscious, is like a master computer which knows the function of every cell, nerve fiber, and tissue in your body. It knows your capacities and your limits. Because your unconscious has a sacred trust to protect you, it will cause certain changes in your body by allowing you to turn, move, twist or bend—but only within your physical capacity and not beyond. In this way, when you feel greater comfort, you will be able to stay within those limits and protect that comfort for prolonged periods of time. As muscle strength and healing occur, you will be able to turn, move, twist or bend to a greater degree—but only within that physical capacity and not beyond it—so that as you continue to enjoy your comfort, you need not fear going beyond your physical capacity or reinjuring yourself.

This second suggestion, called a "splinting technique," can be extremely useful with individuals with chronic, intractable pain syndromes in which there are marked physical limitations. A patient with chronic pain becomes self-preoccupied with his limitations, but when hypnotherapeutic techniques work he may forget his limitations, feel as if he were well, and go beyond his physical capacity. When this occurs, he feels as if he has been "shot down" and believes that the hypnotic techniques do not work when, in fact, they do.

Hypnosis has proven to be a most valued intervention in the treatment of post-traumatic stress disorder (PTSD) (Mutter, 1986). The patient with PTSD has been subjected to an event that is out of the range of usual human experience in which his capacity for adaptive control has been seriously threatened. At the time of trauma, the patient may become disoriented, develop fear of death, and experience pain (Ewin, 1980). Sometimes, the patient has continuing pain, the source of which is obscure to the physician. Hypnosis may be used to explore the source of the physical problem when usual diagnostic techniques have failed to reveal it. The next case describes the utilization of hypnotic exploration.

Case II

A 43-year-old painter was struck by a truck while painting the Seven Mile Bridge in the Florida Keys. He was knocked unconscious and suffered a pelvic fracture, multiple contusions, and spleen laceration which led to an emergency splenectomy. He was placed in a body cast for some months until the pelvis had healed. Following discharge, he experienced pain in his right hip upon weight-bearing on his right foot. X-rays failed to reveal any fractures or abnormalities. He suffered from hyper-irritability, anxiety and depression, phobic withdrawal and nightmares. He was referred to me for evaluation and treatment because of the pervasive psychiatric problems. His past medical history was unremarkable, and there were no known stressors present in his life. Although litigation was pending, there appeared to be no evidence of secondary gain. He was a work-oriented individual who expressed the wish to get well so that he could return to work.

Hypnotic suggestion was first used to diminish anxiety. Subsequently, he was regressed to the incident. As he relived the event, a suggestion was introduced that he had survived and that all the powers that had gotten him through his difficulty were still with him. A posthypnotic suggestion was given that should he have a flashback or dream about his injury his mind would immediately remember that he had survived, and he would continue to improve. Although his nightmares abated and his anxieties diminished, he still complained of persistent pain which was not relieved by hypnoanalgesic suggestions, and it was felt that further hypnotic exploration might be of benefit.

The author recalled a movie, *Fantastic Voyage,* a science fiction tale about a scientist who suffered a brain hemorrhage. In this movie, a submarine with a crew was reduced in size to a minute form by a laser beam so that it could be injected into the bloodstream and travel to the scientist's brain. The laser beam was then used to destroy the thrombus and re-establish circulation. The patient, familiar with this film, was willing to experiment in his own exploration. Hypnotic suggestion was given that he direct his center of consciousness to travel down to his right hip and examine his internal organs and tissue structures as if he were an engineer. After a brief period of silence he exclaimed, "There is a chip on the ball." He was referred back to his orthopedic surgeon. Special oblique films revealed a chip fracture at the head of the femur. He later said, "I knew it wasn't in my head, Doc; I really felt the pain."

Of particular interest was the fact that this individual had only a ninth grade education and knew nothing about medicine or hip fractures. The reaffirmation of his inner knowledge was utilized as a means of ego strengthening to help him recognize that he had greater self-awareness and control over his pain, and he gradually improved. This case, plus many other similar experiences I have encountered in my practice, has led me to believe that the unconscious mind is aware of body functions and dysfunctions; therefore, we can utilize the power of the unconscious as a diagnostic instrument.

Hypnosis has been elevated to a more valued position among other well-established psychotherapeutic techniques. Prominent psychiatric textbooks (Arieti, 1975; Kolb, 1977; Kaplan and Sadock, 1985) include hypnosis as a treatment form. Much has been published about the use of hypnosis in other texts (Cheek and LeCron, 1968; Tinterow, 1970; Kroger, 1977; Wester and Smith, 1984; Crasilneck and Hall, 1985). In addition, there is a growing body of research in hypnosis dealing with the nature or memory, cognitive functioning, and other mental processes. In recent years, many medical, dental and psychology doctoral programs have included hypnosis in their curricula as have many psychiatric residency programs throughout the United States. In sum, the art of hypnotherapy is an extremely valuable adjunct because of its potentially rapid effect which can shorten the course of therapy. It is a skill that should be understood and incorporated in the armamentarium of the psychotherapist.

References

Arieti S (ed): American Handbook of Psychiatry, Vol. V (2 ed). New York, Basic Books, 1975

Barnett EA: Analytical Hypnotherapy. Principles and Practice. Kingston, On., Junica, 1981

Cheek DB, LeCron LM: Clinical Hypnotherapy. New York, Grune & Stratton, 1968

Chiasson A: Hypnosis in other related medical conditions. In Wester WC, Smith AH (eds): Clinical Hypnosis: A Multidisciplinary Approach. Philadelphia, JB Lippincott, 1984

Crasilneck HB, Hall JA: Clinical Hypnosis: Principles and Applications (2 ed). Orlando, FL, Grune & Stratton, 1985

Erickson MH: Personal Communication. Phoenix, AR, 1978

Erickson MH, Rossi E, Rossi S: Hypnotic Realities: The Induction of Clinical Hypnosis and Forms of Indirect Suggestion. New York, Irvington, 1976

Ewin DM: Constant pain syndrome: Its psychological meaning and cure using hypnoanalysis. In Wain H (ed): Clinical Hypnosis in Medicine. Chicago, Year Book Medical Publishers, 1980

Fisher S: The role of expectancy in the performance of post-hypnotic behavior. J Abn Soc Psychol, 49:503, 1954

Frankel FH: Hypnosis as a treatment method in psychosomatic medicine. Int J Psychiatry Med 6, 75, 1975

Fromm E: The theory and practice of hypnoanalysis. In Wester WC, Smith AH (eds): Clinical Hypnosis: A Multidisciplinary Approach. Philadelphia, JB Lippincott, 1984

Hall JA: Clinical Use of Dreams: Jungian Interpretations and Enactments. New York, Grune & Stratton, 1977

Hartland J: Medical and Dental Hypnosis (2 ed). Baltimore, Williams and Wilkins, 1971

Kaplan HI, Sadock BJ (eds): Comprehensive Textbook of Psychiatry IV, Vol 2 (4 ed). Baltimore, Williams and Wilkins, 1985

Kolb LC: Modern Clinical Psychiatry (9 ed). Philadelphia, JB Lippincott, 1984

Kroger WS: Clinical and Experimental Hypnosis (2 ed). Philadelphia, JB Lippincott, 1984

Kroger WS, Fezler, WD: Hypnosis and Behavior Modification; Imagery Conditioning. Philadelphia, JB Lippincott, 1976

Mutter CB: A hypnotherapeutic approach to exhibitionism: outpatient therapeutic strategy. J Foren Sci 26:130, 1981

Mutter CB: The use of hypnosis with defendants. AM J Clin Hypn 27:45, 1984

Mutter CB: Post-traumatic stress disorder. In Dowd ET, Healty JM (eds): Case Studies in Hypnotherapy. New York, Guilford, 1986

Mutter CB, Karnilow A: Hypnosis: A viable option in chronic pain management. J Fla Med Assoc 70, 1086, 1983

Pratt GJ, Wood DP, Alman BP (eds): A Clinical Hypnosis Primer. La Jolla, CA, Psychology & Consulting Associates, Press, 1984

Sacerdote P: Induced Dreams (2 ed). Brooklyn, Theo Gans, LTD, 1977

Sacerdote P: On the psychobiological effects of hypnosis. Am J Clin Hypn 10:10, 1967

Sacerdote P: Therapeutic use of induced dreams. Am J Clin Hypn 10, 1, 1967

Sachs BC: Hypnosis in psychiatry and psychosomatic medicine. Psychosomatics 23:523, 1982

Tinterow MM: Foundations of Hypnosis from Mesmer to Freud. Springfield, IL, Charles C. Thomas, 1977

Werner TR: Hypnosis in psychiatry. In Wester WC, Smith AH (eds): Clinical Hypnosis: A Multidisciplinary Approach. Philadelphia, JB Lippincott, 1984

Wester WC, Smith AH (eds): Clinical Hypnosis: A Multidisciplinary Approach. Philadelphia, JB Lippincott, 1984

Wolberg LR: Hypnoanalysis. New York, Grune & Stratton, 1964

Wolberg LR: Hypnotherapy. In Arieti S (ed): American Handbook of Psychiatry, Vol IV (2 ed). New York, Basic Books, 1975

7 HYPNOSIS IN PSYCHOTHERAPY Part II: Hypnosis in Psychology

CHARLES P. COLOSIMO, Ph.D.

Hypnosis has been used extensively in psychology as a means of influencing human behavior, however with mixed acceptance. As Ernest Hilgard (1971) states about the scientific acceptance of hypnosis: "Modern experiments are bringing hypnotic phenomena out of the fringe area of pseudoscience into the domain of normal psychological science." Even before Hilgard's discussion of the acceptance and non-acceptance of hypnosis in the literature, in scientific practice and in clinical practice psychological practitioners such as William James in his *Principles of Psychology* (1890) and Clark L. Hull in his *Hypnosis and Suggestibility* (1933) were espousing the merits of hypnosis for brief periods of time. Subsequently, there was a lack of interest, however. Even today, there is a question of the merits of hypnosis in clinical practice (Hilgard, 1971; Crasilneck, 1959; Bowers, 1982). Yet this skepticism in the guise of scientific inquiry has led to some fascinating findings in the area of psychosomatic illness, that is, pain, stress disorders, asthma, headaches, hypertension, obesity, and skin disorders.

The use of clinical hypnosis has led into the pioneering fields of behavioral health psychology (Matarazo, 1980), behavioral medicine (Blanchard, 1977), and hypnobehavioral medicine (Colosimo, 1983, 1984, 1986; Milne, 1982). Within these areas of practice have evolved the theoretical applications of hypnosis in cognitive-behavioral therapy (Bowers, 1982; Turk, 1983) and cognitive experiential therapy and hypnosis (Tosi, 1972).

Clinical hypnosis has been isolated from the mainstream of psychotherapy research until recently. Even today the notion of hypnosis in therapeutic effectiveness often is believed to be associated with an arcane set of hypnotic rituals (Bowers, 1982). Hesitancy to use hypnosis in clinical practice is being challenged, however. Bowers (1982) says:

> What the last 25 years of research in hypnosis have taught us, however, is this: it is the hypnotic abilities of the subject or patient, not the special powers or treatment secrets of the hypnotist, that are critical in engendering the various classical hypnotic

phenomena, including some of the more arresting clinical cures that are occasionally reported in literature. In other words, it is a mistake to identify successful hypnotic treatment with a particular set of hypnotic rituals and procedures. Rather, treatment outcome can be said to be hypnotically achieved when and only when it is correlated with hypnotic ability.

In other words, individual differences play a major role in hypnotic ability that reflects treatment outcome rather than the specific differences of the treatment employed (Bowers, 1982; Barber, 1982; Hilgard and Hilgard, 1975). This concept has been important in the psychology literature, especially in personality theory research. Its rigid application to clinical hypnotic applications seems essential in order for the professional psychologist to assert positive treatment outcome in those who have the ability to teach those who lack hypnotic responsiveness to obtain the skill and to reduce the emphasis on procedural concerns.

Behavioral health management or self-regulative skills are emerging as key skills in the self-control therapies. Mahoney and Arnkoff (1978) have stated that "The emergence of self-control as a topic of behavioristic research must be considered a significant and perhaps revolutionary development." Self-control can lead to symptom management if the issues of automatic and vegetative functions are addressed early in psychotherapy (autonomic nervous system regulation). Within the self-confidence from self-regulation of his/her physiological system evolves an eagerness to explore the cognitive system of the psyche. The ability to self-control may lead to giving up control as discussed by Bowers (1982) in terms of "decontrolling cognition." He states:

> In his recent book *Psychotherapy Processes* Mahoney (1980) states that, "there is a strong and pervasive assumption among cognitive-behavioral therapists that feelings are phenomena to be controlled [rather than expressed];" and he goes on to assert that "the conventional practice of avoiding dysphoria during cognitive behavioral therapy [must be challenged]." ...Basically, the argument is that it may sometimes be necessary to lose control in one way (i.e., to experience and display the emotional aspects of a problem) in order to gain control in another way (i.e., to solve the problematic aspects of one's life and circumstances)....the cognitive behavior therapist's emphasis on cognitive control (ignores the nation of psychophysiological control initially in the psychosomatic population)....Pierre Janet, Sigmund Freud, Morton Prince, and a host of other early psychologists, all realized that it was often beneficial to circumvent the patient's willful, active efforts to control thought and feeling, and instead, to engender a psychological state of passive attention in their patients.

This process allows for the emergence of affect, thoughts and fantasies or cognitive emergents which could have surprise value to the patient's treatment. Spanos (1980) suggests that hypnotic responsiveness involves active coping, but that hypnotic subjects make attributions of automatic and nonvolitional control concerning their own behavior. Turk (1983) maintains that giving attention to the events of cognition during hypnosis brings closer the focus on attributional disposition. This brings hypnosis closer to the relevant issues of cognitive-behavioral therapy. As with bio-feedback, cognitive, affective, and social factors plan an important role in hypnosis. Whether hypnosis is used as a part of the treatment regime of the pain patient, the practitioner must consider whether the attitude about hypnosis by the patient is colored by misconceptions. As Turk (1983) says, this image of hypnosis is based on historical caricatures such as a mesmerism (e.g., Svengali in *Tribly*) and stage hypnotists (the request for participants from the audience to come upon the stage and act like an animal, i.e., bark like a dog, quack like a duck or crow like a chicken). Turk further elaborates on the fostering of misconceptions by "inadvertent" anecdotal reports describing "dramatic surgical procedures," such as

> appendectomies, thyraidectomies, cesarean sections, open heart surgery, brain surgery, coronoidectomies, (see Coppolino, 1965; Lassner, 1964; Marmer, 1969; Colosimo, 1984) performed with hypnosis as the sole anesthetic or as an adjunct to more conventional anesthetics. Dramatic accounts of the use of hypnotic analgesia with a variety of severe pain problems also abound (e.g., burns, Crasilneck, Sacerdote, 1966, 1980; trigeminal neuralgia, Sacerdote, 1970; migraine headaches, Basker, 1970).

On the one hand, all hypnotherorists believe in briefing the patient on the misconceptions of hypnosis (alerting the patient to the hypnotic procedures and establishing a belief system in the therapist who is attempting the hypnotherapy) as well as assessing the subject's responsiveness to his adjunctive treatment (Crasilneck, 1976; Kroger, 1977; Wain, 1977). What is seldom discussed in the literature is the role that suggestibility plays in the overall treatment of the subject. Suggestibility does not account for hypnotizability; rather, increased suggestibility is a constant feature of hypnosis. Combating the medieval notions that hypnosis will cast a spell on the subject continues to be the issue in obtaining participants to begin with. In discussing the nature of suggestibility in hypnosis, Kroger (1977) states that "all subjects believe that their responses are produced by the hypnotist." In reality, it is the subject who initiates the acts in response to an appropriate expectant attitude. Turk (1983), Crasilneck and Hall (1976), and Kroger (1973) agree that where criticalness is reduced, a suggested act is usually carried out without the individual's logical process participating in the response. Turk (1983), as well as Kroger, conveys the message that the reduction of critical thinking allows the individual an "openness to information" (similar to Bowers' notion of "decontrol"). The notion of learning the hypnotic phenomena as a cognitive-behavior skills is further noted by Kroger (1973) when he says:

> And when one suggestion after another is accepted in ascending order of importance—task-motivated suggestions—more difficult ones are accepted, particularly if the sensory spiral of belief is compounded from the outset. This is called abstract conditioning and, in part, helps to explain the role that suggestibility plays in the production of hypnotic phenomena.

Kroger continues to emphasize that a favorable attitude further enhances an individual's attitude towards suggestibility. He also reiterates previous authors' claims that it is not so much the technique that is important for hypnosis to occur but the relationship that is important, "the quality of the relationship—the rapport— established between operator and subject." Thus, mere suggestibility per se does not account for hypnotizability, but rather increased suggestibility is a constant feature of hypnosis (Kroger, 1977).

In sorting out the effects of training individuals to become more suggestible in order to benefit more from hypnosis, Barber (1982) states that those low susceptibles (not responsive to direct suggestion) were more susceptible when indirect suggestion was used. (Indirect suggestion is defined as "one in which no response is directly required; rather responsiveness is implied.") Furthermore, pain reduction is experienced in the low susceptible subjects when indirect suggestion is utilized. Barber (1982) asserts:

> It may be, then, that hypnotic susceptibility tests do not measure responsivity to hypnotic suggestion in general but only to direct suggestion. If so, then the notion that clinicians should screen patients prior to hypnotic treatment, in order to avoid wasting time with nonresponsive individuals, should be revised. It is only useful to screen patients with susceptibility tests if we are going to only use direct hypnotic approaches in treatment.

An elaboration on this notion is that an individual's hypnotic skill level is dependent on the imagination of the patient, the ability of the clinician to capitalize on the imagination, and the effectiveness of the relationship to communicate to each other (Barber, 1982). The ability of the clinician to communicate in the language of the patient can facilitate the therapeutic progress or success of hypnosis with the patient's needs. In fact, the patient's ability to monitor pain through his own language base can assure management of his pain. Of course, the management of other psychological concerns such as secondary gain, self-esteem, self-concept, reinforcement of maladaptive behaviors, and family dynamics may have to be addressed while the chronic pain patient is treated.

Assessment

Working with chronic pain patients has been a difficult experience from most clinicians. Further, the use of hypnotherapy has been almost impossible initially with this most difficult patient group (Crasilneck and Hall, 1976; Barber, 1982; Turk, 1983). Biofeedback research is showing that pain patients are more receptive to biofeedback approaches when the emphasis is on the patient's self-regulation training (Blanchard, 1981; Miller, 1975).

The chronic pain patient presented herein was seen on a consult from the oral surgery department. She had been seen frequently in the oral surgery clinic in the past three years for myofacial pain disorder (MPD). The patient had a pain problem present for 14 years. At the age of 26, she first noted symptoms of pain referrable to the temporomandibular joint. The pain radiated into the face and muscles that control the lower jaw. About four years prior to consultation she had a procedure called a right coronoidectomy. This procedure gave her some relief and some increase in the motion of the lower jaw. The relief, however, was temporary, and she continued to have muscle spasm and pain. Her clinical examination was consistent with an internal derangement of the jaw joint. The internal workings of the joint were similar to having a torn or displaced cartilage in the knee. An arthrogram showed that the disc or meniscus of both temporimandibulat joints was dysfunctional. Bilateral TMJ surgery was performed. There was dysfunctional. Bilateral TMJ surgery was performed. There was some improvement in symptoms but pain remained. The pain was referrable to the coronoid process in the lower jaw. The muscle sectioned in the surgery was the temporalis muscle, which with its tendon had become shortened and stiff. Because of these symptoms, the coronoidectomy was performed.

The oral surgeon requested a behavioral medicine consultation before surgery because of the patient's uncontrolled symptoms consisting of masseter spasm. Initially, a behavioral analysis was performed. The behavioral/psychological evaluation of the patient typically includes what Fordyce (1976) referred to as a "behavioral analysis of pain" as well as a general psychosocial history and the Minnesota Multiphasic Personality Inventory. Other psychological tests and/or biofeedback evaluation are included as indicated through the clinical interview. The behavioral analysis is primarily concerned with obtaining information regarding the consistency of reported pain and type of activity, possible direct and/or indirect reinforcement of pain behavior, the presence of superstitious thinking or overguarding, and the potential for excess muscle tension or prolonged stress response. In general, such an evaluation can indicate how much evidence there is to support the "viability," according to Fordyce, of learning (operant) factors as an alternative explanation for the degree and type of the patient's pain behavior. The psychological evaluation also uncovers degrees of evidence as to whether and how much the components of perceived pain (attentional-cognitive factors) and emotional suffering are further contributing to the pain problem. This information can be extremely valuable for organizing a treatment plan that addresses the key factors supporting ongoing pain. A more specific discussion of the behavioral analysis content and process demonstrates more clearly how the following model's components influence operant vs. respondent pain in an individual.

In this case, the patient presented with masseter pain as antecedent to situational stress. The stress precipitated spasm in the masseter muscle area resulting in jaw pain. Behaviorally, she coped with the pain by lowering her activity level, taking medications, eating and talking less and avoiding social situations. As a result, she felt less confident in dealing with her personal problems. Her personal problems were longstanding and numerous, such as marital, sexual and child rearing. She had experienced a poor marriage for the past 10 years as well as having child-rearing problems as the result of the poor communication with her husband. The patient had been sexually abused as a five-year-old child by her step-father and continued to have bad dreams about the abuse. She grew up in a girl's home because "my parents could not take care of me." Therefore, she was experiencing feelings of abandonment and rejection. She reported that "my marriage was to get me out of the home for girls." After two children and a poor relationship with her husband, the patient was contemplating divorce. Whenever she thought about her marital situation, her "jaws tightened and eventually began to spasm."

During the first session, the patient appeared receptive to my suggestions of where to sit in the hospital room, evidenced by a strong presentation of affect about her problems, and an eagerness to self-disclose "to get at the root of my problems." After the clinical interview, I performed an induction in which the patient was able to produce eye closure with the relaxation induction method (I use the relaxation induction methods with new patients who have never been hypnotized). She was able to produce relaxation in all her musculature, arm levitation, glove anesthesia and a post hypnotic suggestion that the spasms in her jaw would subside if medically possible. Suggestions were made that she would become even more susceptible to hypnosis each time she took in three deep breaths, closed her eyes and relaxed her whole body. Furthermore, this introduction to relaxation via biofeedback and relaxation skills allowed the patient to "understand" the process of self-control of her pain.

Intervention Process

Performing the initial pertinent history, behavioral assessment, psychological testing and mental status examination, I began to see pattern of pain behaviors directly related to the patient's relationship to her husband, issues of independence-dependence manifesting themselves in psychosomatic symptomatology. Her expressions of distress for change in her life aggravated her physical discomfort. Feeling out of control of her life, she sought the comforts of the hospital environment, and the oral surgeon became a person she could express her concerns to in a somatic way. The availability of psychological care seemed to enhance this patient's awareness of psychological reasons for her physical concerns. Initially, she seemed very skeptical of attributing her pains to life-age events. However, when the referral by the oral surgeon was couched in terms of "helping you to reduce your pain by way of biofeedback and reduce your stress level," she became interested in "doing whatever I need to do to get rid of the stress." According to Gould (1980), life experiences are ignored by a majority of Americans who believe in a "safe world." When the world becomes unsafe or insecure, they may retreat to the confines of their psychosomatic concerns. This retreat, in turn, leads to a neglect of the transformations occurring. A transformation is an

...expansion of self-definition...and is essentially a license to be, and while operating within that license, a person feels minimal conflict or anxiety and a maximum sense of security. While functioning outside that license, there is anxiety, conflict, and a minimum sense of security until the license is redefined. The boundaries of the self-definition are usually blended into everyday behavior, but became almost palpable when an expansion or growth is taking place via risk-taking behavior in a novel situation. Risk-taking behavior creates anxiety and a sense of internal prohibition against proceeding. The direction of growth and process of transformation are expressed by the tension of vital signals—away from stagnation and claustrophobic suffocation toward vitality and an expanded sense of inner freedom.

In this case, the wife's chewing anger was the result of displaced anger towards her husband—"an internal abstract" (Gould, 1980). She also sensed that her husband was the enemy. This feeling allowed her to deny the transformations occurring in her life is clearly elaborated by Gould, when he says:

At some points in the transformational process there is the experience of warfare. As the drive to expand and become whole meets the provisional boundary of the self-definition in the form of these false ideas, there is an impact and a sense of being arbitrarily held back, analogous to the sensation a child must feel when stopped from climbing out of a playpen...the location of the enemy is always in doubt. It is hard enough to consider that we are often the enemies to our own growth imperative and to accept as fact our ambivalent attitude toward change and internal freedom, but it is doubly hard to keep that focus when at times there are real foes to our progress in the persons of our spouses and bosses. It is temporarily relieving, serves to objectify, and gives hope since the other person, no matter how powerful or important, is much less powerful than the primitive superego images within. Sometimes we make a friend into an enemy unnecessarily with some help from a slippage of logical thinking. "If I hurt, someone responsible for me must be hurting me," or "if he or she isn't completely helpful, he or she must be intentionally hurtful."

Becoming a "friend of growth" to this patient seemed to "free up" her response to therapy. She was able through hypnotherapy to become more familiar with her self-boundaries and less dependent on the therapist for her self-esteem. She practiced self-hypnosis daily in accordance with a structured outline developed by the therapist. Garver (1984) states that "many authorities in hypnosis have maintained that all hypnosis is essentially self-hypnosis. The message to the patient was that she was in charge of her own trance and that she was effecting her own behavior. Her therapy seemed influenced by her personal conviction that she was in hypnosis. Various hypnotic behaviors were pointed out to her during each session to reinforce a sense of self-control and mastery. Kroger (1977) has indiated that "A conviction of hypnosis produces further hypnosis." Furthermore, deeper levels of hypnosis are discovered as the patients practice their hypnotic techniques. This author finds that there is value in having patients produce glove anesthesia, limb catalepsy, hand levitation, and other ideosensory and ideomotor types of hypnotic behavior. The conviction of hypnosis is clearly embedded into the patient.

Outside of psychotherapy, the patient was asked to practice the suggestions for pain relief and increased self-confidence in daily functioning. She would mention her difficulty in "being in hypnosis" when not in my office. (In self-hypnosis the patient becomes both the "sender" and "receiver," which may generate the problems most encountered in self-hypnosis.) In order to reduce the conscious critical thinking from an alerted conscious mind, the author suggested that the patient follow eight steps to self-hypnosis (Garver, 1984). These steps would reduce the "critical screening" that is often generated in the use of self-hypnosis. Garver (1984) relates that ". . . [once] they do not have the therapist to assure them of their depth of trance, they naturally begin to question it." The steps were: 1) Plan the suggestion first and keep it positive; 2) an entry cue, i.e., deep breath, eye fixation; 3) neutral imagery, i.e., relaxing image dissociated from problem; 4) move to suggestive imagery, i.e., insert the positive suggestion from (1); 5) return to neutral imagery; 6) re-orient; 7) post-hypnotic suggestion for post-trance feeling; 8) exit cue. After these steps were demonstrated to the patient, she practiced the procedure aloud and eventually memorized the entire procedure, which she made use of whenever feeling physically uncomfortable and for "boosts" of self-confidence.

Over time, the patient showed more susceptibility towards induction. After skill development in her ability to relax and relieve muscle spasm in her jaws, she was able to utilize auto-hypnosis for general feelings of well-being, self-confidence, and concentration. Her ability to deepen the trance state had improved from a light state initially to a deep state where "out of body experiences" occurred. She was able to completely dissociate herself from her present state of awareness.

The application of biofeedback techniques initially "hooked" the patient into realizing her abilities to control her physiology. The emphasis on biofeedback gave the patient "permission" to explore means of pain management other than traditional medical approaches. In managing her chronic jaw pain, she incorporated personal effectiveness training and social skills into her comprehensive pain management program. This was made possible by more traditional psychotherapy only after the "soma" issues were addressed. In combination with psychotherapy, hypnotherapy was used each session.

Rational Stage Directed Therapy (RSDH) appeared to be appropriate in working with this patient (Tosi, 1984), the emphasis of the hypnotherapy being to give the patient a sense of mastery over her affective physiological, and behavioral functions. The restructuring of her cognitive functioning seemed necessary in order for her to experience a "permanent" life change. According to Tosi (1984):

> . . .The restructuring of the cognitive functions occurs by way of skills that are developed, implemented, and reinforced while the client is in a state of deep relaxation or hypnosis. The hypnotic state amplifies and heightens the cognitive restructuring of emotions, physiological, and behavioral processes. . . .Of central importance is the elaborated ABCDE framework of human functioning. . . .which defined the self as a complex set of cognitive, affective, physiological, and behavioral

functions occurring within a social environment....the fundamental operations of the self occur along time and awareness continua in terms of pervasive experimental themes. The stages of the therapeutic process through which the hypnotic modality was used achieve cognitive restructuring along the continua of time and awareness.

In keeping with the cognitive behavioral perspective, the patient placed herself into a deep trance-like state, in which an elaboration of her current obsessional thinking was magnified:

A)	Event	a	Husband calls patient an unfit person
B)	Cognitive Responses	b	"I can't stand to be called that" (an evaluation of situation)
		b	"He must be right"
		b	"I am an unfit mother—even the kids say so" (An evaluation of self)
		b	"I've got to kill myself or leave"
		b	"I'm leaving him and the kids—I'll show them" (cognitive-symbolic coping strategies)
C)	Affective Responses	c	Panic anxiety
		c	Hostility
		c	Depression, self-doubt and self-defeating thoughts
D)	Physiological Response	d	Rapid heart beat
		d	Muscle constriction of masseters
		d	Increased blood pressure
		d	Facial muscle spasms
E)	Behavioral Responses	e	Unassertiveness
		e	Physical withdrawal from family
		e	Avoidance of husband and children

Interactions between the patient's family members had been strained for some time because of these negative, self-communicating patterns. Her internal dialogue of "being weak minded" and "stupid" strongly suggests to her that she has been weak in the past. She tells herself that she will be unable to do anything about the family situation and therefore concludes that she is a weak, inadequate person, who is destined to remain one. The whole awareness of the effect of these events on the patient was unobserved consciously. She would then experience physiological effects, which would lead to the myofacial pain and muscle spasm. She noticed her anxiety and impotence in the situations, leading to further spasming and discomfort. This dissocation from the situation allowed the patient to cope with her cognitive dissonance and focus attentively on her physical discomfort. Consequently, the events, behaviors, thoughts and feelings occurred without her conscious knowledge.

Assessment of Effectiveness

In order to put the patient's thoughts, feelings, and behaviors more in tune with the situations, hypnotherapy was used to maximize her ability to concentrate and direct attention to the events and her behavioral reactions to those events. In doing so, her conscious mind activities were minimized in order not to interfere with learning activities. Cognitive restructuring of the thought processes allowed this process to occur. At the same time, the unconscious mind or primitive mind could begin to respond to suggestions of personal confidences, assertive behaviors and physical comfort. Hypnosis provided the vehicle whereby the cortical and subcortical brain functioning was integrated (Kroger, 1977; Fromm and Shor, 1979; Tosi, 1980). The patient was able to minimize her bodily reactions to her stressful episodes, thereby limiting her need to focus on physical discomfort. Consequently, the events, behaviors, thoughts, and feelings occurred without her conscious knowledge.

The patient continued to be seen for hypnotherapy with cognitive behavioral therapy utilized to assist in reframing her outlook on her quality of life. She came for sessions twice weekly; then, hetero-hypnosis was performed and a tape made for her to practice daily. This successful practice of self-regulation skills was attained (in a skeptical person) out of a developing relationship and increased self-disclosure by the patient. The relaxation method of induction was utilized to assist the patient in producing a trance-like state. After whole body relaxation was achieved through biofeedback and persistent relaxation training, the patient, while utilizing self-hypnosis, was able to produce glove anesthesia in both her right and left hands (she was unable to produce these physiological changes initially). She transferred this anesthesia to the head, facial, and neck areas (inside and outside her mouth) through hand movements in the mentioned areas. This process produced a "numb and rubbery" sensation that relieved pain. She persisted in the use of self-hypnosis to assist in pain regulation. Later, Spiegal's eye roll method for self-induction was used as she became more confident in her auto-hypnosis skills, decreasing the time required for hypnotic induction time. Hand levitation was also applied to the above procedures to induce further deepening of the trance-like state. Eventually, she performed self-hypnosis procedures several times daily. The patient became quite skillful in managing her pain. As a result, the patient was able to increase her activity level, increase her food intake, and experience less discomfort in her jaw area (free of muscle spasm). As the patient's self-confidence increased, so did her desire to utilize her hypnosis skills when asked to undergo a coronoidectomy procedure by the oral surgeon.

Coincidentally, the patient's psychological disposition had changed as evidenced by the Minnesota Multiphasic Personality Inventory administered initially and prior to the coronoidectomy (see Table 7-1). The more noticeable decline was the patient's

Table 7-1. Minnesota Multiphasic Personality Inventory

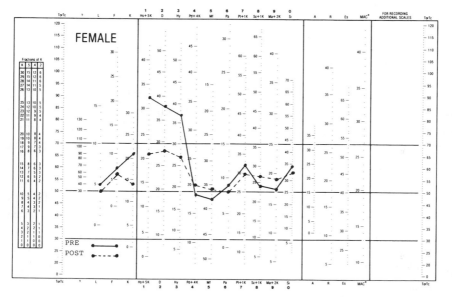

decline in defensiveness as indicated by the K scale and a dramatic decline in the l) hypochondriasis; 2) depression; and 3) hysteria scales. This change suggests lessened somatic conversion, depression, and hysteria. Psychasthenia (7) was reduced and assertiveness (4) slightly increased. Emotionally she was more relaxed, and behaviorally she was able to study for a nursing degree, her life's ambition, in a concentrated manner. One, three and six-month follow-ups confirmed the stability of the therapeutic change.

The decision by the patient to undergo surgery with hypnoanesthesia was significant in assessing the effectiveness of her ability to reduce her pain. She had self-monitored her jaw pain since the onset of therapy. The self-monitoring was broken into segments of monitoring. They were baseline, biofeedback and hypnosis only, rational stage directed hypnotherapy (includes the cognitive-affective domains and clinical hypnosis).

Baseline

Prior to therapy, the patient was asked to record her jaw pain intensity on an hourly basis on a scale of 1 to 10; with 10 being the most severe. (This recording procedure occurred throughout the therapy program.)

Hypnosis Only

Hypnosis only treatment consisted of employing the eight-step self-hypnosis procedure (plan a suggestion, relaxation induction, neutral scene, suggestion, neutral scene, reorient, post-hypnotic suggestion, exit) and biofeedback sessions.

Rational Stage Directed Hypnotherapy

RSDH was utilized for five months. The patient progressed through the awareness, exploration and commitment to positive behavioral change. In the fourth stage, she implemented her changes to result in an internalization of pain process. Finally, behavioral change occurred as the patient's healthy behaviors became more automatic (see previous discussion of RSDH therapeutic progression).

All these stages were experienced hypnotically in conjunction with the development of the restructuring techniques. Although some of the hypnotic exploration of the client's personality was quite complicated, all therapy was eventually directed at educating the patient to restructure her own behavior and to function effectively, independent of therapy. Although past and future contexts were explored, they were useful only in helping the patient adjust more effectively to her present circumstances.

The patient experienced a decrease in pain report in six-month period (even before the coronoidectomy). The intensity decreased from a high rate during baseline (7.5 per week), to slightly reduced during biofeedback and hypnosis (5.5 per week), and was dramatically reduced during RSDH (1.6 per week). Furthermore, in the last five weeks of therapy, the pain was almost nonexistent (0.2 per week). Post-testing was done one week after completion of therapy (see discussion on MMPI above).

Future Trends

The use of clinical hypnosis in the management of chronic pain has many possibilities. Many studies have concluded that hypnosis is effective in treating clinical pain and that susceptibility is a major contributor to outcome. However, for all individuals, depending on their developmental level or psychological sophistication level, hypnosis can be a valuable tool in the psychological management of pain.

No other psychological tool that I know of is so appropriate for creating comfort out of discomfort, with none of the adverse side effects associated with medical treatments of comparable efficacy. The neurophysiological mechanism by which hypnosis enables a person to alleviate suffering is not known. Yet, what is known is that the rate at and degree to which hypnosis enables the modification of pain perception are quite dramatic. Hypnosis is a way in which a person can modify his perception of pain so that the person can become unaware of pain.

The question is when is hypnosis effective as a practical means of long-term relief from chronic pain. From a clinical perspective, it is important to distinguish between the analgesic potential of hypnosis alone and the need for hypnosis to be incorporated into a general psychotherapeutic treatment plan, if it is to be successfully used to provide long-term relief. Many people believe that hypnosis as the sole treatment can alleviate obesity, compulsive behavior, and sexual problems as well as smoking and habit problems. Experienced clinicians are aware that hypnosis can provide comfort and relaxation in the short term for many of the above problems. Yet, the long-term effects are questionable when hypnosis without psychotherapy is utilized. For example, chronic pain is a complex psychological phenomenon affected by many contributing factors. Understanding the patient's situation and the problems that the patient is facing is essential in order for lasting relief to occur. Appropriate use of hypnosis is essential in order to facilitate the long term effects of hypnotherapy. Clinicians who learn hypnotic skills may err if they treat individuals beyond their training and experience. More research is necessary in the use of hypnosis in a variety of psychotherapeutic approaches. Such research could facilitate the advancement of adjunctive therapeutic modalities in the repertoire of clinicians or the incorporation of hypnosis into the routine psychotherapy of chronic pain patients.

Again, it must be emphasized that success with hypnosis requires communication that is sensitive to the needs of the patient, and success depends on the clinician's beginning from the experience of the patient. Therapeutic procedures using hypnosis or biofeedback only may not always effectively modify underlying psychological factors in these disorders. For instance, the use of biofeedback for a migraine headache or a myofacial pain patient may be only the beginning to further in-depth psychotherapy (RSDH) or hypnoanalysis, in which the reduction of pain will occur from restructuring of the patient's irrational ideas which are below the threshold of an awareness. This cognitive restructuring process takes into consideration the role of the unconscious factors along with the knowledge that patients have different ways of coping hypnotically and different ways of experiencing their control (i.e., dissociation, isolation of affect, analegesia). Once a patient has learned to feel comfortable with hypnosis, self-hypnosis procedures can be used frequently to assist posthypnotically in follow-up dental care, dressing changes, immunizations and so on. The additional use of hypnosis in the management of pain and psychotherapy can only facilitate the emotional and physical development of the patient as the clinician becomes more comfortable and integrates hypnosis in patient communication. The skillful use of hypnosis will enable clinicians and patients to benefit from the challenge to relieve pain and suffering and to promote the return of productive and rewarding functioning.

Rapid Induction For The Production of Hypnoanalgesia During Medical Procedures

The purpose of the following procedure is to assist the pain patient in producing analgesia when feeling discomfort during a normal active day or during medical or dental procedures. Complete hypnoanalgesia and muscle relaxation should occur as soon as possible (approximately within 10 minutes).

Verbalization for Induction

I want to see if you would like to feel more comfortable. If so, I would like for you to begin relaxation by taking in three deep breaths. That's it, breathe in slowly, slowly and deeply with your nose and hold the air in your chest and and stomach area for several seconds. Hold, hold the air, now release the air slowly with your mouth opened slightly. (This deep belly breath can facilitate muscle relaxation and reduce tension in contrast to thorasic or shallow breathing, which promotes anxiety and muscle tension and causes hyperventilation.

Now, take in another deep belly breath, hold the air, and exhale slowly. On the third deep breath, I want you to hold the air and let the tension in your chest area be a cue for you to close your eyes and exhale. Each time you exhale, you will find yourself going deeper than the time before. Now, focus on the major muscles in your body. Relax your forehead muscles, just like smoothing out the wrinkles on a blanket; relax your eyes, let all the tension drain out like water pouring out of a pitcher; relax the temples and all the area around and on top of your head. Relax your cheeks and

Comments

Planning Suggestion and developing rapport.

Focus on the pattern of deep breathing for relaxation and comfort for induction. This develops into therapeutic cooperation and initiation of deep relaxation.

Eye closure

Reinforce the depth of trance by focusing on the cue of exhalation.

Dissociation of experience begins and comment on relaxation as each muscle loosens and relaxes.

your jaws allowing your mouth to open slightly and allowing the relaxation to move into your mouth, your teeth and throat area. You may feel warm or tingling sensations in your relaxed areas. Whichever you experience, allow the feelings to continue and move all around the neck area—into your shoulders as they loosen just like two strings were released, and your shoulders feel loose and relaxed. Allow the relaxation to move down your arms to your very fingertips as the warm and tingling feelings allow you to go deeper than you were before. Focus on your shallow breathing as the relaxation moves throughout your chest area and into your stomach as the gentle feelings of relaxation increase even more; relax your buttocks, your thighs, your knees, your calves, your feet and now all the muscles of your body. Allow your whole body to be loose and comfortable just like a rag doll (or Raggedy Andy—if a male).

Confusingly, yet permissively allows the patient to further dissociate his experiences physically and emotionally (a letting-go in a systematic way).

Emphasize complete muscle looseness in an imaginary way, permissive, child-like way.

As you are relaxed like that, allow yourself to drift and float and relax. Also, allow yourself to drift off into infinity and travel wherever you wish. Try to experience all the sounds, smells and good feelings that come with an experience like that. You can be active or you can be inactive with others or by yourself. Just continue associating the deep relaxation with your experience.

Taking for granted the relaxation as a standard part of the experience.

Permissively and indirectly suggesting active use of of imagination engaging the conscious mind.

Now that your conscious mind is occupied with this experience, I would ask your unconscious mind to bring on as much physical and emotional comfort as is medically possible. Allow your mind to drift and float and relax, while your unconscious mind is bringing on numb and rubbery and loose feelings throughout your muscles, joints, just like a relaxation shower starting at the top of your head and flowing down and into every ligament, sinew and cell of your body. This brings on extremely good looseness throughout your body and especially in your facial area— bringing on numb and rubbery sensations

Emphasize unconscious control of pain and elimination of pain.

Analgesia suggestions (emphasizing the analogy to water pouring over the patient's body).

in your jaws, mouth area, cheeks and teeth. Your whole facial area is very numb and rubbery now. Allow one of your hands to bring on even more anesthesia in your jaw joint and whole facial area. Take your hands and fingers and move them throughout your inside and outside of your mouth area. Indicate to me with your left index finger by raising it when total anesthesia has been established (opposite hand raised to the mouth).

Analgesia reinforced to whole body and especially to facial area where surgery will occur.

Continue to travel into wherever you would like. If at any time during the procedure you feel uncomfortable, raise your right index finger (hand closest to therapist) (IV is available for anesthesia as the anesthesiologist is supervising the anesthesia levels).

Further increases patient's confidences in "sealing" anesthesia into facial, mouth and jaw joint area.

I would like for you to continue traveling—you are doing extremely well—

Continue to engage conscious mind activity in dissociation from present unconscious experience (divided consciousness).

Please, when you are ready, I would like for you to regulate the blood flow by allowing it in moderate levels where the the procedure is occurring. After surgery you will find the area healing rapidly with the least amount of discomfort as is medically possible. You may also find your comfort level increasing by leaps and bounds after the procedure is completed—producing more and more hypnoanalgesia.

Unconscious regulating blood flow and vasoconstriction to enhance surgical procedure.

Direct post-hypnotic suggestions begin early for analgesia

Now I would like for you to gradually come back to the present feeling extremely relaxed, refreshed and loose all over. You may find soft sounds, soft music and soft colors and smiling faces relax you by producing even more anesthesia in your mouth area or any part of your body in which you feel any discomfort or wish to feel more relaxed.

Every sensation creates the analgesic experience and with no distractions

Posthypnotic suggestions increase patient's trance.

You are becoming more aware of your feet, your legs, buttocks, arms, stomach, chest and head areas, l0, 9, 8, 7, 6. You are more aware of where you are now, back to the present now, 5, 4, 3, becoming wide awake and alert now, 2, l, open your eyes —wide awake and alert—refreshed as if you took a long restful nap. . .wide awake and alert now. How are you feeling? Relaxed? Comfortable?

Preparation for an end to relaxing, refreshing experience.

Bring patient back slowly, and gradually at his/her pace, watching breathing and reorienting to count down. After 5, increasingly slow counting.

References

Barber J: Psychological Approaches to the Management of Pain. New York, Brunner/Mazel Publishers, 1982

Basker M: Hypnosis in migraine. Brit J Clin Hypn 2:15-18, 1970

Bowers K: The relevance of hypnosis for cognitive behavioral therapy. Clin Psych Rev 2:67-78, 1982

Blanchard E: Behavioral medicine: A perspective. In Williams RB, Gentry WD (eds): Behavioral Approaches to Medical Treatment. Cambridge, Mass., Ballinger, 1977

Blanchard E, Andrasik F: Migraine and tension headache: A meta-analytic review. Behav Therapy 11:613-631, 1980

Colosimo C: Hypnoanesthesia in oral surgery. Presented in symposium on the medical aspets of pain at ASCH Scientific Meeting, Dallas Texas, November 1983

Colosimo C: The use of hypnotherapy in the treatment of chronic pain. Presented in symposium on medical aspects of pain at ACSH Scientific Meeting, San Francisco, November 1984

Colosimo C: A case for the individual treatment of smoking cessation in selected individuals. Presented in symposium on habit disorders at ACSH Scientific Meeting, San Francisco, November 1984

Colosimo C: Outcome research on an outpatient pain program utilizing hypnobehavioral therapy. Presented in symposium on medical aspects of pain at ASCH Scientific Meeting, Seattle, March 1986

Colosimo C: Hypnotherapy in the management of chronic hiccups. Presented in symposium on habit disorders at ASCH Scientific Meeting, Seattle, March 1986

Coppolino CA: Practice of Hypnosis in Anesthesiology. New York, Grune & Stratton, 1965

Crasilneck HB, Hall JA: Physiological changes associated with hypnosis: A review of the literature since 1948. Int J Clin Hypn 7:9-50, 1950

Crasilneck, HB, Hall JB: Clinical Hypnosis: Principles and Applications. New York, Grune & Stratton, 1975

Fordyce WE: Behavioral Methods for Chronic Pain and Illness. St. Louis, C. V. Mosby Company, 1978

Garver R: Eight steps to self-hypnosis. Amer J Clin Hypn 26:232-235

Gould E (ed): Themes of Work and Love. Massachusetts, Harvard University Press, 1980

Hathaway SR: Minnesota Multiphasic Personality Inventory. New York, The Psychological Corporation, 1967

Hilgard ER: Hypnotic phenomena: The struggle for scientific acceptance. Am Scientist 59:567-577, 1971

Hilgard ER, Hilgard JR: Hypnosis in the Relief of Pain. Los Altos, California, 1975

Hull CL: Hypnosis and Suggestibility: An Experimental Approach. New York, Dover, 1933

James W: Principles of Psychology. New York, Holt, Dover, 1890

Kroger W: Clinical and Experimental Hypnosis. Philadelphia, JB Lippincott Company, 1977

Lassner J(ed): Hypnosis in Anesthesiology. Berlin, Springer-Berlag, 1964

Mahoney MJ, Arnkoff D: Cognitive and self-control therapies. In Garfield SL, Bergin AE (eds): Handbook of Psychotherapy and Behavior Change: An Empiracle Analysis. New York, Wiley, 1978

Mahoney MJ: Psychotherapy and the structure of personal revoluations. In Mahoney MJ (ed): Psychotherapy Process: Current Issues and Future Directions. New York, Plenum, 1980

Marmer MJ: Hypnosis and Anesthesia. Springfield, Ill., Charles C. Thomas, 1969

Matarazzo J: Behavioral Health's challenge to academic, scientific and professional psychology. Am Psychologist 37:1-14, 1982

Miller NE: Application of learning and biofeedback to psychiatry and medicine. In Fteedman AM, Kaplan HI, Sadock BJ (eds): Comprehensive Textbook of Psychiatry. Baltimore, Wilkens & Wilkens, 1975

Milne G: Hypnobehavioral medicine in a university counseling centre. Australian J Clin Exp Hypn 10:13-26, 1982

Milne GG, Aldridge D: Remission with autohypnotic relaxation in case of longstanding hypertension. Austrailian J Clin Exp Hypn 2:77-86, 1981

Sacerdote P: The use of hypnosis in cancer patients. Annals of the New York Academy of Sciences 126:1011-1019, 1966

Sacerdote P: Theory and practice of pain control in malignancy and other protracted or recurring painful illness. Intern J Clin Exp Hypn 18:160-180, 1970

Shor RE: Hypnosis and the concept of the generalize reality-orientation. Am J of Psychol 13:582, 1959

Spanos NP: The effects of social psychological variables on hypnotic analgesia: Discovery or experimental creation? J Personality Soc Psychol 39:1201-1213

Tosi DJ, Fuller J, Gwynne P: Case Studies Treating Guilt and Test Anxiety. New York, 1980

Tosi DJ, Howard L, Reardon JP: Modifying migraine headache through rational stage directed hypnotherapy: A cognitive experiential perspective. Intern J Clin Exp Hypn 30:257-569

Tosi DJ: Cognitive-experiential therapy and hypnosis. In Wester WC, Smith AH (eds): Clinical Hypnosis: A Multidisciplinary Approach. Philadelphia, JB Lippincott Company, 1984

Turk D, Meichenbaum D, Genest M: Pain and Behavioral Medicine: A Cognitive-Behavioral Perspective. New York, The Guilford Press, 1983

Wain H: Pain control through the use of hypnosis. Am J Clin Hypn 23:41-46, 1980

Wester WC, Smith AH: Clinical Hypnosis: A Multidisciplinary Approach. Philadelphia, JB Lippincott Company, 1984

8 DENTAL HYPNOSIS

VICTOR RAUSCH, D.D.S.

The dental office is an ideal environment in which the modality of hypnosis can be used in a very structured, direct fashion, with immediate observable results. It can be and should be used as an adjunct to every phase of dental treatment, that is, the preparation, the actual treatment, the post-operative instruction and the post-operative recovery.

As a dental officer with the Royal Canadian Dental Corps (1964-1969), I experimentally developed hypnotic techniques useful in the dental setting. During that time, I used hypnosis extensively in dental treatment. When hypnosis was indicated, no medication was ever used pre-operatively, during the procedure, or post-operatively. From my personal experience of procedures performed, a small sample using hypnosis only are:

1. Reduction of fractured mandible
2. Vital pulpectomy
3. Many extractions
4. Gagging control in severe cleft palate cases during impression taking.

There is a wide range of dental problems in which hypnodontics can be used as a very effective tool.

Hypnodontics in the Past

The experimental data on hypnodontics is sparse. The emotional unpredictability of the majority of dental patients makes the investigation of hypnodontics in an experimental framework almost impossible. The meaningful data we have gained about hypnodontics has come from many clinical reports. Hypnodontic techniques have been developed and used from the end of the Second World War to the present.

Apparently, the first reported case of a tooth extracted under hypnotic anesthesia was by Oudet in 1837 (Hilgard and Hilgard, 1975). Hilgard also reports that in a prisoner of war camp near Singapore in 1945 conditions were primitive and very little anesthesia was available. Surgical procedures were attempted with the aid of hypnosis in 29 cases, of whom 20 proved to be capable of deep hypnosis and four of superficial hypnosis; three were not susceptible, and the other two were treated by suggestion alone without any attempt at producing a hypnotic condition. Dental extractions were performed on 23 of these patients, including many multiple extractions. On being aroused from hypnosis, the patient commonly expressed surprise at finding himself in the operating theater. He refused to believe that a tooth had been extracted until he located a gap in his teeth with his tongue. Post-operative pain was reported by only two of the patients.

Other case reports of dental procedures with hypnosis include:

1. Pulpectomy and pulpotemy on children (Traiger, 1952).
2. Four cases of extractions on hemophiliacs (Lucas, Finkelman, and Tocantins, 1962).
3. Extraction under self-hypnosis on a male physician (McCay, 1963).
4. Extractions with several patients (Petrov, Traikov and Kalendgiev, 1964).
5. Extraction of two abscessed teeth on a 35-year-old woman with multiple sclerosis (Owens, 1970).
6. Extensive extractions on repeated occasions—adult male; chemo-anesthesia contraindicated (Radin, 1972).
7. Several teeth extracted on a 65-year-old male (Weyandt, 1972).

From the above "reported" cases it becomes quite clear that hypnosis is indeed an invaluable tool in the dental armamentarium.

Assessing the Patient

In assessing the effectiveness of any hypnotic approach, we must consider the patient's perspective.

Almost every patient who enters the office automatically experiences some apprehension. The symptoms range from an air of bravado to an almost total unreasonable fear response verging on paranoia. The latter is usually accompanied by physiological symptoms such as cold sweat, pallor, hyperventilation, rapid pulse, dryness of mouth, trembling and, in the extreme, syncope and convulsions.

To account for such reactions, we must face the fact that dentistry is the profession that gives the most physical pain to the largest number of conscious human beings. The inevitable and sometimes unavoidable pain perceived by patients has both psychological and physical components.

To most patients, all dental treatment is perceived as pain. From a psychological perspective, the head and face are the most personal part of the body, being the seat of four of the five senses. Through the oral cavity the personality of the person is expressed in speech. The mouth is also the aperture through which food enters to sustain life. The anxious patient, whether child or adult, has usually been preconditioned by adverse comments from others, reinforcing the belief that there will be terrible pain during dental treatment. It is psychologically impossible to open an individual's mouth and insert into it a variety of sharp metal instruments, cotton rolls, suction tips and clamps without creating powerful unconscious anxieties. The public fears any person such as a dentist, who is authorized by society to "hurt them for their own good."

As responsible dental practitioners, we must treat the psychological as well as the physiological discomfort of the patient. With the advent of our sophisticated drug armamentarium, we are able, in most cases, to manage and alleviate physical discomfort during the actual operative and immediate post-operative phases of treatment. However, the psychological distress related to future treatment is largely left untreated.

The modality of hypnosis, when used as an adjunct to all phases of dental treatment, provides us with a tool which not only enhances the effects of the drugs we use, but allows us, in many cases, to alleviate and sometimes completely eliminate the psychological distress so prevalent in most dental patients.

A simple rule to follow when assessing any patient for hypnosis is to ask the question, "Will hypnosis benefit the patient's psychological, emotional or physical well-being?" In other words, "Does the patient at this time have a need?" If the answer is yes, hypnosis should be used.

Whether a lengthy psychological patient history should be taken prior to the use of hypnosis is a controversial point. A good clinical history is essential in every case; a psychological history to determine the hypnotizability of the patient is, in many cases, counterproductive and unnecessary unless there is reason to suspect a mental disorder. During psychological history taking and testing, the dental surgeon often develops certain expectations of the patient (positive or negative) which may interfere with hypnotic induction and response. Hypnotizability tests in a clinical setting usually serve no purpose.

In most dental situations, the atmosphere, the relationship of dental surgeon to patient, and the anticipated procedures to be carried out are ideal for the elicitation of the hypnotic mind-set and the acceptance of very direct and simple hypnotic suggestions. Reasons why hypnosis is such an ideal modality in clinical dentistry become evident:

1. The patient usually has a need to mentally escape the situation in which he finds himself. The inherent psychological distress produced by simply sitting in a dental chair is very difficult to control.

2. The anticipated discomfort caused by the anticipated treatment, whether justified or not, elicits emotional rather than rational responses in the patient. The patient, therefore, develops a mind-set in which anything that has the potential to alleviate this stressful predicament is acceptable.

3. The patient is usually reclined in the dental chair, putting him into an ideal physical posture to respond to hypnotic suggestions.

4. The dental surgeon has implied permission to physically touch the patient around the face, head, neck, shoulders and arms, making it easy to use non-verbal cues.

5. The dental practitioner, standing or sitting behind the patient, is in a psychologically dominant position.

6. The close proximity of the clinician to the patient allows intense eye contact.

7. The relatively short time span of the treatment phase prescribes a time framework for the patient's response.

Once the decision has been made to use hypnosis, the appropriate and effective hypnotic approach is selected. The key to any successful hypnotic approach or technique is the development of a rapid focused rapport between subject and operator.

Hypnotic Rapport

Hypnotic rapport can be defined as an extremely intense emotional relationship of the hypnotized subject with the hypnotist. The feeling that the particular doctor can help is determined by emotional mechanisms and is independent of any objective, logical appraisal of the doctor's skill. In hypnotic rapport, the subject tends to merge his identity with that of the hypnotist (Meares, 1960).

Rapid hypnotic rapport can be established with the patient by direct eye-contact, a pleasant manner, a reassuring touch on the shoulder and the use of ego-strengthening phrases implying a comfortable experience and a positive outcome. Trust between dental surgeon and patient is essential; thus, the patient's cooperation and participation are assured. Often, hypnotic rapport results in hypnotic trance.

Steps for Hypnotic Induction

1. Establish rapport as quickly as possible.

2. Use eye-contact to hold the patient's attention while you are speaking.

3. Use physical contact to reassure the patient and to give non-verbal cues.

4. Have the patient commit herself or himself to gain cooperation.

5. Use a rapid induction.

6. In the induction, use simple, direct instructions in the present tense.

7. Intersperse the induction with many ego-strengthening phrases.

8. If a specific effect such as anesthesia or analgesia is desired, use ideo-motor response to confirm that the effect has in fact occurred. Trust the ideo-motor signal.

9. Establish a cue for future induction. Give post-hypnotic suggestions for post-operative comfort and future appointments.

10. Alert the patient.

11. Have the patient confirm that he or she is wide awake, alert, and feeling well before leaving the dental office.

Hypnosis can be used with all dental patients in one of two ways—waking indirect hypnosis or direct formal hypnosis.

Waking Hypnosis

Waking hypnosis implies no direct reference to the word "hypnosis" and no structured induction technique.

The most common use of hypnosis in dentistry is to produce relaxation in the patient. Once the patient is relaxed, any dental procedure becomes much easier for the dental surgeon and more tolerable and acceptable to the patient. Through the use of hypnotic rapport and the first four steps of hypnotic induction, waking hypnosis can be extremely effective. If a more profound trance is required for a particular procedure, the dentist can shift to a formal induction technique. The implementation of further hypnotic suggestions depends on the situation, the personality of the operator and the need of the patient.

Formal Induction of Hypnosis

To determine the appropriate formal induction technique suitable for a particular patient, let us ask ourselves one question: "At this time, is the patient experiencing acute physical pain or severe psychological distress?"

If the patient is not in immediate severe pain or distress, more permissive techniques such as progressive relaxation enhanced with ego-strengthening phrases are usually sufficient to produce the relaxation necessary to make the procedure comfortable for the patient.

Instructing the patient in a direct manner to take a deep breath, let the eyes close and let the whole body go limp as the breath is forcibly blown out produces a rapid relaxation response. The suggestion that "with each breath you take and with each word I say you relax deeper and deeper until nothing bothers, nothing disturbs" sets up an automatic deepening technique paced by the patient's breathing and dental surgeon's voice. Specific suggestions can now be incorporated into the verbalization.

If the patient is in acute pain or experiencing severe psychological distress, the short, rapid, authoritarian instructive induction techniques are usually the most successful. For a patient in pain, the top priority is relief as quickly as possible. The patient's mind-set is such that he is less critical and readily accepts suggestions and commands which may under normal circumstances seem to be irrational.

The patient's need for the relief of pain or mental distress dictates the rapidity with which he or she will accept hypnotic suggestions and respond to them.

Verbalization for Treating a Patient in Severe Pain

"I realized you are in extreme discomfort and I can help you. For me to do that you must help me. Listen very carefully to what I say and follow my instructions. Do you understand? (Let the patient commit himself.) Good. Now, look at me and put your finger on the tooth that is hurting. Now, as I touch the area (place a finger on an area adjacent to the tooth where there is no inflammation and gently press), feel the pressure on my finger. The pressure feels good. As the pressure increases, your eyelids become heavy and close. Concentrate only on the pressure. In a few moments you will feel only the pressure. When that happens let this finger (touch and indicate a particular finger on one of the hands) twitch. It will move by itself to indicate to me when you feel only the pressure. (Wait for the ideo-motor response.) That's good!

"The more pressure you feel, the more comfortable the tooth feels. Now, relax very deeply and become aware only of the good feeling of the pressure."

At this point the tooth can be surgically removed. The unacceptable feeling of pain has been integrated into the acceptable, pleasant feeling of pressure. Trust the ideo-motor signal. Do the procedure. Often, as the forceps are engaged on the tooth in question, the pressure produced by the forceps acts as a deepening cue and causes the patient to go into very deep hypnosis.

The Credibility Gap

As hypnotherapists and hypnodontists, we are constantly challenged and put on the defensive by our peers. Even though much progress has been made, only a small percentage of dentists use hypnosis as a modality in their clinical practices. The nature of hypnosis is such that it will not fit every acceptable scientific framework. Consequently, it is disregarded and often shunned. No matter how dramatically the benefits of hypnosis are demonstrated in clinical settings, it is unacceptable as a legitimate healing mode to most dental practitioners.

Twenty years ago, hypnosis, as a useful modality in dental treatment, was still unacceptable and suspect to the dental profession as a whole. As a dental officer in the Royal Canadian Dental Corps, I was the only clinician actively promoting and using hypnosis. My hypnotic approaches did not fit into the framework of "accepted treatment modes" and consequently I was considered "somewhat strange." I was not taken seriously even though my results with hypnosis were very impressive. Let me cite one of my cases.

A patient in severe pain came to the army dental clinic as an emergency case. He was a middle-aged Staff Sergeant, decorated for bravery in the Second World War. A severe dental phobia had prevented the patient from seeking dental treatment for many years. He was now in severe pain, his face was swollen, and extensive infection in the oral cavity was obvious. The patient was hostile and uncooperative. Several attempts by dental clinicians to do an oral examination were unsuccessful. The consensus was that general anesthesia was the only solution to successfully treating the patient. In a confrontational atmosphere, the patient was presented to me and I was "challenged" to demonstrate the efficacy of hypnosis.

The patient obviously had a tremendous need and responded quickly to suggestions of comfort and well-being. I was able to do an oral examination without resistance. The treatment plan was to remove all remaining teeth and fabricate complete upper and lower dentures.

The following day the patient returned to the clinic in a much better frame of mind. He responded immediately to a previously anchored post-hypnotic cue and within seconds achieved deep hypnosis. In the presence of infection and severe inflammation, I surgically removed ten teeth. No premedication or local anesthetic was used. The patient experienced absolutely no discomfort. He demonstrated dramatic bleeding control and total post-operative comfort. Two days later the remaining eleven teeth were removed in a similar manner. At no time did the patient report any discomfort. Healing occurred rapidly without any post-operative swelling. It was indeed a dramatic demonstration of the effectiveness of hypnosis in an almost impossible situation.

Although several specialists witnessed the entire procedure, despite the indisputable evidence their response was both surprising and discouraging to me. When asked, "What do you think of hypnosis now," their answer was: "Until we have further evidence and more study is done, we are not sure." Gradually, I did gain much more support from more open-minded clinicians and was eventually allowed to incorporate hypnosis into the teaching curriculum at the school.

Hope for the Future

In dentistry, as in medicine, outdated traditional teaching methods have created a tremendous barrier to serious investigation and incorporation of hypnotic techniques and principles in the treatment of patients. Our emphasis on solid "experimental" evidence has hindered the legitimization and acceptance of hypnosis in our western approaches to healing.

The nature of hypnosis is such that it cannot be adequately investigated and logically explained with our modern experimental approaches. Hypnosis is a dynamic process; it functions in the realm of subjective experience within each individual. If we hope to gain a deeper understanding and a more predictable result with hypnosis, two important areas must be integrated—clinical and experimental.

A clinical setting provides an ideal framework in which to test and explore the potentials within individuals to control and change biological and physiological functioning of the body.

Experimentally, the monitoring and investigation of various electrodynamic body fields and brain-wave activity during clinical procedures would give valuable insight into the mechanisms involved in hypnotic responses.

In dentistry, the future of hypnosis is exciting and challenging. The nature of dental treatment is such that hypnosis can become an integral part of every phase of dental treatment. At present, there is still a barrier between experimenters and clinicians.

To advance the course of hypnosis we must strike a truce. We must integrate the objectivity of experimental hypnosis with the subjectivity of clinical hypnosis and look at the whole area of hypnosis from a new perspective.

Before anyone involved with clinical or experimental hypnosis can study or use this modality in a meaningful way for self or patient, it is essential that he or she first experience the hypnotic mind-set. Then, everyone would be on common ground, looking from the inside out instead of from the outside in.

If the experimental and clinical groups form a common front, hypnosis will become more credible in a scientific sense, more acceptable to the public and teaching institutions, and most certainly more beneficial to the population as a whole.

The emphasis on self-hypnosis is perhaps the most promising direction the field of hypnosis has taken. The idea that all hypnosis is self-hypnosis has gained more credibility and acceptance among hypnotherapists generally.

Many patients undergoing hypnotherapy today are automatically taught exercises for self-hypnosis. In many cases, self-hypnosis has become a preventive prescription for better physical and mental health. It is used to control stress, insomnia, and chronic pain. It is becoming more apparent that in the proper setting, self-hypnosis is as effective as hetero-hypnosis. Even major abdominal surgery has been performed using self-hypnosis as the sole agent to control muscle relaxation, pain, bleeding, pulse rate, and blood pressure (Rausch, 1980).

The "force" truly seems to reside within each of us. It becomes our responsibility to access, study and activate it.

Sample Case

The following points are demonstrated:

1. Rapid induction
2. Deepening
3. Ideo-motor response
4. Pain control
5. Bleeding control
6. Ego-strengthening
7. Post-hypnotic suggestions
8. Post-operative comfort
9. Cue for self-hypnosis
10. Alerting
11. Waking hypnosis

The patient was a 26-year-old woman with rampant caries in her remaining six upper anterior teeth. She was being treated by another dental surgeon and a diagnosis had been made. The treatment plan was to remove all six upper anteriors and insert an immediate complete upper denture at the same sitting.

Past negative experiences had produced an unreasonable fear in the patient concerning any kind of dental procedure. General anesthesia was suggested, but she was considered a high risk patient and her physician flatly refused to endorse the use of general anesthesia for the removal of her six anterior teeth. She presented herself in my dental office and requested to have the procedure done with hypnosis. She had no previous experience with hypnosis but was prepared to be totally cooperative.

I agreed to do the procedure on the basis that she had a need, and I expected her to respond easily and quickly to suggestions. I had informed her that hypnosis was a natural phenomenon, that she had been in hypnosis many times before without her being aware of it, and that it was simple, easy and safe. I informed her that nothing was expected of her except to follow my instructions and allow herself to flow with the pleasant feelings she would experience. I reclined her in the dental chair, raised my finger above her eye-level, asked her to look at my finger, take a deep breath and hold it. Here is the suggested procedure:

Verbalization	Comments
Hold your breath until my finger touches your forehead. When my finger touches your forehead, let your eyes close, blow out your breath forcibly and let your whole body go limp—Now! (touch the forehead and press firmly on the shoulder as the patient exhales). Keep your eyes shut. Take another deep breath, hold it, let it out now. (Again press on shoulder and repeat for five	Rapid induction By holding the breath, the patient can be paced. The relaxation response is enhanced with each exhalation

deep breaths.) Let your breathing become comfortable and automatic. With each breath you take now and with each word I say, you go deeper and deeper relaxed.

Nothing bothers, nothing disturbs—you are doing just fine—you are safe, comfortable, enjoying the feeling. Your body is safe, comfortable, totally relaxed, working automatically. You now let yourself flow with that feeling of relaxation so deeply that you need pay no attention to your body any more.

As I touch your teeth and the surrounding tissues, those areas become completely numb. Let this finger (indicate a specific finger by touching it) move by itself. It moves by itself when the areas I am touching are completely numb. Good! (The teeth at this point were surgically removed.) Let the sockets fill and the bleeding stop. Turn it off!

You have done extremely well. Enjoy a feeling of well-being and accomplishment. You now become aware of how good you are at hypnosis. After you leave here today, you can use self-hypnosis for your benefit any time it is appropriate for you. Go through the same procedure we used today and you will respond as effectively and easily as you did today. Do you understand? Good.

In a few moments, I will ask you to allow yourself to come to complete alertness. After you do, your mouth remains completely comfortable. Your mouth heals rapidly. The denture feels good. You speak clearly. Nothing bothers, nothing disturbs. Do you understand? Good.

When I count backwards from five to one, you become more and more alert. Your eyes stay shut until I reach one. When I say one, your eyes open, you are wide awake, totally alert, in a good mood, feeling extremely pleased with yourself. You have done very well. Coming back now; five—feeling good; four—more awake; three—smiling; two—just about there; one—wide awake.

Deepening

Total mental dissociation from the physical body and sensations. At this point, many patients report a heightened mental euphoria and awareness. Some claim they are floating and can actually see their bodies lying in the dental chair. Of more clinical interest, total body anesthesia often results at this point of the procedure.

Ideo-motor signal
Stroke the area until the ideo-motor signal is activated.

Bleeding control
The complete upper denture is fitted and inserted.
Ego-strengthening

Teaching self-hypnosis

Post-hypnotic suggestion

Alerting

After alerting, the patient was euphoric. She spoke clearly, had no pain, and accepted the denture immediately. On follow-up, there was no post-operative pain. Healing was very rapid and the total post-operative recovery phase was easy for the patient. She later reported that she used self-hypnosis frequently for her benefit. She felt better physically and very confident mentally. The experience had changed her life.

References

Crasilneck HB, McCranie EJ, Jenkins MT: Special indications for hypnosis as a method of anesthesia. JAMA 162:1606-1608, 1956

Hilgard ER, Hilgard JR: Hypnosis in the relief of pain. Los Altos, CA, William Kaufmann, 1975

Lucas ON, Finkelman A, Tocantins LM: Management of tooth extractions in hemophiliacs by combined use of hypnotic suggestion, protective splint, and packing of sockets. J Oral Surgery, Anesthesia, and Hospital Dental Service 20:488-500, 1962

McCay A: Dental extraction under self-hypnosis. Med J Australia 22:820-822, 1963

Meares A: A system of medical hypnosis. Philadelphia, W. B. Saunders, 1960

Owens HE: Hypnosis and psychotherapy in dentistry; Five case histories. Int J Clin Exp Hypn 18:181-193, 1970

Petrov P, Traikov D, Kalendgiev TZ: A contribution to psychoanesthetization through hypnosis in some stomatological manipulations. Brit J Med Hypn 15:8-16, 1964

Radin H: Extractions using hypnosis for a patient with bacterial endocarditis. Brit J Clin Hypn 3:32-33, 1972

Rausch V: Cholecystectomy with self-hypnosis. Am J Clin Hypn 22:124, 1980

Weyandt, JA: Three case reports in dental hypnotherapy. Am J Clin Hypn 15:49-55, 1972.

9 HYPNOSIS IN MEDICAL PRACTICE

MARLENE E. HUNTER, M.D., C.C.F.P.(C)

In recent years, hypnotherapy has been added to the therapeutic armamentarium in a wide variety of medical problems, including those involving the cardiovascular, the metabolic/hormonal, the gastrointestinal, the respiratory, and the musculoskeletal systems. Hypnotic techniques as practiced by the therapist and as experienced by the patient through self-hypnosis have markedly improved the health of many patients and warrant the attention and approval they are gaining.

As a physician and hypnotherapist, I insist, however, that full and appropriate investigation and treatment of medical clinical problems must precede the utilization of hypnosis as a modality in the management of medical problems. After a case has been investigated and hypnotherapy is indicated, both general and specific hypnotic techniques are introduced to the patient.

For example, every patient can benefit from the following general techniques that apply to most problems.

1. Introductory relaxation. Basic relaxation techniques can be easily and pleasantly adapted for hypnotic experience. Many patients do well in hypnosis even though they may not go any deeper than this light relaxation level. They can employ it as a framework for utilizing the more specific techniques. I usually use a controlled breathing technique wherein "you breathe in" comfortable feelings and "—send them out to tense or uncomfortable parts of the body as you breathe out." It is a simple way to encourage inward focusing and a decrease of global awareness, therefore deepening the level of hypnosis in an easy and unthreatening way.

2. Stress management techniques. These include such basics as problem-solving gimmicks, goal setting, and priorities, basic tools that have application to all problems—medical or otherwise.

3. General imagery of the system involved in the disorder, for example, the cardiovascular system. Patients need to be assured over and over that imagery involved *all* the senses—so many people interpret it to be only visual. Auditory imagery is particularly useful in some cases, for example, the firm throb of the heart. Kinesthetic imagery has infinite adaptability. Give your patients a few suggestions and encourage their imaginations to fly.

Having had some experience of hypnosis while exploring the general techniques, patients are now ready to learn specific techniques that relate to their medical condition.

1. Deciding at which level of function the hypnotic suggestions will be directed. For example, for hypertension one could choose to influence the pump itself (the heart), the tubes (arteries), or the end organs that are affected by the rising blood pressure.

2. Specific imagery is now encouraged, concentrating on the area of the body chosen for intense focusing.

3. Mind/body communication is directly addressed; the patient is encouraged to set up a "dialogue between the subconscious mind and the body—each giving the other the information that it needs to improve function."

4. The patient is invited to encourage the body—through the use of Mind/Body dialogue—to make the best possible utilization of medication so that the least amount necessary to do the job may be taken.

Patients are encouraged to move into the future in their imagination in order to experience the improved health and well-being they are reaching towards.

Cardiovascular System

Hypertension

1. *General approach.* It is easy to understand why relaxation and stress management skills are of great importance when one is dealing with hypertension. As soon as the patient has learned these simple approaches he immediately has something he can do to begin influencing his blood pressure.

2. *Specific techniques* take the patient further into his own resources. He decides the level at which he feels it is most useful to influence the system (with the pump, the tubes, or at the end organ), then creates specific imagery around that particular area. The general suggestion regarding mind/body interaction is given and—very important—suggestions regarding the utilization of medication.

3. *Rehearsal for the future.* The patient is encouraged to experience the sense of well-being that he will have when normal blood pressure is maintained on minimal medication and he enjoys full activity at home, at work and at play.
    I did a small study (Hunter, 1984) of patients with hypertension and reproduced here the table showing the results. As you can see, significant improvement occurred in several cases.

Table 9-1. Study of Patients With Hypertension

Patient	James P. Age 64	Jessie F. Age 43	Trudy R. Age 55	Freda M. Age 48
Medications at 1st Interview	Lasix Aldomet Captopril	HCT	HCT Inderal Aldactone	Moduret Apreso line
B.P. at 1st Interview	200/114	180/105	190/110	220/130
B.P. immediately after 1st session	180/106	160/90	155/80	210/120
B.P. before 2nd Session	210/120	160/100	160/90	220/120
B.P. after 6 weeks	180/105	160/96	150/80	200/110
B.P. after 3 months	176/104	155/95	145/80	160/86
Medication after 3 months	Lasix Captopril	HCT	HCT	Moduret Apresoline

Patients always consider it something of a victory when they are able to decrease their medication substantially; this fact is so reinforcing to them that they are able to make even better use of their own hypnosis.

4. *Case History.* Mr. S. B., a 36-year-old man, an executive in a busy brokerage company, had first been diagnosed as having benign essential hypertension at the age of 27. He responded to the diagnosis by plunging himself even harder into his work, leaving for the office at 6:30 each morning and not getting home until 9 or 10 o'clock at night. He was a bachelor, often commented that "no woman

would have me," and, indeed, his social life was almost nonexistent. He was on high doses of propranolol and a diuretic daily, and at that his blood pressure usually sat around 150/100 mm.Hg. His family physician referred him for hypnosis because the physician felt that the situation would get worse unless Mr. B. took steps himself towards improving it.

When Mr. B. came into the office he was smiling, tense, restless and fast-talking. He told me pleasantly that he was only there at his doctor's request and that he did not expect hypnosis to have anything to offer him. Furthermore, he could take no time out to "waste" on hypnosis. After some discussion about what hypnosis was and was not and the results which one could realistically expect from hypnosis, he agreed to come to an introductory series of four half-hour sessions, and then at the end of that time to reassess the situation.

He was bemused to find that he was a fairly good subject, going easily into moderate levels of trance at the first session. Furthermore, he enjoyed hypnosis. He quickly learned the breathing technique and admitted at the end of the session that he had been able to relieve some of the tension across the back of his shoulders, a fact which surprised him.

In the second session, when I mentioned that we were going to begin by doing some problem-solving techniques, he was obviously dubious that anyone—especially a doctor who called herself a hypnotherapist—could teach him anything about problem-solving. However, as so often happens, once he got into hypnosis this hypercritical attitude faded, and he learned the technique easily. When he came out of hypnosis, he remarked on how useful that type of approach could be.

At the third session, we began with some self-hypnosis techniques. He balked again saying that he did not have time to spend during his busy day on self-hypnosis. I told him that it was important that he comply with my suggestions during this four-week introductory period, and he agreed grumpily that he would set aside 10 or 15 minutes each day as hypnosis time.

At that session, we also began the specific imagery techniques. I suggested to him that he could focus on the pump—the heart—and concentrate on regulating the force, rhythm and tempo of each heartbeat; or he could focus on the tubes—the arteries—especially on arterial walls becoming more elastic and accommodating to the thrust of the heart; or he could focus on the various end-organs in the body such as the kidneys, or the brain, and how they responded to increased blood pressure. He elected to focus on the arteries.

In his imagery he visualized the arterial walls becoming more and more accommodating while maintaining sufficient tone to be effective in carrying the blood out to the tissues. He included a symbolic clearing of any debris or deposits of plaque, restoring the inner lining of the vessels to a smooth, healthy state.

At the fourth session, when we discussed the rehearsal for the future, he saw himself taking less medication, had an image of his doctor's blood pressure cuff registering a lower blood pressure (140/90) and of feeling well and active. He also used his hypnosis to promote modest weight loss and a daily exercise regime.

When he returned in six weeks, he was excited. He had been to his physician the day before and was elated to find that his blood pressure was 140/90. He was still taking the same amount of medication, but was looking forward to reducing it slowly over the next few months. With his hypnosis, he had had no problems in convincing himself about the necessity for the exercise regime and the weight loss. We did two "booster" sessions during which he elaborated on his own imagery, and he was invited to return at any time for reinforcing sessions.

Three months later, his physician told me that Mr. B. had maintained the level of 140/90 mm.Hg. and had been able to reduce his propranolol to two-thirds of the dose that he was taking when he started the hypnosis. While recognizing the role that weight reduction and exercise played in his improvement, the patient praised the role of hypnosis in helping to maintain these modified lifestyle regimes, and the imagery itself was given considerable credit.

Cardiac Conditions

1. *Arrhythmias.* The arrhythmias most frequently encountered are sinus tachycardia/bradycardia, paroxysmal atrial tachycardia and atrial fibrillation. Of these, the sinus arrhythmias and paroxysmal atrial tachycardia are the most likely to be influenced by hypnosis.

   The imagery of the conducting system within the heart can be explained to patients with the aid of a simple diagram.

   For the specific level of interaction, one could choose the impulse as it travels along the conducting system, the nodal system, or the response of the myocardium.

2. *Angina.* The patient who wishes to use hypnosis for the relief of angina will also want to learn some pain relief techniques. Cardiac patients wish to be assured, and reassured, that they can retain sufficient pain to give them warning so that they can take their nitroglycerine when indicated. They feel relieved to know that they can use the hypnosis techniques to be more comfortable without endangering this warning response.

3. *Case History.* Mr. R. W. was a 67-year-old man who had had one heart attack and whose atrial fibrillation was well controlled with medication. He was retired, but he and his wife enjoyed traveling in their motor home, and he was concerned that they would have to curtail these activities if his heart should get

worse or he he should have a further attack. He did suffer from frequent angina and the possibility of another myocardial infarction was always with him. It was his idea to come for hypnosis; he felt that if he were more relaxed the risk of a further MI would be reduced, but he intended to continue with his medication.

He enjoyed learning the relaxation and stress management techniques and, although he was really rather a light subject, he felt that he got considerable benefit from them.

His specific imagery involved opening up new vascular pathways to the myocardium. He had an image of a well-healed scar in his heart muscle—the site of the previous infarct—and had no trouble in interpreting that to be a bridge (a strong, healthy, *living* bridge) between undamaged heart muscle on either side. He understood that if the mycardium received a better oxygen supply his angina would be reduced, and therefore he sensed the need for revascularization. He instructed himself, however, that he would be aware of any angina as a warning to either take his nitroglycerine or stop and rest, whichever was appropriate.

The patient also learned some basic pain relief techniques in case he should have an anginal attack even though he always carried two or three nitro tablets with him. The pain relief approach most comfortable for him was a dissociative approach where he placed himself a little distance from the discomfort in his chest, as if there were a cushioning balloon between him and the pain.

Mr. W. has not had another infarct in three years and very seldom has angina. His improvement may be due to many factors, but he feels strongly that hypnosis played an important role.

In both these case histories, the role of hypnosis has been of prime importance in the management of lifestyles. However, the sense of well-being and mastery that these patients have enjoyed through their own self-hypnosis and imagery is of equal importance. How we think and how we feel has a direct impact on physiological function, and it seems prudent to enjoy the additional benefits of these simple and enjoyable techniques.

Metabolic/Hormonal System

Thyroid Function

1. The general approach to improving thyroid function is again introductory relaxation, stress management, and imagery of the thyroid system—the hypothalamus, the pituitary, the thyroid gland and the end-organs.

2. Specific techniques revolve around imagery of the level of interference, mind/body interaction, and utilization of medication.

3. *Case History.* Mrs. D. S. was a 43-year-old woman who had had a severe attack of thyroiditis 10 years before. She had been on thyroid replacement therapy all that time, taking Eltroxin 0.2 mg. daily. She had been referred to me for an entirely different problem, which had responded well to hypnotherapy, and she asked me one day whether I thought it was possible for her to use hypnosis to aid in restoring normal thyroid function and to help her reduce or get rid of her thyroid replacement therapy. It was essential for her to have the support of her family physician and to have him monitor carefully her thyroid function during treatment; with some reluctance he agreed to cooperate.

The patient considered several possible areas of influence within the system. She thought she might affect the neurotransmitters passing information from the hypothalamus to the pituitary gland; she considered focusing on the pituitary gland; she was interested in encouraging the thyroid gland itself to put out more hormone, and she gave a passing thought to the tissue response. She decided to concentrate on the thyroid gland itself and conjured up her own image of what that gland looked like, with thyroid cells releasing their various hormones in a symbolic way.

The patient persuaded her doctor to stop her thyroid replacement therapy after she had been involved in this imagery for several weeks, and she promised that she would have her blood checked regularly.

That was four years ago. She has not taken any thyroid replacement since then and her thyroid levels are normal. Of course, it is possible that her thyroid has had the potential of normal activity for many years, but was dampened by the replacement therapy. She feels strongly, however, that she is responsible for the improvement, and it has done much for her self-confidence and self-esteem.

Disorders of Ovarian Function

Disorders of the ovarian function include:

1. Menstrual cycle disorders including premenstrual tension, dysmenorrhoea, and irregularities.

2. Infertility.

3. Menopausal distress, particularly hot flashes.

The addition of hypnotherapy to the therapeutic armamentarium for disorder of ovarian function is one of the most interesting and rewarding uses of hypnosis in the treatment of medical problems. Several case histories come to mind.

Case History. A young woman in my own practice, Mrs. A. M., suffered from agonizing dysmenorrhoea, which followed a week of almost insufferable premenstrual syndrome. The premenstrual symptoms were so distressing that she had seriously considered suicide on at least two occasions, and only the realization of the grief it would cause her family prevented an attempt.

In the week before her period, she became extremely bloated, put on 10 to 15 pounds, had pain throughout her body, endured blinding headaches, and felt the black pall of depression so heavily that she wondered if it would ever go away. The dysmenorrhoea began several hours before her period started and was profound through the next two days. At the time, the patient had been married for about six months, and these 10 days of distress every month were seriously affecting her marital relationship.

She had tried all sorts of medications from vitamin B6 through various other diuretics, a host of analgesics, and most of the anti-prostaglandin medications. She did get some relief with anti-inflammatory preparations but—almost in retribution— the gastric irritation was profound. As she was nauseated and vomiting anyway, the effect intensified the problem.

When I suggested hypnosis, the patient was skeptical but willing. She enjoyed her introductory sessions and found that she could achieve fair levels of hypnosis with little effort. However, her next period was looming and she felt, desperately, that she must have relief or she would have some sort of breakdown. Therefore, I taught her the principles of self-hypnosis right away so that she would have tools immediately available to her. She welcomed the simple suggestions that she begin to find ways to use the new tools effectively so that her body could respond more comfortably to variations in hormone levels throughout her cycle. When she came back after 10 days, she reported that although it had been a very trying time she felt that she coped better than in the past. There was no great relief, but she was able to function in a relatively normal way throughout those days.

We started on some more specific techniques. The patient was good at both visual and kinesthetic imagery and created for herself a little scenario of the way her body and emotions had been responding to the variations in estrogen and progesterone levels, and—when she had that scenario firmly in her mind—she created a second one wherein she responded much more comfortably. In this second scenario, her body rid itself of excess fluid, there was much less engorgement of the pelvic structures, her weight stayed steady, and she was free from headaches. This was a big order, and she worked on it over a period of several months, reporting slow but steady improvement. Her daily hypnosis session involved some relaxation, some positive thoughts about what she was doing, and then focused on the imagery. One of the most notable and early effects was that the depression became much less severe and she knew that it would last only a few days. She decided to continue taking a diuretic (vitamin B6) and incorporated her body's positive response to the diuretic into the imagery.

With these aspects of the situation under better control, she began focusing on the dysmenorrhoea. She used imagery here, too, thinking of the uterus relaxing its spasm and comfortably shedding the endometrial lining. She continued to take a non-steroidal anti-inflammatory agent, choosing the one that had been least aggravating to her stomach. This combination approach was markedly successful for her.

Infertility—Case History. In any practice, one has a patient who deperately wants to have a baby. All her investigations have proven normal, her husband's investigations have also been normal, and yet she has not conceived. Two such patients—one in my own practice and one who was referred to me—stand out. Both had been trying for more than six years to get pregnant. Both were healthy young women, well into their thirties, with all investigations "normal." Hypnosis was thought to be the final card in the deck, and we were not sure whether it was going to be an ace or a deuce. But I felt that with such an emotionally-laden subject as infertility hypnosis was a very suitable modality. Since the approach was basically the same with each woman, I will describe one case in detail.

Mrs. A. S., aged 35, had been married for 10 years.

Although her husband's family began to make comments on her wedding day about the importance of having children, she and her husband decided to postpone having children for at least two years, and she used oral contraceptives. Her periods had been regular, with normal flow and duration, and there was no reason to think that oral contraceptives would be detrimental.

After two years, the couple decided to start a family. One year later she had still not conceived. Both went for investigations and both were pronounced fit, anatomically normal, hormonally in balance, and apparently fertile. Friends and family began asking questions about their delay in producing children. Mrs. S. found this very hard to cope with, because by now she was becoming anxious herself.

Five years elapsed. The patient had become convinced that the failure to conceive was her fault.

She began to do her own imagery, which was mostly concerned with feeling and seeing herself holding a baby in her arms. There was no doubt in her mind that this was a baby she had borne herself. Four months later she became pregnant. At the end of the first trimester, she had a spontaneous abortion.

Eight months later she was referred to me. After inquiring in detail about her past history, I thought it reasonable to incorporate the above imagery in the approach I used; the most important part of each session was having her walking into the future experiencing holding that baby.

I also incorporated imagery surrounding receptivity of her body to the sperm and the endometrium ready to enfold and nurture the fertilized ovum. We focused on the reduction of tension and the acceptance of the fact that her body did know how to conceive and that we were merely promoting the most advantageous conditions.

Nearly two years passed before she again conceived. This time the pregnancy has been normal, and at this writing she is due to have her baby. She is convinced that hypnosis played a major role in her childbearing.

One other patient had a similar background. Finally conceiving after nearly nine years, she had a healthy boy and another healthy boy two years later.

Menopause. Menopausal symptoms can be categorized under various "F's": fears, flushes and fatigue. Techniques for relieving these symptoms can also be categorized into "F's": facts, fantasies and facilitation.

Fears. Fears also fall into "F's"—fat, faculties, fecundity and femininity. The very term "middle-aged spread" refers to the extra pounds that women put on when their estrogen-progesterone cycle begins to change.

Because of the bizarre symptomatology that so often accompanies the menopausal years, many women really do wonder if they are beginning to lose their mental faculties. It is a fear that is seldom brought out into the open unless the physician asks about it. Women comment on how forgetful they have become, how their moods are unpredictable, that they cannot sleep, and that they do not always grasp things as quickly as they used to. They may become concerned about "running to the doctor for every little thing" and wonder whether they are becoming neurotic.

Although the situation is becoming better, in the past unfortunately there has been among the medical community an implication that menopausal women *were* neurotic and that tolerance on the part of the doctor was all that was required to soothe the distraught woman with a pat and a platitude.

The onset of the menopause symbolizes the end of reproductive life. Although many women welcome it, to others it is a distressing thought, as if something they had been able to do—some physical function they had been able to perform —is no longer available.

Also, for many women the loss of femininity is a dreaded prospect. Such a loss is reflected in the end of fecundity and such physical problems as painful intercourse due to atrophic vaginitis, constantly leaking urine from stress incontinence, weight gain, change in body shape due to osteoporosis, weathering of the skin, with its wrinkles, lines, creases and moles, thinning of the hair, and other similar symptoms, the cause is the changing hormone status, not only of estrogens but also of androgens, with tissue breakdown rather than tissue restoration being the predominant pattern. In addition, there are distressing irregular and unpredictable periods— scanty one time and flooding the next.

Flushes. The hot flush (or flash) is the hallmark symptom of the menopausal woman. It can be extremely uncomfortable, cause great embarrassment when the woman turns red at a time when she wants to appear calm, wake her up at night, interfere with making love, drench her with unbecoming sweat, and be the subject of almost as many jokes as mothers-in-law. For the victim, the hot flush is not funny. Another "F"—frustration—becomes her constant companion.

Fatigue. This is a very common problem. Many women say that they have not been so tired since their children were pre-schoolers. Changes in metabolism, hormone levels and possible factors such as anemia from months of flooding periods predispose to tiredness.

The therapeutic "F's" are particularly important.

Facts. If ever a patient needed facts, it is the bewildered woman—so used to being capable, confident and in control of her body—who presents with these disturbing menopausal symptoms. She needs to understand how the changing ovarian and adrenal functions affect her emotions, her intellectual functioning, and the many physical changes such as the effect on mucous membrances, on bones, skin and muscle, on blood vessels, on her metabolism in general.

She needs to know the role of hormone replacement therapy both for the prevention of osteoporosis and the relief from hot flushes, vaginitis (and therefore dyspareunia), and menstrual irregularities. Medications (not only hormones but also calcium and iron replacements and those which assist with thermal regulation), attention to nutrition, and the working out of a practical activity program facilitate relief.

With regard to fancies and fantasies, hypnosis can play its major role. Never was the rebuilding and nurturing of self-confidence and positive body image more important than with menopausal patients. Ego strengthening techniques in hypnosis can be invaluable. Relaxation and stress management will help the woman organize and cope with the bewildering assortment of problems that come her way.

Imagery plays a significant role. The first symptom most women want to tackle is the hot flush; this symptom invites imagery of cooling situations—mountain streams, shady copses, fields of snow, ice tinkling in tall cool drinks. With practice and application, a woman may be able to invoke her subconscious to reconize a hot flush even before her conscious mind does and begin the cooling process at a subconscious level, thereby modifying the intensity of the flush or even removing it from conscious awareness.

Imagery surrounding the metabolic and hormonal processes themselves will facilitate her body's making the best possible physiological adjustments. It will promote good utilization of medication and adherence to good nutritional and activity patterns.

Hypnosis can be used to rehearse difficult situations or to look into the future when these distracting years are over and the woman is once more able to rely on her moods, her brain and her body. She can enhance mind/body interaction— sometimes to a remarkable degree. Hypnosis for the relief of symptoms and the promotion of physiological regulation is a tool we should offer every woman experiencing distressing menopausal symptoms.

Male Sexual Dysfunction

Impotence. Erectile dysfunction is one of the most disturbing disorders of male sexuality. For many years, it was thought that 95 percent of "impotence" was psychogenic. We now know that such a conclusion has done a tremendous disserve to thousands of men who suffer from such distressing disorders.

The difficulty can be with initiating and/or with maintaining an erection. It is of importance that all organic factors have been considered and ruled out or corrected. In particular, one needs to remember the effects of medications such as tranquilizers or anti-hypertensives and the effect of other disorders, such as diabetes, on male sexual function.

There is much that hypnosis has to offer the man who suffers from poor or short-lived erections. Once again—as with the menopausal woman—ego strengthening, improved self-image (both physically and emotionally) and general stress and relaxation techniques are the cornerstones of good therapy.

Specific imagery is helpful, but I have found this to be one area where language is of prime importance. With careful choice of vocabulary, one can create a much more sublte and non-directive approach.

Case History. Mr. L. H., a 64-year-old man, was referred for hypnosis because of his great distress at his diminished erectile function. He had been sexually very active until about five years before and he felt that the waning that occurred at that time was because of his age. He was then able to achieve erection about two-thirds of the time and tolerated this frequency although it frustrated him.

In the subsequent three years, he was diagnosed as having moderately severe hypertension and placed on anti-hypertensive medication. He had also required a transurethral prostatic resection which left him with a post-surgical fistula; this had not responded to conservative therapy and had to be excised. His wife found the fistula very disturbing and made reference to "that dirty old thing" when the home care nurse came to change the dressings. The patient was also greatly distressed when he had a spontaneous and uncontrollable erection on two occasions when the nurse was changing the dressing. He told me about these incidents with embarrassment, reiterating that they had had nothing to do with sexual desire. The nurse was calmly reassuring in a matter-of-fact way.

At the time he came for his initial consultation, his anti-hypertensive medication had been reduced to a fairly low dose and his fistula was entirely healed. However he now "failed" on almost every occasion. He assured me that his wife was a willing partner, responding to and often initiating sexual advances.

The first two hypnotherapy appointments were devoted as usual to relaxation and stress management techniques and the learning of a self-hypnosis approach. At the end of each of those sessions, I gave the subconscious some "homework."

I chose my words carefully: "You will find that a strong, sturdy core of understanding is building up within you. It becomes a tower of strength which you can maintain as the days and weeks pass. You can use this strong core of understanding in very positive ways."

The patient came back for his second session a bewildered but happy man because he had "tried" four times and succeeded twice! For him, a 50 percent improvement was progress indeed. He said to me, "I don't remember your saying anything about erections at all—so what has happened?" I assured him that his subconscious was interpreting the techniques that he was learning in a way that was prompting good sexual function. I repeated the same type of suggestions, using similar vocabulary, at the end of the second session.

He came once more, telling me that the progress had been maintained and that he had again succeeded on half of the occasions that he had "tried." I suggested that the word "try" was a hidden saboteur, best left unused. He looked thoughtful, nodded, and said he would try—laughing as he caught himself—he rephrased, saying, "I'll do it." During the session we did some specific imagery of the male reproductive system and what triggers a sexual response, focusing on aspects that had been part of his good sexual life in earlier years.

He did not return for another session, but I saw him socially a year later, and he came up and quietly said with a big smile, "Still batting .500."

Premature Ejaculation. This dysfunction is so frequently the result of tension and anxiety—which the patient will readily acknowledge—that it is useful to take that approach first. Ego strengthening is obviously important. Rehearsal of good sexual function, where the man is able to restrain the ejaculate for increasing periods of time, is a simple and helpful technique.

Diabetes

Diabetes can be modified, particularly in those patients who experience wide swings of blood sugar levels. The approaches are similar to those described for thyroid dysfunction. A patient whose blood sugar had ranged from 47 mg% to 470 mg% in one day had, over months of hypnotherapy, modified this to an outside range of 134 mg% to 374 mg%; this case has been described by the author elsewhere (Hunter, 1984).

Gastrointestinal System

Dysphagia (including globus hystericus). Disorders of swallowing, where organic causes have been ruled out, frequently respond well to hypnotic intervention because they are so often caused or exacerbated by tension and anxiety. The patient can be reassured that the body often reflects anxiety in physical ways and that it is appropriate to use relaxations and imagery to relieve the problem. Most people are not aware of the physiology of swallowing, and it is useful to explain it to them— particularly the fact that the three swallowing waves each need time to complete their rhythm. This is one area where imagery (and do not forget kinesthetic imagery) can be very helpful. For patients' rehearsal for the future, begin with very easy to swallow, delicious foods in small mouthfuls. Have them savor each mouthful as it is carried from the mouth down the esophagus, through the cardiac sphincter into the stomach.

Functional vomiting. This is a particularly distressing disorder for the victim and for family, friends and acquaintances. It is vitally important to rule out organic causes; a misdiagnosis here could be very serious.

Assist the patient in evoking a good image of the organs of digestion and how they work. Sketches or drawings often help. In most cases, the image will be very symbolic, anyhow, and any image that has meaning to the patient is acceptable.

Having achieved the working tools of hypnotherapy, one then focuses on specific applications. Vomiting disorders also respond well to carefully chosen language— particularly relating the symptoms to idioms in common English usage, for example, "You make me sick," "I'll throw that back at him next time," "It makes my gorge rise," "I'm sick and tired of it all," etc. When these phrases are used in hypnosis in the form of questions, the link between the subconscious and the idiom is easily established. For the patient who comes in with nausea, vomiting and fatigue, where no organic cause can be found, it is worth asking, in hypnosis, "What are you sick and tired of?" The patient may tell you. In hypnosis, one tends to take questions and statements literally, and this is to the advantage of the therapist. The patient may answer, "My boss," "My mother's constant nagging," "The heavy commuter traffic into the city," or give other similar answers. One then has a place to start a more focused inquiry, and directive therapy can begin.

Peptic ulcers. Gastric and duodenal ulcers are so commonly lumped into the "stress disorder" package that the patient himself will firmly implant them there. He may say that his job, his domestic difficulties, his college courses, or his hockey training club cause too much pressure, that is why he has an ulcer. He readily agrees that relaxation and stress management are vital components of therapy and reaches out for them.

Therapeutic approach should be directed to the smooth normal functioning of the stomach itself, including its musculature, its acid-producing cells, and its role in the digestive process. Special attention should be focused on healing and how healing occurs. Imagery or an ulcer crater with a heaped-up edge, inflamed, swollen and painful is important so that the image of the *healing* ulcerated area can displace the active, painful ulcer. Patients must continue whatever medication is appropriate while hypnotherapy is in progress.

Ulcerative colitis. Ulcerative colitis has many similarities to peptic ulcers, higher in the digestive tract, and the general approach is very similar.

Case History. Mr. J. B. was a 27-year-old man, who had first been diagnosed as having ulcerative colitis eight years before. He was intense, artistic, and articulate. I first met him in the hospital when he had been admitted for a severe flare-up. He had been on intravenous steroids which were now bringing the inflammation under control; but his doctors had warned him that surgery was imminent.

Interestingly, he had had some experience with transcendental meditation three years previously. In fact, he had felt much better for at least a year during which he did his TM twice a day. However, he began to miss his meditation and soon was doing it very seldom if at all. For the year before I met him, he was in a chronic state of exacerbation and had been on two occasions extremely ill.

We began his therapy when he was still in the hospital and I saw him there on two occasions. We did the routine techniques, which he enjoyed, but he was impatient to get on with the "real therapy."

Besides being intense, artistic and articulate, this young man was angry. Furiously angry. He did not know at what or at whom, but he did acknowledge that he often felt "consumed by rage," and he commented that sometimes he felt as if he were being eaten up inside.

We proceeded with great emphasis on imagery and on vocabulary. His imagery included the kinesthetic awareness of peristaltic action (smooth, wave-like), of the delicate lining of the large bowel, of the mucus-secreting cells whose function it is to protect that delicate lining, of the villi and the cells which continue the absorption process, and the collecting of the waste residue prior to evacuation. He began to realize that the mucous so commonly found in the stools of colitis sufferers was really nature's protective mechanism, a fact which gave him an entirely different response to that mucous. He understood that when there was blood in the stool the mucous layer had not been able to protect the tender lining of the alimentary canal.

In his imagery, he went down inside his colon and searched for areas that were in a state of disease—whether or not there was actually an ulcer there. If he intuitively felt that there was activity, then he began the mind/body dialogue to provide the information that was necessary to soothe, comfort and relieve the area of all irritating factors. The phrase "irritating factors" can be interpreted by the subconscious to include everything from chemical imbalance to a nagging wife. I suggested that he focus his own healing concentration on the area which he felt was diseased, stressing that it was important to heal from the very deepest cellular layer first and then to heal successive layers until the final healing layer restored the epithelium.

He was pleased to set up a routine of doing self-hypnosis at least once a day, and usually did two or three short sessions (three or four minutes) and one long 20-minute or half-hour session every day.

The immediate benefit was relaxation of tension and anxiety within him, which he appreciated very much, as it greatly lessened the discomfort in his abdomen. He was discharged from the hospital and continued to come for "booster" sessions every few weeks. He gradually weaned himself off his medication and has been in remission since that time. He was encouraged to go regularly for check-ups even though he was not having symptoms, and he has done that, albeit somewhat reluctantly. Certainly, the situation has improved dramatically, and he has high expectations of avoiding surgery.

Respiratory System

Hyperventilation syndrome. Since this syndrome is a common component of anxiety attacks, it is important to seek the cause of the anxiety. However, patients are invariably confronted to know that they have a tool right within themselves, immediately available, to counteract any further hyperventilation episodes. This knowledge in itself reduces anxiety.

Asthma. One of the most rewarding of all hypnotic interventions is that of helping a child gain mastery over his asthma, especially if the asthma is severe enough to have interfered with the child's social life and school activities. The youngster of eight or nine who cannot spend a night at a friend's house or go on a school field trip for fear of getting an asthmatic attack when away from his support system is a sad youngster indeed.

There are many ways to approach the problem, and the one that I use is controversial, but it has proven successful on every occasion when I have used it—and I have used it often.

When the child is comfortable, I ask him in hypnosis to simulate for me an asthma attack. Depending on the age of the child, I ask him to remember what it is like, or imagine himself in a field of flowers, or have trouble breathing like he does when he has an attack. Children are able to follow this instruction well, and within a short time—usually less than a minute—they are wheezing loudly enough to hear the rhonchi without a stethescope.

I congratulate the child on having done well. My next comment is a reassuring phrase such as, "You can come back to normal now." Occasionally a child will gasp, "I don't like this any more," and I will say, "Of course, I can understand that. You can do whatever you need to do to be more comfortable." The child will then spontaneously release the bronchospasm and breathe normally.

Children are intuitive and intelligent. They understand that having treated an asthmatic attack and then "come back to normal" they now have a tool by which they can always help themselves "back to normal." All I say is, "Isn't it nice to know that you can always do that?"

Eight-year-old S. L. was one such asthmatic patient. He had been having trouble since the age of four and required daily medication to prevent an attack and much more stringent intervention should an attack be triggered. He was unable to spend the night at a friend's house or go on a school field trip because he dared not be away from support. Although it had been explained to him that he could easily contact his parents and doctor from a friend's house, he was unwilling to take a risk. A field trip was out of the question.

I asked his mother if I could take him to a seminar I was giving on hypnosis with children and she agreed; we then asked the child if he would go. He, in turn, agreed when I explained that he would be helping to teach doctors how to treat children with asthma.

We proceeded as I have outlined above. He was one of the children who gasped, "I don't like this any more!" and I said to him, "What would you like to do about it?" He replied that he wanted to get back to breathing normally, and I said, "I can understand that." Just do whatever you need to do to make that happen." Within 30 seconds, his discomfort had subsided. It was a very impressive demonstration.

That was the *only* occasion on which I did hypnosis with this lad, and yet to his parents' astonishment he improved dramatically from then on. Although he maintained a low dose of bronchodilator on a daily basis for the next six months, he never again had a serious attack.

Musculskeletal System

No chapter on medical problems would be complete without a mention of that devastating disease, rheumatoid arthritis. If the therapist does nothing else than teach the patient some hypnotic pain relief mechanisms, he has reduced the helplessness of the rheumatoid patient greatly in beginning to free him from the victim role. Hypnosis can also provide a framework in which the patient can release some of the pent-up anger that, in turn, produces pain. Many patients need permission to be angry. Hypnosis gives them a safe way to explore their inner feelings and to find that those feelings are acceptable after all.

References

Ader, R: Psychoneuroimmunology. New York, Academic Press, 1981
Antonovsky, A: Health, Stress and Coping. San Francisco, Jossey-Bass, Inc., 1979
Hunter, ME: Psych Yourself In: Hypnosis and Health. Vancouver, B.C., SeaWalk Press, 1984
Lynch JJ: The Broken Heart. New York, Basic Books, Inc., 1977

10 THE INTERFACE BETWEEN BIOFEEDBACK AND HYPNOSIS: THE BIOTIC BAND ™

SHIRLEY SANDERS, Ph.D.

Thermal biofeedback as a primary form of psychotherapy for the patient with psychophysiological disorders is currently effective, popular and replicable. These elements interact so as to place thermal biofeedback in a privileged position vis-a-vis other forms of therapy. Because of the visibility and usage of this methodology, it is important to view thermal biofeedback within a broader hypnotherapy context, looking at the interface of thermal biofeedback to developmental concepts such as the transitional object (Winnicott, 1953) and hypnosis. The resulting integration should be of interest to the clinician working with psychophysiologically disordered patients as well as the researcher who has the tools to put this integrated hypothesis to the test. This chapter limits its observations to the clinical situation and to relevant theoretical concepts, making no claim for generalization outside of the examples cited. The introduction will briefly describe thermal biofeedback, the transitional object, and hypnosis.

Thermal Biofeedback

Thermal biofeedback may be conceptualized as a procedure in which peripheral thermal reaction is monitored, processed and conveyed back to the patient so that the patient can learn to deliberately alter that activity in a given direction. Farnhill (1980) found that relaxation combined with handwarming and measured by biofeedback equipment tended to develop the subject's awareness of a bodily state conducive to symptom relief. Crosson (1980), in a study involving biofeedback, skin-temperature, imagery and relaxation, found that only those subjects receiving biofeedback and biofeedback plus suggestion and imagery demonstrated evidence of learned temperature control. Feamster (1976) found in the treatment of Raynaud's disease that biofeedback and hypnosis led to an increase of finger temperature. Wickeramsekera (1976) surveyed numerous research studies in an attempt to clarify ways in which biofeedback, behavior therapy and hypnosis have contributed to the arrangement of conditions which increase subjective involvement with words. Kline (1979) discussed hypnosis as an integrative and amplifying procedure in relation to biofeedback and behavior therapy. Hypnosis appeared effective in linking cognitive to affective reactions within a feedback loop of sensory and motor imagery. Kline's interest lay in the dynamics observed within the biofeedback and behavior therapy situations as studied within the environment of hypnosis.

A dynamic interpretation of biofeedback may be discussed informally at workshops and in clinical situations, but surprisingly little literature has appeared. Modern society too often prefers to use machines in a magical, omnipotent manner and at the same time to ignore the patient's potential capability of imagery and the impact of imagery on his or her body. In work with psychophysiological disorders, a dynamic approach to biofeedback and hypnosis appears promising.

The patient's thermal activity may be monitored by a feedback device that records the activity, for example, a biotic band (Biotemp Products). A biotic band is simply a wrist band containing liquid crystals that reacts to changes in temperature by the regrouping of the crystals to display a given temperature between the ranges of 70 and 99. The biotic band has been shown to be reliable within the limits of plus or minus .05 degrees. A change of temperature by more than one degree is a significant change. The patient is instructed to alter the temperature by imaging scenes, experiences, feelings until the temperature changes. The sequence reflects the construction of an ongoing loop between a physiological process, for example, peripheral body temperature, and the measurement of that process, the reading of the temperature. In the examples to be presented, the temperature was monitored by a biotic band which was chosen because it was relatively inexpensive, readily available for home practice, and reliable. The patient keeps and uses the band at home as well as in the treatment session.

Like other therapies, biofeedback requires the active participation of the patient. Unless the patient is willing to concentrate and to image, mastery of temperature alteration does not occur. In essence, within the biofeedback paradigm, the power of change resides in the willingness of the patient to imagine, to concentrate, to participate actively in order to bring about alteration of temperature. While biofeedback provides the information that something has changed, the capacity for change resides in the patient. In this manner, biofeedback minimizes dependency and maximizes autonomy.

According to Green and Green (1979), who studied the application of thermal biofeedback within clinical situations, the use of thermal biofeedback rests on the fact that peripheral skin temperature is a function of vasodilation and constriction. Thus, when the peripheral blood vessels are dilated, more blood flows through them and the skin warms. By measuring the temperature in the extremities, then, one can get an indication of the amount of blood level constriction. Secondly, because constriction and dilation of blood vessels are controlled by the sympathetic nervous system, one can get a second indirect measurement of the amount of sympathetic nervous system activity. In this manner, biofeedback provides the opportunity for the patient to exert some control over autonomic responses.

Certainly, this measurement is interesting. It is important, however, to know what images, thoughts, feelings can exert such a powerful influence on the sympathetic nervous system. Cognitive awareness of the "trigger" for change is the key to the development of true self-control. The process of imaging the trigger and receiving feedback enables validation of one's ability to affect one's physiology. The identified thoughts, images and feelings which accompany the change allow the patient to believe in his/her ability to change and consequently to rely less on the measuring instrument and on the therapist while relying more on himself or herself. Is there not a leap from instrumental regulation to self-regulation, much like the leap described by Freud (1911) in his description of a developmental "passing"? Tolpin (1971) went on to describe the essential "leap" from maternal regulation to self-regulation as illustrated by the phenomenon of the transitional object.

Transition Object

Winnicott (1953) introduced the concept of the transitional phenomenon when he indicated that an object, a thought, or a concept could be experienced in a very specific way, for example, in the intermediate area of experience. In this arena of experience, one has the capacity to experience both external and internal reality in a blended manner. He believes that there is an intermediate area of experience to which both inner reality and external life contribute. A baby's blanket reflects an outer source of soothing, warming experience as well as the baby's fantasies, body memories and wishes. Even a popular song, for instance, may be appreciated for fine realistic qualities, while at the same time it contains a wealth of fantasy, imagery and primary process experience.

Winnicott clearly indicates that any object, thought or concept can become a transitional object—it need only be experienced in the intermediate area of experience. By this definition, an infant's babbling or humming can become a soothing intermediate area of experience as a transitional phenomenon. Even adults can experience this intermediate mode of experience since the task of reality acceptance never ends and one needs to escape the strain of relating inner and outer reality. Relief from this strain is provided by an intermediate area of experience which is not challenged. In our practices, our patients make symbolic references to transitional objects and transitional phenomena. The transitional object and the transitional phenomena provide something very valuable: time out, a quiet, soothing place. While Winnicott at one point says that a transitional object must be chosen, he does acknowledge that initially the infant is given the sheet, the blanket. What is really created is the transitional space (Coppolillo, 1967).

Coppolillo describes transitional objects and transitional experience as necessary elements in psychological development in that they mediate those ego structures which will permit socially appropriate and mature forms of object relatedness. Certainly, these new formations are important in the process of learning and growing.

The transitional mode of experiencing while insuring the ego optimal autonomy from inner stress and environmental problems eventually becomes the buffer for soothing itself. In this way, learning can be fostered.

In one sense, the concept of transitional object functions as a bridge between the inner and the outer, the imagined and the real, the soothing comfort of security and the fantasy of safety. The bridge is partially constructed from the primary tools of sensory motor channels, continuously providing stimulation from sensory organs: olfactory, kinesthetic, tactile, visual, thermal and body memories. This inwardly directed stimulation generates a natural tendency to anticipate, to expect, to believe, to trust the very foundations upon which self-help, autonomy and independence are nurtured. Erickson (1956) has described a developmental series of life crises beginning with basic trust, then autonomy, and has discussed their ongoing importance throughout the life-growth cycle. On the other hand, precursors of transitional objects are objects that have a unique capacity for consoling, are not discovered or invented, but are administered, for example, a pacifier.

Hypnosis

Hypnosis is an altered state of consciousness in which the person exhibits focused attention and heightened imagery experience and can alter certain types of physiological experience such as peripheral body temperature, blood pressure, physical relaxation and cognitive-emotional experience (Crasilneck and Hall, 1985). A hypnotic environment would facilitate the development of a transitional object experience (Baker et al, 1983). It is a matter of debate whether hypnosis fosters response to biofeedback training (Andreychuk and Scriver, 1975). In this author's view, hypnosis can enhance such response.

Case Examples

The following case examples illustrate the use of the Biotic Band as a transitional object.

Donna, a 48-year-old female, was referred by her internist for itching, burning sensations and rash of nine months duration. Donna had been seen by a number of specialists: the dermatologist, the gynecologist, the internist—all to no avail. She had tried a number of medications, but found no relief. She came to my office under tremendous stress, revealing pressure of speech and tight body tension. She communicated a well-rehearsed review of symptoms in great detail, without stopping for breath. She was unable to relate everyday stress to her symptoms, and she was not psychologically-minded, apparently unable to shift gears from body language to psychological language.

Taking out the Biotic Band, I explained that we would use this band to measure temperature in her lower arm. She looked puzzled, and I explained that by learning to control the temperature in her arm she could learn to be more in control of her body. Since to start we needed a "baseline," it was necessary for her to keep a recording of her temperature four times a day, plus whenever she felt warm, itching or was aware of the rash. The diary of temperature recordings should also contain descriptions of what she was doing at the time of measurement and how she was feeling. Her initial reading in the office was 90 degrees, which was high compared to my other patients. Donna responded positively to my attention and my explanations and seemed immediately struck by the band. She stroked it, was quite inquisitive about how it worked, and seemed relieved.

In the second visit, she returned the diary of baseline information. Nonetheless, she was having a very difficult time with the rash on her chest. Even at the moment, she said she felt hot, itchy and red. We recorded the temperature reading on the band, which indicated 92 degrees. A review of her diary made it clear that she was comfortable when her temperature was below 90 degrees. So we chose cooling as the target behavior. I asked her to close her eyes and tell me what she thought might feel cool. This question stimulated self-directed imagery, which could be monitored through verbal report and appropriately reinforced by the therapist.

Donna replied to the suggestion: "I am walking into a cool pool of water." I asked her to imagine that she was walking into a cool pool of water—to describe what it would look like, feel like, smell like, how it was to walk in the water. This suggestion was intended to expand and more fully develop the patient's involvement in the imagery. She readily described walking into the water in a very concrete manner mentioning "goose bumps" as she moved more deeply into the imagery experience. She revealed all the recognized signs of hypnosis—slow reaction time, relaxed musculature, focused attention, slower respiratory rate, vivid imagery and a sense of time distortion. She described becoming cooler and feeling more comfortable, with the rash receding. I noticed that her temperature had dropped to 88 degrees. I asked her to open her eyes and to look at the band. She was pleased to see that she had really cooled and was surprised at how much better she felt. She praised the soft comfort of the chair, the quietness of my voice, and the soothing quality of the office. She appeared to have a very positive reaction to me as a soothing, caring, nurturing person.

We practiced the imagery twice more, and she was instructed to practice the cooling imagery three times a day and whenever she felt particularly warm. Before leaving, she touched the band, stroked it, and asked several questions about it. Out in the waiting room her fascination with the band continued as she asked my secretary how it was made.

Her third visit revealed significant relief of the symptoms during the week. Her practice sessions had gone well and her temperature had stayed in the 80's range.

The fourth week she began to recognize her panic in the face of stress—getting "hot and bothered" when her husband was late for dinner. She recognized how helpless she felt. As she explained this tendency to feel out of control, her temperature shot up above 90 degrees. She experienced rapid relief with the vivid image of walking into a cool pool of water.

She now practiced regularly and realized that panicking was counter-productive. Labeling her reaction as an emotion enabled her to gain distance from it and ultimately to control it. She remained fascinated with the band for two months; at that point she said that now she could monitor her temperature directly without the band. She knew how to cool and she no longer needed the band. The patient continued in psychotherapy two months longer, directly exploring verbally those situations which had led to panic. Developmentally, she seemed to have progressed from body language to psychological awareness.

What Happened in This Case

Initially, Donna felt helpless and out of control over her body. Like the infant who has been prematurely abandoned, she did not know how to soothe and quiet herself, and her feelings led to panic. She found relief and soothing calm in my office. Indeed, my office, my chair, and my voice were experienced as the calm in the midst of the storm. The band enabled her to reexperience the calm even when away from the office. It seems that the band took on properties of a transitional object in that it provided an intermediate mode of experience, which symbolically provided a bridge from the office to real-life experience, from the comfort and soothing experienced in the office to the comfort and soothing wished. In the office, she became aware that she could soothe and quiet herself and be in control of her body. This relief was reinforced by her practice away from the office. The image she created was prescribed, and it affected her arm cooling and body cooling, leading to physiological change, changing from discomfort to comfort, from loss of control to control, from passivity to activity. The band represented a link to the office—to the orange chair—where she felt in control. Even at home, or away from home, the bank transcended time and space. Donna created an intermediate space which permitted her to grow, to help herself, to become cool, calm and collected.

Second Case Example

Bill, a 45-year-old engineer, was referred by his internist for migraines, a problem he had endured for 20 years, since his marriage. He had been to see numerous physicians, neurologists, super-specialists, and he had even tried thermal biofeedback at a competing university, but the procedure had been a failure. Although he had learned to raise his temperature by 15 degrees, he continued to have migraines. I asked Bill to record his temperature as measured by the band four times a day and to record what he was doing and feeling at the time. In addition, he should measure his temperature whenever he had a migraine, which he claimed was every day. Upon his return the following week, the baseline readings indicated that Bill was more uncomfortable when his temperature was warm. So again, the target behavior was cooling.

Bill chose placing imagined ice and snow first on his neck then on his forehead and eyes to cool. He became quite involved in expressing the vivid detail of placing cold ice and snow on sensitive areas of his face, such as his eyes. The imagery led quickly to a hypnotic state in that the patient was able to experience sensory distortion and time distortion. I introduced hypnoanesthesia in the form of numbing which followed quite directly from images of ice and snow. He was surprised to notice that the numbing led to a neutral feeling different from pain and discomfort. His temperature had dropped two degrees. After the imagery was completed, he was instructed to practice four times a day and also when he had a migraine.

Bill also seemed fascinated by the band, how it was made, what led to the changes in color and number. When he returned the following week, he announced that he had experienced only one migraine and that cooling really seemed to help. He expressed very positive feelings about me as someone who was nurturing and caring. He continued to show an interest in the band and was very motivated to practice. As he became more confident of his ability to recognize when he was getting hot, usually stressful times at home and at work, and instead became more confident of his ability to cool and to recognize the pleasant neutral state, he became less interested in the band, saying he could regulate his temperature without it. Treatment at this time became more psychological as Bill began to explore ways he could express his anger and frustration and to learn better ways of coping.

These two examples, although the diagnosis was different for each, reveal certain similarities.

1. Both patients were centered initially on the experience of their symptoms and their bodies. Developmentally, they spoke in body language as opposed to recognition of psychological stress.

2. Both patients had failed other treatment attempts.

3. Both patients developed positive transference feelings towards me as a caring, nurturing person.

4. Both patients were ambivalent about change, feeling that help was impossible.

5. Both patients reacted with interest and curiosity towards the Biotic Band and the fact that by using their imagination they could cool.

6. The band represented a soothing, calming influence begun in the office and reinforced through self-practice at home. The descriptions of their experience suggested the creation of an intermediate space.

7. As the patients gained mastery in controlling their temperatures and their symptoms, they were able to give up the band. They were able to self-monitor their temperature directly.

8. These experiences parallel the description of the transitional object which is part outside stimulation (mother-doctor) and part inside stimulation (sensory-motor and imagination) resulting in an intermediate area of experience which is unchallenged. Through biofeedback and hypnosis these patients learned to be autonomous in dealing with their symptoms, their feelings, and their lives. The band represented a temporary bridge from their symptoms to a reduction in their symptoms, but more importantly it led to new learning and greater autonomy.

The wearing of the Biotic Band by the patient can be much like the holding of the transitional object by the child: it proves the illusion of security and safety. Through playful activity of self-hypnotic imagery, the patient consoles self, feels support and security, and strengthens his or her ability to comfort and soothe. This new mastery over discomfort results in the integration and reintegration of body parts into the totality of the body image.

The adult patient's ability to take control of his or her bodily functions, such as becoming warmer or cooler, involves an initial denial of reality because the creation of an image counter to immediate experience constitutes denial. The patient compensates for helplessness by making the passive active, by making a positive change. In so doing, the patient initiates the disappearance of discomfort—the return of safety and relaxation is fostered. In essence, the use of thermal biofeedback can create an intermediate space similar to that described by Winnicott's transitional object.

References

Andreychuk T, Skriver C: Hypnosis and biofeedback in the treatment of migraine headache. Int J Clin Exp Hypn 23:172-183, 1975

Copeland D: Transitional objects and development; transitional phenomena and regression. Paper presented to the American Psychological Association, August 25, 1981, Los Angeles, CA.

Coppolillo HP: Maturational aspects of the transitional phenomenon. Int J Psychoanalysis 43:237-246, 1967

Crasilneck H, Hall JA: Clinical Hypnosis: Principles and Applications. Second Edition. New York, Grune & Stratton, 1985

Crosson B: Control of skin temperature through biofeedback and suggestion with hypnotized college women. Int J Clin Exp Hypn 28(1):75-87, 1980

Edmonston, Jr. WE: The Induction of Hypnosis. New York, Wiley, 1986

Erickson EH: Childhood and Society. New York, Norton, 1956

Farnhill D: Subjective versus objective reports of digital skin temperature in the treatment of Raynaud's disease. Australian J Clin Exp Hypn 8(1):75-87, 1980

Feamster HJ: Raynaud's phenomenon biofeedback, and hypnosis. Newsletter for research in Mental Health and Behavioral Sciences. 18(1):20-22, 1976

Freud S: Formulations Regarding Two Principles in Mental Functioning. Standard Edition. 12, 1911

Gaddini B: Transitional objects and the process of individuation: A study in three different social groups. J Amer Academy Child Psychia 9:347-365, 1970

Green, Green A: Beyond Biofeedback. New York, Delacorte, 1977

J-42 Feedback thermometer (registered trademark). Cuyborg Corporation, Boston, 1977

Kline MV: Hypnosis with specific relation to biofeedback and behavior therapy; theoretical and clinical considerations. Psychotherapy and Psychosomatics 31(1-4):294-300, 1979

Sanders S: The biotic band as a transitional object. Presidental Address, Division 30, American Psychological Association. Los Angeles, 1982

The Biotic Band (reg. TM) Biotemp Products, Inc. 1950 W. 86th Street, Indianapolis, Indiana

Tolpin M: On the beginnings of a cohesive self. Psychoanalytic Study of the Child. 26:316, 1971

Wickeramsekera IA: Biofeedback, Behavior Therapy and Hypnosis: Potentiating the Verbal Control of Behavior for Clinicians. Chicago, Nelson Hall, 1976

Winnicott DW: Transitional Objects and transitional phenomena. Int. J Psychoanalysis 34:89-97, 1953

11 HYPNOSIS IN THE TREATMENT OF PAIN

HAROLD P. GOLAN, D.M.D.

Pain, that dreaded and frequent human experience, can be controlled by hypnosis. Although many studies, both clinical and experimental, have been done on the relief of pain through a variety of hypnotic techniques, the exact how or why of such pain alleviation is still obscure (Crasilneck and Hall, 1975). It is a fact, however that a patient in pain, either chronic or acute, may be well served by hypnosis and the hypnotherapist.

What can be said about pain? Pain is a common expectation with any surgical intervention, dental treatment, accident, burn, or even an exasperating experience. There are pain models such as headaches, dysmenorrhea, arthritis, acute musculoskeletal spasms which may have no external cause (Des Jardens, 1983). It is estimated by Mutter and Karnilow (1983) that as many as one in three Americans experiences chronic pain. About 70 percent have low back pain; 10 percent have headaches. Pain is one of the most frequent symptoms which bring patients to physicians and dentists. Hilgard and Hilgard (1975) note that pain treatment has become the primary task of the physician.

We know pain exists. We have experienced it. Yet the explanation of what it is and exactly how the body uses its nervous system to create sensations of pain—which vary from individual to individual experiencing similar noxious or experimental stimuli—is theoretical. Bonica (1953) states that pain must be considered as a psychobiological phenomenon which is not easily classified as a sensation or emotion. The conversion of sensation into a painful experience is largely an emotional reaction involving many processes. The emotional reaction to pain requires much attention during management because it often constitutes the most relevant aspect of the pain phenomenon.

Cheek (1968) says that pain is a consciously perceived, uncomfortable awareness. Melzack and Wall (1963) give a neurophysiological model of pain which embraces social and cognitive determinants. Hilgard and Hilgard (1975) distingush at least three components: 1) sensory pain; 2) suffering; 3) mental anguish.

The response of pain is conditioned by variables including pain tolerance, age, gender, family, socioculture and environmental factors. Sternbach (1978) says that the person's cultural context, level of anxiety, personality characteristics, social learning experiences regarding responses to illness in addition to the meaning attributed to the situation and prevailing enforcement contingencies will all have a bearing on the pain experience. The differentiation of acute from chronic pain is critical. In acute pain, nociception is of greater significance than in chronic where the conditioning variables are more important. Although Bonica (1979) says that chronic pain is a condition which has lasted at least six months, St. Amand (1984) states that pain which has lasted at least six weeks is chronic.

Des Jardens (1983) comments on the production of pain. In acute pain, there is a cell injury which releases fatty acids from the cell. This in turn releases histamine, bradykinin within cells, and prostaglandins to produce pain. Arachidonic acid is the precursor of prostaglandins, which are important in fever, headaches, asthma, ulcers, diarrhea, dysmenorrhea, pain, inflammation. Chronic pain models may have a different cause, hormonal perhaps, which probably produces the histamine, bradykinin and protaglandins.

How Hypnosis Works

McGlashan, Evans and Orne (1969) showed that the hypnotic pain relief differed from placebos. Hilgard (1975) noted that hypnotic induction alone ("neutral hypnosis") did not produce pain relief. The primary response to pain is anxiety. Decrease of anxiety seems to be a factor in hypnotic lessening of pain (Shor, 1962), as Alexander (1977) mentioned in a pain symposium. Thus, fear, stress and anxiety seem to be factors in increasing physiological responses of the pain process. Hypnosis can be invaluable in reducing the emotional factors surrounding any pain process, acute or chronic (Wain, 1982). St. Amand (1984) states that pain is both a symptom and an illness and that the most common cause of the symptom is stress and anxiety. Stress precipitates the symptom; then the symptom becomes a further cause of anxiety. Needless to say, the pain is real, whether it is imagined (precipitated by an accident or surgery which has psychological overtones) or organic.

According to Crasilneck (1975), hypnosis produces pain relief by a possible neurophysiological mechanism. He uses the example of a 14-year-old, white female who had received a head injury some four years before he saw her. She had increasing epileptic seizures for which anticonvulsive drugs were ineffective. The right temporal lobe of the brain was the seat of the electroencephalographic discharge which produced the seizures. It was decided to do a temporal lobectomy with electroencephalographic monitoring. If general anesthesia were used, the alpha waves would be flattened out and could not be monitored. Hypnosis, however, does not produce alterations in the brain wave pattern, a fact which occasioned the decision to use hypnosis and local anesthesia. Four rehearsals were done.

During the nine-hour procedure it was notable that when a blood vessel in the hippocampal gyrus was being coagulated the patient suddenly came out of trance. She was immediately rehypnotized. The surgeon then purposely restimulated the same area. Again the patient awakened from trance. She was rehypnotized. The proper area was destroyed by cryosurgery. The patient recovered well with no further abdominal discharge.

Not only is a neurophysiological basis to hypnotic pain relief possible, but there is at least one brain pathway which creates the trance of hypnosis. We then can postulate a scientific neurological theory regarding hypnosis.

Crasilneck and Hall (1975) argue that there is some central inhibition of pain perception, perhaps analogous to that obtained when psychosurgery is done for relief of intractible pain and perhaps related to the Melzack-Wall "gate theory," with a central hypnotic change as the "gate-closing" stimulus.

Pain can be experimentally produced as Hilgard and Hilgard (1975) demonstrated so well in their cold pressor and ischemic studies. Hypnosis has been shown to be effective in pain reduction in such situations.

Pain can be organic in origin. Hilgard and Hilgard (1975) state that pain is a prominent symptom in cancer, obstetrics, surgery and dentistry. The source of these pains is related primarily to organic disease (cancer), definable stress (obstetrics) or to interventions made in the course of treatment (surgery and dentistry). These pains have minimum psychological roots. Their alleviation by hypnosis produces a convincing demonstration of hypnosis as a psychological and physiological method of pain control. Crasilneck and Hall (1975) say that organic pain patients were unusually good subjects for hypnosis and that all such pain can be removed for a controlled period of time in these patients.

Organic pain can be acute or chronic. Acute pain patients with illnesses such as ulcers can have symptoms which subside quickly or slowly. It is difficult to classify a patient who may have a chronic illness, such as ulcers, which may produce acute attacks that may last for relatively short times or persist for weeks with varying degrees of discomfort.

Studies of Hypnosis in Pain Control

Crasilneck and Hall (1975) have an excellent bibliography on the history of hypnosis use in pain control, anesthesia and surgery. Hilgard and Hilgard (1975) offer outstanding material on experimental pain. Bassman and Wester (1984) give a modern detailed description of headache alleviation. Barber (1982) notes Ericksonian methods of treating both acute and chronic pain. Many authors have detailed hypnotic treatment for pain states. Wakeman (1978), for example, describes its use for burns in a controlled study which compares patients according to severity of burns and age. Autohypnosis was taught for hypnoanesthesia, dissociation and reduction of anxiety and fear. Hypnosis was found to be an effective method of pain reduction. Ewin (1984) gives an excellent example of burn pain treatment by outlining verbiage stressing the imagery of coolness.

Golan (1965) describes a consultation case of a 60-year-old white female who was burned by fire which killed her husband and severely burned her over 65 percent of her body. She was on the danger list at the Peter Bent Brigham Hospital in Boston. Two months after she had received grafting to her face, she was despondent, crying, had to receive a general anesthetic daily for dressing changes to all four limbs, was losing fluids and electrolytes because the dressing changes could not be done at will. The general anesthetic daily precluded necessary ingestion of liquids and fluids. She had been so severely burned on her arms and legs that there was no area for an intravenous injection. She was hysterical about painful dressing changes. On the first visit, as therapist I explained hypnosis, and the patient agreed to participate. During the trance, I explained pain physiology, necessity of changing dressings, need for her by her children and grandchildren. I had her imagine her limbs were like pins and needles, and took her on a trip mentally to the mountains while one leg dressing was changed. Post hypnotic suggestions were given for better eating, drinking, sleeping, general well-being and autohypnosis practice.

On the second visit, the patient informed me that no sleeping pill had been necessary for the first time in her hospital stay. She had not seen her hands since the accident, and the plastic surgeon was fearful of further depression when she viewed them. So negative hallucination was used in the suggestion that she disregard her hands even if they looked bad to her because they were going to look different when she left the hospital. The suggestion that she imagine her limbs to be as insensitive as thin, light, steel rods was given as dressings were changed on her other leg. On the third visit, verbiage was used to motivate the patient to live, to get well, to prepare for further grafting and walking out of the hospital. Suggestions were given that with autohypnosis she could have her dressing changed at will. On this visit both hand and arm dressings were changed during trance with no untoward depressive results.

On the fourth visit both leg dressings were changed; on the fifth all four limb dressings. At this point, she was literally able to stand on her own two feet and was eager to show me. On the sixth visit all four dressings were changed with the operator only verbalizing during two; on the seventh visit the operator just watched during dressings. During the next month, the patient had general anesthesia only for successful grafting to her hands and was discharged. About four months following admission, the interested case was presented at Grand Surgical Rounds.

Chronic Pain Control

Pain control by hypnosis in cancer has been an important factor in treatment. Imagery innovations are being continually improved (Erickson, 1966; Olness, 1981; Sacerdote, 1962, 1968, 1970, 1980, 1982; Barber, 1982; Newton, 1982-83; Margolis, 1982-83). Of the 400,000 cancer deaths in the United States, the incidence of severe pain in the terminal stages is estimated at 60-80 percent by Bonica (1979) so that any pain reducing mechanism takes on importance. Reports of the use of hypnosis have noted varying degrees of success in helping pain in cancer patients. Hilgard and Hilgard (1975), using reports of Butler (1955), Lea, Ware and Munroe (1900), (1900), Cangello (1972), mention an average about 50 percent of patients improved. Wolfe (1962) and Erickson (1966) report pain-free states obtained in terminal cases. Newton (1982-83) and Simonton (1978) report hypnosis as being a very important adjunct to treatment.

Sacerdote (1982) states that the two most important factors in the treatment of chronic pain are: 1) the patient's individual talent for hypnosis; 2) the therapist's ability in eliciting hypnotic responses appropriate and adequate for bringing about useful perceptual changes. The inventiveness and creativity of the therapist inter-reacting with the motivation of the patient seem to bring the desired effect.

Others recently have described treatment of chronic pain states very well, for example, Bassman, Wester (1984), Barber (1982), Hilgard and Hilgard (1975), Crasilneck and Hall (1975).

Relaxation Through Hypnosis

Wain (1982), Sacerdote (1982), and others have enumerated various hypnotic pain strategies. Relaxation alone very often brings about a diminution or lessening of pain of whatever origin. The pain threshold of the patient seems to rise as a patient's relaxation response occurs (Benson, Beary and Carol, 1974). Some of the changes include a decrease in oxygen consumption, carbon dioxide elimination, heart rate and respiratory rate.

Hypnosis seems to bring about a very effective form of relaxation. The one advantage that hypnosis produces over other related forms of relaxation, such as transcendental meditation or "The Relaxation Response," is that by using hypnosis the therapist is able to direct the treatment, changing strategies as the occasion demands. The rapport which occurs at the very outset of a therapist/patient relationship is far deeper than in a treatment setting in which hypnosis is not used. The feeling of warmth and caring which the patient subconsciously feels from his doctor has an important bearing not only on the degree of relaxation which is produced but also on the entire treatment.

Pain patients have their own concerns and unconscious misconceptions, hopes, expectations and doubts as well as those of referring physicians and family friends (Sacerdote, 1982; Cheek, 1968). These are intangible factors that can enhance or inhibit success. Thus, some authors have doubts on the use of susceptibility tests. Barber (1980) states that a susceptibility score reflects only responsiveness to a particular hypnotic approach and is not a predictor of general responsivity to hypnosis. Sacerdote (1982) says, "I do not believe most clinicians would be helped by adopting the routine use of susceptibility tests. They would more likely harm than help patients."

This writer believes that susceptibility tests fail on two counts. The first is that the patient, whether experiencing acute or chronic pain, may have a high motivation to lose his or her pain. This fact alone could make this patient's response far higher in the pain situation than it would at other times.

Golan (1975) has an example of a case of retrobulbar hemorrhage with a patient who has an Edwards valve in his heart which caused the man to have postural hypotension resulting in a "drop attack." He struck his eye on a sharp projection. He could have neither general nor local anesthesia. This patient would be ordinarily classified at the lowest end of the scale of susceptibility tests, but for this one hour operation carried out successfully with hypnoanesthesia, he was a superb subject. The second reason for failure of the tests is that if a susceptibility test is given and the patient scores low, the expectation of the doctor is lessened. The doctor's lowered expectation may preclude the successful use of hypnosis for for the pain problem at hand.

Procedures With Patients

The operator must use his creative imagination as well as exercising the patient's creative imagination so that he tailors his words and suggestions to the patient's particular problem and personality. This writer will list the protocol he uses for each hypnosis patient; segments can be lengthened or shortened depending on the patient, but some kind of checklist is necessary when one is seeing many patients for hypnotherapy.

The patient who has completed a physical history form is personally escorted into the office by the doctor who greets the patient with a warm handshake. The following subjects are introduced:

1. Explanation of hypnosis

2. Emotional history of patient including education, family, vocation, likes, dislikes

3. Induction

4. Importance of body to good health (Spiegel and Spiegel, 1978); Ideomotor questioning about situation (Cheek and LeCron, 1968)

5. Relaxation exercise

6. Autohypnosis

7. Sense of humor approach

8. Therapy for specific ailment and stress control

9. Glove anesthesia, 95 percent
   Arm catalepsy, 5 percent

10. Repetition of some of above

11. Termination

The emotional history is important in that the operator can discover many facets of the patient's perception of himself in relation to his problem. Blau (1982) has formulated the following questions to ask pain patients; the answers yield clues to the operator for treatment:

1. How can I help you?

2. When did you have the pain for the first time? How often now? How long does it last?

3. Where does the pain start? How does it travel? Deep (like bellyache) or superficial (skin)?

4. What brings the pain on? Can anything aggravate it, increase or make it worse? What have you tried to reduce pain?

5. What is the pain like? How bad is the pain?

6. Do you notice anything else when you have pain?

7. What has been your previous treatment? What do you think caused the pain? Why are you seeking help now?

Pain Strategies

Pain strategies are many with hypnosis (Wain, 1982):

1. Direct abolition of pain

2. Indirect permissive hypnotic abolition

3. Amnesia

4. Hypnotic analgesics

5. Hypnotic anesthesia

6. Hypnotic replacement of symptom

7. Hypnotic displacement of pain

8. Hypnotic dissociation

9. Hypnotic reinterpretation

10. Hypnotic time distortion

11. Hypnotic diminution

12. Ego strengthening (Hartland, 1966)

13. Electric light switches (Sacerdote, 1982; Cheek and LeCron, 1968)

These techniques can be used on both acute and chronic patients depending on the strategies the operator chooses. An example of hypnotic replacement of the symptom by Golan (1971) is on a patient with tic doloureux (major trigeminal neuralgia), a disease which is considered a very painful affliction. The patient had been having paroxysms of severe, lancinating pain lasting from 15 to 60 minutes. During the first session, it was suggested to him that he would substitute a very heavy feeling lasting only a moment or two. At the next visit, the patient did not accept the suggestion of heaviness but translated the tic into "a momentary feeling of pickiness." He had chosen his own pathway to replace his original symptom. If the therapist can get the patient to manipulate his symptom of pain in any way, he is on the way to successful therapy.

In regard to the detailed treatment of chronic pain, many excellent descriptions have noted the need for psychological intervention as part of the treatment plan (Bassman, Wester, 1982; Barber, 1982). This writer accepts the treatments outlined by therapists who use psychological adjuncts because their results have been rewarding. The problem to many physicians and dentists who have had no psychological training is what to do with pain patients in situations in which psychiatric or psychological treatment is resisted or where outside help in the form of pain clinics or adequately hypnosis-trained psychological therapists is not available.

It has been the writer's experience that even in severe cases of chronic pain the use of physiologic controls, such as anesthesia, catalepsy, displacement, and replacement, produces adequate results. Once the patient is aware that he can control one part of his body, he then can control other parts of his body. Somehow the patient subconsciously or consciously comes to the realization that he can cause physiological change. Once this occurs, treatment is rapid. The use of physiology rather than psychology may well be the way therapists with no psychological training might treat pain patients.

Crasilneck and Hall (1975) compare the use of hypnotherapy and psychotherapy and say that hypnosis offers distinct advantages. "It is focused directly on those problems of immediate concern to the patient—pain relief, maintaining appetite and interest, and being reassured that his condition will not lead to abandonment. Hypnosis has the added advantage of being a more structured situation than psychotherapy." Wakeman and Kaplan (1978) use no other forms of counseling or interpersonal intervention in their treatment of pain control in burns. Other authors have used some of the other pain strategies for adequate treatment.

Hypnosis has been used extensively for acute pain situations. Deltito (1984) says that safe, quick pain control remains one of the physician's major duties. He has used hypnosis with orthopedic injuries, acute burns, menstrual discomfort, renal calculi, herpetic lesions, muscle spasms, dental syndromes. He notes that whether a given injury will be translated into suffering is determined in large part by 1) the context; 2) the patient's sense of loss or control; 3) his attention to the pain; 4) his general level of anxiety; 5) his expectation of how the injury will interfere with his present lifestyle and future plans.

Patients with chronic conditions such as phantom limb pain, present special problems since the pain is acute but occurs only some of the time. It can be modified by the five postulates of Deltito (1984). Siegel (1979) has described a 54-year-old white female who had persistent phantom limb pain from an above-the-knee amputation. Hypnotic anesthesia provided successful treatment for condition.

Schafer and Hernandez (1978), in the first premise of their paper on "Hypnosis, Pain and the Context of Therapy," say that acute uncomplicated pain is not desired by the patient and is therefore directly amenable to hypnotic intervention, proportional to the patient's ability to utilize hypnosis.

Many patients have chronic diseases which have exacerbations of acute pain. Zeltzer, Dash and Holland (1979) have used hypnosis for pain control in sickle cell anemia. Patients were able to reduce 1) frequency and intensity of pain crises; 2) need for heavy analgesics; 3) frequency of emergency room visits; 4) frequency and length of hospitalizations for pain.

Use of Hypnosis for Hemophiliacs

Another chronic disease which necessitates pain control for acute situations is hemophilia. Hemophilia is a hereditary male disease which is the most important constitutional anomaly of blood coagulation (90 percent). The bleeding time is prolonged and may last for hours. Hemorrhage, usually following trauma but sometimes spontaneous, is the essential symptom. Hematomas can be large and life threatening. The severest cases can result in complete inactivity, making education and employment difficult. One million units of the six million units of blood collected in blood banks, hospitals and mobile centers are used for about 25,000 men, who average about 10 transfusions a month.

Hemophiliac patients facing dental treatment are apprehensive because they have usually been hospitalized many times, have had narrow escapes, have seen

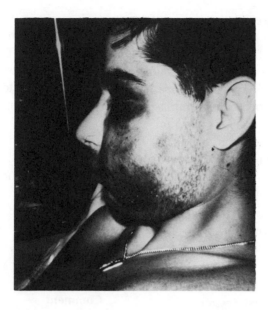

relatives die of the ailment. The following case will introduce a life-threatening situation in a 28-year-old white male (Fig. ll-l) called N.S. who sought to avoid pain in a dental setting. Pertinent history reveals hemophilia, grade 1 (antihemophilic globulin factor 0-1 percent, normal 65-136 percent. Past pertinent history reveals hemophilia discovered at three weeks of age, hundreds of past transfusions, limited mobility of joints (bleeding into joints, resolution, connective or scar tissue impedes movement). Emotional history reveals a man who is not working, would like further education, has a girlfriend. Present situation is that of a very nervous, tense, frightened person who has psychophysiologic bleeding areas on his face. His dental condition is one of many caries, some gaping empty spaces between anterior teeth, need for complete dentistry in the form of prophylaxis, restorations, full crowns.

In his home town, about 40 miles south of Boston, N. S. received an injection of novocain for a mandibular inferior dental block to anesthetize a region of his lower jaw. The trauma of the injection caused a massive hemorrhage in the tissues of his neck and face. Bleeding such as this causes pressure on the trachea, restricting the airway, and can sometimes end fatally. The insertion of an endotracheal tube may precipitate further bleeding. Tracheostomy is also not indicated. N. S. was rushed to Childrens Hospital in Boston where he was given four complete exchange transfusions (about l00 pints of blood) to stop the hemorrhage. His blood had to be completely exchanged because of the number of past transfusions from which he had developed circulating anticoagulants. It was a terribly frightening experience for him, part of Erickson's "experimental learning."

The dental resident responsible for N. S., Dr. Leonard Carapezza, now a pediatric dental specialist in Wayland, Massachusetts, requested a consultation with this writer about the use of hypnosis for pain control. General anesthesia was precluded by the Anesthesia Service and local anesthesia had resulted in near tragedy.

I met N. S. first in a dental outpatient operatory in the Dental Department of Childrens Hospital. After being introduced to N. S., I mentioned that many people with problems like his had been helped with hypnosis. I told him that I was going to take as good care of him as I possibly could. The one thing uppermost in any patient's mind is his situation. He wants and needs reassurance that he is in good hands. It is rewarding for the therapist to be called into consultation because the patient is then expecting more effective treatment from a "specialist." Expectation usually increases results, especially in hypnosis. Four prerequisites have to be met before any patient seeks treatment: 1) a patient has to realize that a disease exists; 2) he has to accept it personally; 3) he has to realize the threat or ramifications of the disease; 4) he has come to the conclusion that perhaps something can be done about it. N. S. met these qualifications.

Verbalization in First Session

"I'm going to explain what hypnosis is and what it is not. Hypnosis is nothing like you have seen on a TV screen or the stage because in that kind of situation people will do almost anything to be part of the show. They'll act silly. They'll bark like dogs at the suggestion of the stage person. In real life that is just not true. We use hypnosis every day. It's a natural, normal physiological function that we use all the time. For instance, at this moment, would you wiggle your toes around in your shoes? And suddenly you feel your shoes. Now why didn't you feel your shoes a moment ago?"

"I wasn't thinking of my feet."

"Right, but you have this marvelous ability then for your body to have selective control, for your body to make itself anesthetic to your shoes, your wristwatch, your clothes all day. And this is the quality we're going to teach you now to use in order to help you help yourself with your problem. There is a great deal to be said about hypnosis. You're not zombied out, you're not asleep; for instance, if the telephone rings, you'll be able to hear it. You'll be able to hear the nurse working around

Comment

Patient is immediately brought into participating. It's "you do your part. I'll do my part." This principle will follow in therapy itself, "The doctor will do his part, you'll do your part."

the operatory. But you'll only pay attention to the sound of my voice when we start. You won't be asked to do anything silly. We certainly will not invade your privacy by asking you to answer questions that might cause any kind of embarrassment. And the whole thing is very, very simple, easy, an everyday experience. Do you have any questions?"

"No, I don't."

"I should like to ask you some questions now. I'd like to find out a little bit more about you than appears on the history chart which lists your medical records. Did you enjoy school?"

Emotional history

"Yes, I'd like more education so that I could work. I'm also afraid to smile because of the way my teeth look."

"Do you have friends?"

"I do like a girl very much and want to be with her a lot."

"What do you like to do?"

"Movies, television, reading."

Rapport—You like to read. I do also. Like the same thing.

"Do you know I still visit the library every week. Anything you don't like?"

"Dentistry."

"Well, you might be pleasantly surprised at how you feel about dentistry once you learn how to use hypnosis.

Expectation of successful therapy and treatment—Hope—

"We're going to spend a great deal of time on helping you help yourself.

Self-reliance

"If you would just rest your head back, close your eyes, and just relax yourself very completely, as I speak to you you'll find your whole body will begin to relax and from the tip of your toes to the very top of your head you're going to feel whole muscle systems relax, ankles, knees, muscles of your thighs. The whole lower part of your body. Muscles of your middle, muscles of your chest, muscles of your shoulders, arms, hand, muscles of your neck, face foreheard. Everything about you is becoming more and more relaxed, and with each breath that you take you'll go a little bit deeper into relaxation, and a little bit deeper and a little bit deeper. Everything about you is easy, calm, comfortable and

Induction—simple eyes closed induction. Eyelid catelepsy will occur within 10-30 seconds and deepen

Tieing relaxation to doctor speaking to patient

Tieing physiology to deepening. The patient must breathe so that with every breath he has to deepen.

relaxed. It is said that the relaxation produced by hypnosis is the deepest a body can have. Even in night-time sleep we move around every six or seven minutes. In hypnosis we can stay still for long, long periods of time. And as I speak you'll find, too, that as I continue talking everything about you is going to get more deeply into relaxation. You're doing very, very nicely indeed. Very, very nicely.

Tying relaxation to doctor speaking to patient

Praise liberally throughout session.

"Now we're going to talk about you a little bit. From the time you were a little boy you had to take care of yourself. There is nobody else in this world who can take care of your body for you. Your parents, who love you very much, couldn't be the ones to cross the street with you to watch out that a car wouldn't hit you. Even as young as 5 years old you had to do this yourself.

"Your girlfriend, who loves you very much can't take care of your body for you. You have to be the one to take care of it. Your body is your most prized possession. Only you can take care of it. You owe your body the respect of good health, good medical health, good dental health and we're about to show you how you can have this. Bad teeth are a threat to your health.

Spiegel's techniques of self-preservation

"I should like you, in the privacy of your home, to practice feeling like this or getting into this state of relaxation at least six times a day. You'll do this with a finger signal, the touch of your first finger and thumb of your left hand. It will be so that no one will know when you're doing it, unless you tell them, not your friends, not your relatives, no one. This is a private signal to you. When you do this signal, you're going to be in control all the time. If the doorbell rings, if the telephone rings, if anything demands your legitimate attention you'll be able to open your eyes instantaneously and carry out your daily activities without any feelings of heaviness or tiredness. Notice how good you feel right now. You can learn to reproduce this feeling at any time you need it or want it. You'll feel

Autohypnosis specifically taught

so good doing this. You're going to remember this hand signal because you're going to use this so many times that it will become second nature to you. And you'll be able to use it not only for this problem, but you'll be able to use it for any medical or dental situation, for injections, examinations, for yourself.

Hypnosis not limited to this situation alone

"You're doing this very nicely. Everything about you is easy, calm, comfortable, relaxed. The purpose of this practice is that whenever any kind of stressful situation occurs you'll be able to touch those fingers together and a wave of relaxation, self-reliance, self-control will come over you. You can practice for a moment, several minutes, or even put yourself to sleep this way. You're doing very nicely indeed. You'll have this concept, the concept of being in control of your body rather than your body controlling you. You may swallow whenever you like. You can do whatever you want to do and, as you do, you'll go even deeper into relaxation and enjoy this whole experience as being a necessary one to you.

Self-control

Large new concept

Whatever patient does, swallowing here, use it as a deepening technique.

"You'll go through this process with a sense of humor. A smile and you'll say, 'My gosh, is this really happening to me?' And everything is going to be so rewarding."

"I'm going to ask you to focus your attention on your right hand. Would you do that? Just imagine that you have taken off your mitten or glove on a freezing cold day here in New England. You know how your hand gets like a block of wood or a piece of ice with tingling, pins and needles. Let your hand get cold, or feel pins and needles. You may want to interpret that feeling. It's as though your hand has gone to sleep or has an anesthesia. Some people have measured a temperature change of 10-11 degrees. Every operation known to medical science has been done with this hypnoanesthesia provided the motivation was high enough. I'm sure you know about Indian fakirs who lie on a bed of nails or Greek fire walkers who walk across glow-

Hands and fingers are being stroked by therapist. Touch enhances the whole sensation.

ing embers without burning their feet. They use a very similar technique to what you are doing.

"With every breath you take you'll go a little bit deeper and deeper into relaxation and everything about you is easy, comfortable.

"Just signal me by raising the first finger of your right hand when you feel the cold in that hand. (Finger gives traditional slow, jerky movement upward.) In a few moments, not just yet, when I ask you to open your eyes, remaining in this deep state of relaxation, you'll compare your hand to mine. Notice how pale your hand has become. Notice how the veins stand out from what you have imagined. Let's rehearse this again. When you open your eyes, remaining in this deep state of relaxation, you'll look down at the back of your hand. Notice how different in color it is and notice the veins standing out because of the cold feeling. Remember what you saw. Then close your eyes, going even deeper.

"Now you may open your eyes. (Patient looks down, compares his hand to the ruddiness of operator's hand, sees the vasoconstriction.) Now you may close your eyes going even deeper. This experience has shown both you and me how good you are at this state of relaxation. Realize that something physical has happened from that marvelous mental process of yours and this is going to be important for our future discussion.

"You've done very nicely, indeed, because you can see how very powerful this whole process has been, that you can actually create a difference in a part of your body which you have learned to control. The only reason we have chosen your hand is that it is visible and easily accessible. What does this portend for the future? If you can have this kind of control over one part of your body, you can control any part of your body or your whole body. You can use this anesthesia for many things, including the work on your mouth. You can numb

Cheek's ideomotor signaling

Ego strengthening

Physiological control realization by patient is extremely important

Therapy for operative work and bleeding control

the gums and the teeth. You can do this whenever you need it or want it. Some patients control their bleeding, and so can you.

"You know how important good health is to you. Good teeth are needed to chew food, which is the source of life, itself, for us. I know you want to look well so that you can smile at your friends instead of hiding your front teeth. But, most important, you can have your teeth fixed with a minimum of discomfort and trouble and a maximum of ease. You know what happens when you get frightened. You get small bleeds. Your heart rate goes faster and you breathe fast. Notice how good you feel right now. Your heart rate is normal, breathing normal. If you can do this now, you can do this at any time, but particularly in the dental chair. It will all seem to pass so quickly. You know about pain. Well, lots of it is emotional. That is, we remember the part that is anticipated and remember the last pain. You now have a way, by relaxing, to get rid of the anticipated and remembered pain, about two-thirds, and what's left usually can fall into a higher threshold of pain because of the relaxation. You're doing great. Easy, comfortable, relaxed.

"You'll remember all of your dental work as an interesting experience. You'll close your eyes when you sit down in the chair, relax the way you are doing now. You'll hear the nurse working, the noise of the motor, the gurgling of the suction, sounds like the telephone, and conversation. Pay no attention to them. Take yourself away to the beach or wherever you'd like to go in your imagination. But you'll be able to produce the same kind of feeling in your teeth and jaws that you did in your hand, a feeling of numbness and anesthesia. Don't mind anything that goes on except the sound of my voice or the voice of the doctor when he talks to you. You'll have various instruments in your mouth, things going under the gum for restoring your teeth. You'll be pleasantly

Motivation—Anesthetics important to patient

No promise of anything you don't absolutely know about. Let patient choose the amount of discomfort he may need. Norman did not have any discomfort.

Time distortion

Language patient can understand. Speak in a way patient can understand.

Amnesia for dental operative work.

Dissociation also

Dry run of operative work

surprised at how well things will go. Your mouth can remain open for long periods of time without any strain. Remember, eating is essential to life itself. Self-preservation is the first rule of life.

Hope. Expectation. Catalepsy

Motivation

"We're giving you a two-pronged approach, Norman. We're giving you the approach of relaxation when you touch those fingers together and a wave of relaxation, self-control, self-reliance will come over you, and we're giving you an anesthesia to use at will.

"I also suggest that you keep this anesthesia of the hand for five full minutes following the termination of this state of relaxation as a further sign to you that you have control and something physical has happened from that marvelous mental process of yours. Now, Norman, we're going to repeat some of what we have said to make certain you have understood everything."

Physiological control by patient

Here Spiegel's technique, Cheek's ideomotor signal, relaxation, autohypnosis, sense of humor approach and therapy are briefly repeated. Once the patient is in trance something repeated several times will be remembered.

"In a few moments, Norman, not just yet, when I ask you to open your eyes, you're going to feel so good. You're going to be happy, happy that you have found this medium. Cheerful, smiling, going to feel just tip top. Everything about you is going to feel so vibrant and alive. Every nerve, every muscle, every blood vessel feeling just so good. There'll be no feelings of heaviness or tiredness. You're going to look forward to everything that the rest of the day brings you and what the future brings you. You're going to do just fine. Whatever you do this evening, dinner with your family this evening, perhaps reading, talking, everything is going to take on a rosy glow because of how successful and how good you are at this whole procedure. When you open your eyes in just a few moments, Norman, there'll be no feelings of heaviness or tiredness. Everything about you will be

Termination started

Much time is spent in termination. The patient should feel exhilarated about the whole hypnotic experience.

Expectation of success

cheerful, happy. You'll be proud of yourself
that you are so good at this. You're going
to feel fine remembering that you're going
to keep this anesthesia for five full minutes
following the termination of this trance as
a further sign to you that something physical can happen from this marvelous mental
process of yours. And now, Norman, feel-   Rising voice
ing just great, completely aroused, you may
open your eyes. Do you have any comments or questions?"

"I sure do. I feel good. My hand is
numb."

"You did very well, of course."

"I understood everything you said.
Both hands are numb. This right hand
really can't feel a thing."

The total time involved in this first visit was about 30 minutes. There were
four weekly sessions with the hypnotherapist. The therapist spoke during the whole
first dental operative appointment following the explanation and therapy. Simple
operative procedures (restorations) were carried out by Dr. Carapezza as the patient
was pre-warned by phrases like this: "Pay no attention to the sound of the motor.
Take yourself far away from here mentally, allowing your teeth to be as insensitive
as possible from your anesthesia. You're doing very well. I'm pround of you. You're
very good at this." Touch is used liberally as a non-verbal technique. Whenever
the high-pitched motor was used, the operator would hold the patient's forearm and
signal by finger pressure. Successful operative work was now completed.

The second session found the patient able to accomplish much more since
he had a week to practice at home before this visit. More complicated procedures,
such as full crown preparation, were attempted and completed successfully. The
therapist spoke only during about half of this session, using non-verbal communication the other half. During the third session only non-verbal communication was
used. Again, long complicated dental procedures were successfully accomplished.
During the fourth session the therapist, available on request, was in the hospital
corridor while the patient, using autohypnosis, was in the dental operatory.

Hours of further dental procedures were completed without pain, without any
loss of blood even though Tofflemyer retainers below the gingiva were used, full
crowns were placed, and prophylaxis accomplished. The patient retained a positive
attitude throughout treatment because he was able to be a partner in his own therapy
and could use hypnosis at will.

The approach used on this patient with hemophilia that is, a combination of
relaxation, physiological control, dissociation, time distortion, ego strengthening,
motivation, expectation, hope, autohypnosis, partnership in therapy, touch, amnesia,

imagery, anesthesia—has been successful for me in patients with both acute and chronic pain. Hypnosis offers one pragmatic, clinically-oriented solution to the problems of patients in pain.

References

Alexander L: Pain Symposium. ASCH Annual Meeting, 1977

Barber J: Hypnosis and the unhypnotizable. Am J Clin Hypn 23:4, 1980

Barber J, Adrian C: Psychological Approaches to the Management of Pain. New York, Brunner/Mazel, 1982

Bassman SW, Wester WC: Hypnosis and pain control. In Wester WC, Smith AH (eds): Clinical Hypnosis: A Multidisciplinary Approach. Philadelphia, JB Lippincott, 1984

Benson H, Beary JF, Carol M: The relaxation response. Psychiatry 37:37, 1974

Blau JN: Pain. Brit Med J 285 (6350) 1249, 1982

Bonica JJ: Pain. Philadelphia, Lea and Febiger, 1953

Bonica J: Importance of the Problem. In Bonica JJ, VentaFridda (eds): Advances in Pain Research and Therapy, Vol. 2. New York, Raven, 1979

Butler B: The use of hypnosis in the care of the cancer patient. Brit J Med Hypnotism 6:9, 1955

Cangello UW: Hypnosis for the patient with cancer. Am J Clin Hypn 4:215, 1962

Cheek, DB, LeCron LM: Clinical Hypnotherapy. New York, Grune & Stratton, 1968

Crasilneck HB, Hall JA: Clinical Hypnosis. New York, Grune & Stratton, 1975

Deltito JA: Hypnosis in the treatment of acute pain in the emergency department setting. Postgrad Med J 60:263, 1984

Des Jardens PJ: Lecture. Boston City Hospital, Dept of Dent and Oral Surg, 1983

Erickson MH: The interspersal hypnotic technique for symptom correction and pain control. Am J Clin Hypn 8:198, 1966

Ewin DM: Hypnosis in surgery and anesthesia. In Wester WC, Smith AH (eds): Clinical Hypnosis: A Multidisciplinary Approach. Philadelphia, JB Lippincott, 1984

Golan HP: Placebos and suggestion in psychosomatic disease. J Am Soc Psychosomatic Dent and Med 12:4, 1965

Golan HP: Control of fear reactions in dental patients by hypnosis: Three case reports. Am J Clin Hypn 13:4, 1971

Golan HP: Further case reports from the Boston City Hospital. Am J Clin Hypn 18:1, 1975

Hartland DJ: Medical and Dental Hypnosis. London, Balliere, 1966

Hilgard ER, Hilgard JR: Hypnosis in the Relief of Pain. Los Altos, CA, William Kaufmann, 1975

Lea P, Ware P, Monroe R: The hypnotic control of intractible pain. Am J Clin Hypn 3:1, 1960

Margolis EG: Hypnotic imagery with cancer patients. Am J Clin Hypn 25:2-3, 1982-1983

McGlashan TH, Evans R, Orne MT: The nature of hypnotic analgesia and placebo response to experimental pain. Psychosom Med 3:227, 1969

Melzack R, Wall P: Pain mechanisms: A new theory. Science 150:971, 1965

Mutter CB, Karnilow A: Hypnosis: A viable option in chronic pain management. J Florida Med Assoc 70:12, 1983

Newton BW: The use of hypnosis in the treatment of cancer patients. Am J Clin Hypn 25:2-3, 1982-1983

Olness K: Imagery (self-hypnosis) as adjunct therapy in childhood cancer. Am J Ped Hemonc 3:3, 1981

Sacerdote P: The place of hypnosis in relief of severe protracted pain. Am J Clin Hypn 4:3, 1962

Sacardote P: Psychophysiology of hypnosis as it relates to pain and pain problems. Am J Clin Hypn 10:4, 1968

Sacardote P: Theory and practice of pain control in malignancy and other protracted recurring painful illnesses. Int J Clin Exp Hypn 18:160, 1970

Sacardote P: Hypnosis and terminal illness. In Burrows GB, Dennerstein L (eds): Handbook of Hypnosis and Psychosomatic Medicine. Amersterdam, Elsevier, 1980

Sacerdote P: Techniques of hypnotic intervention with pain patients. In Barber J, Adrian C (eds): Psychological Approaches to the Management of Pain. New York, Brunner/Mazel, 1982

Schafer D, Hernandez A: Hypnosis, pain and the context of therapy. Int J Clin Exp Hypn 26:3, 1978

Shor, RE: Physiological effects of painful stimulation during hypnotic analgesia under conditions designed to minimize anxiety. Int J Clin Exp Hypn 10:183, 1982

Siegel EF: Control of phantom limb pain by hypnosis. Am J Clin Hypn 21:4, 1979

Simonton OC, Matthews-Simonton S, Creighton JL: Getting Well Again. Los Angeles, Tarcher-St. Martins, 1978

St. Amand A: Strategies for success. ASCH Annual Meeting, San Francisco, 1984

Sternbach R: Clinical aspects of pain. In Sternbach RA (ed): The Psychology of Pain. New York, Raven Press, 1978

Wain H: Presentation on pain. N E Soc Clin Hypn, Boston, 1982

Wakeman RJ, Kaplan JZ: Experimental study of hypnosis in painful burns. Am J Clin Hypn 21:1, 1978

Wolfe LS: Hypnosis and pain: A clinical instance. Am J Clin Hypn 4:3, 1962

Zeltzer L, Dash L, Holland JD: Hypnotically induced pain control in sickle cell anemia. Pediatrics 64:4, 1979

12 HYPNOTIC TREATMENT OF ANXIETY

GARY R. ELKINS, Ph.D.

Anxiety predominates as a primary feature of most emotional disorders. In everyday life, the concept of anxiety is familiar as a fearful anticipation or worry about some future or past events. At one time or another, the discomfort of anxiety inevitably touches the lives of the majority of people, and the experience of extreme and disabling anxiety is frequent. It is estimated that up to five percent of the population in the United States suffers with anxiety disorders or phobias (Kaplan and Sadock, 1985). Because of the pervasiveness of anxiety and its destructive effect on human lives, any tool that successfully combats the condition is welcome. Hypnotherapy is such a tool. Many studies substantiate the usefulness of hypnosis in treating patients with anxiety disorders.

The Nature of Anxiety

The symptoms of anxiety are manifested as a sense of intense apprehension, fear, panic, or impending doom. The physical symptoms most commonly experienced during an anxiety attack are heart palpitations, chest pains, choking, vertigo, dizziness, sweating, paresthesias, and trembling (American Psychiatric Association, 1980). The patient may feel an urge to run, hide, or avoid the situation.

Although fear and anxiety are similar at a biological response level, anxiety and fear differ. A fear response relates to some observable threat and lasts only as long as the event or danger is present. Anxiety continues even after the danger has been removed and results in emotional symptoms. Freud (1936) is noted for making this distinction. He conceptualized anxiety as originating from intrapsychic disturbances or disequilibrium. At a basic level, anxiety functions as a signal to the ego of some conflict or threat. If the individual's defenses are sufficient (i.e., denial/repression), then the anxiety is reduced. However, if the individual's defenses are inadequate for coping, then neurotic anxiety symptoms result. Sullivan (1953) proposed that chronic anxiety begins with a fear of parental rejection. Jenkins' (1968) research supports this with the finding that highly anxious patients are likely to have parents who set high expectations and then are rejecting and critical of their child's actual accomplishments.

In comparison, behavioral theorists (Lazarus, 1971; Kroger and Fezler, 1976) conceptualize anxiety as the result of learning via classical or operant conditioning. Within this paragon, a stimulus which naturally elicits fear occurs in contiguity with some neutral stimulus. By repeated pairings, the fear becomes associated with a previously neutral stimulus and produces anxiety.

The behavioral explanation of anxiety is further elaborated by the addition of an operant conditioning model. The organism seeks to learn some behavior which allows it to avoid the anxiety-arousing stimulus. This avoidance behavior is thereby reinforced as it is effective in reducing anxiety.

The cognitive-behavioral therapists such as Ellis and Harper (1975) also acknowledge the learning and conditioning aspects of anxiety but have advanced a cognitive formulation. The primary concept is that what a person tells him or herself about an event rather than the event itself is the actual cause of emotional reaction. Anxiety is the result of faulty perceptions and "irrational beliefs" such as labeling some event as awful or believing one cannot stand a reality as it exists. For example, anxiety may result when an individual is convinced that being rejected for a date is terrible, and that he/she cannot stand it. A less anxious person would view the same event as unfortunate or undesirable, but not as terrible.

While there are differences among these conceptualizations, practitioners are in general agreement that the treatment of phobias and other anxiety disorders must go beyond purely analytic methods alone. The patient must confront the anxiety-arousing situations either imaginably or in vitro. Hypnosis is useful in enhancing a variety of therapeutic modalities, including systematic desensitization (Shurman, 1979), uncovering analytic methods (Gruenewald, 1982), cognitive restructuring (Boutin, 1978; Elkins, 1984), and teaching relaxation and self-hypnosis (Crasilneck and Hall, 1985).

Aspects of Therapy for Anxiety

The presentation of anxiety is often complicated by secondary symptoms of depression. Barnett (1984) has commented on the almost universal finding of low self-esteem among anxiety neurotics. Chronic anxiety results in sleeplessness and inability to cope with life demands. It is unfortunate that patients often fall into a trap of excessive use of tranquilizing drugs, sleeping pills, and alcohol in an attempt to deal not only with the anxiety but also with the pessimism and helplessness that inevitably occur (Coleman, 1976). Certainly, these reactions must be addressed as a part of the total psychotherapeutic program.

Clinically, the specific treatment of anxiety includes five primary components. *First,* the source of anxiety must be uncovered. Even cases of "free-floating" anxiety can be related to the patient's anticipation of some events or expectations. For example, the agoraphobic commonly has a great anticipation about the possibility of becoming anxious in public. Thus, the patient anticipates anxiety and becomes anxious about its possible occurrence. This may be termed a "fear of becoming anxious." Thus, a pattern of withdrawal begins as the patient seeks to avoid such feelings.

Secondly, there is a suggestion to the patient of improvement. The suggestion may be direct or indirect and is facilitated by the use of hypnosis (Mott, 1982). The patient is able to develop a positive expectation for the future.

Third, the patient is encouraged to adopt a new view of the feared object. The goal is to help the patient change beliefs and perceptions in order to distinguish between real and imagined danger.

Fourth, relaxation methods are utilized to enhance the patient's coping skills and to reduce anxiety. Relaxation forms the basis of desensitization techniques and is best accomplished in hypnosis.

Fifth, there is a "working through" of the anxiety by confrontation with the feared object or situations. The patient is encouraged to engage in the feared behavior and increased confidence is achieved as he/she does so.

Systematic Desensitization/Relaxation—The Literature

A considerable body of evidence exists attesting to the efficacy of systematic desensitization in reducing anxiety (Cooke, 1966; Paul, 1969). Treatment procedures in systematic desensitization follows the approach developed by Wolpe (1969).

This procedure involves constructing a hierarchy of anxiety-arousing events and presenting these in vivo while the patient is deeply relaxed. More recently, however, the actual need to construct a hierarchy has been questioned (Mahoney, 1974) and the procedure has been criticized as lacking in generalization of facts beyond the desensitization hierarchy.

In place of the counter-conditioning model, "relaxation as self-control" procedures have been developed to broaden the treatment effects (Goldfried, 1971; Suinn, 1976). In self-control relaxation training, relaxation is utilized as a general copying skill. Patients are taught to reduce not only the anxiety for which they sought assistance but also related anxieties.

Denny (1974) compared active, passive, and vicarious desensitization in the treatment of test-anxious clients. Also included in the study were self-control relaxation and untreated control groups. The active desensitization group required the subjects to describe their visualizations of the scenes used in the hierarchy. In the vicarious desensitization group, subjects observed the desensitization treatment of another client. Four measures of anxiety were included as dependent variables. The self-control relaxation procedure was found to be the most effective on all measures of anxiety and exceeded that shown by any of the desensitization groups.

Similar results have been reported by Edie (1972) and Chang-Liang and Denny (1976). An interesting comparative study was reported by Deffenbacher and Shelton (1978). The effectiveness of standard systematic desensitization versus self-control anxiety management therapy in the treatment of test anxiety was evaluated. Therapy consisted of five weekly sessions for both treatment groups. Pre- and post-treatment measures included ratings of test anxiety and general measures of nontargeted anxiety. Both procedures proved to be effective; however, greater changes were obtained through the self-control relaxation groups. Further, the self-control relaxation therapy resulted in greater generalization to non-targeted anxieties.

Elkins (1980) studied the effects of self-control relaxation therapy in combination with Ellis' (1975) cognitive therapy methods in the treatment of communication anxiety. Subjects were assigned to three groups: (Group 1) cognitive restructuring combined with self-control relaxation therapy, (Group 2) cognitive restructuring alone, or (Group 3) no treatment. The combined therapy approach was most effective in reducing both anxiety and in increasing assertiveness.

Hypnotherapy

Hynotherapeutic methods have been widely utilized in treating patients with anxiety disorders. Hypnotic inductions often involve a component of relaxation which achieves anxiety reduction. It is not surprising that behavioral methods which depend upon relaxation and mental imagery are often greatly enhanced by hypnosis. Hypnosis also has become increasingly popular in psychoanalytic treatment of anxiety. More analytically-oriented therapists have developed hypnotic methods of uncovering, abreaction, symptom substitution, and ideomotor questioning (Barnett, 1984). It should be emphasized, however, that hypnosis is appropriately used in an adjunctive way. The patient is treated "in hypnosis" rather than "by hypnosis." It is not the hypnotic state per se that is therapeutic, but the context it provides for the facilitation of psychotherapy and goal achievement.

Several case studies have been presented which combine hypnotherapy and behavioral methods such as systematic desensitization (Marks, Gelder, and Edwards, 1968; Deiker and Pollock, 1975; Daniels, 1976; Melnick and Russell, 1976; Timm, 1977; Spies, 1979; Frutiger, 1981), relaxation (Marks, Gelder, and Edwards, 1968; Horowitz, 1970; Spiegel, Frischholz, Maruffi, and Spiegel, 1979), and guided imagery (Golan, 1971; Deyoub and Epstein, 1977; Cohen, 1981; Van der Hart, 1981). Also, Lawlor (1976) described a combined hypnotic intervention and family therapy in the treatment of school phobic children.

In a case study, Crasilneck and Hall (1985) reported a 30-year-old business executive who was considering leaving his job because he experienced such intense anxiety that he was unable to make verbal presentations during business meetings. He was not able to sleep at night before the presentations and was losing weight.

Hypnotic treatment included hypnoanalytic probing which revealed underlying guilt and anxiety about past sexual activities and affairs. During hynotherapy, he was able to increase his self-concept and came to the conclusion that having affairs was not necessary to bolster his self-concept and his anxiety reduced. He was also taught self-hypnosis to achieve relaxation.

Shurman (1979) presented several cases illustrating the combined use of hypnosis and desensitization in the treatment of agoraphobia and anxiety. Cooley, Ciotti, and Henninger (1981) found desensitization facilitated by post-hypnotic dream suggestion to be more effective than systematic desensitization alone in the treatment of snake-phobic subjects. Elkins and Saltzberg (1981) reviewed the use of hypnosis in the treatment of social anxiety and concluded that hypnosis significantly facilitated the reduction of anxiety and could also be used to increase assertiveness. Mordey (1965) used hynotherapy procedures to treat a patient with stage fright.

Horowitz (1970) compared three methods for reducing fear of snakes. All methods involved hypnosis and included: a) relaxation while recalling fearful snake-related events; b) fear arousal during recall; and c) post-hypnotic suggestion for the elimination of snake-phobic feelings. All methods led to a decrease in anxiety while patients in the no treatment control condition did not significantly change. Boutin (1978) demonstrated the adaptation of cognitive therapy in an integrated hypnotic treatment of test anxiety.

As is evidenced by these studies, anxiety has been investigated on different levels of behavioral, cognitive, and hypnotic treatment. It is apparent that hypnosis is successfully used with a wide range of diverse psychotherapeutic methods. While generally positive outcomes have been reported, there are many unanswered questions about the relative efficacy of the different treatment modalities. Unambiguous conclusions must await further research and controlled evaluation of both differing and perhaps overlapping of treatment methods.

Assessment of Effectiveness of Hypnotherapy

Anxiety is largely a subjectively felt phenomena. While it is easily identified by the individual who is anxious or in discomfort, it is much more difficult to objectively measure or quantitate. Therefore, the effectiveness of hypnosis in the treatment of anxiety states necessarily depends upon subjective self-ratings by the patient. In fact, this has been the primary assessment method used in case reports of hypnotherapy. Although useful information about an individual patient is communicated, such ratings lack precision and do not allow for comparison of treatment modalities across different patient populations in research.

These limitations may be overcome to some extent through the use of objective psychometric scales such as the MMPI (Hathaway and McKinnley, 1948), the State-Trait Anxiety Inventory (Spielberger, 1966), and other anxiety scales. Anxiety inventories are useful in obtaining pre-post ratings of anxiety and are appropriate measures in hypnotic treatment procedures. Such scales have the advantage of being relatively convenient methods requiring a minimal amount of therapist and patient time.

Behavioral therapists have been more reliant upon observational methods. These involve finding some behavior that a patient is unable to perform because of anxiety. The patient is asked to attempt the behavior, and objective ratings of his or her performance are obtained. Researchers, in particular, should be encouraged to provide measurable outcome of hypnotherapeutic methods. When possible, measuring techniques include a combination of self-reports and more behaviorally-based assessment criteria. For the clinical practitioner, they are most likely to involve the use of psychometric instruments and some report or observation of changes in what the patient is actually able to do as a result of successful anxiety control and reduction.

Future Trends

There is an established clinical and experimental research base attesting to the effectiveness of hypnosis in the treatment of patients presenting with anxiety disorders. Furthermore, in recent years there has been a proliferation of behavioral and "stress management" studies which appear to have much in common with some aspects of hypnosis. In fact, some reports of the use of "mental imagery" and "relaxation" may be indistinguishable from aspects of classical hypnotherapy. While some authors may not acknowledge this overlap, the implications for clinical hypnosis and research are unaltered. It is my expectation that this trend will continue significantly. Perhaps it would be useful to define "hypnotic methods" as encompassing therapeutic relaxation and other methods which may not appear in the hypnosis literature but are nonetheless applicable to it.

Without doubt, the clinical literature will bring forth new methods of hypnotic induction and anxiety management. I suspect that there will be a greater integration of hypnosis with both cognitive-behavioral and psychoanalytic therapies. There has been some suggestion of a coalescence of the various schools of psychotherapy into a more integrated and eclectic model.

Case Study

The following is a case illustration of the successful assessment and intervention process with an anxious and phobic male. While no transcript of induction and treatment applies to all patients, a number of treatment principles are illustrated.

T.L. was a 27-year-old single male who was self-referred regarding a history of anxiety and phobic behavior. The patient related that he had "always been kind of tense and nervous." However, he felt that he was able generally to cope with these feelings. He had completed high school without difficulty and gone on to a university where he completed a degree in management. He was an only child, and after graduation from school, he returned to the small town where his parents lived and went to work at a local business.

The patient related an incident that took place three years prior to his consultation with this author and when he was driving home after visiting a girlfriend in a city 60 miles away. He had been to a party, had been drinking, and had an argument with the girlfriend. While driving home, he became acutely anxious and began to hyperventilate, pulled over to the side of the road, and was eventually taken to a hospital and evaluated for a brief period of time with no illness found. Since that time, he had become increasingly phobic of driving cars and feared driving his car alone, especially at night. He had less difficulty driving as long as there was another person in the car with him.

During the initial interview, the patient presented himself as a well-dressed and cooperative young man. He appeared somewhat nervous and occasionally stuttered over words. Review of his current status revealed that he was well-adjusted socially, and no other difficulties or stressors were noted.

The patient was administered psychometrics which included the MMPI and State-Trait Anxiety Inventory. On the MMPI, the patient obtained a normal profile with the exception of significant elevations on scales 7 (psychasthenia) and 9 (mania), indicating a significant amount of felt anxiety. On the State-Trait Anxiety Inventory, the patient achieved a percentile rank of 82 on the state anxiety scale. He received a percentile rank of 52 on the trait anxiety scale. The diagnostic formulation was that the patient had a history of being somewhat over-anxious. It was further postulated that he had become conditioned so that he had developed a phobic avoidance of driving an automobile and in addition had marked anticipatory anxiety.

The patient was asked to subjectively rate the amount of anxiety he would expect to experience in a variety of driving situations with 0 equaling no anxiety and 100 representing the most severe anxiety.

Session 1

Verbalization

"The first thing I want to know is that the difficulty that you have been having with feeling anxious while driving is primarily due to a problem of learning. You mentioned earlier that you had always been somewhat more anxious than average. I believe that you are right about that, and I be-

Comment

Pre-induction talk directed toward providing the patient with a model for understanding the persistent anxious feelings.

lieve that this is part of the reason why you became anxious in the first place on the day when your problem with driving began about three years ago. You had had an argument with your girlfriend, and you may have been somewhat more tensed up or perhaps you were worried about your driving because you had been drinking at the party. While you were driving home, you began to feel more anxious, and then as you became more anxious perhaps you felt that there was something seriously and physically wrong.

"Often, when people hyperventilate, they begin to think that they are going to suffocate or that they are having a heart attack. You now know that neither of these things happened; rather hyperventilation is simply a symptom of anxiety which will pass. Also, you know how to breathe into a paper bag and to eventually stop any hyperventilation feelings. However, that feeling of intense anxiety that you had became associated with driving and all the things involved with driving, the feel of the steering wheel, the interior of the car, driving down the highway, and so on. After that, each time you attempted to drive your car, the anticipation and the anxiety began to come back. By now, you have begun to avoid driving and, of course, each time you avoid it the anxiety is reduced somewhat.

Communication of reassurance, empathy, and rapport.

Reinforcement and instruction in self-management of hyperventilation.

"Now, you can overcome this problem through the use of hypnosis and relaxation techniques. You may not know how to do it, but it will be an interesting experience for you to learn how. Now, I'm going to describe in a general way what we are going to do. First, you need to learn how to put yourself in a state of hypnosis. Perhaps you've been in hypnosis many times but not been aware of it. The experience is somewhat like daydreaming as you become deeply, deeply relaxed.

Build positive expectation of successful hypnosis and symptom reduction.

Building a foundation for later instruction in self-hypnosis.

"Today, it is important only that you have the experience of hypnosis. You may notice some change after today or it may come later. Also, I want you to have some experience of hypnosis such as having your hand and arm feel light and weightless or simply having a heavy and relaxed feeling. During the later sessions, I am going to ask you to imagine driving in a lot of different situations while maintaining a relaxed, calm feeling. You may be surprised to find out how well you will be able to do this in hypnosis. Eventually, you will be able to drive your car without difficulty or be able to achieve a sense of relaxation whenever you need and want it.

Positive expectancy and anticipation for treatment outcome.

"Now, to begin the induction, I want you to get very comfortable in the chair and take a few moments to settle into the chair and let yourself become more and more relaxed. Now, I want you to pick out some spot on the wall and focus your attention on that spot. As you focus on that spot and the more you focus on that spot, allow your body to become more and more relaxed. Just deeply, deeply relaxed. Just as though you were becoming as limp as a rag doll, limp and relaxed and quiet. And, as you focus more and more on that spot, drifting into a deeper and deeper state of hypnosis, just allowing all the things around that spot to begin to fade into the background as you are able to focus more and more on that spot, you can drift into just as deep a state of hypnosis as you want to in order to accomplish the things that you want to accomplish today.

Begin induction emphasizing concentration and relaxation.

"Feel that sense of relaxation spreading through each and every muscle, each and every fiber in your body, deeper relaxed, calm and quiet and peaceful. At this time, I want you to take a deep, deep breath of air, all the air that you can hold in your lungs and hold the air and feel the tension. And, as you exhale, allow your eyelids to close and allow all the tension to go out with the air as you become so completely relaxed and comfortable and quiet. From the top of your head down to your feet, limp and relaxed and quiet. And, for the next few moments, the most important thing you have to do is to achieve

Anxiety reduction during therapy session through relaxation.

a sense of relaxation, drifting just as deeply into hypnosis as you need to go and with each breath you exhale getting deeper and deeper relaxed.

"And I want you to notice all the sensations of relaxation, the sensations of relaxation that begin at the top of your head and eventually spread down to your feet. And you can experience that like a wave of relaxation. It spreads bringing a sense of relaxation, warmth, and calm. Feel that wave of relaxation now as it spreads across your forehead. Just let the muscles of your forehead release and relax and feel that wave of relaxation as it passes across your face, mouth, and jaw. Just allow the muscles of your jaw to release and relax. As your neck goes limp, perhaps your chin will fall by itself down towards your chest or perhaps your head will simply sink deeper and deeper into the pillow. Allow your shoulders to slump and allow your hands to rest exactly where they are. Notice how heavy your right hand is becoming in comparison with your left hand, so limp and heavy that no tension remains and your arms rest there all by themselves, allowing your breathing to become more comfortable now, deeper and deeper relaxed with each and every breath that you exhale. And allow that wave of relaxation to spread across your chest and stomach and across your lower back and shoulders, just allowing all the tension to flow out as that wave of relaxation spreads down your legs, past your kneecaps, down into your calves, and down into your feet.

"And, as you concentrate on that relaxed feeling, I want you to give yourself the suggestion that your right arm is becoming very light, very light and weightless. Very light and weightless and so light that it can begin to drift up from the arm of the chair. Perhaps you may want to imagine that a helium-filled balloon is attached to your wrist by a string and notice the color of that balloon and watch it as it drifts up towards the ceiling, tugging and

Describe progressive relaxation and release of muscle tension.

Therapist speaks softly.

Focus on relaxation and associated proprioceptive stimuli.

Anxiety reduction during therapy session.

Demonstration building patient conviction and belief in hypnotic processes.

pulling at your wrist, pulling up, up, up, pulling your arm up higher and higher, more and more light, more and more relaxed as your arm drifts up all by itself, very relaxed and comfortable. And, as your arm goes up, the rest of your body simply becomes more relaxed. And, that's a comfortable, interesting feeling. And, take the time to enjoy it and relax.

Associate hypnotic behavior with anxiety reduction.

"You've been able to accomplish something very important here today and you know that you have had a learning experience. You didn't know how to go into hypnosis and you may not know at what point you began to learn. However, you have been able to achieve something very important . . . a sense of relaxation, drifting into a deep and comfortable state of hypnosis and you can feel pleased with that. Pleased and comfortable and relaxed. And, just allow your arm to begin to drift back down towards the arm of the chair. That's right. Just allow that arm, that right arm, to become heavier as it drifts back down towards and touches the arm of the chair. So comfortable and so pleasant.

Reinforcement.

"And this is a sense of relaxation that you can achieve here in the office or at home. You can keep the tape recording of this session. I want you to practice it every day for the next two weeks, once a day practicing and achieving this same sense of relaxation. Just take a few moments to notice how you feel emotionally and physically. Just remember that feeling and know that you can bring it back whenever you need it and whenever you want it. I am going to begin counting now from the number I to the number 3, and as I reach the number 3 you can alert yourself, feeling refreshed and relaxed and comfortable and confident. A feeling of confidence and competence and security. I . . . 2 . . . 3."

Therapist emphasizing patient self-control of anxiety.

Instruction in daily self-hypnosis practice.

Sessions 2 Through 6

"You have been practicing the self-hypnosis for relaxation, and you have been able to

Pre-induction talk.

accomplish a greater sense of relaxation and self-control. Perhaps you realize that you are already beginning to conquer your anxiety and fear of driving. If at any time you experience any feeling of anxiety, you can reduce it by utilizing the self-hypnosis technique in achieving that sense of relaxation. Today, I am going to ask you to go into hypnosis and, while you are relaxed, I am going to ask you to imagine, to vividly imagine, driving your car under a variety of circumstances. We will start out with a scene that is relatively simple and, as you are able to visualize that while staying relaxed, I will ask you to imagine a lot of other driving scenes.

"Begin the process of relaxation now and focus your attention on a point on the wall or ceiling. Take a deep, deep breath of air, all the air you can hold in your lungs. And, as you exhale, allow your eyelids to close and allow your body to go limp and relaxed. For the next few moments, shift your attention to your breathing, concentrate on your breathing, and each time you breathe out, think the word 'relax' silently to yourself. Relax. And allow your body to respond to that word each time you exhale, relaxing deeper and deeper and just letting all of the tension begin to flow out. For the next few moments, allow relaxation to become the most important thing you have to do. For the moment, other things can be set aside so that you can concentrate on becoming more relaxed and achieve that fully and completely. As you relax deeply, allowing more and more tension to release, I'd like for you to imagine a wave of relaxation that spreads from the top of your head slowly yet completely and eventually down to your feet. A wave of relaxation that brings a sense of mental calm and quiet as the muscles relax deeply.

"And I want you to now visualize that you are driving in your car. Visualize that you are in your car and you are driving out on the highway. It's a warm summer day and your father and your mother are in the

Anticipation of further success.

Create patient expectancy and anticipation.

Relaxation-induction.

Visual imagery.

car with you. And notice all the sensations of driving, the sound of the engine and the wind as it goes past your car. And, whenever you are able to visualize that, I want you to allow the index finger of your right hand to raise so I'll know that you are there. And allow a slight sense of anxiety to develop as you are there driving the car. That's right, you're doing very well. And give that feeling of anxiety a number which represents the amount of discomfort you feel. Just nod your head when you've done this. That's right, very good. Now, I want you to take a deep breath of air and as you exhale allow all the anxiety and tension to go out. Just bring that feeling of anxiety down, become more and more relaxed. And, whenever you've achieved that sense of relaxation, complete relaxation of 0 to 5, let me know by again raising the index finger of your right hand. That's right. Very good.

Create anxiety during therapy session.

Reduction of anxiety via self-control hypnosis.

Reinforcement.

"You're doing very well. Now, I want you to visualize driving your car down the highway once again on a warm summer day. You are alone, and that's all right because you have a sense of control and you can achieve and maintain a deep sense of relaxation. Visualize driving the car now. You are in the car alone. Notice the scenery along the highway as it passes your window. Notice the green fields and the pavement of the highway. You are alone and perhaps you have the radio on. Take a few moments to listen to the music. And, when you are there, just raise the index finger of your right hand. That's right. Very good. Now, allow that feeling of anxiety to return. More and more anxiety. Feel your shoulders as they begin to tense up. Feel a slight shaking feeling, more and more a sense of anxiety. More and more anxiety. And, whenever you are there, give that level of anxiety a number. And, whenever you have done this, simply nod your head so I'll know you've accomplished that. That's right, and now bring the level of anxiety down. More and more relaxed. Perhaps

Emphasize self-control.

Visual imagery-desensitization.

Therapist's voice becomes tense and louder.

you'll want to take a deep, deep breath of air now, and as you exhale, relax twice as much. Each time you exhale, that serves as a cue for you to become deeply relaxed. So deeply relaxed and comfortable, you can accomplish that at any time.

Anxiety reduction suggested. Therapist's voice soft and calm.

"You have done very well today in conquering your anxiety. Perhaps at times you can already visualize yourself driving down the highway with no sense of anxiety whatsoever. Just a relaxed, confident and competent feeling. Each time you experience hypnosis, you are achieving more and more control and freedom from any feelings of anxiety. I am going to begin counting now from the number I to the number 3. As I reach the number 3, you can alert yourself, feeling refreshed and relaxed with an even greater sense of control and comfort. I . . . 2 . . . and 3. Alert and refreshed."

Post-hypnotic suggestion. Reinforcement of accomplishment.

Post-hypnotic suggestion emphasizing patient control and responsibility.

References

American Psychiatric Association, Diagnostic and Statistical Manual of Mental Disorders, 3rd ed. APA, Washington, D.C., 1980

Barnett EA: Hypnosis in the Treatment of Anxiety and Chronic Stress. In Wester WC, Smith AH (eds): Clinical Hypnosis: A Multidisciplinary Approach. Philadelphia, JB Lippincott, 1984

Boutin, GE: Treatment of test anxiety by rational stage directed hypnotherapy: A case study. Am J Clin Hypn 21:52, 1978

Chang-Liang R, Denny DR: Applied relaxation as training in self-control. J Counsel Psych 23:183, 1976

Cohen S: Phobia for bovine sounds. Am J Clin Hypn 23:266, 1981

Coleman JC: Abnormal Psychology and Modern Life. Glenview, Ill, Scott, Foresman & Co., 1976

Cooke G: The efficacy of two desensitization procedures: An analogue study. Behav Res Ther 4:17, 1966

Cooley LE, Ciotti J, Henninger KM: Augmentation of systematic desensitization of snake phobia through post-hypnotic dream suggestion. Am J Clin Hypn 23:231, 1981

Crasilneck HB, Hall JA: Clinical Hypnosis: Principles and Applications. New York, Grune & Stratton, 1985

Daniels LK: Rapid in-office and in vivo desensitization of an injection phobia using hypnosis. Am J Clin Hypn 18:200, 1976

Deffenbacher JL, Shelton JL: Comparison of anxiety management training and desensitization in reducing test and other anxieties. J Couns Psych 25:277, 1978

Deiker, TE, Pollock DH: Integration of hypnotic and systematic desensitization techniques in the treatment of phobias: A case report. Am J Clin Hypn 17:170, 1975

Denny DR: Active, passive, and vicarious desensitization. J Couns Psych 21:369, 1974

Deyoub PL, Epstein SJ: Short-term hypnotherapy for the treatment of flight phobia: A case report. Am J Clin Hypn 19:251, 1977

Edie CA: Uses of AMT in treating trait anxiety. Unpublished doctoral dissertation, Colorado State University, 1972

Elkins GR: Hypnosis in the treatment of myofibrositis and anxiety: A case report. Am J Clin Hypn 27:26, 1984

Elkins GR: Rational restructuring and relaxation training in the treatment of communication apprehension. Unpublished doctoral disseration, Texas A & M University, 1980

Elkin GR, Saltzberg LH: Hypnosis in the treatment of social anxiety. J Counsel Psychother 4:95, 1981

Ellis A, Harper R: A New Guide to Rational Living. Englewood Cliffs, N.J., Prentice-Hall, 1975

Freud S: The Problem of Anxiety. New York, W. W. Norton, 1936

Frutiger AD: Treatment of penetration phobia through the combined us eof systematic desensitization and hypnosis: A case study. Am J Clin Hypn 33:269, 1981

Golan HP: Control of fear reaction in dental patients by hypnosis: 3 case studies. Am J Clin Hypn 13:279, 1971

Goldfried MR: Systematic desensitization as training in self-control. J Consul Clin Psychol 37:228, 1971

Gruenewald D: A psychoanalytic view of hypnosis. Am J Clin Hypn 24:185, 1982

Hathaway S, McKinnley J: Minnesota Multiphasic Personality Inventory. New York, The Psychological Corporation, 1948

Horowitz S: Strategies within hypnosis for reducing phobic behavior. J Abn Psychol 75:105, 1970

Jenkins RL: The varieties of children's behavioral problems and family dynamics. Am J Psychiatry 124:1440, 1968

Kaplan HI, Sadock BJ: Modern Synopsis of Comprehensive Textbook of Psychiatry IV. Baltimore, Williams & Wilkins, 1985

Kroger WS, Fezler WD: Hypnosis and Behavior Modification: Imagery Conditioning. Philadelphia, JB Lippincott, 1976

Lawlor ED: Hypnotic intervention with school phobic children. Int J Clin Exp Hypn 24:25, 1976

Lazarus A: Behavior Therapy and Beyond. New York, McGraw-Hill, 1971

Mahoney MJ: Cognition and Behavior Modification. Cambridge, Mass., Ballinger, 1974

Marks IM, Gelder MG, Edwards G: Hypnosis and desensitization for phobias: A controlled prospective trial. Bri J Psychiatry 114:1263, 1968

Melnick J, Russell RW: Hypnosis versus systematic desensitization in the treatment of test anxiety. J Coun Psychol 23:291, 1976

Mordey T: Conditioning of appropriate behavior to anxiety producing stimuli: Hypnotherapy of a stage fright case. Am J Clin Hypn 8:117, 1965

Mott T: The role of hypnosis in psychotherapy. Am J Clin Hypn 24:241, 1982

Paul GL: Outcome of systematic desensitization: II. Controlled investigations of individual treatment, technique variations, and current status. In Frank CM (ed): Behavior Therapy: Assessment and Status. New York, McGraw-Hill, 1969

Shurman, OS: Postnoxious desensitization: Some clinical notes on the combined use of hypnosis and systematic desensitization. Am J Clin Hypn 22:54, 1979

Spiegel D, Frischholz EJ, Maruffi B, Spiegel H: Hypnotic responsivity and the treatment of flying phobia. Am J Clin Hypn 21:108, 1979

Spielberger CD: Anxiety and Behavior. New York, Academic Press, 1966

Spies, G: Desensitization of test anxiety: Hypnosis compared with biofeedback. Am J Clin Hypn 21:108, 1979

Suinn RM: Anxiety management training to control general anxiety. In Krumboltz JD, Thoresen CE (eds): Counseling Methods. New York, Holt, Rinehart & Winston, 1976

Sullivan HS: The Interpersonal Theory of Psychiatry. New York, W. W. Noron, 1953

Timm S: Systematic desensitization of a phobia for flying with the use of suggestion. Aviation, Space and Environmental Medicine 48:370, 1977

Van der Hart O: Treatment of a phobia for dead birds. Am J Clin Hypn 23:263, 1981

Wolpe J: The Practice of Behavior Therapy. New York, Pergamon, 1969

13 PEDIATRICS AND HYPNOTHERAPY: A CASE MANAGEMENT APPROACH TO JUVENILE MIGRAINE

KAREN OLNESS, M.D.

Hypnotherapy has many applications in pediatrics, including both primary and adjunct uses (Gardner and Olness, 1981). This chapter, which assesses hypnotherapy with children who have migraine, provides a good example of hypnotherapy as a primary treatment.

Objectives for the reader in studying this case history are to be able to:

1. List a differential diagnosis in a child presenting with headaches.

2. List diagnostic criteria for juvenile migraine.

3. Determine whether or not hypnotherapy is appropriate for a given child.

4. Make decisions regarding appropriate hypnotic techniques for a child with migraine who wishes to learn self-hypnosis.

5. Determine effectiveness of interventions.

Foundations

There are clinical reports of the successful use of hynotherapy with children from two centuries ago, beginning with the work of Mesmer. Subsequently, John Elliotson and James Braid, English surgeons, reported clinical success in performing surgery on children using hypnoanesthesia. Bramwell, an English psychotherapist, around the turn of the century, reported the successful application of hypnotherapy in children with behavior and habit disorders (Tinterow, 1970). Application of hypnosis in pediatrics was mentioned in the American journal, *Pediatrics,* in 1987 (Witmen) and was then not mentioned in an American pediatric journal again until 1975 (Olness). In the past decade, more than 20 articles documenting successful clinical applications of hypnosis with children have appeared in American pediatric journals (see references), and two textbooks on pediatric hypnotherapy have been published (Gardner and Olness, 1981; Hilgard and LeBaron, 1984). In addition, research data is beginning to appear which documents the ability of children to self-regulate certain autonomic processes which are facilitated by training in hypnosis (Olness and Conroy, 1985; Olness and MacDonald, 1986; Deubner, 1977; Presky, 1979; Congdon and Forsythe, 1979). Such studies indicate that children learn to control certain autonomic processes more rapidly than do adults and are also capable of achieving desired clinical outcomes more quickly than adults.

The child's application of innate imagery skills seems generic to learning and application of self-hypnosis. While it is recognized that the imagery of the child is important to child development and related to play patterns, creativity, and adult achievements, there is relatively little basic research related to effects of imagery on physiologic responses or to changes in imagery associated with puberty. The child therapist should take time to assess a child's imagination and learning styles prior to embarking on a hypnotherapeutic course. Some children prefer auditory imagery; others have excellent olfactory imagery. Therapists who work with children benefit by staying up to date in children's television, movies, songs, books, and classroom instruction methods as well as by considering a particular child's age, interests, development state, fears, skills, and attention span.

Children rarely sit quietly during a hypnotic induction process. They also resist approaches that may remind them of authority figures or chores at home or situations in which they have no control. Facilitating the child's personal sense of mastery or control is essential to therapeutic success. Phrases that give the child control include, "When you are ready, just go ahead," "Please show me how you do that," and "Take as much time as you need."

A number of clinical reports agree on a 75 to 80 percent success rate in application of hypnotherapy in pediatrics (that is, attainment of original goal such as dry beds or comfort during painful procedures). Failures may reflect inappropriate assessments, inappropriate explanation to the child or his/her family, or inappropriate hypnotherapeutic strategies. There is data to support the theory that incorporation of a suggestion may not be evident for many months; early lack of responsivity may be interpreted as failure (Kohen, Olness, Colwell and Heimel, 1984). Therefore, long term follow-up of patients is important.

Overview—Juvenile Migraine

Migraine affects approximately six percent of all children in the United States and the Western world. Its onset may occur at a very early age before a child is able to communicate the source of distress. Migraine is a poorly defined symptom complex which may include multiple causes (Shinner and D'Souza, 1981; Glueck and Bates, 1986; Egger et al., 1983; Gascon, 1984; Houts, 1982). Research data has confirmed the complexity of the diagnosis, pathogenesis, and treatment. Recent articles note that severe migraine in boys may reflect primary and familial lipoprotein abnormalties (Labbe and Williamson, 1983); another study notes that many children with migraine have food allergies which trigger the symptoms (Werder and Sargent, 1984). At this time, it seems incorrect to explain migraine in terms of blood flow changes alone or as a psychogenic entity. The following definition, used in this chapter, is currently acceptable among neurologists. It is likely that research will sort out a variety of causes for this condition now defined with a group of symptoms.

Juvenile migraine diagnoses require:

1. Unilateral head pain severe, with entirely symptom-free periods separating the headache episodes.

2. Associated nausea and/or other gastrointestinal symptoms.

3. Family history of similar headaches.

4. Other associated neurologic changes.

Treatment of juvenile migraine has included aspirin, acetaminophen, ergotamines in children over 10 years of age, propranolol prophylaxis, phenobarital, phenytoin, and methysergide (Diamond and Medina, 1975; Hoelscher and Lichstein, 1984; Olness et al., 1986). Recent double blind crossover studies with propranolol raise doubt about its efficacy (Olness, MacDonald and Uden, 1986; Forsythe, Gilles and Sillsman, 1984). There is data to indicate that children who receive long-term medications are more likely to take non-medicinal drugs in adolescence. This fact, coupled with known undesirable side effects from usual migraine drugs, makes it highly desirable whenever possible to teach self-regulation methods for control of migraine symptoms. A number of such studies, uncontrolled and using self-hypnosis and/or biofeedback, have encouraged the teaching of these methods to children. Our own recent prospective, controlled study concluded that self-hypnosis was superior to either propranolol or placebo in management of juvenile migraine (Olness and Libbey, 1986).

Assessment—Case Study

Liz is a 12-year-old girl referred by her neurologist as a possible candidate to learn self-hypnosis for management of her migraine symptoms. The neurologist sent a letter indicating that she had migraine symptoms for five years with recent increasing frequency. An electroencephalogram, CAT scan, and neurologic exam, all conducted within the past six months, had been negative. The neurologist had prescribed acetaminophen, fiorinal, and rest.

The therapist must make an important decision at this point. Is he/she comfortable with the previous evaluation? Does he/she accept the results? Much of this decision depends on previous knowledge of the referring child health professional. Children diagnosed as having migraine have subsequently died from brain tumors or cerebrovascular accidents. Our recent study of 80 patients referred consecutively for hypnotherapy found that 25 percent had previously unrecognized significant biologic bases for the presenting symptoms (Olness and Libbey, 1986). Most of these diagnoses would not have been amenable to hypnotherapy, and further delay in diagnoses would have compromised the child's condition. Careful consideration as to possible causes of symptoms cannot be overemphasized. Children diagnosed as having migraines may have sinusitis, temporomandibular joint syndrome, brain tumors, cerebrovascular malformations, food allergies, dyslipoproteinemias, carbon monoxide poisoning, lead poisoning, subdural hematomas, and other causes.

In the case of the representative patient, let us assume that we have confidence in the neurologist but will, nonetheless, ask questions in the initial interview to get more details about the symptoms. Not infrequently, answers will provide suggestions for further diagnostics.

When setting up a first appointment, it is appropriate for the therapist to invite both parents, with care not to demand this. Schedules may make it difficult for both parents to come, could increase stress, and decrease the likelihood of a successful relationship with the parents. If the child is under 10, it is usually easiest for the child if the entire family is seen together initially. When the child seems comfortable, he/she can then be seen alone. With respect to usual hypnotherapeutic plans, the child is seen alone in subsequent visits. The accompanying parent may be invited in at the conclusion of each session. The therapist should avoid seeing the parent alone while the child is left sitting in the waiting room. It is preferable to schedule times for the parent to come in alone or for a telephone discussion.

It is important to establish the child's and parents' expectations at the beginning and the end of the interview. Expectations may change from the beginning to the end. We use a general questionnaire to be completed prior to an initial interview and also provide a number of specific questionnaires with respect to specific presenting complaints such as bedwetting, soiling, etc. We also ask that parents of children under 10 bring along family photo albums, baby books, and school reports. The photos provide a stimulus to the child and facilitate rapport.

Initial Interview

I asked that the mother be present for the initial part of the interview but directed most questions to Liz:

Physician: *Good morning, Liz. I know a little about you from the letter sent by Dr. M. and from the questionnaire you've completed. I know that you have been sent to me by your coach, to teach you ways of controlling your headaches. You don't know much about me, and I'd like to tell you something about me. I'm a pediatrician. That means I take care of children and teenagers. I see patients for different kinds of problems and many for problems of pain. I've helped myself with the kind of approach I will tell you about. You can think of me as a coach. Before we begin, it would help to know some of your ideas about your symptoms, what helps, what doesn't, and what you want to get out of this visit. Please tell me the very first time you can remember a headache and what it was like.*

Child: *The first time I remember was when we were on a plane going to Florida. That was the first one.*

Physician: *How long did it last?*

Child: *Until sometime after we landed, and I had another on the flight back.*

Physician: *Did you think the headache had something to do with flying?*

Child: *I thought—I didn't know. Later, my mother said maybe it was from air pressure changes.*

Physician: *How old were you then?*

Child: *Eight.*

Physician: *Do you get the headaches in a certain place on your head?*

Child: *Yes, always the same place.*

Physician: *Where is that place? (Patient points to her right temple area.)*

Physician: *Do you have any other symptoms with your headaches?*

Child: *No, just sleepy.*

Physician: *Do you sneeze? Vomit? Have a feeling of chills or fever?*

Child: *Sometimes I feel nauseated.*

Physician: *Are you able to eat when you have the headache?*

Child: *Yes, I do eat.*

Physician: *How long do the headaches last?*

Child: *About five hours.*

Physician: *If zero is no pain and 10 is the worst pain you can imagine, what number is your average headache?*

Child: *About seven or eight.*

Physician: *When you have a seven or eight headache, is there anything you've learned to do to feel better?*

Child: *I just rest.*

Physician: *And if you were to keep going with a seven or eight headache with your play or school, what would happen?*

Child: *It would just get worse.*

Physician: *Did you sometimes keep going with the headache?*

Child: *Yes, lots of times.*

Physician: *How often do you have these episodes?*

Child: *At least once, sometimes twice a week.*

Physician: *What is the worst part about the headache?*

Child: *Not knowing when it will come. I don't like that.*

Physician: *So when you had had the headaches for a while, your mom took you to see a doctor about them? Do you remember that and what medicine was suggested?*

Child: *Yes, he told me to take Tylenol.*

Physician: *Did you take Tylenol? Did it help?*

Child: *I took it, but it didn't make much difference. And the headaches got worse, so last year Mom took me to see Dr. M.*

Physician: *He's your neurologist, right? And what did he do?*

Child: *He did some tests, brain waves, and X-rays, and he said I should see you.*

Physician: *What idea did he give you about what I would do?*

Child: *Well, he said you could teach me some ways to help myself through hypnosis or biofeedback—and you wouldn't give any shots.*

Physician: *That's right. I won't. What do you think hypnosis or biofeedback is?*

Child: *I don't know. I saw a guy with a pendulum on television.*

Physician: *I don't have any pendulums. What I can teach you is very similar to what the Olympic champions were taught to help them control their bodies better. Did you see the Olympics last summer?*

Child: *Yes, I watched the gymnasts, mostly.*

Physician: *Many of the Olympics competitors were taught ways to self-regulate their bodies, to prepare themselves mentally as well as physically. They had coaches who helped them. And I will help you if you want to practice. The average Olympic competitor had to practice daily for eight or nine weeks until he or her self-regulation practice was automatic. You're younger. You can probably learn faster. But you will need to think about practicing 10 minutes twice a day for a month, then, depending on how you do, once a day for another month. After that, you can probably practice just two or three times a week and again if a migraine should start. How does that sound?*

Child: *When should I practice?*

Physician: *It would be best in the morning and afternoon. You'll have to work that out depending on your schedule. Some days you might have to practice morning and evening or afternoon and evening. Do you want to begin today or think about it and learn later?*

Child: *I'd like to start now.*

Physician: *Great. Let me tell you a little about pain and how this works. No one knows for certain why migraines start. Food is a factor for some people, allergies for some people, and, whatever the cause, stress seems to make them feel worse. We know that the pain of migraine and other kinds of pain can be reduced and elimi-*

nated by self-hypnosis exercises. There are different ways and types of exercises, and I'll give you a choice of several. We know that the body makes its own natural pain killer. We know that joggers put out extra amounts of that substance. Maybe when we teach self-hypnosis to children and teenagers they put out more of their natural pain killer. Maybe they control pain because their brain understands the pain signals in a new and different way. We're not sure how—we do know that just by thinking humans change body processes. If I ask your mother how her body reacts when she gets nervous or upset about something, she can probably tell me. (I turn to her mother.)

Mother: *I perspire and my voice gets shaky.*

Physician: *And I used to get pain in my upper abdomen. What about you, Liz?*

Child: *My heart beats fast.*

Physician: *And all of us make those changes just by thinking in a certain, scared, nervous way. We can change our thinking, learn to control body processes in a more positive way. So now I'll ask your mom to leave, not because she can't know what you will learn, but because I want you to be the one to tell her about it. (The mother leaves.)*

Physician: *Today, we'll begin a relaxation exercise only. We won't say a thing about pain. You can get yourself comfortable and follow along with what I say and practice the same mental exercise at home. I know from your questionnaire and from what you like to do that you have a good imagination—so we'll start with using your imagination.*

When you're ready, get comfortable in that chair, or move to one of the others, if you prefer, and then take a few long, deep breaths. Notice how your chest expands and how the muscles in your chest stretch as you take in air. Take a good deep breath, hold it, that's fine. Then let it go and notice the feeling of relaxation as you let that air go out. The muscles relax. Everyone relaxes when breathing out several times a minute.

Close your eyes and pay attention to the feeling of your chest wall muscles each time you breathe out. That's good. And, with each breath out, think of extending that loosening, that relaxing from those chest muscles into another muscle group. Loosen your tummy muscles (following her breathing). Good. Now let a flow of loosening and relaxing move into your upper legs—each time you breathe out a little more loosening. Let the muscles loosen all the way to your toes—when you're ready. Please follow your own pace and speed. Just let my coaching be a general guide to you. As you breathe out you gradually loosen your back muscles—shoulder muscles. . .upper arms. . .lower arms. . .hands. Sometimes, the hands feel warmer as they relax more and more. When you're ready, loosen your neck muscles, first a little, then a bit more so your head is so comfortable on your neck. Loosen your face muscles, around your mouth, around your eyes, even the tiny muscles of your scalp. . .and when you've relaxed and loosened all of your muscles as much as you wish to at this time, please give me a signal by raising one of your fingers to say "yes." I'll be quiet until you give the signal.

(She gives the signal.)

That's fine. Now let your imagination find that golden dragon you enjoy reading about, find the dragon and go off to some wonderful place, just as slowly or as quickly as you choose. Let the dragon go where you choose, enjoy what you see, enjoy going in the direction you choose. . .and keep going until you find a special, favorite place where you can rest, be safe, comfortable. Just so I know. I don't need to know where the place is. When you're there, give me a signal with your finger again, just so I know.

Enjoy that special, safe, lovely place—-the colors, the sounds, and what you can do there. Enjoy as long as you want to, right now, and when you're ready, slowly, comfortably, easily you can open your eyes and enjoy the rest of the day.

Intervention Process

The written questionnaire and the initial interview provide guidelines for decisions about initial intervention strategies. However, it is important to check with the patient at the conclusion of the initial session and at the beginning of each subsequent session regarding what was helpful, what was not, what was liked, what was not liked. It is useful to make initial choices for children on the basis of developmental stages as well as to recognize that a child may require a different approach a year or two later as he/she matures. The following is a summary list of some options for initial hypnotherapeutic strategies based on age and developmental stages:

Early Verbal (2-4 years)
Story telling
Thinking of favorite place
Speaking to child through his/her favorite stuffed animal
Watching another child on videotape

Preschool and early school (4-6 years)
Favorite place imagery
Imagining favorite song
Think of animals, changing their colors and numbers
Focus on coin or other object held in front of child
Watching videotape
Imagining self as bouncing ball
Computer game hookup
Finger lowering

Middle Childhood (7-11 years)
Favorite place
Thinking of favorite activity
Imagining riding a horse or bike
Eye fixation on coin or hand
Hands moving together
Imagining favorite music
Imagining flying blanket

Adolescence
Progressive relaxation
Imagining sports activity
Eye fixation
Imagining driving
Hand levitation
Imagining favorite music

Regardless of the choice of initial induction, it is important to encourage the child's control, to agree on a signal from the child regarding his/her readiness to proceed to the next step, and to be flexible. With respect to coaching for control of migraine, we have used a protocol involving four visits. A general relaxation oriented induction is taught at the first visit. No mention is made of pain. At the second visit, a week later, pain control methods are offered and explained. The initial exercise is reviewed and refined, the child then practices a pain control method, and peripheral temperature is monitored. Additional pain control methods are taught at the third visit two weeks later, and a review session is held a month after the third visit. Children then telephone their progress and only occasionally request review sessions.

First Training Session

Physician: *Good morning, Liz. How are you?*
Child: *Fine. I'm doing great.*
Physician: *You have a new hairdo. It looks very nice.*
Child: *Yeah. My friends and I, we saved our babysitting money, and we all went to this one stylist. So we all look alike.*
Physician: *You saved your money for something special. That's impressive. Tell me, how is your practice going?*
Child: *Good. I did it twice a day except one day when I got home too late. And I didn't have any headaches this week.*

Physician: *That's terrific. And you haven't even learned pain control officially yet! What questions have you about your practice and what you're doing?*

Child: *Well, none really, except sometimes I only practiced 10 minutes. Is that okay?*

Physician: *I usually suggest that people practice 15 or 20 minutes each time in the beginning. After they've practiced for a few weeks, most don't need to practice that long because the relaxation becomes automatic. That's your goal. Sometimes, if the results aren't what patients expect or what, I suggest they practice longer. Since you're doing well, I think that 10 minutes is fine.*

What seemed best about the practice? What was good? What was least helpful?

Child: *I really like to imagine that golden dragon and my favorite place. It makes me feel so comfortable.*

Physician: *That's great. Let's stay with that and add a few more exercises that you can practice if you wish. First, we need to talk a bit about nerves, sensations, and pain. Did you study those yet in biology?*

Child: *Yes, but not much. I have some idea.*

Physician: *Well, we all have nerves bringing many signals into our brain, and we're not aware of all of them at any one moment. They bring in signals of heat or cold, or wet or dry, of smells, of sounds, of sights. We notice some more than others. It's really difficult to pay attention to more than a couple at one time. I'll flip on this tape recorder. Please listen to the music, at the same time noticing how your right foot feels on the floor and focusing on the smell sensation from this bottle of perfume I'll open. (There is a pause.)*

Child: *That's really hard. It's almost impossible. (She laughed.)*

Physician: *Somehow our bodies turn off some signals so we notice or focus on others. So we know how to do that unconsciously. What I would like to teach you is to switch off pain signals deliberately, knowing that you're doing it.*

Child: *I'd like that!*

Physician: *We'll repeat the exercise like we did before with two changes. I'm going to put this little biotic band on your middle left finger. This measures temperature, and the colors change as the temperature of your finger changes. As you relax, the temperature usually goes up. We'll look at it at the start and at the end of our practice session. After you're relaxed, I'll ask you to give me a signal when you are ready to practice control of the nerves that transmit pain from your hands. That signal would be asking you to lift a "yes" finger, whichever you want to be a "yes" finger. Do you have questions?*

Child: *Can I talk?*

Physician: *Sure, anytime you wish.*

(The induction then proceeded in the same manner as during the first session, with the following addition when Liz had reached her favorite place.)

Physician: *That's good. I see by your signal that you are in that special, comfortable, favorite place. Just enjoy it, what you see, hear, feel there, and part of you can easily listen to what I say that's important to you while the other part of you just enjoys your special place. We talked about nerve signals, and we know that each of our brains has a system for controlling those signals. We don't know exactly how that system works so you can imagine your own system. You can choose one of the systems, a switch system with a dimmer switch controlling pain signals or a flipswitch or a pushbutton switch or some other switch. Or you might use a computer and type in instructions to your computer brain. Maybe you prefer to think of a panel of lights and you can punch lights on and off. Take all the time you need to choose your control system. I'll wait. When you have a system, just lift your "yes" finger so I will know.*

(After 30 seconds her right pointer finger slowly lifted.)

Physician: *That's good. You have your system. Would you mind telling me what it is?*

Child: *Like a Commodore Computer.*

Physician: *That sounds like a good idea. Now, when you're ready, type in the control signal to turn off the pain signals coming to your brain from one of your hands. Turn it off for a definite period of time like three minutes or seven minutes or five minutes. When it's off, let me know by lifting your pointer of the hand which you have turned off.*

(Almost immediately the left pointer lifted.)

That was fast. Now you can keep your eyes closed or open. I am going to touch your hands alternately with a paper clip. It's interesting to notice the difference between the one you turned off and the one you left on.

(Liz nods her head—After the paperclip check, she smiles.)

Now, I have a small needle. Please look at it. I will touch your hands again with this needle. Tell me how it feels.

Child: *Like a feather on my left. It's sharp on the right.*

Physician: *You've done very well for the first time. Be sure you've given yourself the instruction to put the signals back on at the appropriate time, and then return to enjoying your favorite place for a few more minutes. Enjoy, take your time, and when you're ready, slowly, comfortably, easily you can open your eyes and enjoy the rest of the day.*

(After three minutes Liz opened her eyes, stretched slightly, and looked at the bioband which registered an increase of six degrees Fahrenheit. She smiled.)

Physician: *You did very well. Now you can practice in the same way, just focusing on the signals from your hands. Next time, we'll start to focus on signals from the area of your headaches. You can take the bioband home with you. Please bring your headache diary on the next visit.*

Liz was seen a third time two-weeks later. Her headache diary indicated one six-hour headache. She said that it was milder than usual and gave it a number five. At the time of the third visit (20 minutes), I asked her to go through the review up to the point of pain control on her own without cues from me while I observed. I asked that she lift a "yes" finger when she was comfortable in her favorite place. At that point, the pain control was rehearsed with additional suggestions for signals coming from her head. Again she did well.

At the time of the fourth visit, a month later, her headache diary indicated that she had aborted two headaches by excusing herself from her classroom, going to the nurse's office, and spending 10 minutes reviewing her self-regulation exercise. She was very pleased. At this time, I suggested she could reduce her practice to one daily. Subsequent follow-up by phone at monthly intervals for one year indicated that she had rare headaches which she controlled. She took no medications.

Assessment of Effectiveness

Although hypnotherapy can be used in acute situations involving pain and anxiety with children who have no previous experience, most pediatric applications are in chronic or semi-chronic conditions. In an acute situation, the endpoint is rapid comfort, and it is easy to determine if it was reached and when.

Adequate evaluation of effectiveness of most hypnotherapeutic efforts demands pre-intervention data and long-term post-intervention data. In the case of a symptom such as nocturnal enuresis, it is important to get a baseline of number of dry nights. Baselines can be acquired in many chronic conditions including episodes of wheezing, numbers of tics, frequency of cough, numbers and duration of pain episodes. With respect to some situations involving pain, families are unwilling to control without intervention for very long. In the previously mentioned migraine study, a baseline of headache frequency was obtained for one month prior to initiation of the study. Frequency of symptoms must be charted during the period of training in self-hypnosis and for some time thereafter. Children may be given headache diaries, calendars, stickers. It is important to solicit parental assistance in keeping these records, but it is also important not to take the responsibility away from the child.

Programming of voluntary or involuntary physical responses, whether via athletic coaching, piano teaching, or training in self-hypnosis, may require a gestation period before the desired outcome is realized. We reported a study of obese teenage girls in which the only girls who achieved and maintained the desired weight reduction two years after the study were those who regularly practiced the self-hypnosis exercise. This phenomenon, reported clinically by others, is one which makes it difficult to interpret short-term studies.

Thus far, our follow-up of juvenile migraine sufferers indicates that they continue to retain self-regulation skills in spite of reduced practice frequency over a five-year period. In spite of symptom reduction, we encourage them to pursue new diagnostic avenues, for example, food allergy, in efforts to determine exact triggers for the migraine syndrome.

Future Trends

The science of cyberphysiology, which refers to human steering or self-regulatory abilities, is in its infancy. Greater understanding of cyberphysiology with respect to children has major implications for health, including acute and chronic disease treatment, public health programs, and health care costs. Those who work with children wonder if early acquisition of self-regulatory abilities via training in self-hypnosis or biofeedback may result in healthier adults. Pilot studies in schools demonstrate that it is possible to teach children self-regulation of body processes as a means of stress reduction. Children learn how forcing tachycardia or tachypnea will, within minutes, cause them to perceive negative images and feelings, while raising peripheral temperature or reducing the respiratory rate will trigger comfortable feelings. Deliberate focusing on pleasant images results in stabilization or autonomic responses. Both clinical and research observations indicate that autonomic responses, formerly viewed as reactive reflexes, can be modified by learning which is significantly dependent on control of internal images. It is hoped that child health workers, parents, and teachers will learn how anticipatory guidance can help children become aware of the power of their internal images very early.

References

Congdon PJ, Forsythe WI: Migraine in childhood; a study of 300 children. Develop Med Child Neurol 21:109-121, 1979

Deubner DC: An epidemiologic study of migraine and headache in 10-20 year olds. Headache 17:172-180, 1977

Diamond S, Medina JL: Autogenic training with biofeedback in children with migraine. In Luthe W, Antonelli F (eds): Therapy in Psychosomatic Medicine. Proceedings of the 2rd Congress of International College of Psychosomatic Medicine, Rome, 1975

Dikel W, Olness K: Self-hypnosis, biofeedback, and voluntary peripheral temperature control in children. Pediatrics 66:335, 1980

Egger J, Carter CM, Wilson J, Turner MW and Soothill JF: Is migraine food allergy? A double-blind controlled trial of oligoantigenic diet treatment. Lancet 2:865-869, 1983

Ellenberg L, Kellerman J, Dash J, Higgins G, Zeltzer L: Use of hypnosis for multiple symptoms in an adolescent girl with leukemia. J Adolesc Health Care 1:132, 1980

Forsythe WI, Gillies D, Sillsman: Propranolol in the treatment of childhood migraine. Devel Med Child Neurol 26:737-741, 1984

Gardner G: Hypnotherapy in the management of childhood habit disorders. J Pediatr 92:934 1978

Gardner G and Olness K: Hypnosis and Hypnotherapy with Children. New York, Grune and Stratton, 1981

Gascon GG: Chronic and recurrent headaches in children and adolescents. Pred Clin N A 31:1027-1051, 1984

Glueck CJ, Bates SR: Migraine in children: Associated with primary and familial dys-lipoproteinemias. Ped 77:316-321, 1986

Hilgard JR, LeBaron S: Hypnotherapy of Pain in Children With Cancer. Los Altos, CA, William Kaufmann Inc., 1984

Hoelscher TJ, Lichstein KL: Behavioral assessment and treatment of child migraine; implications for clinical research and practice. Headache 24:94-103, 1984

Hogan M, Olness K, MacDonald J: The effect of hypnosis on brainstem auditory responses in children. Am J Clin Hypn 3:91-94, 1985

Houts AC: Relaxation and thermal feedback treatment of childhood migraine headache: A case study. Am J Clin Biofeedback 5:154-157, 1982

Johnson RL: Use of hypnosis with enuretic adolescents. JCAM 2:39, 1981

Kellerman J, Zeltzer L, Ellenberg L, Dash J: Adolescents with cancer: Hypnosis for the reduction of the acute pain and anxiety associated with medical procedures. J Adolesc Health Care 4:76, 1983

Kohen DP: Relaxation/mental imagery (self-hypnosis) and pelvic examination in adolescents. JDBP 1:180, 1980

Kohen DP, Olness K, Colwell S, Heimel A: The use of relaxation-mental imagery (self-hypnosis) in the management of 505 pediatric behavioral encounters. JDBP 1:35, 1984

Labbe E, Williamson DA: Temperature biofeedback in the treatment of children with migraine headaches. J Ped Psy 8:317-326, 1983

LeBaron S, Zelter L: Behavioral incentive for reducing chemotherapy-related nausea and vomiting in adolescents with cancer. J Adolesc Health Care, in press, 1986

Lewenstein LN: Hypnosis as an anesthetic in pediatric ophthalmology. Anesthesiology 49:144, 1978

Olness K: The use of self-hypnosis in the treatment of childhood nocturnal enuresis: A report on forty patients. Clinical Pediatrics 14:273-279, 1975

Olness K: Hypnosis in pediatric practice. Curr Prob Pediatr 12:1, 1981

Olness K, Conroy M: Voluntary control of transcutaneous oxygen flow in children. Int J Clin Exp Hypn 33:1-5, 1985

Olness K, Kohen D: Suggestion and hypnotherapy in pediatric practice. Ross Currents 26:17, 1984

Olness K, Libbey P: When you hear hoofbeats, think of zebras. Presentation, scientific meetings, ASCH 1986

Olness K, MacDonald J: Self-hypnosis and biofeedback in the management of juvenile migraine. JDBP 2:168, 1981

Olness K, MacDonald J: Headaches in children. Pediatrics in Review, in press, 1986

Olness K, MacDonald J, Uden D: Self-hypnosis in treatment of juvenile classic migraine. Ped, in press, 1986

Olness K, McParland FA, Piper J: Biofeedback: A new modality in the management of children with fecal soiling. J Pediatr 96:505, 1980

Presky AL, Sommer D: Diagnosis and treatment of migraine in children. Neurology 29:506-510, 1979

Sarles RM: The use of hypnosis with hospitalized children. J Clin Child Psychology 4:36, 1975

Shinner S, D'Souza B: Migraine in children and adolescents. Pediatrics in Review 3:257-262, 1981

Tinterow, MM: Foundations of Hypnosis: From Mesmer to Freud. Springfield, IL, Charles C. Thomas, 1970

Varni JW, Katz ER, Dash J: Behavioral and neurochemical aspects of pediatric pain. In Russo DC, Varni JW: Behavioral Pediatrics: Research and Practice. New York, Plenum, 1982

Werder DS, Sargent JD: A study of childhood headache using biofeedback as a treatment alternative. Headache 24:122-126, 1984

Williams DT, Singh M: Hypnosis as a facilitating therapeutic adjunct in child psychiatry. J A Acad Child Psychiatry 15:326, 1976

Williams DT, Spiegel H, Mostofsky DL: Neurogenic and hysterical seizures in children and adolescents. Am J Psychiatry 135:82, 1978

Witmen L: The use of hypnotism in education. Pediatrics 3:23-27, 1897

Zelter L, Dash J, Holland JP: Hypnotically-induced pain control in sickle cell anemia. Pediatrics 64:533, 1979

Zelter L, LeBaron S: Hypnosis and nonhypnotic techniques for reduction of pain and anxiety during painful procedures in children and adolescents with cancer. J Pediatr 101:1032, 1982

14 HYPNOSIS FOR SMOKING CESSATION

WILLIAM C. WESTER, II, Ed.D.

A variety of studies support the fact that hypnosis can be a valuable tool in the treatment of smoking. Some of the studies have major limitations because of the self-report methodology used. For example, Wagner, Hindi-Alexander and Horwitz (1983) evaluated the Damon group hypnosis smoking-cessation program and found that 113 out of 783 subjects who participated had not smoked in one year post-treatment. An aggressive method of data collection accounted for 48 percent from questionnaires and 31 percent from telephone surveys. Even with this aggressive approach, the authors listed the self-report methodology as a major limitation.

There are many variables which influence statistical outcomes. Horwitz, Hindi-Alexander and Wagner (1985) examined the relationship of health beliefs, social support, use of nonsmoking areas, and objecting to another person's smoking with long-term abstinence and relapse. Results showed that ex-smokers coped with smokers in their environment, avoided smokers in public places and received considerable support from friends and spouses. In contrast, recidivists prior to treatment had been unable to quit smoking for extended periods. Following treatment, recidivists did not cope with smokers, were more likely to participate in more hypnosis. The study recommended including coping skills training into smoking cessation programs and restrictions on smoking in ex-smokers' environment.

Level of susceptibility of the patient and hypnosis versus relaxation are other significant variables. Schubert (1983) found that smokers in hypnosis groups who were in the upper two-thirds of the group in terms of hypnotic susceptibility reduced cigarette consumption substantially more than smokers in relaxation groups who were in the upper two-thirds of the group in terms of hypnotic susceptibility.

Agee (1983) in a general review of the literature found that individual versus standardized suggestions appears to be the major differentiating variable in determining success.

Rentchnick (1985) reports that the success of hypnosis treatment often depends on the patient's personality. He further states that ex-smokers should alter their lifestyles by learning relaxation techniques to ensure long-term success from any treatment.

Types of Smokers

The variables discussed above have been found to be of prime importance to this writer. A significant amount of time is spent to develop rapport, determine individualized motivations, assess health beliefs, review support systems available to the patient, estimate level of susceptibility, select an induction procedure based on the patient's personality, and finally, to highly individualize all suggestions. In addition to the fact that people are chemically addicted to nicotine, Christen and Cooper (1979) describe six psychological types of smokers. Each person's habit is unique and thus there is no "typical" smoker.

1. Stimulation (10 percent of smokers)
   This type of smoker is stimulated by the cigarette. He or she uses cigarettes to wake up in the morning and for energy to keep going.

2. Sensorimotor Manipulation (10 percent of smokers)
   This type of smoker enjoys touching and manipulating the cigarette with the hands, flicking the ashes, and making a production of lighting the cigarette.

3. Pleasurable Relaxation (15 percent of smokers)
   This type of smoker gets real, honest pleasure from smoking. This type smokes to enhance pleasurable feelings accompanying a state of well being.

4. Tension Reduction (30 percent of smokers)
   This type of smoker uses cigarettes for the tranquilizer effect in moments of stress or pressure. Cigarettes are used by this type to cope with problems.

5. Psychological Addiction (25 percent of smokers)
   This type of smoker feels totally dependent upon his cigarettes. This type is constantly aware when he or she is not smoking and begins craving for the next cigarette when putting out the present one. Tapering off will not work. "Cold turkey" is the only solution.

6. Habit (10 percent of smokers)
   The habitual smoker gets very little satisfaction from his habit and performs it somewhat automatically. He may smoke a cigarette without realizing it or even wanting it.

As will be seen in the case presentation, this writer tries to personalize the procedure from start to finish. Making the patient accountable for himself or herself is essential.

Nuland and Field (1970) used an "active personalized approach focused on the commitment to stop." They fed back during hypnosis the patients' own reasons for quitting smoking.

Huggan (1985) states that the hypnotherapist's role is to help the patient quit, not make him or her quit. He also emphasizes that time given to discussion of the nature of hypnotherapy and aspects of withdrawal is of great benefit. This writer agrees with Huggan in that negative suggestions, such as instructing patients to have a foul taste in their mouths if they continue to smoke, is to many a challenge that will be tested. Motivation is still the primary factor in success.

Facts

Some patients want to hear specific facts about the negative effects of smoking and various aspects of withdrawal. The American Cancer Society, the U.S. Department of Health, local heart and lung associations and many other organizations will supply the therapist with packets of current factual information. Some of the facts present- ed to my patients include the following:

> In the next 12 months, cigarette smoking will cause 300,000-350,000 deaths. This is three times the number who will die in automobile and other accidents (United States Department of Health, 1983). A 25-year-old two-pack-per-day smoker will have a life expectancy of 8.3 years shorter than a non-smoking contemporary (American Cancer Society, 1980). The life expectancy of a 35-year-old is 78 compared to 73 if he smokes. Of the 100,000 people who will die this year from lung cancer, 85 percent of the deaths will be caused by smoking. Over 30 percent of all cancer deaths are attributable to smoking. A person who smokes a pack of cigarettes per day is two to five times more likely to have a heart attack than a non-smoker of the same age. In monetary terms, smoking-related illness costs an estimated $14 billion per year in medical expenses and another $26 billion in lost production (United States Department of Health, 1983).

Immediate Rewards of Quitting

Within 12 hours after a person has his or her last cigarette, the body begins to heal itself. The level of carbon monoxide in the system declines quickly and the heart and lungs begin to repair the damage (National Institute of Health, 1980). Quitting smoking is not impossible. There are now more than 34 million ex-smokers in the United States (United States Department of Health, 1983).

Case Study

CJ, age 66 had been smoking since high school. The longest she had gone without smoking was one and one-half days. Her husband, age 68, "smokes a great deal." This couple have been married 45 years and have three children. This woman is a college graduate and holds a responsible position in the community. Her health is good and there is no reported psychiatric history. During the clinical interview, she stated that she wanted to quit smoking because of:

1. "Health."

2. "It's a dirty habit—It's a bad habit."

3. "I like to get along with people. It bothers me to make people uncomfortable."

Based on her own motivation and history, the following procedure was used:

Progressive Relaxation/Imagery Procedure for Smoking Cessation	Comments
"Just sit back in the chair now and relax and let yourself be comfortable. Just close your eyes, listen to my voice, focus in on what I am saying, and let yourself relax. One of the best ways to begin to relax is to take a few moments, focus in, and concentrate on your breathing. Get in tune with your entire breathing process. . .think about it, sense it, feel it, experience it. Sense and feel air coming into the body as you inhale; sense and feel some air leaving the body as you exhale; begin to feel the relaxation, particularly in the chest muscles each time you exhale. Also note the nice rhythm produced each time you inhale and exhale. . .a very comfortable, relaxing rhythm. . .much like a metronome. . .just inhaling and exhaling. As this very normal breathing process continues, you will find that you are able to relax more thoroughly and more comfortably, and as I continue to talk with you, your breathing will assist you in relaxing even more deeply. . .even more completely. . .and at the same time I would like you to focus your attention on the top part of your head. . .your scalp. . . much like you did with your breathing, get in tune and in touch with your scalp, feelings in your scalp, sense and feel the muscles, the skin tissue, the hair follicles, and pay particular attention to the muscles of the scalp, allowing those muscles to become just as comfortable and just as relaxed and smooth as you would like. The mind is a very powerful thing, and anything that you need to do to enhance that feeling of smoothness and comfortableness in	Initial relaxation with focus on patient being responsible for relaxation Eye closure and focusing of patient's attention on therapist's voice Deep-breathing exercise Patient begins to be aware of bodily responses and changes Reassurance that what is happening is normal Reinforcement that the patient's own process will bring about a deeper state of relaxation Transfer of patient's breathing awareness to bodily awareness Use of the phrase "as you would like" continues to reinforce that the patient is in control and can function accordingly Permission to relax even further

those muscles is perfectly all right; for example, think of something smooth, like a quiet lake early in the morning. . .not even a ripple on the water, just as smooth as glass, or smooth like a plastic table top. . .just very smooth, and then just let that feeling of smoothness and comfortableness and relaxation just filter through all of the muscles in the scalp, and then just as if you were taking a relaxation shower, let that feeling of comfort and smoothness and relaxation just flow down into the muscles in the forehead. When we frown or get angry we get little wrinkles in our forehead, and just let those muscles smooth out and become relaxed and comfortable. . .flowing, comfortable relaxation. . .now, down into the muscles of the forehead, the temples, the cheeks, down into the chin, around the mouth, just all of the facial muscles now comfortably and thoroughly and more deeply relaxed. . .such a good feeling, and that feeling of comfort and relaxation can continue down into the muscles of the neck. . .the front, the back, the sides of the neck, down at the base of the neck where we get sort of tense or tight at times, flowing, comfortable relaxation across the shoulders, across the shoulders now, and down the arms, down the arms and through the elbows and forearms and the wrists and the hands. . .comfortably, thoroughly relaxed. The hands and sometimes even the scalp may tingle a little, may feel a little warm or a little cool; that sensation doesn't have to happen, but if it does it's very normal and natural. . .there is nothing to be concerned about. . .just enjoy the deep comfortable relaxation. Your breathing is excellent now, it has slowed down nicely, comfortably, and as that feeling of relaxation and comfortableness continues to flow down through all the muscles in the back and the sides and the chest and down into the waist. . .you can just sense yourself relaxing more deeply and completely, more thoroughly and more deeply relaxed . . .and as that feeling of relaxation and

Introduction of imagery

On-going reinforcement of the relaxation process

Many patients experience physiological change. This suggestion makes these feelings, if they occur, seem normal and natural.

Therapist continues to watch for nonverbal cues and then reinforces the behavior seen.

More direct suggestion about patient experiencing a deeper level.

Deepening experience

Deepening method

Awareness of physical and emotional relaxation

comfort comes into the waist area and down into the hips, you may sense a feeling of heaviness in the entire body, a feeling of heaviness more completely and more thoroughly relaxed, flowing, comfortable relaxation, down through the hips and down into the legs, down through the legs, down into the ankles, and finally into the feet. . .the entire body, all of the muscles in the body, thoroughly comfortable, and deeply relaxed. . .listening to my voice, focusing in on what I am saying, and just letting go. . .complete, total, relaxation.

"In order to relax even deeper simply listen to my voice. As I count backward from 7 to 0 just let yourself relax even more deeply and more completely. 7 deeper and deeper now 6. What you are going to experience is very interesting. As you physically relax deeper and deeper you will—5—also experience an internal emotional relaxation. 4 a calm, peaceful and tranquil feeling. 3 that's right, just deeper and deeper relaxed. 2 nothing to worry about, just letting go completely, both physically and emotionally. 1 almost completely and totally relaxed and 0 deeply relaxed. Your mind is a wonderful marvelously creative mental process. As I continue talking you will find that your conscious mind can be doing something entirely different from your subconscious. You will hear everything I am saying consciously, but you don't have to pay close attention—just enjoy what you are thinking and seeing in your mind. The subconscious will take in and hold and store everything important to you. I would like your conscious mind thinking of and enjoying a thought, an image or perhaps a very clear picture in your mind of a favorite or special place. Perhaps you will get a picture in your mind of a favorite place you have been or somewhere you would like to go. It's your favorite place, so just enjoy it. Let yourself really experience your favorite place. For example, persons who may think of times they went to the beach and ocean can see themselves there

Introduction of permissive imagery

Example used to have patient experience image via sensory experiences

Pause

Conscious/subconscious distinction

First major suggestion to increase patient's motivation

FORMAT FOR SMOKING CESSATION

JUST SIT BACK IN YOUR CHAIR NOW AND RELAX, AND LET YOURSELF BE COMFORTABLE. EASE INTO RELAXATION AND CLOSE YOUR EYES, LISTEN TO MY VOICE, FOCUS ON WHAT I AM SAYING, AND LET YOURSELF RELAX.

ONE OF THE BEST WAYS TO BEGIN TO RELAX IS TO TAKE A FEW MOMENTS, FOCUS IN, AND CONCENTRATE ON YOUR BREATHING. GET IN TUNE WITH YOUR ENTIRE BREATHING PROCESS... THINK ABOUT IT , SENSE IT, FEEL IT , EXPERIENCE IT.

IF YOU CAN, BREATH SO THAT YOUR ABDOMEN, RATHER THAN YOUR CHEST EXPANDS THEN CONTRACTS..... THATS IT.... AND DELIGHT IN THE RELEASE OF ANY TENSION EACH TIME YOU LET THE AIR OUT.

① 12 Months - 300,000 - 350,000 die
② 35 y.o. life expectancy 73 instead of 78
③ of 100k people who die this yr 85% die
of CA
to sm-
④ are 30% of all CA deaths attrib. to smoke
⑤ Person smokes 1ppd is 2 to 5x more likely to
have ♡ ctl
⑥ Shot glass of

—out for their morning walk, feeling the warmth of the sun, hearing the waves lapping in against the shore, smelling the salt air or someone fixing breakfast, perhaps even seeing a shrimp boat off shore or coming in from an early morning catch. So whatever you are thinking just enjoy your favorite place and let yourself experience it. As you are enjoying that experience with your conscious mind, your subconscious is now very aware. You are going to experience some interesting things in the next few days and for weeks to come. You don't have to try to figure out why—just enjoy what your subconscious mind is doing for you. Your motivation to quit smoking is going to be higher than it has ever been. Each day you will find yourself feeling more relaxed, comfortable, confident and very much in control. There will be less tension, less anxiety, less tightness and little or no withdrawal. As a result of being more relaxed, confident, comfortable and in control, there will be no need for a cigarette. Your subconscious is also going to remember something very important. Your body is very important to you and you need your body to live. You want to respect and care for your body. Smoking is a poison to your body. Since you do not want to poison yourself in any way you will stop smoking immediately and continue to be an ex-smoker. Remember, your body is important to you and you need your body to live.

"We know that if you took a regular drinking glass (8-10 oz.), filled it completely with tar and nicotine from cigarettes, and drank it you could be dead before 12 minutes. You do not want to poison yourself—even slowly—and therefore will stop smoking immediately and remain an ex-smoker."

Second major suggestion—general suggestions with ego strengthening phrases

Third—decrease patient's need and lower chance of withdrawal

Fourth—increase patient's awareness of life, health—introduction of the fact that smoking is a poison

This suggestion is not necessary in all cases—use when patient tells you that something strong is needed to get him/her to quit

Fifth—begin to reinforce the fact that the patient is NOW an ex-smoker

At this point, I introduce other motivations elicited from the patient during my intake interview. Health is almost always one of the stronger motivations and is covered within the above poison sequence and the need to care for and respect one's body. For example, my case study gave me two additional ideas during the pre-induction talk. These ideas are now incorporated as follows:

"In addition to respecting your body, you can feel so proud that you are now in control and no longer subject to this bad and dirty habit. Everywhere you go people will appreciate the fact that you are not smoking—no longer making people feel uncomfortable. Just enjoy your favorite place now. I am going to count from 1 to 5 and when I reach 5 you will open your eyes and will be completely alert. Just take your time now—just like getting up in the morning. 1 slowly and easily begin to alert. 2 feeling good. 3 knowing that you are now an ex-smoker. 4 more alert now—almost completely alert. And 5—open your eyes—completely alert."

Sixth—the idea of "bad and dirty" came from patient in pre-hypnotic interview

Seventh—the idea of people not liking her and upsetting people came from patient in pre-hypnotic interview

Counting technique to fully alert patient

Over the years, I have found that a personal approach enhances the hypnotic procedures. At the end of the hypnosis session, I give all of my patients the following "Tips for New Ex-Smokers":

1. Clean and store away all ashtrays.

2. Exercise if there is any withdrawal tension. Check with your physician regarding proper exercise if you have any health problems.

3. If there is an urge to smoke—sit down and relax, take a deep breath, hold it for 5-10 seconds and release it slowly.

4. Increase fluid intake—juice, water, diet drinks, etc., (no caffeine).

5. Decrease caffeinated coffee and alcohol.

6. If needed—get a supply of sugarless gum or use carrot/celery sticks if you feel you need something in your mouth.

7. Talk with another non-smoker or someone who has recently quit for any positive strokes.

8. Send your daily post cards for 7-10 days.

9. Keep thinking—"I am now an ex-smoker."

10. Call if you have any problem. Do not smoke that first cigarette and you will be fine.

I go over the list step by step making special suggestions based on the history. For example, in the case of CJ, her husband was a heavy smoker. (He came in several weeks later and had also quit.) I told my patient to ask him to cooperate by using one ashtray and limiting his smoking to one area. The post cards are very important as a follow-up. I told CJ that I needed to know how she was doing each day and to call if there was a problem and before smoking. After I get card 7 or 10, based on how much the patient is smoking, I call the patient, congratulate him or her and request cards at six months and one year. CJ's cards read as follows:

Card 1: So far I'm an "ex-smoker" with built-in alarm system it seems! Not as hard as I feared...as yet!

Card 2: I can't believe this is really working! A little concern about appetite—I am hungry.

Card 3: Lots of stress today with breakdown of our transportation system. So far—so good.

Card 4: I still regard this "event" as a miracle after so many years. This morning at breakfast a little anxiety but not long lasting. Deep breathing helps. My appetite worries me—I am hungry, but seem to have some control.

Card 5: Very, very stressful day both at office and home. Still no cigarettes, but ate lots (a worry, I'm really hungry).

Card 6: Good day—no problems and still no smoking. Took a long walk this morning—no breathlessness—no morning coughing. Wow!

Card 7: Good day—no problems. Sometimes a mild wish I could have a cigarette. Never any thought of having one really. My husband is amazed at my success, and will be calling you.

Sixth Month Card: This card is just over six months—but neglected to send. Still holding on—no cigarettes.

One Year Card:

Dear Dr. Wester,

Well, it's been a year since I sat in your parking lot and smoked my last cigarette! I'm still not smoking and don't think I ever will again. It's amazing to me that it has been comparatively easy. Thank you for coming in so early on Good Friday for my son. I'm so glad I came to see you a year ago. Sincerely, CJ. (Patient's son also came in and quit smoking.)

The case of CJ is fairly typical of many smoking cases I see. I see the majority of cases for one session. Several sample cards can be kept in your desk and then reviewed as "here are some examples of the types of card I want you to send me each day for seven days." This is a powerful suggestion that can be given before or after the hypnotic session. I ask each patient to leave any cigarettes he or she has with me to be pitched. I also collect the lighter and place the lighter on my bookcase shelf with many others. Once again, this is a subtle suggestion that all of the people who have contributed to my lighter collection have stopped smoking.

The emphasis throughout this paper has been on a highly individualized approach based on all available data and variables. If you spend the time and show the concern described in the case presentation, your results statistics will increase. For those patients who do not quit, the personal approach will encourage them to come back for second appointments. If they ask to come back, I insist that they smoke no more than five cigarettes per day for at least three days prior to the appointment. Once again, I am putting the responsibility on the patients. If they are motivated to follow this suggestion, the chances of their stopping smoking after the second visit are increased.

References

Agee LL: Treatment procedures using hypnosis in smoking cessation programs: A review of the literature. J Amer Soc Psychosomatic Dentistry and Medicine 30:4, 1983

American Cancer Society: Dangers of Smoking...Benefits of Quitting, 1980

Christen AG, Cooper KH: Strategic withdrawal from cigarette smoking. CA-A Cancer J for Clinicians 29:2, 1979

Horwitz MB, Hindi-Alexander M, Wagner TJ: Psychosocial mediators of abstinence, relapse, and continued smoking: A one-year follow-up of a minimal intervention. Addictive Behaviors 10:29, 1985

Huggan DK: Smoking and hypnosis. Practitioner 229:603, 1985

Nuland W, Field PB: Smoking and hypnosis. A systematic clinical approach. Int J Clin Exp Hypno 18:290, 1970

Reaney JB: Hypnosis in the treatment of habit disorder. In Wester WC, Smith AH (eds): Clinical Hypnosis: A Multidisciplinary Approach. Philadelphia, JB Lippincott, 1984

Rentchnick P: Treatment of tobacco addiction. Medicine et Hygiene 43:1611, 1985, French

Schubert DK: Comparison of hypnotherapy with systematic relaxation in the treatment of cigarette habituation. J Clin Psych 39:2, 1983

United States Department of Health and Human Services, Public Health Services [PHS 83-50199], 1983

Wagner TJ, Hindi-Alexander M, Horwitz MD: A one-year follow-up study of the damon group hypnosis smoking cessation program. J Oklahoma State Medical Assoc 76:12, 1983

15 HYPNOSIS IN THE TREATMENT OF OBESITY

WILLIAM RUSS, Ed.D.

Some 10 years ago, fresh from post-graduate training and a workshop sponsored by the American Society of Clinical Hypnosis, I accepted the referral of my first client, who was coming expressly in the hope of using hypnosis to treat obesity. She was a large woman, of German extraction, well over six feet tall and weighing some 265 pounds. In her late sixties, she was widowed and lived alone. A note from her doctor certified that she was in good health and that it would benefit her to enter a program designed to help her lose weight. Her only complaint in the way of health was arthritis, which primarily affected her hands. I completed her history and noted that there were no contraindications, but did wince when she told me that never since reaching adult growth had she weighed under 225 pounds. Now she thought it would "be nice" if she were able to reach a target weight of 215 pounds. She agreed to a program that combined elements of self-hypnosis and behavior modification in a regime of exercise and dieting.

With all the enthusiasm and optimism of the uninitiated, I went to work with protocols cobbled together from my ASCH Workshop Syllabus (1973) and Kroger and Fezler (1976). We met together for six sessions, and she lost nine pounds and then plateaued out around a 10-pound loss. She was having difficulty sticking to her diet and complained about having hunger pains in her stomach which were making her nervous. Since she had reported increasing success with self-hypnosis and had satisfactorily demonstrated arm levitation in the office, I went back to my Kroger and pulled out the "mountain cabin scene with glove ancsthesia." I varied the instructions so that after the patient's hand had become satisfactorily numb, instead of touching her cheek she laid her hand just below her ribcage and let the numbness flow into her stomach. Although this procedure was effective, when she came in for her next session she said, "This is my last visit and I came by to tell you that I appreciate all you have done for me." "But you have not lost the weight," I objected. "Yes, I know," she said, "but I have decided I am no spring chicken who needs to lose weight and, besides, coming here I have learned something more useful. I am now able to let my hands go numb so they are not bothered by the arthritis, and I have been able to take up my knitting again!" I did not argue with her. **183**

We have much to learn from our clients. If she were part of an experimental study, my German lady would have been counted as a "failure" or, at least, as "not significant"; but as a clinician I take a more positive view of the outcome. Hypnosis proved to be an effective tool in working with this client even though it was not used effectively in dealing with her obesity.

The issue of the effectiveness of hypnosis in work with obese clients has not yet been clearly defined in the literature. There is little evidence of the effectiveness of an induction in the successful outcome of an obesity treatment (Mott and Roberts, 1979) and "when hypnosis is successful in treating obesity its efficacy is probably attributable to non-hypnotic factors which may include a structured program, positive treatment expectancies and encouragement" (Wadden and Anderton, 1982). At the same time, we have evidence that gastro-intestinal functions such as hunger contractions, stomach secretions, and a variety of other functions can be modified through the use of hypnosis (Sarbin and Slagle, 1979). Goldstein (1981) found that demonstrating to a subject that he or she is in a trance produces a significantly more successful result in a weight loss program. The key word here is "program" because the obese client is a complex of physical and psychological factors (Rodin, 1982). To attempt a cure with only hypnosis as a tool would be like approaching your automobile with the intention of rebuilding the carburetor with only a screwdriver. A screwdriver can be a very important tool in that operation, but you will quickly find out that you need some wrenches and other items as well. In building a therapeutic strategy, the the clinician can increase the effectiveness, or leverage, by combining with hypnosis elements that include strategies from behavior modification, cognitive, psychoanalytic and other therapies along with medical consultation and proper education of the client in regard to causes and effects of obesity.

This chapter is offered as a process guide for those new and intermediate level therapists who intend to use hypnosis in their work with obese clients. It is not exhaustive, nor obviously the only way of doing things, but it is intended as a framework of considerations and a developing process that beginning therapists can use and modify in their own practices.

Initial Considerations

Before your secretary picks up the phone, you ought to decide how willing you are to work with a group of clients as opposed to an individual. Kline (1982), Kroger (1977), and others have found that group treatments for obesity are rewarding and effective. I, however, agree with Reaney (1984) that "hypnotic suggestions have the greatest impact when paired with the unique characteristics of individual patients." There is also a wider variety of techniques available to the clinician working with an individual client as well as increased effectiveness in the ability to pace and respond to client changes. Furthermore, when I have worked with groups, I invariably have found that many of the participants, on their own initiative, request individual sessions.

When a client calls for a first appointment, unless the therapist is a physician willing to do his own work-up, the client should be told that medical consultation is required. We ask for a physician referral in writing, not only because obesity is a medical as well as a psychological problem but also because, as Udolf (1981) points out, there are some special problems for which these clients will need to be screened. Besides anorexia nervosa and other eating disorders of which the physician may have knowledge, the client may be on medications that play a role in the obesity or require special dieting instruction due to some medical condition. If a client is unable to produce a satisfactory note from his or her doctor and I am unable to contact the physician by phone, I discontinue the session and ask that it be rescheduled when the consultation can be completed. This insistence upon medical consultation very rarely causes difficulty, and the seriousness with which it is taken helps form the mental set for the client that therapy is an active process with shared responsibility.

Interview

Most clinicians begin working with clients by asking what they hope to achieve and what their motivation is. With obese clients, I also pay close attention for indications of tendencies to respond to internal cues such as "I feel so bad about myself," "it makes me sick to be so fat," "I eat when I'm upset," or external cues, such as "a bad time is at dinner; everything I see goes into my mouth," "my clothes don't seem to fit anymore," and "I'm embarrassed whenever my wife looks at me or I see myself in a mirror." Answers to the questions "How insightful is this person?" and "Is one motivation more likely than another to be successful in attacking the problem?" and similar questions help being to build a "theory of personality" for the person.

Then there is the reluctant client. The sullen, dumpy housewife, who sits in the chair and tells me that "My husband said he'd pay for me to get myself in shape," may be a candidate for marital or individual therapy but not for hypnosis. Not long ago, I had an obese teenager with the money to pay for the therapy session stuck in his shirt pocket by his mother. After I determined that he did have some interest in losing weight and since he was employed part-time, I suggested that he work out a plan with his parents whereby he would be responsible for a "fair share" of his treatment. He did so, and when he returned he was able to make progress enough so that I count him a success. Often, when I have had a spectacular failure, I have found out afterwards that the client was in conflict with a third party over the issue of weight. Look carefully at your client's environment and life situation so that you may distinguish what aspects constitute support and what aspects constitute barriers to change. A family and social environment usually exerts the most influence over a long period of time. Beware of the husband who leaves out chocolates and candies for his dieting wife. If that issue is not dealt with, you are doomed to failure.

Assuming you find a supportive or at least a neutral environment for change, next get a measure of sedentary versus active lifestyle. Most overweight people focus on their eating habits to the exclusion of the calories that they should be burning up. What are their hobbies, what do they do for fun, what is their daily schedule? One key question should be, "If you lose weight, how would it change your life? What would change?"

Take a good weight history, but keep in mind that many overweight people do not know what they weigh! Ask how long it has been since they weighed themselves and if they have a scale at home that gives a relatively accurate reading. If you do not have a doctor's scale in your office, now is the time to acquire that tax deduction. What past dieting attempts have been made and how successful they were is important. Another question is, "What do you feel you ought to weigh?" I distinguish between what my clients have read in a book or been told and what weight they might be willing to make a legitimate effort to attain. In the same vein is the question, "How long do you think it will take for you to get to that weight?"

As you take the weight history, distinguish between adolescent versus adult onset or obesity. There can be important clinical differences between severely obese people who experienced that condition as adolescents compared to persons who became overweight as adults:

> Juvenile onset obesity can be conceptualized as an extremely visible physical deviation not unlike any other type of physical handicap. The ramifications of this handicap may include teasing by peers and family, other aversive social interactions, and an adequate opportunity to learn appropriate social skills. Thus, the obese youngster develops an extremely poor self-concept and body image. These negative and painful experiences, occurring as they do during a time when issues related to the body in general are highly salient, may exert a continuing psychological influence irrespective of whether the person succeeds in losing weight at a later time. These experiences and evaluations about one's self would seem to result in quite different long-term effects than those manifested in an individual whose body was not deviant during the adolescent period but who became obese after marriage, childbirth or at some point in middle age. (Leon, 1982)

Along with a disturbed body image, persons who were obese as adolescents often have deficits in social skills which may have to be addressed during therapy. Likewise, changes in the family may occur as the formerly obese person becomes more assertive and independent, as he or she learns and tries out new social roles. Interpersonal and marital problems often can be anticipated and addressed.

If you find a client who has a disturbed body image, who plans in detail every eating experience, is intensely preoccupied with a sense of food and becomes extremely anxious over even a small weight gain, you should consider clinical assessment to rule out any serious psychopathological disorder. There may be feelings in society today that people who are overweight are somehow "strange" and mentally imbalanced. Silverstone (1982), Mendelson (1982), and others conclude that the prevalence of neuroticism and psychoticism is no greater in obese than non-obese persons and that one can expect obese individuals to vary in their emotional health as much as a normal-weighted population. Leon et al. (1979), in a study of the massively obese, demonstrated the addictive nature of eating patterns in these individuals, using the McAndrew scale from the MMPI. Because food consumption is a continuous, strongly learned pattern, client issues such as the decision-making process, the commitment to change, the problem behavior, and the development of effective self-control techniques are important to the therapist.

It is impossible to anticipate, much less discuss, all the possibilities when you are considering a client as a potential candidate for the treatment of a weight problem. However, one question "new" hypnotherapists often bring up is, "What about tests of hypnotizability?" Cohen (1984) reviews data from a survey of a group of experienced clinicians and concludes that "none of the tests of hypnotizability have yet to prove their efficacy to even a significant minority of clinicians." The most important consideration is the therapeutic alliance, and many clinicians believe that the tests are not only not indicated nor helpful but that they might even produce an anti-therapeutic bias. And there is some evidence that "depth of trance" does not correlate with outcome either (Cohen, 1978).

When I have enough information to begin formulating "a theory of personality" and approach to therapy for the client, I introduce him or her to the idea that there is more than just hypnosis involved in any effective program of weight control. Usually clients are asked to keep track of their weight and body measurements on a chart. Some bibliotherapy or readings may be assigned. One effective paperback is *How to Lower Your Fat Thermostat,* by Remington, Fisher and Parent (1933), because it emphasizes the importance of exercise, is well researched and corrects many false ideas people have about dieting. A program of regular exercise is discussed, and some structure is suggested. For example, most people find that walking is the least objectionable exercise, but most experts agree that moderate exercise needs to be continued for longer than half an hour to be effective. So I recommend that in the beginning my clients walk 15 minutes out and 15 minutes back. If they are walking the same route, they can carry a "talisman" such as a rock or stick and at the end of their trip out set it down and head back. The next day they pick it up, carry it a few yards further on, set it down and head back. By giving instructions, you can help the client gain control over the amount of time he or she exercises or the amount of effort put into the exercise or both.

Next, the idea that self-hypnosis will be an important part of the program is introduced. The rationale for clients is that self-hypnosis will help them learn new habits of behavior more quickly and gain the ability to manage deprivation feelings. "The need to define, execute, and maintain effective control over deprivation feelings has been singled out as the major factor in the therapeutic success or failure in the correcting or modifying habituation disorders" (Reaney, 1984). After discussion and definition of deprivation in relation to eating, Assagioli (1970) suggests giving the client a small pack of cards, on each of which is lettered in bold print an "evocative word" defining an affective state that has been found to enhance feelings of well-being. These words are: will, harmony, calm, energy, relax, wisdom, enthusiasm, goodness, joy, courage, love, silence, confidence, simplicity, serenity, gratitude, patience. Clients are asked to select the words that are meaningful to them and to meditate on one or more of these words during a self-hypnosis exercise several times a day. Reaney (1984) suggests a "self-hypnotic grace before meals," in which the evocative words may be used or more direct suggestions may be made.

Besides giving a rationale for hypnosis and the use of self-hypnosis, the therapist should correct any misconceptions clients may have about hypnosis. They need to understand that no one can take over their mind; they will remain in control; hypnosis is not sleep; it is a form of special concentration and a normal kind of experience so that they should not expect anything bizarre. I also make the point that in dealing with habits the depth of trance is not important and that, with practice, nearly anyone can do what is necessary to achieve the goals.

Beginning the Therapeutic Encounter

Until this time you, the therapist, have been a relatively passive note taker and question asker. As you begin to discuss the elements of a proposed program and move into a description of hypnosis, be sensitive to the fact that you are moving to the foreground in your client's consciousness and beginning to direct his or her attention more actively. As this occurs, a veteran therapist will often recognize that the client is experiencing trance and choose to use that experience. My bias is that the induction should be part of the therapeutic encounter, not a separate entity. If you notice that your client is in a trance, you may want to attempt to "anchor" the experience as described by Lankton (1980). This is a process of providing a stimulus that will become deliberately associated with a particular experience, in this case, the trance. Simply shifting the tone of your voice and saying, "You can experience that again also" may be enough of an anchor to help your client retrieve the experience when, at a later time, you shift your voice to the same tone and use a similar phrase. If "anchoring" can be done naturally and within the context of your preparatory talk, then the fact that a portion of what you did is out of your client's consciousness is to therapeutic advantage.

During this preparatory talk, you may also set about deliberately including a trance using a conversational induction. Here is an example:

You're right, your mind can work on more than one thing at a time. Have you ever had the experience of finding yourself in your driveway with your car keys in your hands? Or the lights go up in a theatre; it was a good play or show and you had to kind of shake yourself to get re-oriented? Or maybe you've been reading or watching a television show when someone has tapped you on the shoulder and said, "Haven't you heard a word of what I have been saying?" (keep at it until you get a positive response). Notice each time you did that you were thinking about something, concentrating on it. But that's what hypnosis is. It's a special kind of concentration and people go into trance many times a day. It's a natural kind of thing. They just don't always use it. And now you're going to use it to do something that you want to do very much. Learn a new habit, a new way of eating, of feeling your body, of moving. Think of your mind for a moment as a television set. You can turn the selector and tune in one channel, but there are always a lot of other channels going on at the same time. You've got a top part of your mind and a bottom part of your mind; a conscious and an unconscious. (But gear this to the sophistication level of your client.) You can do many things at once. For example, there was a time when you didn't know how to walk. You learned how to walk (foreshadowing an "early learning set" [Erickson, 1978] if you choose to use it). Over your lifetime of experience, you have learned to do many things. You can walk through your house with the lights out and pick up your toothbrush and brush your teeth (foreshadowing symptoms substitution if desired). You have many habits, and you can learn new habits and forget old habits. You can learn to eat in a new way or in an old way and enjoy bending, stretching, moving, the feel of muscles sliding over muscle, to do some new things or old things.

Many clients will be in a trance at this point, and you may ratify it in a number of different ways. Simply stating, "You know you're in a trance, don't you?" is an effective double bind (Erickson, 1979). The fact that some clients move in and out of trance throughout a session should not be of concern and can even increase the effectiveness of the work that is done with them. Keep in mind that clinically hypnotic depth tends to increase with experience. Kline (1982) points out that signs of increased responsiveness are found in the ease of imagery, in the ability of the client to become more quickly and deeply relaxed, and in the ease of the induction of emotional states such as calmness, confidence and strength. I have found all these things happening without having to resort to the use of artificial "deepening techniques." Clients come to therapy motivated for hypnosis and "suggestibility is determined by context" (Deyoub and Wilkie, 1980).

There are a myriad of techniques of induction offered to the clinician in the literature. Each has its own advantages and disadvantages. The "early learning set" of Erickson (1973; Erickson, Rossi, 1979) is a comfortable conversational approach that has the advantages of being both indirect and of moving quickly to developmental issues on an unconscious level. On the other hand, this procedure takes time and seems to lose some of its effectiveness with those clients who think concretely and are not "psychological minded." With these clients, an eye fixation technique, lid closure, arm levitation and other similar techniques (ASCH Syllabus, 1973; Kroger,

1977) can be more effective. They are direct techniques that allow the ratification of a trance, but they are also open to challenge by the client. Such a challenge is infrequent, but all clients are resistant at some level, and if control is an issue with the client I usually try to stay away from direct techniques of induction. Frequently, I find it useful to use the eye roll from Spiegel's Hypnotic Induction Profile (1978). While I do not use the eye roll test from the HIP as a test of hypnotizability, it does clinically allow me to judge the ability of the client to become involved and concentrate on trance work. It also creates a positive response set and has some elements of misdirection and confusion techniques in it:

> Now that you've explained to me some of the things that you are concerned with, it would seem that what you want to do has to do with your body. So, to help you focus down on your body, I would like you to do one thing on the count of 1, two things on the count of 2, and three things on the count of 3. On the count of 1, roll your eyes back in your head as far as you can, as though you were going to look out the top of your skull. On the count of 2, slowly close your eyelids over your upturned eyes and inhale from your diaphragm deeply. On the count of 3, let your eyes relax behind your lids, let your breath out and focus on a feeling of floating. It can be imaginary; and with your permission I'd like to occasionally touch your wrist like this (touch your client's wrist with your thumb and forefinger as though you were feeling for a pulse). Then I'll talk to you. Ready? Now look at me. 1. Look up...that's right. Very good. 2. Slowly close your eyes...inhale. 3. Breathe out. Eyes relaxed. All the way...just as though you're letting all the tension drain from your fingertips and toes. Now float. (Gently grasp your client's wrist at this point and lift from the arm of the chair. You may note arm levitation, deep regular breathing or trembling of the eyelids and proceed as you wish. Another more indirect way of ratifying trance is to proceed as follows [from Erickson, 1978]). The only important thing now is the activity of your unconscious mind. Your conscious mind can do whatever it wishes—talk to itself, listen to the sound of traffic, ask questions...but your pulse has changed. Your blood pressure has changed. Your breathing has changed and you're showing that relaxed concentration a hypnotic subject can show. But you don't need to pay attention to your relaxation, to your comfort. I can tell your unconscious mind that you are an excellent hypnotic subject. And whenever you need to or want to, your unconscious mind will allow you to use it, to help you become that kind of person you truly wish to be. See yourself...feel yourself...strong, slender. Now I'm going to talk to you. (This last part is often modified according to the therapeutic strategy that makes most sense for the client with whom you are working.)

Imagery and relaxation techniques, as described by Kroger and Fezler (1976), and inductions such as the "early learning set" take time, but more quickly move on therapeutic issues. For example, you can modify the "beach scene" to access feelings of well-being and health through exercise:

> (in part)...The feel of cool hard-packed sand beneath your feet as you walk. Step after step. Muscles sliding over muscles. You feel the warmth of the sun on your back. Smell and taste the salt in the air. There's a residue of it on your lips if you lick them. (Often a client at this point will lick the lips.) And now you notice your

shadow stretched out before you. Slender and vigorous. With each step that you take, your toes reach out and touch your shadow. Step after step. Muscle sliding over muscle. Rhythmically, running now...breathing deeply. There's a light sheen of sweat on your forehead. And now you slow to a walk. Your arms swinging comfortably at your sides. Your limbs feel heavy, relaxed. A cool ocean breeze cools your brow. And you're at peace. It's good to be alive. You feel strong and relaxed.

This excerpt is part of a proposed induction, in this case emphasizing the kinesthetic sense, taste and smell as channels of experience. Notice the linking up of sensory states and emotional feelings and attitudes. This kind of work can be very effective, particularly with those clients who respond readily to internal cues, or it can be used to sensitize a client to internal cues.

Trance Work

Beginning hypnotherapists are understandably concerned with induction of hypnosis as though it were a separate entity. But, with experience, induction becomes secondary to the selection and weaving of appropriate techniques into a therapeutic regime. In a very readable text, (Adelstein (1981) suggests an approach:

> There are no hard and fast rules to govern the selection of techniques, nor the sequence of techniques; only general guidelines can be offered. The first is to remember that hypnosis is no magic; like other forms of therapy, it does not always work, and even when it does, it can often be supplemented by other modalities. The use of traditional methods of therapy and the use of medications may be indicated along with the use of hypnosis, and the therapist should employ whatever seems the most appropriate at the time....Many patients seek therapy for problems that do not have an important, repressed, underlying dynamic. For these patients attenuation of affect, relearning techniques or simple direct suggestions will be the techniques of choice. Because a therapist may not always know if there are important underlying dynamics or not, before he attempts to remove a symptom he should consider at least a brief exploration via idea-motor responding....The patient is asked, "Does this symptom serve some useful purpose for you? If it were removed, would that cause you any further trouble? Are there any reasons you should not give up this symptom at this time?"

If the answers to these questions are all "no," there is no point in unnecessarily complicating the therapy. Direct suggestions for symptom substitution combined with imagery and instructions for self-hypnosis can be effective. Suggestions that require changed attitudes and a different way of understanding are also recommended and seem to have the most long-term impact. Here are some examples by Cooke and VanVogt and Reardon combined from the ASCH Syllabus (1973) to which clients have responded quite well:

> Your body already has in storage an abundance of fat. Your body has no need for additional fat. Your body is ready to use this fat that you stored up. As this fat is used, you look the way you want to look. As this fat is used you feel the way you

want to feel strong, energetic, vigorous. Because your body has no need for fat now you have no appetite for fats, sweets, and starches. Because you wish to be slender and strong...(and so on). You won't be using your stomach as a garbage disposal, but only eating when you are hungry. The strangest thing is going to happen when you're halfway through your meal. You will feel so satisfied and contented, that you won't be able to put another morsel of food into your mouth. The satisfied feeling will remain with you until the next meal. You will have no desire to eat or drink between meals, while watching TV, or before going to bed. Want it to happen. Expect it to happen; and it will happen. Your body is your best friend, so don't treat it like an enemy. But you can substitute your relaxation for your fattening, junky food. By controlling the muscles of your arm and your hand you can control everything you put into your mouth. Food is no longer so important to you.

For the teaching of self-hypnosis, I like to use the three-part meditation technique of Spiegel and Spiegel (1978). The client is given instructions to enter a state of focused concentration on three statements that are essentially a syllogism: 1) for my body, not for me, overeating is a poison; 2) I need my body to live; 3) I give my body this respect and protection. The client is then asked to consider what this means to him or her in a special sense and to have a vivid fantasy or image. Unlike the conscious mind which uses words, the unconscious mind uses a language of imagery, sensation and feeling. So to change one's habits effectively, the message needs to be translated into the language of the unconscious mind. Most clients seem to appreciate this kind of explanation, and it makes their work more effective. Brief images or "scenes," based on topics taken from the patient's history that seem relevant, are important in getting him or her started.

For example, one woman, who had been a dancer as a young child and who was currently signed up for an aerobics class, was told that she could "feel the chalked grip of her hand on the brass barre. You open your mind's eye and see yourself in a black leotard, reflected in mirrors around the room. You have the whole room to yourself. As you lift a leg and touch the barre, bending, stretching, you lower your leg (and so the imagery continues in an exercise room until she becomes conscious of the sound of music, lets go of the barre, begins to dance, music rises to a crescendo and she finds herself in the center of the room perspiring, feeling loose and relaxed. The door opens. Someone special looks at her, smiles and says 'how good you look, how strong you are.')" In this case, the woman later told me that at home she was writing messages on a pad to herself (notes on the meditation) and was "dancing them out...it felt good...to control myself is to control my appetites," she said. Notice how she modified the instructions given to her for self-hypnosis and used them in a larger context.

If you question your clients afterwards as to what their experience was and how they used it, you will almost always find deviations and modifications on what you "thought" you had communicated and they had learned. This is healthy. By the very fact that your clients have sought you out, you know they are motivated to make positive changes in their lives. Sometimes, too, they will give you wisdom that you can pass on to other clients. Some years ago, two of my clients independently reported a modification of the self-hypnosis exercise I had prescribed that I have since found very useful. Later on, I did see the same general idea reported in a journal. Basically, it goes like this:

> The fat thermostat: when you awaken in the morning. Before you move while you're still in that relaxed twilight zone somehow step back, walk down, float down deep inside yourself until you come to a place where there's a doorway through which you step into a control room. For some, it's made of bricks and iron, for others perhaps of stainless steel and plastic. It really doesn't matter but you notice gauges, levers, dials and rheostats. And now you notice one labeled energy and your hand reaches out, turns it, pushes it higher and higher. You can feel the metabolic engines rumble. They begin to burn up increasing amounts of unnecessary, unwanted fat. And now you notice one labeled energy and your hand reaches out, turns it, pushes it higher and higher. You can feel the metabolic engines rumble. They begin to burn up increasing amounts of unnecessary, unwanted fat. And now you notice one labeled appetite and your hand reaches out, pulls, turns it down, down until you only have the urge to eat enough to keep (amount of weight desired) pounds of yourself alive. And now in the center of the controls you see something like a box with a dial on the top and underneath is labeled "fat thermostat" and your hand reaches out and turns it down, moving the set point down so all of the activities, the processes come together in a balance five pounds less than what you weighed the day before, turning it down (number) down, (number), etc). You feel deeply pleased with yourself and this experience stays with you throughout the day (have the client leave the room, go back "upstairs" where they open their eyes and feel refreshed and alert).

Direct suggestions assume an uncomplicated client with straightforward motivation and low levels of any underlying resistance. I haven't come across many such clients in my practice. For this reason, the use of indirect suggestions and metaphors should nearly always be part of treatment plans. "A uniformly startling revelation to many therapists who have learned to induce and stabilize hypnotic states is that they do not have an understanding of how best to make treatment interventions in the trance once it has been established. Once the idea of using direct suggestions has been surrendered, what then?" (Lankton and Lankton, 1983). The use of multiple level communications, metaphor, paradox, symptom prescription, double binds and other Ericksonian techniques offers a methodology that either circumvents resistance or, in some cases, uses it. Both the description and application of these techniques are included in many of the works cited at the end of this chapter.

Termination

If possible, I try to provide the client, at the end of an interview, with an "anchor" that will in the future help him or her retrieve the experiences, suggestions, and commitments from the work just done. As mentioned earlier, an anchor is "any stimulus that evokes a consistent response pattern from a person" (Lankton, 1980). Because of the nature of overeating and the frequent emphasis in clients on their own "hand to mouth behavior", I frequently use the following protocol to achieve an anchor experience:

> . . .Consider that most of the things you do in life have to take into account other considerations or other people, but in your eating behavior you're in business for youself and by controlling the muscles of your arm and your hand you control everything you put into your mouth and so you learn a new gesture, a gesture of respect for your body. In a moment, one of your hands, arm, I don't know which one, perhaps the one that feels lighter than the other one, lifts from the arm of the chair. And your hand is drawn toward your face, not carrying poison to your mouth but in a gesture of respect. Your fingertips brush the side of your mouth, your cheek, as though you were brushing back a strand of hair. But when your fingertips touch your cheek you have a deep feeling of confidence, confidence in yourself. You will never overeat again. Never underexercise again. One of your hands lifting now, breaking contact with the arm of the chair. As though your fingers are drawn to your face by invisible strings, closer, you don't know just when they'll touch but when they do there's a deep feeling of confidence (and so on until the fingers touch the cheek), a deep feeling of calmness and confidence. You need never overeat again. Hold that feeling. Hold it tight in that hand. Let those fingers curl into a fist now. Every time you make that fist you can re-experience your confidence, confidence in yourself. Open your eyes. Look at your fist. You have learned more today than you know. And it will be even easier next time. You can be deeply pleased with yourself. Feel refreshed and alert. Let me feel your hands. They're warm.

Several different things are going on here. We ratify the trance by giving opportunity for an arm levitation (if it does not occur, do not worry, just reach over and lift the arm or ask the client to "go ahead and lift it" quite openly; the important thing is to complete the gesture). We have a modification of hand to mouth behavior that moves away from the satisfaction of oral needs to good feelings and confidence building. I've had clients tell me later that just making a fist throughout the day helped them access feelings of confidence in all kinds of situations. Finally, there's the important suggestion that the client will do it even better and learn more next time. Depending on circumstances, any of these areas could be added to or modified with a particular client.

Continuing the Work

Weight loss does not occur in a smooth curve, and if you prepare your client for the fact that there will be setbacks and unevenness in progress you will be ahead of the game. By reinforcing your gains with ego-building techniques and using behavior modification procedures, you should see continuing progress. However, when it does not occur, clinical re-evaluation of the client and situations should be done. In fact, you should continually be revising your personality theory for each client.

Some clients request the use of tapes. I generally resist those clients initially, on the grounds that if they "listen to my voice" they will not be listening to their own inner voice. That's where the real work of self-hypnosis is done. If the client insists, I do provide a tape, and some clients have done well and testified to the usefulness of tapes.

The number of sessions and length of time that therapy continues depend on many factors. Unfortunately, unless the client has a liberal insurance policy, financial considerations frequently play a large part in determining the number of sessions you can plan for with the client. Three to six sessions are the usual range, with the ideal of a follow-up session in six months. If this is not possible, you can ask clients to send you postcards in the mail with their name, a number that represents their weight or waist size, a simple communication on how they are getting along, perhaps even just a smiling face or a frown. Phone call follow-ups on these cards can be very rewarding and give you the opportunity of doing "telephone inductions" and the revivification of suggestions (another topic entirely).

By outlining a therapy session, I have presented some techniques and considerations that are central to therapeutic work with obese clients. Mine is not the only way of working with clients, nor are these suggestions and recommendations meant to constitute a "theory of therapy" in working with obese clients. Rather, I hope that beginning and intermediate therapists will find attitudes here as well as specific recommendations that will make his or her work with obese clients more effective and rewarding.

References

Assagoli R: The Technique of Evocative Words. P.F.R. Issue No. 25. Psychosynthesis Research Foundation, 1970

Cohen SB: Tests of susceptibility/hypnotizability. In Wester WC, Smith AH (eds): Clinical Hypnosis: A Multidisciplinary Approach. Philadelphia, JB Lippincott, 1984

Cohen N, Murray A: Locus of control as a predictor of outcome in treatment of obesity. Psychological Reports 4:805, 1978

Cook CE, VanVogt AE: The Hypnotism Handbook. Alhambra, CA, Borden Publishing, 1956

Deyoub PL, Wilkie R: Suggestions with and without hypnotic induction in a weight reduction program. Int J Clin Expn Hypn 28:333, 1980

Edelstein MG: Trauma, Trance and Transformation. New York, Brunner/Mazel, 1981

Erickson M: An induction technique. In A Syllabus On Hypnosis and a Handbook on Therapeutic Suggestions. Chicato, The American Society of Clinical Hypnosis—Education and Research Foundation, 1973

Erickson M, Rossi E: Hypnotherapy: An Exploratory Casebook. New York, Irvington, 1979

Goldstein Y: The effect of demonstrating to a subject that she is in a trance as a variable in hypnotic interventions with obese women. Int J Clin Exp Hypn 29:15, 1981

Hartland J: Medical and Dental Hypnosis, 2nd ed. Baltimore, The Williams and Wilkins Company, 1971

Kline MV: Hypnotherapy in the treatment of obesity. In Wolman BB (ed): Psychological Aspects of Obesity: A Handbook. New York, Van Nostrand Reinhold, 1982

Kroger WS: Clinical and Experimental Hypnosis. Philadelphia, JB Lippincott, 1977

Kroger WS, Fezler WD: Hypnosis and Behavior Modification: Imagery Conditioning. Philadelphia, JB Lippincott, 1976

Lankton S: Practical Magic. Capistrano, CA, Meta Publication, 1980

Lankton SR, Lankton CH: The Answer Within: A Clinical Framework of Ericksonian Hypnotherapy. New York, Brunner/Mazel, 1983

Leon GR: Personality and behavioral correlates of obesity. In Wolman BB (ed): Psychological Aspects of Obesity: A Handbook. New York, Van Nostrand Reinhold, 1982

Leon GR, Kolotkin R, Korgeski G: MacAndrew addiction scale and other MMPI characteristics associated with obesity, anorexia, and smoking behavior. Addictive Behaviors 4:401, 1979

Mendelson M quoted in Leon GR: Personality and behavioral correlates of obesity. In Wolman BB (ed): Psychological Aspects of Obesity: A Handbook. New York, Van Nostrand Reinhold, 1982

Mott T, Roberts J: Obesity and hypnosis: A review of the literature. Am J Clin Hypn 22:3, 1979

Reaney JB: Hypnosis in the treatment of habit disorders. In Wester WC, Smith AH (eds): Clinical Hypnosis: A Multidisciplinary Approach. Philadelphia, JB Lippincott, 1984

Remington D, Fisher G, Parent E: How to Lower Your Fat Thermostat. Provo, UT, Vitality House International, Inc., 1983

Rodin J: Obesity: Why the losing battle. In Wolman BB (ed): Psychological Aspects of Obesity: A Handbook. New York, Van Nostrand Reinhold, 1982

Sarbin TR, Slagle RW: Hypnosis and psychophysiological outcomes. In Fromm E, Shor RE (eds): Hypnosis: Developments in Research and New Perspectives, 2nd ed. New York, Aldine Publishing Company, 1979

Silverstone JT quote in Leon GR: Personality and behavioral correlates of obesity. In Wolman BB (ed): Psychological Aspects of Obesity: A Handbook. New York, Van Nostrand Reinhold, 1982

Spiegel H, Spiegel D: Trance and Treatment: Clinical Uses of Hypnosis. New York, Basic Books, 1978

The American Society of Clinical Hypnosis—Education and Research Foundation. A Syllabus on Hypnosis and a Handbook of Therapeutic Suggestions. Chicago, 1973

Udolf R: Handbook of Hypnosis for Professionals. New York, Van Nostrand Reinhold Company, 1981

Wadden TA, Anderton CH: The clinical use of hypnosis. Psych Bull 91:215, 1982

UNIT THREE
SPECIALIZED APPLICATIONS OF HYPNOSIS

16 HYPNOSIS IN CLINICAL NEUROLOGY

THOMAS L. FEHER, M.D.

Hypnosis is a form of communication. Gaining and maintaining the subject's attention is of paramount importance for successful hypnosis to take place (Davidson and Coleman, 1977). But many patients afflicted with neurological dysfunction have, as part of their dysfunction, deficits in their communication and/or attending abilities; there are, of course, many neurological disorders in which these higher functions remain intact. This chapter will discuss the various neurological dysfunctions for which hypnosis may be of value in improving the clinical status of the patient and point out some of the difficulties of treatment with ways of circumventing these difficulties.

The areas where hypnosis has been used in neurology are broad and include many of the more frequently seen conditions (Table 16-1). However, the degree of effectiveness in these conditions is difficult to ascertain. The literature contains a little information, and much of what is presented consists of case reports and empirical data (Chiasson, 1984; Crasilneck and Hall, 1985; Kroger, 1975; Panov, 1969); essentially, there are no controlled trials of hypnosis in neurological dysfunction. Therefore, although we refer to the literature, much of what is reported represents the author's own experience in his clinical practice.

Pain

Much has been written on the use of hypnosis in treating pain, and there is a chapter on that subject elsewhere in this text. The reader can review this material and that from other sources (Crue, 1983; Elton, 1979; Hilgard and Hilgard, 1975; Pinsky, 1983; Sacerdote, 1973; Savitz, 1983; Spiegel,1983; Toomey and Sanders, 1983; Wadden and Anderton, 1982), as the presentation here is brief and generalized. Nonetheless, the neurologist sees many patients with a wide variety of painful complaints, this author more than most by virtue of 11 years as director of a pain control center.

The approach to pain is variable, and, particularly if the problem is of long standing, lasting success rarely occurs if attention is focused merely on the physical symptom and neglects consideration of emotional, social, economic and other **199**

Table 16-I. Neurological Conditions in Which Hypnosis May be of Value

I. Pain
    Headache
    Radicular pain
    Neuropathy
    Arachnoiditis
    Neoplastic pain
    Neuralgia
    Atypical facial pain
    Muscle spasm
    Phantom or deafferentation pain

II. Spasticity
    Cerebral palsy
    Spinal cord injury
    Stroke
    Head injury
    Multiple sclerosis
    Other neurodegenerative processes

III. Movement Disorders
    Tremor
    Tics
    Torticollis
    Blepharospasm
    Basal Ganglia disorders
    Writer's cramp

IV. Seizures

V. Hyperkinetic Disorders

VI. Speech/Swallowing Dysfunction

VII. Other Conditions (In which non-specific effects of hypnosis might improve function)
    Multiple sclerosis
    Myasthenia gravis
    Seizures
    Narcolepsy
    Heim-syndromes
    Hemiparesis
    Nerve Palsies
    Neuropathies
    Motor neuron disease

factors. Similarly, our approach tends to include the use of hypnosis as *one* of the tools the patient learns to use. He is encouraged to employ other techniques and the help of other members of the pain treatment team to help regain control of his symptoms and often the various aspects of his life inevitably affected in any chronic pain syndrome (De Piano and Salzberg, 1979; Kellner, 1975; Kline, 1979). These techniques may include the use of biofeedback, counseling, body mechanics training, a physical therapy or aerobics program, devices such as TENS (Transcutaneous Electric Nerve Stimulator), medication adjustment, vocational or goal planning activities and considerable education about pain and the myriad factors that can influence its perception and duration.

On the other hand, if the pain is of shorter duration or an approach such as the one described above is not necessary or appropriate, we tend to use hypnosis in the manner described elsewhere in this text, although always considering the possibility that some of the above techniques might be of value.

Spasticity

Any disease of destructive process affecting the central nervous system can bring about spasticity as a significant symptom. Often this symptom is severe enough to seriously hamper mobility, interfere with the process of rehabilitation, or even render a limb useless even though sufficient motor power is present otherwise to allow it to function. Spasticity can also hamper adequate sphincter control and thereby significantly diminish effective functional abilities. Most of the available drugs used to treat spasticity, such as benzodiazepines, baclofen and dantrolene, leave sedation, tolerance, serious side-effects and limited effectiveness to be contended with. Here hypnosis can be very useful (Chappel, 1964). Simply reducing tone sufficiently to allow for increased range of motion can make an enormous difference in the patient's ability to care for himself or to be cared for. Skin care can become less difficult: transfers, dressing and other simple activities may become less of a chore.

Working with children who have cerebral palsy can be particularly rewarding; the techniques are simple and the rewards in terms of potential functional improvement are great (Gardner and Olness, 1981; Secter and Gelberd, 1964; Spankus and Freeman, 1962). We have worked with physical therapists teaching them hypnotic techniques that can be used even with pre-verbal and non-verbal children to bring about striking reduction of muscle tone during therapy sessions, and these techniques can in turn be taught to parents for treatment at home.

A further benefit from the use of hypnotic training in patients with spasticity is that most can learn to use these techniques successfully themselves and thereby increase their sense of self-mastery; this feeling is often either lacking or very limited in their lives. Even when self-hypnosis is not possible, the family or care-givers can be trained and bring about for the patient a feeling of control close to home.

Movement Disorders

Neurological dysfunctions which are movement disorders can have a particularly broad group of manifestations and degrees of severity. At best, a movement disorder can be nothing more than an annoyance (either to the patient or to those around him); at worst, it can bring about a degree of helplessness that is devastating. Of all the movement disorders, the one drawing the most attention in hypnosis literature is an unusual one, the syndrome of Gilles de la Tourette (Crasilneck and Hall, 1985; Erickson, 1963; Lindner and Stevens, 1967).

Many movement disorders are much more commonplace and respond well to hypnosis as either a primary or adjunctive form of therapy (Smith, 1979; Spithill, 1984; Stein, 1980). Patients with benign tremor, torticollis, writer's cramp, blepharospasm and simple ties have proved particularly rewarding to work with. Conversely, patients with Parkinson's disease (Crasilneck and Hall, 1985), one of the most common extrapyramidal disorders, have done considerably less well, perhaps because the author tends not to use hypnosis as long as the response to medication is satisfactory; by the time the patient becomes refractory to drugs there may be a degree of cognitive dysfunction present sufficiently severe to mitigate the effectiveness of hypnosis as a treatment.

The author has worked with only one patient with Huntington's disease (Moldawsky, 1984), with a moderate reduction in the severity of the involuntary movements on a short-term basis. But this is a progressive disease, and when the dementia which occurs becomes significant the effectiveness of hypnosis may become minimal.

Seizures

There is literature on the use of hypnosis in seizure disorders, much of it related to the treatment of pseudo-seizures, and as an adjunct to distinguish the latter from true seizures (Glen and Simonds, 1977; Gross, 1979; Guberman, 1982; Mostofsky and Balaschak, 1977; Owen-Flood, 1952; Peterson, 1950; Spiegel, 1983). In this author's and other neurologists' experience, most patients who have pseudo-seizures have true seizures as well; in addition, some patients with only "true" seizures can have significant psychopathology. Some patients with epilepsy use their seizure disorders in a very manipulative manner, using either self-induction of seizures or medication non-compliance to produce seizures for a secondary gain. Psychotherapeutic techniques, with or without hypnosis, are an important aspect of treating these patients. On the other hand, there are patients, particularly those with partial complex seizures and those with a clear aura or a progression ("march") of symptoms, who can be trained in hypnotic techniques that may decrease their seizure frequency and/or reduce the amount or types of medication necessary for control. The technique that appears to provide the most success is by post-hypnotic suggestion and training to trigger the induction of trance by the occurrence of the earliest recognizable symptom of the seizure.

Another group of seizure patients who often benefit from the use of hypnosis are the patients whose seizure control becomes more tenuous during times of stress (Kroger, 1977; Maher-Loughnan, 1980). These patients become much easier to maintain in a seizure-free state if they successfully learn self-hypnosis as part of a stress management program. Obviously, hypnosis in no way precludes the appropriate use of an adequate medication regime.

As a warning, we must say that the diagnosis of "pseudo-seizures" is one which should only be made after extensive evaluation neurologically, including, if possible, electroencephalographic telemetry under closed-circuit television monitoring. Interictal EEGs can be negative in a significant percentage (15-20 percent) of patients with bona fide seizure disorders (Prensky and Coben, 1984). The clinical manifestation of the seizure may be atypical in the extreme, and the circumstances surrounding the seizure may look "made to order" for a behaviorally mediated display; nonetheless, the seizure may be genuine.

Hyperkinetic Disorders

There are children seen by practitioners because of complaints of excessive activity, difficulty with concentration, disruptive behavior and other similar problems. Often, these children have learning difficulties as well. The behavior may be primarily school-related; at times, it is more evident in the home environment. When such behavior is present to a significant degree, it makes these children pariahs in most social situations and sometimes the bane of their family's existence.

Many etiologies have been suggested to explain this behavior, including dietary factors, environmental causes, "minimal brain dysfunction," specific attentional abnormalities, family dynamics and other causes. The problem is that of trying to give a single identity to multiple conditions. By careful assessment of the complaint, which involves not only attention to the child and his behaviors but a realistic assessment of the home and school situation, one can sort out the factors involved.

Often, a more longitudinal approach is appropriate, to assess behavior over a greater period of time and to develop an accurate baseline from which changes can be more readily measured. This approach involves cooperative effort on the part of parents, teachers, school nurses and/or psychologists, and the treating practitioner. Frequently, behavioral and other "psychological" approaches can produce very rewarding results. Sometimes it is necessary to use medications as well, but the percentage of children who actually require these is relatively small. Having a baseline of measured behaviors is particularly valuable, for the child can be given alternating trials of medication and placebo on a "blind" basis and behavioral changes can be observed and compared with baseline data.

Sugar and dietary additives are often suggested as potential etiologic factors, but studies to date seem to indicate that these have little if any influence.

Hypnosis can be a useful adjunctive treatment in the care of children with such behavioral problems, and reports of the successful use of this technique are present in the literature (Crasilneck and Hall, 1985; Gardner and Olness, 1981; Illovsky and Fredman, 1976). However, with the diagnostic confusion noted above, a certain degree of reservation must be maintained regarding the condition for which the child is being treated.

Speech and Swallowing Disorders

Another group of neurologic disorders include the aphasic or dysphasic syndromes, the dysarthrias and the various forms of dysphagia. There is little information on these areas in the hypnosis literature; there are reports of usefulness of hypnosis in stuttering and other similar speech disorders (Smith, 1979), and some case study reports on its use in functional swallowing disorders, but for the neurologic patient who has his disability on the basis of actual brain injury the contribution from the literature is minimal (Crasilneck and Hall, 1970, 1985; Kroger, 1977; Magonet, 1961). We are currently assessing hypnotizability as related to specific areas of neurological damage, but insufficient data have been collected to warrant even preliminary conclusions.

Obviously, when a patient has a severe deficit in comprehension, our ability to make therapeutic suggestions is significantly hampered. Our experience is that these patients can enter into an apparent hypnotic state, or at least one of deep relaxation and immobility, and come out of that state at an appropriate cue. However, we cannot say that any significant improvement of their communication deficit occurred because of this or, in fact, that they were truly in hypnosis. On the other hand, when comprehension is less significantly affected, many of these patients are well able to respond to therapeutic suggestions. Again, one needs to be very cautious in interpreting whether any change occurs as a result of the suggestions or is merely a reflection of the normal rehabilitative process. Essentially, all of the patients seen were involved in an ongoing rehabilitation program. It appears that the more non-specific results of hypnosis, that is, a reduction in anxiety and an increased feeling of self-mastery, were as much related to clinical gains as to any specific suggestions.

Most patients with dysarthria have no significant problems with comprehension. If the dysarthria is related to pseudobulbar palsy, cognitive loss or attentional disturbances are sometimes present, and little obvious response to the induction may be noted. On the other hand, the remainder of the patient group all showed some ability to respond to suggestion, and the speech pathologist felt that the gains made in breath control and intelligibility of speech were faster and more easily accomplished in this group than was usual. But there was no attempt to set up any type of formal study and the patients *were* involved in an intensive rehabilitation program.

Patients with dysphagia proved to be a most interesting group to use hypnosis with, although the results were often frustratingly transient. There were, of course, some patients who had such severe dysfunctions that feeding enterostomies were put in place and considered permanent early in their course of treatment. There were six other patients, however, who had extensive evaluations for their swallowing difficulties which persisted considerably beyond the point at which on a clinical basis effective swallowing could have begun to return. Two of the patients eventually proved to have dyskinesias of their swallowing apparatus and required continuation of their feeding jejunostomies. For the other four, no reason for their persistent difficulties could be found. Three of the four were young head-injured patients with brain stem and diffuse hemispheric involvement. Although operating at a reduced cognitive level, they were unable to respond to hypnotherapeutic techniques often used with young children, that is, playing "let's pretend" or getting involved in a story told by the operator (Levine, 1980). The fourth patient was a middle-aged male recovering from an anoxic encephalopathy secondary to a cardiac arrest. He was able to respond at least to the point of quieting down when working with the author, but no progress could be made in his difficulty with swallowing. The three youngsters improved to the point of getting all their nutrition orally, although with two of the three eating was an extremely slow process.

Other Neurological Conditions

Other neurological conditions are reported to be or are potentially amenable to improvement with the use of hypnosis. Some of the reports are single case studies which are of great interest if reproducible results can be obtained by others, such as Chiasson's (1984) report of obtaining eye closure with a Bell's palsy patient. Others are frankly questionable, not whether the operator perceived the reported response, but whether the degree to which recovery occurred was on some basis other than the neuropathologic process involved. Some results reported with patients with multiple sclerosis would rival the miracles at Lourdes, and one must suspect that significant underlying anxiety, hysteria or some other psychopathology responded rather than the underlying disease.

There is certainly, however, considerable potential for benefit in using hypnosis with multiple sclerosis patients (Crasilneck and Hall, 1985; Kroger, 1977; Spiegel, 1933), but the benefit is more realistically to be expected over the longitudinal course of the disease. Fewer and less severe exacerbations are noted in many multiple sclerosis patients who have learned to use hypnosis; also, lessening muscle tone (see section on spasticity) can have benefits in the form of increased functional ability. The problem with trying to draw conclusions about clinical improvement in a disease process with as variable a clinical presentation and course as multiple sclerosis is that there is no way of conclusively determining clinically that the treatment produced the observed outcome. As more becomes known about the underlying immunologic aspects of this disease, it may become possible to study the results more objectively.

Myasthenia gravis is mentioned only theoretically. Crasilneck and Hall (1985) discuss it in passing, but the author was unable to find any specific reports in the literature on the use of hypnosis in this disease and has had no opportunity to use hypnosis with any myasthenic patients. However, this disease is clearly on a neuro-immunologic basis, and the opportunity to alter the clinical and immunologic picture is important to consider (Adlercreutz et al., 1982; Behan and Spreafico, 1984). Myasthenia gravis is by no means a common disease, but most university teaching hospitals have such patients, and possibilities for a well-controlled study exist.

Narcolepsy falls under the category of hypersomnolent sleep disorders; traditionally the syndrome includes paroxysmal bouts of sleep, cataplexy, sleep paralysis and hypnagogic hallucinations. Although the author has not used hypnosis with any of his narcoleptic patients, there is one report in the recent literature indicating a beneficial response to hypnosis, at least for the treatment of sleep paralysis (Nardi, 1982). Whether other aspects of this syndrome would be responsive to hypnosis has not been determined.

Hemipareses and other so-called "hemisyndromes" are most often the result of strokes, although head injury, tumor and other neurologic catastrophes can also produce these syndromes (Cedercreutz et al., 1976; Johnson and Korn, 1980; Milos, 1975). Hypnosis has been used adjunctively in the rehabilitation of these patients and reports have shown enhanced performance in therapies and better functional improvement in groups in which hypnosis was used (Allen, 1984; Crasilneck and Hall, 1970, 1985, Speigel, 1983; Vodovnik et al., 1979). In the author's experience as well, hypnosis appears to produce some beneficial effect with these patients. However, the impression (which is currently being tested in a controlled clinical trail) is that right hemisphere injured patients have more difficulty undergoing trance induction than patients with left hemispheric damage. Probably this process can be further localized to more specific areas of brain injury, and this is the goal of the study.

There are two more groups of neurological diseases that should be commented upon before the practical aspects of methodology with neurological patients are discussed. The first are the neuropathies, of which there are many, of different etiologies. Every effort to discover the specific etiology of the neuropathy and to treat it specifically should be made. Nonetheless, the etiology often remains obscure, and even when it is known, treatment results may be disappointing. This author has never proved objectively that hypnosis significantly affected nerve function in his patients, but the response to hypnosis of the more subjective complaints of numbness, paresthesias, dyasthesias and other sensory symptoms can be very gratifying, affording at least partial relief from these complaints and often allowing for the return of an undisturbed night's sleep when other inducements have failed. Again, using hypnosis does not preclude other attempts at treatment that might be useful, such as TENS, medication therapy, etc.

A last group of patients are those with motor neuron disease. Again, Chiasson (1984) has reported some encouraging results with the use of hypnosis. This author has not had the opportunity to use hypnosis with any such patients, but he would not hesitate to recommend its use; there are no alternative successful therapies yet. Even if the only result proves to be non-specific, that is, relaxation of muscle tone, reduction of anxiety, and increased feelings of self-control and self-mastery, that response would be worthwhile in a disease with such a dismal outlook.

Case Studies

1. P.R., a 38-year-old T-7 paraparetic female, was seen because of persistent severe spasms in her legs, sufficiently severe to interfere with her transfers, wake her from sleep, and, most distressing for the patient, cause her to be fearful of attempting any sexual activity. She had been tried on multiple spasmolytic agents, including diazepam, dantrolene and baclofen, without any appreciable lessening of symptoms, even at dosage levels which produced significant sedation. Although the patient had intermittent urinary tract infections, no other genito-urinary pathology was present and the symptoms were present even in the presence of sterile urine.

   The patient responded well to a simple reverse levitation induction and proved to be an excellent hypnotic subject. She was able to visualize herself floating effortlessly in a soothing warm pool of water, which relaxed all of her muscles completely. This visualization was extremely effective in decreasing her muscle tone, and she was able to perform a transfer successfully while in trance. Subsequent training in self-hypnosis enabled her to utilize her skills to achieve the necessary results.

   An important note is that a prior attempt (by a psychologist seeing the patient) at muscle relaxation under hypnosis using a progressive relaxation type of approach was unsuccessful and frustrating for the patient because of the impaired sensation in her lower extremeties. She could not, in essence, tell whether her legs were relaxed or not. The more successful approach made use of a more diffuse sensation of relaxation, which was well within the patient's impaired abilities.

2. F.L., a 19-year-old boy, had suffered from a mixed form of seizure disorder since early childhood. His major motor seizures were well-controlled on hydantoin, but he also suffered from partial complex epilepsy which had been resistant to treatment with a number of anticonvulsant combinations, even at near-toxic levels. He was understandably upset, not just because of the seizures themselves, but also because of the interference with his social life and, most importantly, because he was unable to get a driver's license until his seizures were in control.

His seizures always began with an aura involving the hearing of music. The melody was a familiar one to him, but he was never able to reproduce it or think of it interictally. This onset was followed by some automatisms which included lip-smacking and some vocalizations. The whole episode typically lasted 30 to 40 seconds, and the patient had as many as 12 seizures in a day. Hypnosis was induced by an eye-fixation technique, an ideomotor questioning technique was established, and the suggestion was made that he would become aware of the sound of the musical aura, but that nothing more than his awareness of the music would occur. When he indicated that he could hear the music, suggestions were made that the music would produce a feeling of great quietness, peacefulness and well-being, with that feeling growing stronger and more complete while he slowly counted up to 100 in his mind. The suggestion was also made that this feeling would come on even when the music began spontaneously, or if he should, by chance, hear the music played elsewhere. He was given instructions for practicing this sequence of events on his own, and these instructions were repeated after the hypnosis session was terminated.

The patient became very facile at using this technique, with excellent results. He was able to modify it over a period of time so that he eventually did not need to count, but could trigger the desired result merely by taking a deep breath at the onset of the aura. He continued to need medication with multiple agents, but the dosages were reduced considerably.

3. J.A. was a 19-year-old college student near the end of her freshman year when she was struck by an automobile and suffered multiple severe injuries, including a severe closed head injury. After a stormy hospital course which included a prolonged coma, the patient finally became more aware of her environment and able to participate actively in an intensive rehabilitation program. Although she had a spastic quadriparesis with superimposed extrapyramidal and cerebellar signs, she progressed to a degree of mobility that ensured her ability to be cared for at home without skilled nursing. She was able to communicate effectively, and though she showed cognitive impairment and some emotional lability, she was

generally pleasant and cooperative. However, she could not progress to oral feedings. Careful assessment by appropriate members of the rehabilitation staff and multiple consultant physicians, testing by roentgenographic and manometric studies, all failed to produce an etiology; the mechanism for effective swallowing was there, but when food was placed in her mouth, she would chew it and move it around in her mouth but would not swallow it. In desperation, hypnosis was tried. Prior psychometric and behavioral assessments had indicated the patient was effectively functioning at a five to six-year-old cognitive level, and induction was designed to be effective at that age level. The patient was asked to pretend that she was a beautiful princess who had gone on a unicorn hunt and become lost, and considerable time was spent having her walking through the woods "getting tireder and tireder, hungrier and hungrier" until she finally had to rest beneath a shady tree. The princess was subsequently found and awakened by the rest of the party, who had been searching for her. When they discovered her, they found her with a unicorn sleeping next to her, its head in her lap, her hand resting on its head. There was, of course, much joy throughout the kingdom, and a feast with delicious foods was prepared.

Everything went smoothly throughout the session. The "princess" closed her eyes on cue, demonstrated ready hand levitation and catelepsy to be able to rest her hand on the unicorn's head, and actually was observed to make small mouthing and licking movements when the feast was described. The jejunostomy tube feeding prior to the session had been omitted, and the session was scheduled for just before the dinner hour. The patient chewed her food vigorously with seeming relish—and spit it out. Two subsequent sessions went the same way. Finally, the author, also in desperation, decided to personally observe an actual feeding session, only to find that the staff had inadvertently been successfully using negative suggestion for weeks. There, piled high next to the dinner tray, was a stack of towels which the staff carefully unfolded, one by one, and held under the patient's chin so she would have something to spit into. The towels were gone at the next meal, and J.A. swallowed everything edible on her tray.

A Look at the Future

It is ironic that during the "golden age" of hypnosis, many of the most prominent neurologists of the time, including Charcot, Dejerine, Forel, Korsakov, Freud, Babinski and Brown-Sequard, were intimately involved in the study of hypnosis, whereas today there appears to be little interest in hypnosis on the part of neurologists (Feher, 1983). This is unfortunate not only from the point of view of the patients who could be served by hypnosis, but also from the absence of neuroscientists who could be investigating hypnosis with the vast array of tools currently available. There are some indications that relevant changes in the direction of research are taking place.

Of great interest in the study of the nervous system and those diseases which affect it is the area of immune mechanisms and their possible etiologic relationship with certain neurologic disease states (Ader, 1981; Adlercreutz et al., 1982; Behan and Spreafico, 1984; Bowers and Kelly, 1979; Kurokawa et al., 1977; Rogers et al., 1979; Sternbach, 1982). With the further discoveries in the growing field of what has been awkwardly termed psychoneuroimmunology—that is, the way in which internal and external events, working through the central nervous system, can effect changes in the immune system, and how these changes can consequently bring about either disease states on the one hand, or lessen the effect of disease states on the other—one hopes that neuroscientists will begin to systematically study processes such as hypnosis to shed much-needed light on how this intriguing aid works and brings about its remarkable effects.

References

Ader R (ed): Psychoneuroimmunology. New York, Academic Press, 1981

Adlercreutz H, Kuoppasalmi K, Narvanan S, Kosunen K, Heikkinen R: Use of hypnosis in studies of the effect of stress on cardiovascular function and hormones. Acta Med Scand (Suppl) 660:84-94, 1982

Allen BL: The Use of Hypnotherapy in the Rehabilitation of Cerebral Vascular Accident Patients. Dissertation Abstracts International 44(11), May 1984

Behan PO, Spreafico F (ed): Neuroimmunology. Serono Symposia Publications from Raven Press, Vol. 12. New York, Raven Press, 1984

Bowers KS, Kelly P: Stress, disease, psychotherapy and hypnosis. J. Abn Psychol 88:490-505, 1979

Cedercreutz C, Lahteenmaki R, Tulikoura J: Hypnotic treatment of headache and vertigo in skull injured patients. Int J Clin Exp Hypn 24:195-201, 1976

Chappel DT: Hypnosis and spasticity in paraplegia. Am J Clin Hypn 7:33-36, 1964

Chiasson SW: Hypnosis in other related medical conditions. In Wester WC, Smith AH (eds): Clinical Hypnosis: A Multidisciplinary Approach. Philadelphia, JB Lippincott Company, 1984

Crasilneck HB, Hall JA: The use of hypnosis in the rehabilitation of complicated vascular and post-traumatic neurological patients. Int J Clin Exp Hypn 28:145-159, 1970

Crasilneck HB, Hall JA: Clinical Hypnosis: Principles and Applications, 2nd ed. Orlando, Florida, Grune & Stratton, Inc., 1985

Crue BL Jr.: The peripheralist and centralist views of chronic pain. Seminars in Neurology 3(4):331-339, 1983

Davidson RJ, Goleman, DJ: The role of attention in meditation and hypnoisis: A psychobiological perspective on transformations of consciousness. Int J Clin Exp Hypn 25:291-308, 197

De Piano FA, Salzberg HC: Clinical applications of hypnosis to three psychosomatic disorders. Psychol Bull 86:1223-1235, 1979

Elton D: Hypnosis and Chronic Pain. Presented at the 8th International Congress of Hypnosis and Psychosomatic Medicine, Melbourne, Australia, August 1979

Erickson MH: Experimental hypnotherapy in Tourette's disease. Am J Clin Hypn 7:325-331, 1963

Feher TL: A neurologist looks at hypnosis. Presented at The 26th Annual Scientific Meeting of the American Society of Clinical Hypnosis, Dallas, Texas, November 1983

Gardner GG, Olness K: Hypnosis and Hypnotherapy with Children. New York, Grune and Stratton, Inc., 1981

Glenn TJ, Simonds JF: Hypnotherapy of a psychogenic seizure disorder in an adolescent. Am J Clin Hypn 19:245-250, 1977

Gross M: Hypnosis—A diagnostic tool in epilepsy. Presented at the 8th International Congress of Hypnosis and Psychosomatic Medicine, Melbourne, Australia, August 1979

Guberman A: Psychogenic pseudoseizures in non-epileptic patients. Can J Psychiatry 27:401-404, 1983

Hilgard ER, Hilgard JR: Hypnosis in the Relief of Pain. Los Altos, California, William Kaufmann, Inc., 1975

Illovsky J, Fredman N: Group suggestion in learning disabilities of primary grade children: A feasibility study. Int J Clin Exp Hypn 24:87-97, 1976

Johnson K, Dorn ER: Hypnosis and imagery in the rehabilitation of a brain-damaged patient. J Ment Imagery 4:35-39, 1980

Kellner R: Psychotherapy in psychosomatic disorders. Arch Gen Psychiatry 32:1021-1028, 1975

Kline MV: Hypnosis with specific relation to biofeedback and behavior therapy. Psychother Psychosom 31:294-300, 1979

Kroger WS: Clinical and Experimental Hypnosis, 2nd ed. Philadelphia, JB Lippincottt, 1977

Kurokawa N, Suematsu H, Tamai H, Esaki M, Aoki H, Ikemi Y: Effect of emotional stress on human growth hormone secretion. J Psychosom Res 21:231-235, 1977

Levine ES: Indirect suggestions through personalized fairy tales for treatment of childhood insomnia. Am J Clin Hypn 23:57-63, 1980

Lindner H, Stevens H: Hypnotherapy and psychodynamics in the syndrome of Gilles de la Tourette. Int J Clin Exp Hypn 15:151-155, 1967

Magonet A, Philip MD: Hypnosis in dysphagia. Int J Clin Exp Hypn 4:291-295, 1961

Maher-Loughnan GP: Clinical applications of hypnosis in medicine. Brit J Hosp Med, May 1980

Milos R: Hypnotic exploration of amnesia after cerebral injuries. Int J Clin Exp Hypn 23:103-110, 1975

Moldawsky RJ: Hypnosis as an adjunct treatment in Huntington's disease. Am J Clin Hypn 26:229-231, 1984

Mostofsky DI, Balaschak BA: Psychobiological control of seizures. Psychol Bull 84:723-750, 1977

Nardi TJ: Treating sleep paralysis with hypnosis. Int J Clin Exp Hypn 29:128-140, 1982

Owen-Flood A: Hypnotism in epilepsy. Brit J Med Hypnot 3:49, 1952

Panov AG, Lobzin VS, Belyankin VA, Kulagin YM: The use of autogenic training in neurologic practice. Zhurnal Neuropatalogii i Psikhiatrii 68:813-816, 1969

Peterson DB, Sumner JW, Jones GA: The role of hypnosis in the differentiation of epileptic from convulsive-like seizures. Am J Psychiatr 107:428-433, 1950

Pinsky JJ: Psychodynamic understanding and treatment of the chronic intractable benign pain syndrome—treatment outcome. Seminars in Neurology 3(4):346-354, 1983

Prensky AL, Coben LA: Electroencephalography. In Baker AB, Baker LH: Clinical Neurology, Vol 1. Philadelphia, Harper and Row, 1984

Rogers MP, Dubey D, Reich P: The influence of the psyche and the brain on immunity and disease susceptibility: A critical review. Psychosom Med 41:147-164, 1979

Sacerdote P: Applications of hypnotically elicited mystical states to the treatment of physical and emotional pain. Int J Clin Exp Hypn 25:309-324, 1977

Savitz SA: Hypnosis in the treatment or chronic pain. Southern Med J 76:319-321, 1983

Secter II, Gelberd MB: Hypnosis as a relaxant for the cerebral palsied patient. Am J Clin Hypn 6:364-365, 1964

Smith F: Hypnosis in the treatment of tics and stammering. Presented at The 8th International Congress of Hypnosis and Psychosomatic Medicine, Melbourne, Australia, August 1979

Spankus WH, Freeman LG: Hypnosis in cerebral palsy. Int J Clin Exp Hypn 10:135-139, 1962

Spiegal D: Hypnosis with medical/surgical patients. Gen Hosp Psychiat 5:265-277, 1983
Spithill AC: Treatment of monosynaptic tic by hypnosis: A case study. Am J Clin Hypn 17:88-81, 1984

Stein VT: Hypnotherapy of involuntary movements in an 82-year-old male. Am J Clin Hyp 23:128-131, 1980

Sternbach RA: On strategies for identifying neurochemical correlates of hypnotic analgesia. Int J Clin Exp Hypn 30:251-256, 1982

Toomey TC, Sanders, S: Group hypnotherapy as an active control strategy in chronic pain. Am J Clin Hypn 26:20-25, 1983

Vodvnik L, Roskar E, Pajntar J, Gros N: Modeling the voluntary hypnosis-induced motor performance of hemiparetic patients. IEEE Transactions on Systems, Man and Cybernetics 9:850-855, 1979

Wadden TA, Anderton CH: The clinical use of hypnosis. Psychol Bull 91:215-243, 1982

17 INVESTIGATIVE HYPNOSIS

RICHARD B. GARVER, Ed.D.

Forensic hypnosis has come a long way since the court case of *People v. Ebanks* (1897), in which the court held that "the law of the United States does not recognize hypnotism." Throughout this century, the primary focus of forensic interest in hypnosis has been the controversy over whether an individual may be coerced with hypnotic suggestion to carry out antisocial behaviors (Orne, 1979) and how that coercion may affect legal responsibility. Nevertheless, within the last 15 years, there have been legal cases throughout the country which have utilized hypnotic techniques for different purposes. In these cases, hypnosis was used to enhance the recall of a witness who observed a crime or a victim whose memory could then aid in uncovering new information which might exonerate him of the alleged offense (Crasilneck, 1980a; Mutter, 1983). Such information has been used in recent years to furnish additional leads in the investigative phase of the case and to provide eyewitness testimony in court.

The history of investigative hypnosis is replete with abuses which has tainted the credibility of its use and contaminated the end product as evidence. Two extreme attitudes have resulted. One posture (Reisner, 1980) dictates that either a mental health professional or a law enforcement officer may perform the hypnotic function and stipulates that most of the information gained is reliable and accurate, deemphasizing the likelihood of confabulatio and misperceptions. Some "experts" have testified in court to the veracity of this procedure (*State v. Nebb,* 1962). The truth is that no one is able to discern or predict the truthfulness or accuracy of information obtained from a hypnotic interview until it is independently vertified or corroborated.

The other extreme position (Diamond, 1980) indicates that no matter how the hypnotic conference is conducted, or by whom, or with what safeguards, any witness who is hypnotized to enhance his recall should not be allowed to testify on matters pertaining to the hypnotically obtained information or any information that he had prior to the hypnotic interview. In other words, because of the hypnotic interview, the testimony of this witness has been contaminated. Both of these positions are extreme and difficult to support with scientific data. The real problem inherent to information obtained in an investigative hypnotic session involves the clinical procedures which have been adapted for the forensic setting.

Clinical Techniques in a Forensic Setting

Explorative or analytical hypnotherapy is often a treatment of choice for the amnestic patient (Crasilneck, 1980b). In such instances, various uncovering methods such as ideomotor responses, automatic writing, movie or T.V. screen techniques and/or others are frequently used. The purpose of these procedures is to uncover repressed or unconscious memories which may be utilized therapeutically. When these modalities are used to enhance the patient's memory of past events, the accuracy or veracity is not of chief importance. If the patient believes such information to be true, then it is genuinely true for him/her, and it is all "grist for the mill" in the psychotherapeutic process.

When these same techniques are used, however, for the purpose of enhancing the recall of a witness, a victim, or a defendant, the usefulness of such information depends upon its accuracy and factual integrity. Unfortunately, neither the patient nor the therapist can accurately discern fact from fiction as it is produced in the hypnotic state. Quite often there is highly detailed and precise information recovered; but interspersed with this information may be pseudo and screen memories, confabulation, and other misinformation in considerable detail. No one can ascertain the accuracy and validity of that information as it is presented. It is, therefore, a necessity that such knowledge be verified by independent corroboration of the investigative agency. Never should this hypnotically enhanced information stand on its own merit or be accepted as valid.

To be sure, the probing hypnotic interview not only utilizes a variety of clinical hypnotic skills to uncover information, but is often a therapeutic as well as clinical process. The hypnotic subject is often recalling (hypermnesia) or reliving (revivification) a prior incident which was traumatic. Though these clinical techniques may provide subjects with better control over an experience after the fact than when they were involved in it, yet the memory contact with the experience is sufficient to produce an abreaction.

Major Issues: Clinical and Forensic

Probably the most significant issue is the validity and reliability of the investigative hypnotic interview. This issue has been argued in many court cases, with one in particular, *Frye v. United States* (1923), noting that any scientific principle or technique must be "sufficiently established to have gained general acceptance in the particular field in which it belongs." This has come to be known as the *Frye Rule* and has generally excluded hypnosis as a reliable means of retrieving memory.

Hypnosis per se is not the primary reason for this unreliability; it is the human memory which is the offender. Human memory is fallible and continuous and, as Hilgard and Loftus have pointed out in their research on eyewitness testimony, one does not have to be hypnotized to produce invalid or unreliable information (Hilgard and Loftus, 1979; Putnam, 1979). For instance, a person may witness a crime and remember what was perceived fairly accurately. However, after reading an account of that crime or a similar crime in a newspaper, or after being questioned in detail on different occasions by law enforcement personnel, that person may have his original memory influenced by the recollection of similar variables which contaminate the primary and initial memory. The investigative hypnotic interview may add to the contamination with other confabulated material and pseudo or screen memory. Hypnosis intensifies the focal point of the event and invariably firmly convinces the subject of his certitude regarding the event.

Additionally, the conduct of the interview itself significantly affects the amount of distortion or contamination of this hypnotic memory. Provocative and leading questions while the person is in a suggestible state, such as "Do you see the man holding the gun?" could certainly produce a memory rather than recall one. Also, techniques which significantly alter the actual perception of the occurrence present further problems. For example, under hypnosis a witness 100 yards away, in a dimly lighted area, may be told that he can see the suspect much closer by using a huge spotlight and a zoom lens, bringing him within a few feet of the suspect for a closer and more accurate view. The hypnotic subject, wanting to please and capable of accepting these suggestions as reality, will produce a highly detailed report of the episode, often believing it to be an accurate one.

With the possibility of such misperception and distortion and with so much at stake in our criminal justice system, should we continue to utilize the hypnotic technique?

Another important question is: whom do we consider qualified to conduct such an interview? Should it be a law enforcement officer trained in hypnotic techniques, who normally conducts a non-hypnotic interrogation, or should it be a mental health professional qualified in the use of clinical hypnosis?

There is considerable controversy over this issue. Some observers say the law enforcement officer who conducts non-hypnotic interviews as a part of his regular duty may be well trained in hypnotic skills and well qualified to examine witnesses. (Reiser, 1980). Others (Orne, 1979) believe that only the mental health professional should conduct the interview because he is familiar with the hypnotherapeutic techniques and is best qualified to handle a psychologically traumatic interview.

There are established and respected hypnosis societies, the Society for Clinical and Experimental Hypnosis (1978) as well as the International Society of Hypnosis (1979), which have resolved that it is unethical for members to train lay individuals in the use of hypnosis, to collaborate with laymen in the use of hypnosis, or to serve as consultants to laymen practicing hypnosis. These societies are strongly opposed to the training of police officers as hypno-technicians and to the daily use of hypnosis by a police officer. When hypnosis is a necessary adjunct to law enforcement, they recommend that trained psychiatrists or psychologists with experience in the forensic use of hypnosis should be employed.

A moderate, middle ground posture is suggested by proponents of "The Federal Model." Among these are the Air Force Office of Special Investigations (Hibler, 1979; Teten, 1979), the Federal Bureau of Investigation (Ault, 1979; Garver, 1979), and other federal investigative agencies. They believe that an investigative hypnotic interview is an excellent paradigm when conducted by a team of mental health professionals working in conjunction with trained law enforcement persons.

In this format, the mental health professional is in charge and is not only accountable for the hypnotic conference but is also responsible, especially, for the timely and adequate conduct and hypnotic rendering which is utilized. The law enforcement officer has been trained by mental health professionals to conduct the actual interview within the framework of the altered state, hypnosis. In this model, care is taken to control the amount of information wittingly and unwittingly presented to the subject, and all interactions with the subject before, during, and after hypnosis are videotaped. Information gleaned from a scrutinized hypnotic problem does not end up in court but is utilized for investigative leads. However, the interview should be conducted with sufficient planning as though the information were going to be introduced as testimony in court. For this reason, it is important that the agency using hypnosis as an investigative aid have an established course of action before conducting hypnotic explorations.

Two issues are likely to be involved in any legal attack on hypnotic interview testimony; one is the credibility of the technique, the other, the validity of the information. Each of these are important areas in a hypnotic inquiry and must be considered in the planning for the admissibility of hypnotically enhanced testimony in court.

The following criteria can be used as a guideline in planning and achieving a hypnotic interview (Garner, Kenney, 1983):

1. Screening. There should be thorough screening before the decision is made to use hypnosis. First, the interviewee's participation in this technique must be voluntary. Then the witness or victim needs to have had perceptual access to the specific event and to persons involved. Important variables are the interviewee's visual acuity (to include color vision and distance vision); auditory acuity; time perceptions; whether or not he/she was wearing corrective lenses; his/her state of mind at the time; whether he/she was under the influence of alcohol or drugs; and whether he/she had a psychiatric history. In short, did the person being interrogated have reasonable opportunity to perceive that which occurred? This significant screening should be established in the examination of a potential witness or victim, especially before the hypnotic interview.

2. **Location.** Once the decision has been made to conduct an in-depth inquiry with hypnosis, the location for the interview becomes important. It should be a comfortable or private setting either in the doctor's office, in the interviewee's home, or in a private room within the confines of the law enforcement agency. Moreover, the interrogation should always be in a neutral setting not directly related to the crime. Personnel in the room should be limited to mental health professions (doctors), law enforcement persons trained to conduct hypnotic interviews (hypnotic coordinators), the case agent, family or friends of the interviewee whose presence may increase his comfort level, and appropriate support personnel to record the interview. The author strongly recommends that the entire forensic hypnotic conference be videotaped because the videotape then becomes an item of evidence.

3. **Mental health professionals.** The doctor should be a clinical psychologist or psychiatrist with special training in hypnosis, who is not an employee of a law enforcement agency, who uses hypnosis frequently in his practice, and who has experience in forensic hypnosis. If the case goes to trial, the credibility of the doctor as an expert witness rests on his/her professional credentials, so these points should be considered carefully.

4. **Pre-knowledge.** It is important that the hypnotic coordinator and doctor have no detailed knowledge of the crime to insure their impartiality in the administering of the probe. While it may seem incongruous that one would interview in depth and not have any knowledge of what is to be covered, the disclosure of facts will be determined in the protocol of the examination when the interviewee relates (at a conscious level) all the facts he/she can recall about the event in question. The hypnotic interview is based upon pertinent information in the interviewee's conscious recall.

5. **Video equipment and operator.** The video operator should be briefed on what to expect during the interview and constantly mindful that this recording may be shown as evidence in a trial. The video operator should be informed that the interrogation may take several hours so that a sufficient supply of videotapes is on hand. He should be instructed to signal the hypnosis coordinator approximately five minutes before a tape needs to be changed. If available, a time-date generator and sound mixer for three microphones should be used to insure good quality sound. Superimposing the date and elapsed time on the video tape is important, but if a time-date generator is not available, a simple wall clock behind the conference setting may be used in order to visually display the continuity of the interview.

6. **Hypnosis consent forms and others aids.** Hypnosis consent forms should be available for the interviewee, doctor and hypnosis coordinator to sign before the hyp-

notic interview. The contact of the consent agreement should conform to the local laws of the city and/or state. If a female is to be interviewed, there should be a chaperone present. If the purpose of the interview is to obtain a composite of the subject, there should be a selection of mug photographs and an artist or Ident-a-kit operator in attendance. However, a photographic line-up that has previously been shown to the interviewee should never be used in a hypnotic interrogation, as it may invalidate the selection process. Other useful investigative aids are maps of the area in question; firearms identification publications; and photographic displays of vehicles. An example of a hypnosis consent form is shown at the end of this chapter. When these criteria are met, the actual interview may begin.

After the induction of hypnosis in the interviewee, he/she should be requested to recall a place in time, just prior to the incident in question, a time when he felt relaxed and comfortable. At this point, the interrogator may begin with questions such as "What do you see?" or "Tell me what you are looking at now." As hypnosis is a highly suggestible state, it is important in forensic hypnotic questioning to acquire facts in a non-leading manner. Queries such as "Do you see the green car?" or "Are you looking at the man with the gun?" are inappropriate questions as they may suggest ideas. Utilizing non-leading questions, the hypnotic coordinator and the doctor may assist the interviewee with recollection of events chronologically, thereby allowing him to relate what happened as it unfolds sequentially.

There is some controversy as to approaches among authorities in the field of hypnosis (Crasilneck, 1980a; Garver and Kenney, 1984; Gravitz, 1980; Hibler, 1980; Mutter, 1983; Orne, 1979; Reisner, 1980) from the most sterile approach of allowing the witness an uninterrupted flow of narrative recall without any questions from the investigator about specifics to the other end of the continuum where the investigator abuses the state of suggestibility and invades the imagination of the witness to "create" a memory rather than allowing the witness to recall one.

The usefulness of the information obtained is determined by independent verification and corroboration. Less contamination is likely to occur if the hypnotic coordinator is reasonable with the questioning technique. For instance, it would be inviting confabulation for the interviewer to suggest that adequate lighting existed when in fact it did not; to suggest that the light is growing brighter, and in a few moments the interviewee will be able to see the subject's face, when, in fact, no such light actually existed in the first place. It is, however, reasonable to concentrate all attention on one area as though to focus a spot light on that site, but never to increase beyond actual reality the former conditions of perception. It is unreasonable to suggest that the interviewee is observing someone at 100 yards and then to suggest that he use the zoom lens of the camera in his mind to bring that individual in to a 10-foot radius. It is advantageous and creative to use hypnotic and imagery techniques to increase the selective attention of the interviewee. However, when creativity leads to distorted perception, then the hypnotic coordinator is responsible for the contamination. There should be no undue pressure placed on the interviewee to please the examiner or produce additional information, especially if there is no other factual disclosure available.

Moreover, no matter how accurate and realistic an evaluation of a properly conducted interview may seem, there is both fact and fiction, and truth and confabulation interwoven in the testimony. It is unusual to find any hypnotic exploration that is either all good or all bad; totally precise or totally inaccurate. The only way to determine what is a true rendition and what is not is by independent verification and cooroboration. If only a few details obtained from a hypnotic interview are substantiated and confirmed and a considerable portion of the probe is found to be uncorroborative and inaccurate, this fact in no way contaminates or detracts from the authenticated verification of the disclosed data. It has been successfully argued by the author in federal court, *United States v. Harrelson* (1982), that a jury should have a right to hear hypnotic testimony. If, indeed, this hypnotic testimony to be presented in court can be verified or corroborated independently and fits the facts of the case, the jury deserved to know that the state of consciousness is not the culprit. Human memory is both fallible and continuous. Hypnosis is a suggestible state, and interviews during this state may enhance and magnify both accuracy and erroneous recall. However, the faulty concept was there in the first place—as was the accuracy.

The Interview

The hypnosis coordinator begins the interview by stating the place, date, time and identity of persons present; presents the purpose of the problem; obtains verbal affirmation that the participation of the interviewee is voluntary; acquires permission of the subject to record the entire interview on video tape; apprises the individual of what will happen in the interview; and discusses the credentials and function of the mental health professional who will actually manage the hypnosis.

It is important that the interviewee comprehend that the doctor is there to insure his well-being during the hypnotic interview. The doctor discusses the state of hypnosis, and if the interviewee is comfortable with and accepts the technique the hypnosis coordinator reads aloud a hypnosis consent form, discusses it with the subject, and asks if there are any questions before he requests signatures.

Following the above protective legal conformities, the hypnosis coordinator asks the person being examined to recount in his/her own words what can be recalled of the incident in question. The interviewee should not be led or questioned during recitation, and should be allowed to report the details in any order he desires. This critical aspect of the interview serves as the basis for any questioning during the hypnotic state. At this point, the hypnosis coordinator uncovers and retrieves through divulgence what transpired during the incident. This phase is, in effect, the hypnosis coordinator's roadmap for following the path of the data source to be extrapolated and expanded on the basis of absolute recall.

The doctor induces hypnosis and transfers rapport to the hypnosis coordinator who proceeds to conduct the intensive interview. At its conclusion, the hypnosis coordinator, before terminating the videotape of the interview, returns rapport to the doctor, who questions the interviewee about his feelings and well-being, and upon receiving a positive response dehypnotizes the subject.

Post-Interview

Following the appropriate protocol of the hypnotic interview, a detailed analysis and evaluation is made by the mental health professional. This analysis includes an assessment of the mental status of the interviewee before, during and after the interview, a description of the induction methods, the utilization of trance management procedures, an evaluation of the interviewee's responses to all hypnotic techniques, and the incorporation of any other behavioral observations made of the interviewee concerning his/her demeanor. No comment should be made regarding the doctor's opinion on the veracity of the information gleaned, since that is not relevant. The hypnotic coordinator should evaluate the interviewee's responses based upon his knowledge of the interrogation, both hypnotically and nonhypnotically, and all new information of the case agent, who is always present throughout the interview. As the case progresses, the merit, worth, and conformity to truth of the hypnotic interview can be further evaluated by the hypnotic coordinator and the case agent to determine the accuracy and usefulness of the hypnotic information.

It is important that the prosecuting attorney be advised of the fundamentals of this modality so that he understands the source, the essence, and the intrinsic worth of hypnotically enhanced information and the fact that there are vulnerable aspects to hypnotic testimony given in a trial. The prosecuting attorney should be provided with any literature that might better enable him to understand forensic hypnosis, should be supplied with detailed information with which to prepare his case, and should be assisted in developing his strategy in court. Because of the many misconceptions regarding hypnosis, with even more misinterpretation surrounding the subspeciality of forensic hypnosis, it is necessary that the prosecuting attorney understand the role of the doctor and the hypnotic coordinator in this process. The prosecuting attorney must establish the doctor's professional credential and credibility as an expert witness in the field of forensic hypnosis, as well as the credentials of the hypnosis coordinator.

Ideally, the hypnotic interview should be conducted in such a manner, with appropriate safeguards and procedures, that information forthcoming can be independently verified and corroborated. The hypnotic information is not required to stand on its own merits in court, but to provide investigative leads which will facilitate the apprehension, arrest, and conviction of the perpetrator of the offense. Even though the interview itself may never be required in court, as stated before, it is important to prepare for an interview as though it will be an issue during the trial.

Within the past 10 years, the author has conducted well over 200 forensic hypnotic interviews, with more than 100 probes initiated for the Federal Bureau of Investigation and other federal agencies. The "Federal Model" or teamwork approach unquestionably has the best track record over any other modality. In only one case (*United States v. Valdez,* 1984), which used the "Federal Model," the interview failed, and should have been aborted at the onset because the witness, a Texas Ranger, had prior knowledge of the case involving the suspect.

However, in the landmark federal case of the *United States v. Harrelson* (1982), investigative hypnosis using the "Federal Model" was pivotal in providing information and testimony of several witnesses. The videotaped hypnotic interviews and the hypnotically enhanced testimony of these witnesses were accepted as evidence during the trial, which led to the conviction of Charles Harrelson for the assassination in May, 1979, of Federal Judge John H. Wood, Jr. In the author's extensive testimony, he stated and demonstrated that both confabulated material and factual data were produced under hypnosis by these witnesses. The defense made the point to the jury that a hypnotic interview was not a truth telling device, nor an assurance of truth or accuracy; and that, in fact, hypnotized witnesses can err in their perceptions. The author agreed. He also testified that because a portion of information furnished by a witness during a hypnotic interview was in error or confabulated, that did not preclude the acceptance of accurate hypnotic testimony which had been *independently* verified and corroboratd. Therefore, with that precedent, and the experience of many other cases in which this paradigm was used, the author recommends the following guidelines as a reasonable and prudent course of action for investigative hypnosis:

Guidelines

1. The investigative hypnotic examination should be the responsibility of a psychologist or psychiatrist with specific training in its use.

2. The interrogative part of the conference should be accomplished by a law enforcement officer with special training in conducting interviews in the hypnotic environment.

3. The mental health professional and the law enforcement investigator should work as a team. It is wise and discretionary that they not be informed about the facts of the case in any detail, lest the inquiry become biased and contaminate the information desired. The law enforcement interviewer should not be involved in the investigation of the case, and the mental health professional should be independent of responsibility to the prosecution or investigating agency.

4. All conferences of the interview team, with the individual to be hypnotized, should be videotaped.

5. Before the hypnotic interview, a brief mental evaluation of the interviewee should be conducted by the mental health professional.

6. Before the hypnotic interview, the person to be questioned should be given an opportunity to provide a conscious detailed recital of the experience. It is important to have a record of what the witness describes in conscious recall before the hypnotic interview.

7. While conducting the interview, the consultation team should be careful not to prompt the witness with any new components to the description of his/her experience and should be especially careful not to alter the perceptual reality of the incident in any way.

8. The number of people present in the room during the interview should be kept to a minimum, but may include the prosecuting and/or defense attorneys, the case agent, a chaperone when appropriate, or a close friend or family member at the request of the interviewee.

9. Finally, all information gleaned from the hypnotic interview must be independently corroborated by other evidence before it is used as an investigative lead or is presented in court.

A special panel for the council on scientific affairs at the American Medical Association published a report to evaluate the scientific evidence concerning the effects of hypnosis on memory (JAMA, 1985). The Society for Clinical and Experimental Hypnosis summarized the findings of the panel in their newsletter (April, 1985). The Council of Scientific Affairs recommended the following:

> The use of hypnosis with witnesses and victims to enhance recall should be limited to the investigative process. Specific safeguards (detailed below) should be employed to protect the welfare of the subject and the public and to provide the kind of record that is essential to evaluate the additional material obtained during and after hypnosis.
>
> Prior to the induction of hypnosis in an investigative context, a psychological assessment of the subject's state of mind should be carried out and a detailed history of the individual's recollections obtained in a nonleading fashion. Statements such as "I can't remember anything" should not be accepted at face value but should lead to careful exploration of whatever memory is available. Clinical, forensic, and

experimental experience indicate that several nonhypnotic techniques may facilitate recall; for example, repeated recall efforts, even when the subject claims to remember nothing more, can enhance memory. If, after repeated attempts to obtain recall, the decision is made to use hypnosis, it is essential to elicit the subject's expectations and fantasies about hypnosis and to deal with misconceptions. Before proceeding with hypnosis, informed consent should be obtained from the subject.

Hypnosis should be conducted by a psychiatrist or psychologist, skilled in the clinical and investigative use of hypnosis, who is aware of the legal implications of the use of hypnosis for investigative purposes within the jurisdiction in which he or she practices. The clinician conducting the hypnosis sessions should take care to avoid leading or inadvertently cueing the subject. A complete tape and/or precise written record of the clinician's prior knowledge of the case must be made. Complete videotape recordings of the prehypnotic evaluation and history, the hypnotic session, and the post-hypnotic interview showing both the subject and the hypnotist should be obtained.

Ideally, only the subject and the psychiatrist/psychologist should be present when the subject is hypnotized. At times, exceptions may be necessary, such as allowing a law enforcement official who is not familiar with the details of the case to provide special expertise, such as a forensic expert or police artist, or such as permitting the parent of an anxious child to remain in the room. The needs for the presence of additional individuals must be weighed carefully against the added risk of inadvertently cueing the hypnotized person.

Although the specific form of hypnotic induction is relatively unimportant, some test suggestions of known difficulty should be given to provide information about the subject's ability to respond to hypnosis; standardized hypnotizability tests may also be used. Regardless of the specific procedure used to focus the subject's attention in hypnosis on the events to be remembered, the hypnotist should elicit at least one free narrative recall first and avoid any questions about specifics; instead, encouraging remarks without specific content (such as "go on," "continue," or "yes") should be used. After obtaining unpressured, free recall in hypnosis, it may be necessary to ask more specific (but nonleading) questions. Before asking such questions, it should be made clear to the subject that the response, "I don't know," is acceptable.

The subject's response to the termination of hypnosis and the posthypnotic discussion about the experience of hypnosis are of major importance in assessing the subject's response to hypnosis. The videotape recording should include the complete posthypnotic discussion.

Medical responsibility for the health and welfare of the subject cannot be abrogated by the investigative intent of a hypnotic session.

Finally, the Panel recommends that the American Medical Association encourage continued research: 1) to help clarify the effects of hypnosis on recall; 2) to enhance understanding of the kinds of functional amnesia that affect some victims and witnesses of crimes; and 3) to shed light on the nature of normal and pathological human memory.

It is satisfying to know that yet another subspecialty of our discipline, hypnotherapy, is of valuable use to our criminal justice system, but with that knowledge we accept the responsibility of insuring that this professional tool is used appropriately and wisely.

Appendix 17-1

Consent for Hypnosis

ON: _____

AT: _____

I,_____, hereby agree voluntarily and freely, to undergo hypnosis and be interviewed under hypnosis in order to assist with an investigation. I understand that a video tape recording will be made of the entire interview and that this method of preservation of the interview may be used, as to be determined by my attorneys, for any lawful purpose connected with this investigation.

_____, a mental health professional, has explained the procedures to be used during the course of this hypnosis session and any questions I had concerning this procedure have been answered to my satisfaction. The purpose of this interview under hypnosis is to assist my memory in recalling _____

_____

_____

_____

_____

_____

_____

Interviewee

Witnesses:

_____

Mental Health Professional

_____

Witness

References

Ault RL: FBI guidelines for the use of hypnosis. Int J Clin Exp Hypn 27:449-451, 1979

Ault RL: Hypnosis—The FBI's team approach. FBI Law Enforcement Bull 49:1, 1980

Council on Scientific Affairs report on scientific status of refreshing recollection by the use of hypnosis. J Am Med Assoc 252:1918-1923, April 5, 1985

Crasilneck HB: The case of Dora. Am J Clin Hypn 24:94-97, 1980a

Crasilneck HB (Panelist): Psychogenic amnesia and forensic hypnotherapy. East Tex State Univ Commerce, TX, 1980b

Diamond BL: Inherent problems in the use of pretrial hypnosis on a prospective witness. Calif Law Rev 68:2, 1980

Frye v. United States, 293F. 1013, 34 A.L.R. 145 (D.C. Cir. 1923)

Garver RB: An overview of forensic hypnosis: Where are we going? Paper presented at the American Psychological Association Eighty-seventh Convention, New York, 1979

Garver RB, Kenney JW: Investigative Hypnosis (Videotape) on on Guard Series #21. San Antonio, TX, Marinco, Inc., 1983

Garver RB, Kenney JW: The collection and preparation of hypnotically enhanced testimony. Am J Clin Hypn, 1984

Gravitz MA: Forensic uses of hypnosis: Discussion. Am J Clin Hypn 23:103-111, 1980

Hibler NS: The use of hypnosis in the United States Air Force investigations. Paper presented at the American Psychological Association Eighty-seventh Convention, New York, 1979

Hibler NS: Administrative aspects of forensic hypnosis. Presented at the Twenty-Third Annual Scientific Meeting of the American Society of Clinical Hypnosis, Minneapolis, 1980

Hilgard ER, Loftus EF: Effective interrogation of the eyewitness. Int J Clin Exp Hypn 27:342-357, 1979

International Society of Hypnosis: 1979 resolution. Int J Clin Exp Hypn 27:453, 1979

Mutter C: The use of hypnosis with defendants. Presented at the Twenty-Sixth Annual Meeting of the American Society of Clinical Hypnosis, Dallas, 1983

Orne MT: The use and misuse of hypnosis in court. Int J Clin Exp Hypn 27:311-341, 1979

People v. Ebanks, 117 Ca. 652, 49 P. 1049 (1897)

Putnam WH: Hypnosis and distortions in eyewitness memory. Int J Clin Exp Hypn 27:437-448, 1979

Reiser M: Handbook of Investigative Hypnosis. Los Angeles, LEHI, 1980

Society for Clinical and Experimental Hypnosis: 1978 resolution. Int. J Clin Exp Hypn 27:452, 1979

Society for Clinical and Experimental Hypnosis Newsletter: Refreshing recollection by the use of hypnosis 26:1-5, April 1985

State v. Nebb, No. 39, 540 (Ohio Com. Pl., Franklin Co., May 28, 1962)

Teten HD: The FBI's policy and concerns in the use of hypnosis. Presented at the American Psychological Association Eighty-Seventh Convention, New York, 1979

United States v. Harrelson, 754 F.2d 1182 (5th Cir. 1985)

United States v. Valdez, 722 F.2nd 1196 (5th Cir. 1984)

18 ADMISSIBILITY OF HYPNOTICALLY REFRESHED TESTIMONY

DENNIS E. SIES, J.D., Ph.D.
WILLIAM C. WESTER, II, Ed.D.

Judicial attitudes toward hypnosis and judicial approaches toward hypnotically adduced evidence have oscillated markedly over the past century. Issues involving hypnosis first appeared in American courts in the late 19th century.[1] At that time, judicial wariness of hypnosis and hostility to hypnotically adduced evidence was manifest.[2] In 1897, the California Supreme Court seemed to speak for all American courts when it declared that "the law does not recognize hypnosis."[3] The evidentiary problem of hypnotic evidence largely vanished shortly after that pronouncement, and it remained dormant until the late 1950's and early 1960's when hypnosis received recognition and widespread use by the various branches of the medical community.[4] Medical recognition and use spawned increased investigatory use by law enforcement agencies and soon the evidentiary problem of hypnotically refreshed testimony was again before the courts.[5] This time the judiciary did not view hypnosis with a hostile eye, and the late 1960's saw the beginning of a decade of uncritical acceptance of hypnotically refreshed testimony. In 1977, at the end of the decade, one writer stated that "The older cases, in which suspicion of such evidence [hypnotically refreshed testimony] was sufficient to summarily deny its admissibility are no longer of persuasive weight."[6] In the same year, two other commentators boldly asserted that courts would soon take the next step and admit statements made by witnesses while under hypnosis.[7] What these writers did not foresee was yet another pendulous change in the attitude of a significant segment of the American judiciary.[8] Renewed skepticism caused some courts to admit hypnotically refreshed testimony only after careful scrutiny convinced them that the proposed testimony was both reliable and probative. The same doubts caused other courts to exclude hypnotically refreshed testimony per se. As a result, there have developed three judicial approaches to the question of admissibility of hypnotically refreshed testimony, and none clearly commands a majority. Currently, the law is in a state of flux.

This chapter was adapted from: Sies DE, Wester WC: Judicial Approaches To The Question of Admissibility of Hypnotically Refreshed Testimony. Since this article was published in the *De Paul Law Review* (Volume 35, Book No. 1, 1986) the Uniform System of Citation has been used for style and annotation. Reprinted with permission of the *De Paul Law Review*.

To place the evidentiary problem of hypnotically refreshed testimony in proper perspective, this chapter examines the nature, methodology, and uses of hypnosis. The chapter then traces the development of the three currently competing judicial approaches to hypnotically refreshed testimony. Finally, an analysis of those three approaches leads to the conclusion that both the approaches of per se exclusion and of per se admissibility contain significant analytical flaws and practical difficulties. The approach of per se exclusion is especially pernicious in its effects. In contract, the third approach, that of guarded admissibility, recognizes the risks of hypnosis but uses procedural safeguards and balancing tests to minimize or negate those risks, thus allowing reliable and relevant evidence to reach the trier of fact. It is, therefore, the preferable approach.

The Art and Science of Hypnosis

Although this chapter focuses on an in-court admissibility of testimony of a previously hypnotized witness, a general review of hypnosis is first required for a full understanding of the evidentiary concerns facing the courts. The following sections briefly survey the nature, methods, and uses of hypnosis as a medical-therapeutic technique, and examine the utility of that technique when it is transposed into judicial settings.

Nature and Methodology

Hypnosis may be defined simply as an altered state of awareness or perception.[9] This altered state of mind is characterized by "heightened suggestibility as a result of which unusual or extraordinary changes in sensory, motor and memory functions (cognitive processes) may be more readily experienced."[10] The subject's altered state of consciousness is achieved by a process known as induction, in which the hypnotist induces a hypnotic state, with the cooperation of the subject.[11] Various induction techniques may be used,[12] but the processes have in common the establishment of rapport between the subject and the hypnotist, progressive relaxation by the subject, and progressive narrowing of the subject's attention as a result of the specific suggestions by the hypnotist.[13] The resulting hypnotic state may be separable into several levels, or stages, with each level manifesting distinct characteristics.[14] A fully hypnotized subject may experience a broad range of mental, emotional, physical responses and effects, including *inter alia,* alterations in heartbeat and respiration, production of hallucinations and fantasies, and recovery of forgotten memories.[15]

Induction techniques need not be complicated. Each professional develops his own style based on individual training and experience. Induction of hypnosis can be direct or indirect. Use of indirect, subtle suggestions has gained popularity among practitioners working therapeutically with patients. Most forensic work involves direct techniques such as progressive relaxation, eye fixation, or imagery. The subject is simply asked to close his eyes and then given suggestions that all muscles of the body are relaxing in a progressive way from the top of his head to his toes. The progression can be followed with a "deepening" technique such as asking the subject to count or to imagine being in his favorite place. A variety of "tests" can be used to check on the level/depth of trance.[16]

There is some controversy about level and depth of trance. Some believe that it is important for the subject to achieve a very deep trance in order for hypnosis to be effective. Others contend that the subject will develop the proper depth of trance in order to reach a predetermined goal. In most cases a light-medium state is appropriate. One of the older scales of trance level was devised in 1931 and is still used to demonstrate the kinds of phenomena associated with the different stages of trance.

1. Hypnoidal—general relaxation, fluttering of the eyelids, eye closure and complete physical relaxation.

2. Light trance—catalepsy of the eyes, limb, catalepsies, rigid catalepsy and glove anesthesia.

3. Medium trance—partial amnesia, posthypnotic anesthesia, personality changes, simple posthypnotic suggestions, kinesthetic delusions, and complete amnesia.

4. Deep (somnambulistic) trance—eye open trance, bizzare posthypnotic suggestions, complete somnambulism, positive and negative visual and auditory hallucinations, and post-hypnotic amnesias.[17]

A forensic hypnosis session usually consists of four phases: prehypnosis, induction and trance-deepening, recall, and termination. The most common techniques used to elicit information and to enhance recall include: age regression, revivification, screen techniques, and hyperamnesia.[18] In age regression, the hypnotist directs the subject back to a particular age in the subject's life, enabling the subject to role-play the age, including age-appropriate behavior.[19] In revivification, the subject actually relives a past event, once again experiencing all of the cognitive, emotive, and sensory factors present to the subject at the time of the event.[20] Screen techniques are a form of regression in which subjects are told they can see the past event(s) in question unfolding on a movie or television screen. Hyperamnesia is the simplest of the memory restoration techniques, enabling recall simply as a result of the relaxation effect produced by hypnosis, which allows the mind to release memories stored in the subconscious even though the subject could not volitionally release them while not hypnotized.[21] The first three methods, respectively, require the subject to role-play, relive, or watch past events as they happened and to describe them in detail. Hyperamnesia is of greater use as an enhancement technique, when a subject remembers portions of an event but is unsure of details.

History and Uses of Hypnosis

Hypnosis has had a long, colorful, and somewhat checkered history. While the nature of the phenomena of hypnosis described *supra* was not understood until relatively recently, the practice of hypnosis is at least as old as recorded civilization.[22] Although primitive practitioners may have used hypnosis to establish and maintain their positions of tribal power, the primary historical use of hypnosis has been therapeutic.[23] Evidence indicates that hypnosis was used by Assyrian and Babylonian priests over 50 centuries ago to cure various afflictions, and that induced hypnosis was a regular form of therapy in Egyptian "sleep temples" over 30 centuries ago.[24] It was similarly practiced by primitive doctors and medicine men in ancient India, Africa, and pre-Columbian America.[25]

Early attempts to establish hypnosis as a science, or, more accurately, as a pseudo science, can be traced to the efforts of Franz Mesmer, a Viennese physician in Paris, who attracted attention in the late 18th century by developing a theory and practice of medical therapy which he called "animal magnestism."[27] Mesmer believed that all reality was filled with an invisible fluid, that illness was the product of an imbalance of this fluid in the body, and that, by using magnets and an elaborate ritual, he had the power to cure illness by increasing the flow of magnetic fluids in the body.[28] Situating his patients in a tub filled with glass, iron fillings, and cold water, Mesmer, wearing flowing robes and accompanied by soft background music, touched iron rods protruding from the tub to the afflicted parts of the patient's body, inducing a "convulsive crisis" in the patient.[29] In reality, the "crisis" was "a true state of hypnosis, produced through suggestion and the patient's own beliefs and expectations of cure."[30] Mesmer and his techniques were thoroughly discredited by an investigatory commission of the French government,[31] and it was not until the middle of the 19th century that an English physician, James Braid, was successful in bringing a measure of scientific credibility to hypnosis.[32]

Additional incremental research and experimentation during the next century resulted in gradually increasing levels of use, popularity, understanding, and legitimacy of hypnosis. In 1955, the British Medical Association officially endorsed hypnosis as a therapeutic technique.[33] The American Medical Association gave a similar endorsement in 1958, stating that hypnosis has "a recognized place in the medical armamentarium and is a useful technique in the treatment of certain illnesses. . ."[34] Two years later, the American Psychological Association recognized hypnosis as a branch of psychology by establishing a special Hypnosis Division (Division 30).[35] Today, hypnosis is widely accepted by the various branches of the medical community and "has been used in the treatment of various illnesses and addictions, including:

smoking, asthma, burns, chronic pain, grief, impotency, obesity, migraine and tension headaches and warts."[36]

Forensic Application and Benefits

The growing popularity and use of hypnosis by the medical community for therapeutic purposes stimulated an interest in and use of hypnosis for forensic purposes.[37] Since one of the traditional salient uses of hypnosis was memory restoration and enhancement, the technique appeared to have great potential for law enforcement agencies as an aid in enhancing the memory of witnesses and victims.[38]

In the late 1950's and early 1960's, many of the dangers and deficiencies of hypnosis as a memory refreshing device were unknown,[39] and evidentiary problems relating to the testimony of previously hypnotized witnesses had not yet manifested themselves in court. At the same time, the number of psychiatrists and psychologists professionally trained in hypnotic techniques was not large, and the services of these individuals were fairly expensive. Moreover, it is easy for laymen to quickly learn techniques of hypnotic induction, at least superficially.[40] Thus, for one or more of the above reasons, a pattern emerged in which many law enforcement agencies did not rely exclusively upon trained psychiatrists and psychologists to perform hypnosis, but instead established ad hoc and regular training programs for their own selected personnel. By 1978, police in a large number of large cities and agents of the Federal Bureau of Investigation and Alcohol, Tobacco and Firearms Bureau had received training in hypnosis.[41] By 1981, it was estimated that at the local, state, and federal levels between one and 10,000 detectives and police officers had received some training in hypnosis.[42] Recently, perhaps partly because of growing criticism by professional and scholarly organizations of the use of hypnosis by inadequately trained law enforcement personnel,[43] and partly because of growing judicial concerns about evidentiary problems related to the testimony of previously hypnotized witnesses,[44] there has been increased attention and effort in the law enforcement field to standardize training procedures and improve the competency of law enforcement practitioners of hypnosis.[45]

Hypnosis is of significant potential benefit not only to law enforcement authorities in criminal investigations, but to lawyers in the pre-trial discovery process, in either criminal or civil litigation. It may be that a witness has been the victim of a crime or accident and has suffered such physical and/or emotional trauma as to cause varying degrees of amnesia or psychological blocking of the memory of the traumatic experience. It may be a witness suffers such trauma and consequent memory loss or block simply by the fact of witnessing a crime or tragic event. It may be simply that a witness has a poor memory or that the memory of the witness has eroded due to the passage of time.

In all of the examples *supra,* hypnosis may be of considerable value in assisting the witness to recover lost or repressed memories. Alternatively, it may be that the witness has a perfectly normal memory, but nonetheless one which could be further enhanced through hypnosis, as one forensic hypnosis expert explains:

> Hypnosis, much like a surgeon's scalpel, cuts through inhibitory fears enabling the subject to experience a relaxed, concentrated state of awareness in which all five senses are heightened to a marked degree. He thinks and remembers better because the conscious mind swings aside permitting direct access to the vast repository of the subconscious.[46]

Problems with Hypnosis in a Forensic Setting

Although hypnosis is a valuable procedure for memory retrieval and enhancement, its use is not without dangers. The hypnotic state is one of heightened suggestibility. In this state there is the danger that false memories will be created by the subject's desire to please, by his expectations of appropriate behavior for hypnotized individuals, or by his ready acceptance of either deliberate suggestions or inadvertent cues by the hypnotist.[47] The subject may confabulate, attempting to fill in gaps in his memory with logical deductions of what should have occurred.[48] Fantasies known as "screen memories" may be produced by the subject as a defense to prevent the retrieval of real but traumatic memories.[49] Since hypnosis is no guarantee of historical accuracy, hypnotic recall may contain error or distortion due to the erosion of memory over time and/or the subconscious intermingling of memory of the original event with memory of subsequent events.[50] Lastly, it is possible for a subject to willfully lie if he has motivation to protect himself or another.[51]

It must be emphasized, however, that these problems are not peculiar to hypnotized subjects, but may be found with non-hypnotized persons.[52] Moreover, many of these problems can be avoided by the use of hypnosis only with appropriate subjects and under appropriate circumstances. Hypnosis makes "no promises other than to confuse, mislead, and misdirect resources if it is not carefully applied."[53] It should not be viewed as a "short cut" in the investigative process and it should be used sparingly in serious and difficult cases where there are no suspects, where there are disinterested but forgetful or traumatized witnesses, and where there is the likelihood that information derived from hypnosis can be independently verified.[54]

Restricting hypnosis to proper subjects and investigative uses is not sufficient, however, in avoiding hypnotic hazards. The key safety factors are the training and conduct of the hypnosis specialist.[55] One does not need to be a surgeon to make an abdominal incision, but training in medicine and surgery is essential in knowing what to do next. Similarly, induction techniques are easily learned, but when hypnosis is performed by an unqualified person, the results can be detrimental to the interests of justice and to the health of the subject. Hypnosis should, therefore, be conducted by a competent professional "possessing an advanced level of training and experience directly related to eyewitness recall, hypnosis, and the application of forensic hypnosis techniques."[56] Ideally, the professional should be a psychiatrist or a psychologist whose qualifications and conduct are regulated by state statutes and administrative regulations as well as by professional codes.[57] Such professionals can use recall techniques appropriate to types of memory loss and are skilled in the art of using non-leading questions and appropriate suggestions designed to minimize the possibility of distorted recall.[58] Moreover, the trained professional can detect behavior that indicates that the subject wants to help so badly that he is risking distortion by pushing himself, and the professional can employ a variety of techniques to deal with this problem.[59]

The reliability of procedures used and the qualifications of the hypnosis specialist are valid evidentiary concerns. As will be seen in the following sections, however, courts have proposed safeguards which adequately address these concerns.[60]

The Case Law

Although hypnosis has had nearly a century of legal history in the United States,[61] it has had little impact upon case law until recently. Most judicial activity in this area has taken place only within the past 20 years, and that activity has centered on the question of admissibility of the testimony of previously hypnotized witnesses.

Brief History and Contemporary Patterns

The earliest cases involving hypnosis appeared during the 20-year period 1895-1915 and involved the use of hypnosis by the defense, either in the form of using a state of hypnosis as a defense to a crime,[62] or regarding the admissibility of exculpatory statements made by a defendant under hypnosis.[63] Other cases dealt with alleged seduction of the hypnotized subject by the hypnotist.[64] One scholar has summed up the early judicial history of hypnosis by stating:

> Judicial hostility was manifest, and in none of these cases did the interjection of the hypnosis issue have any appreciable effect. The result was that just as suddenly as the problem of hypnosis had become important in American criminal law, so it lost its importance, and from 1915 until 1950, there was but one reported case dealing with any medical-legal aspect of hypnosis. (citations omitted)[65]

While there have been exceptions,[66] the overwhelming authority in this skimpy line of cases since 1895 is that statements made by the defendant under or as a result of hypnosis are inadmissible, and it matters not whether they were made in or out of court, nor whether they were made on a voluntary or involuntary basis.[67] Judicial rationale for such exclusion has, of course, varied with the facts of the cases, but in general has ranged from "bald conclusions that such evidence is *prima facie* inadmissible"[68] to justifications such as "the self-serving and hearsay nature of the accused's exculpatory statements, the involuntary nature of a defendant's statements which have proven to be inculpatory, and the lack of qualifications of the hypnotist."[69]

As previously discussed, official approval and increased use of hypnosis by the various branches of the medical community in the 1950's and 1960's gave impetus to a similar increased forensic use of hypnosis in criminal investigations and in the discovery process generally. This process in turn produced an ever-growing number of previously hypnotized witnesses. The eventual result was a flurry of judicial activity in the past two decades in an issue area that had previously been largely dormant. The context was somewhat different, however, for now the previously hypnotized witnesses were generally not defendants but victims, or even more commonly neither victims or defendants but simply individuals who had witnessed a crime or accident, and who had been hypnotized in the process of their cooperation with litigating attorneys and/or law enforcement agencies. Should the courts exclude the testimony of these individuals as they had previously excluded the testimony of defendant witnesses? In dealing with the issue, the courts groped for decisional rationale, used different tests, applied the same tests in different ways, and, not surprisingly, reached different conclusions. "Judicial analysis of hypnosis," as two commentators have noted, "has been uncertain, if not inconsistent, in finding an appropriate definition of the qualities of hypnosis, and thus the proper application, if any, of hypnosis to the resolution of disputes within the judicial system."[70]

The results of this uncertainty and inconsistency was a drastic, and continuing, splintering of opinion among jurisdictions. Worse, many state high courts found themselves in the embarrassingly sticky situation of rendering authoritative pronouncements, only to modify or overrule their decisions within a few years, or, in some cases, within a few months. What had become the majority position in the states over a period of time from 10 to 20 years ago has, during the past few years, been relegated to a distinct minority position. As of mid 1985, there was no majority position among the states on the issues of admissibility of hypnotically influenced testimony. Rather, at least three different approaches have emerged, and the approach which appears to be the emerging trend is *contra* that taken by the two federal circuits most active on the issue.[71]

The Admissibility Approach

Courts using this approach will admit hypnotically influenced testimony, leaving to the trier of fact the role of according the proper weight to such testimony. The case which established this approach in the modern era was *Harding v. State*.[72] In

Harding, the previously hypnotized witness was not a defendant, but a victim who had been abducted, raped, and shot. There was corroborating evidence that she had been shot and raped, and that she was with the alleged assailants during the night in question, but the trauma of the experience had impaired the victim's memory, and her recollection of events varied during her first three interviews with the police. About a month after the night in question, the victim was, at the instigation of the police, hypnotized by a clinical psychologist. While in a hypnotic state, and "without prompting,"[73] she was able to recall the events and incrimate the defendant. Given a post hypnotic suggestion to remember what she had related under hypnosis, she recounted the same story at trial.[74]

The admission of her testimony was upheld on appeal, the court finding that the witness had "recited the facts and stated she was doing so from her own recollection. The fact that she. . .achieved her present knowledge after being hypnotized concerns the question of the weight of the evidence which the trier of facts, in this case the jury, must decide."[75] In examining the victim's testimonial evidence, the court found other indicia of reliability in the corroborating facts, the credentials of the hypnotist, and his testimony that he did not prompt the victim and had no reason to doubt the truth of her statements.[76] In addition, the court noted that the trial judge had instructed the jury to give the hypnotically refreshed testimony no more weight than any other testimony presented in the trial.[77]

The *Harding* court did not treat hypnotically refreshed testimony as scientific evidence or the product of a novel scientific device, but rather as just another means of refreshing the memory of a witness. Testimonial lapses in memory are common and the principle of "present recollection refreshed" is well established in the law of every American jurisdiction.[78] The principle allows the memory of the witness to be refreshed by various means, including leading questions or the perusal of a document or memorandum.[79] Once convinced that the witness is clearly unable to testify due to a lapse in memory, the courts have been extremely liberal regarding what may be used to refresh memory. "Anything may in fact revive a memory; a song, a scent, a photograph, even a past statement known to be false."[80] Or, as another court has stated, it could be "the creaking of a hinge, the whistling of a tune, the smell of seaweed, . . .the taste of nutmeg, the touch of a piece of canvas."[81] Once the witness testifies that his memory has been revived, it is his continued testimony, and not the device or artifice that revived his memory, that is admitted into evidence. The reliability and credibility of that testimonial evidence are matters of weight for the trier of fact.

Although the Maryland court reversed itself 15 years later,[82] the approach it established in 1968 was widely followed by courts in other states[83] during the next decade. As recently as 1983, one court observed that "until 1980 the *Harding* rule has been uniformly, almost automatically, followed in other jurisdictions and still commands a majority."[84] Other courts tended to embrace *Harding* uncritically,[85] and added nothing to *Harding's* rationale other than to point out that skillful cross-examination of the previously hypnotized witness would act as a safeguard and would assist the trier of fact to evaluate the reliability of the witness' testimony.[86] While some courts did reconsider the issue and overrule themselves, others first adopted, or reaffirmed their earlier adoption of, the *Harding* rule, even after the Maryland Court of Appeals overruled *Harding* in 1983.[87]

There have been relatively few cases involving the admissibility of hypnotically refreshed testimony in federal courts.[88] Among the Federal Circuit Courts of Appeal, most have not addressed the issue at all, two have only tangentially touched the issue,[89] and another has dodged the issue.[90] The two circuits which have directly tackled the issue adopted, at least initially, a position similar to *Harding*.

The Ninth Circuit has, among federal courts, been the leader in ruling on hypnotically refreshed testimony. In *Wyller v. Fairchild Hiller Corp.*,[91] it applied a *Harding* approach in a civil case. In *Wyller,* the victim-plaintiff was the sole survivor and only eyewitness of a helicopter crash. His recollection impaired by the trauma of the accident and a four-year delay in litigation, he underwent hypnosis prior to trial to refresh his memory.[92] On appeal the court rejected the defense argument that the plaintiff's posthypnotic testimony was "inherently untrustworthy."[93] The court stated that the witness "testified from his present recollection, refreshed by the treatment."[94] It noted that the defense "was entitled to, and did, challenge both the remembered facts and the hypnosis procedure itself by extensive and thorough cross-examination"[95] of the plaintiff and the hypnotist. It ruled that "the credibility and weight to be given such testimony were for the jury to determine."[96]

The following year, in accord with *Wyller,* the Ninth Circuit in *Kline v. Ford Motor Co.*,[97] found that although the victim-plaintiff had undergone hypnotic refreshment of her memory she was competent to testify because "she was present and personally saw and heard the occurrences at the time of the accident."[98] The court noted that the "device by which recollection was refreshed is unusual," but "in legal effect her situation is not different from that of a witness who claims that his recollection of an event that he could not earlier remember was revived when he thereafter read a particular document."[99]

Three years later, the Ninth Circuit extended this approach to criminal cases in *United States v. Adams,*[100] although the court now observed that hypnosis "carries a dangerous potential for abuse," and, as a result, recommended certain minimal procedural safeguards to protect against that potential.[101] It nevertheless reasserted its position that "the fact of hypnosis affects credibility, but not admissibility."[102]

The Fifth Circuit Court of Appeals has rendered similar discussions. In *Connolly v. Farmer,*[103] the court addressed the issue in a round-about fashion, holding it need not reach the question of whether the trial court's refusal to admit into evidence physician testimony and tapes that plaintiff made under hypnosis was error because the plaintiff was allowed to give his posthypnotic testimony. "In effect, the jury did learn the results of the hypnosis, and no prejudice to plaintiff resulted from the exclusion of either the doctor's testimony or the tapes."[104] In *U.S. v. Valdez*,[105] the court directly addressed the issue and adopted a rule of admissibility of hypnotically refreshed testimony, albeit differing from *Harding* in requiring that "adequate procedural safeguards" be followed.[106]

The two circuits discussed *supra* continue, as of 1985, to admit hypnotically refreshed testimony, although they both now require procedural safeguards against the hazards of this testimony.[107] Federal district courts generally favor admission of such testimony.[108]

The Eclipse of Harding and the Rise of Alternative Approaches

Increased use of hypnosis, growing recognition in research reports of limitations and problems inherent in the use of hypnosis, and emerging criticism of the *Harding* approach eventually combined to create new patterns of judicial attitudes toward, and treatment of, hypnotically refreshed testimony. Although distinct from each other, the new patterns had two things in common: a rejection of the uncritical acceptance of hypnotism as a method of refreshing memory and, therefore, an unwillingness to freely admit hypnotically refreshed testimony into evidence.

Emerging then, in the mid to late 1970's, was a new form of judicial analysis which reflected the concerns mentioned *supra*. Courts began to address, at least implicitly, one or both of the following two questions: Is hypnosis so inherently unreliable that, as a matter of law, the results of the procedure should not be admitted into evidence, either because the use of hypnosis has destroyed the competence of a witness or because the hypnotically refreshed testimony of a witness would unduly prejudice or mislead the trier of fact? There is, of course, another question hidden within this one: Unreliable as to what? As a truth-detection device, or as a memory refresher, or as an interview technique? Courts can, and have, answered the first question in different ways because they viewed the nature and purpose of hypnosis differently, although the decisions are not always clear as to the court's opinion of the nature and purpose of the procedure. In any event, if the answer to the first question is affirmative, that is, if hypnosis is considered inherently unreliable, then the analysis stops here, the evidence is not admitted, and the second question is not reached. If the answer is negative, or at least ambiguous, then the second question is addressed: Admitting that there are certain problems with the process of hypnotic interview and defects in hypnotically refreshed memory, are there procedural safeguards which may be employed to minimize those hazards to the point where the testimonial product of hypnosis may be safely admitted to reach, and be evaluated by, the trier of fact?

One of the problems associated with the first question is finding a standard to measure reliability. If hypnotic evidence is considered the same as any other evidence, then the only standard is the Federal Rules of Evidence and the corresponding state evidence codes which do not mention reliability but which liberally state that relevant evidence is generally admissible,[109] and evidence is relevant as long as it is probative regarding any fact of consequence to the determination of the action.[110] If, however, hypnotic evidence is considered as *scientific* evidence, then the courts may choose between two standards of admissibility: (1) The so-called "reliability" or "relevancy" test, which has been identified with Professor McCormick, and which is nothing more than the "probative/prejudicial test of the Federal Rules.[111] (2) The judicial rule of evidence known as the *Frye*[112] test, established by a 1923 decision of the United States Court of Appeals for the D.C. Circuit. The widely-quoted passage establishing the test reads:

> Just when a scientific principle of discovery crosses the line between the experimental and demonstrable stages is difficult to define. Somewhere in this twilight zone the evidential force of the principle must be recognized, and while the courts will go a long way in admitting expert testimony deduced from a well-recognized scientific principle or discovery, the thing from which the deduction is made must be sufficiently established to have gained general acceptance in the particular field in which it belongs.[113]

In addition to these two rules or tests, some courts have borrowed from both to create a hybrid test, the exact nature of which, of course, will vary as to the jurisdiction and the case.[114]

If the McCormick relevancy test is used, a foundation is laid via expert testimony on the reliability of the technique, and the evidence derived from that technique is then admissible, if it is relevant and not found by the court to be unduly prejudicial, misleading, cumulative, etc.[115] As Professor Giannelli explains:

> Under the relevancy approach, novel scientific evidence is treated the same as other kinds of evidence. Thus, if an expert testifies that an innovative technique is valid, a court could find that evidence derived from that technique is probative. Admissibility, however, would not be automatic. As with all relevant evidence, a court would have discretion to exclude the evidence if the probative value were outweighed by considerations of undue prejudice, misleading the jury, and undue consumption of time.[116]

If the *Frye* test is used, the proponent of the evidence has a stronger burden, the showing not only that the technique is in the demonstrable, or working, stage, but that it is "generally accepted" as reliable by the appropriate scientific community. As Giannelli states: "In contrast to the relevancy approach, it is not enough that a qualified expert, or even several experts, believe that a particular technique has entered the demonstrable stage: *Frye* imposes a special burden—the technique must be *generally accepted by the relevant scientific community.*"[117] Clearly, then, of the two tests, *Frye* is the more difficult and restrictive regarding the admissibility of scientific evidence.

Whether hypnosis, a technique which has been employed for at least 4,000 years, should be treated as novel scientific evidence; whether *Frye* is superior to the relevancy test in determining the scientific reliability of hypnosis; and whether *Frye* should be applied to eyewitness testimony are all questions which are discussed *infra* in section IV of this chapter. For now, it is sufficient to note that in the decade following *Harding,* no federal appellate court and no state supreme court applied the *Frye* test to the hypnosis. Apparently, the courts either were not overly concerned with the reliability of hypnotically refreshed testimony, or they did not consider such testimony to be scientific or the product of a scientific technique or device, or they preferred to leave the question of reliability, as a component of credibility, to the trier of fact, or some combination of the above. "Most courts," according to two commentators, "have circumvented the issue by either defense counsel's failure to raise it before the trial, or simply by treating the issue, ipso facto, as a matter of credibility for the trier of fact."[118]

In the mid to late 1970's as judicial concern over hypnotic reliability increased, courts became more disposed to view hypnosis as a science and hypnotically refreshed memory as a scientific product. They also became increasingly disposed to choose *Frye* as the test of hypnotic reliability reliability as one court recently explained: "Given the mysterious and unfamiliar nature of hypnosis and its significant potential for abuse, a number of courts have approached the problem of hypnotically refreshed testimony as courts have historically dealt with other novel scientific methods or procedures: through application of the test set forth in *Frye*"[119]

Interestingly, this was not true in the federal courts, which continued to ignore or refuse to apply *Frye.* The federal courts either continued to follow the *Harding* approach of free admissibility,[120] or refused to consider hypnotically refreshed evidence as scientific evidence, or rejected *Frye* as the appropriate test of reliability, or employed some combination of the above.[121]

In the state courts, however, beginning with the 1980 case of *State v. Mack,*[122] the *Frye* test was planted, took root, and flourished. Since *Mack,* every state supreme court which had elected not to follow, or which abandoned, the *Harding* approach has invoked and applied, in some fashion or another, the *Frye* test. But the consistent use of *Frye* has not produced consistent results. Some courts, like that in *Mack,* applied *Frye,* found hypnosis not generally accepted and, hence, unreliable with respect to one or more purposes. These courts proceeded either to bar testimony regarding both post and prehypnotic memories, or to bar hypnotically refreshed testimony while admitting testimony relating to prehypnotic memory. Other courts, however, applied *Frye,* found hypnosis to be generally accepted and, hence, reliable with respect to one or more purposes, provided that various procedural safeguards had been employed to minimize the possibility that unreliable testimony would result from a previous hypnotic session. These courts proceeded to admit hypnotic evidence that had been subjected to such safeguards.

Guarded Admissibility: Procedural Guidelines, and Balancing Tests

The first state supreme court to clearly articulate and adopt a delineated procedural approach was the New Jersey Supreme Court in the 1981 case of *State v. Hurd*.[123] By the time the court reviewed *Hurd, State v. Mack*,[124] using the *Frye* test and rejecting hypnotic evidence as unreliable, had been decided. Thus, the New Jersey Supreme Court had three alternative models to choose from: the free admissibility approach of *Harding;* the per se exclusion approach of *Mack*, and an alternative procedural safeguard model which had been roughly sketched by the Ninth Circuit and which had been fine-tuned and applied by some lower state courts. Indeed, one of those lower state courts was the trial court in *Hurd.*

   This alternative model recognizes the hazards of hypnosis, especially, perhaps, the dangers of confabulation and hypersuggestiveness, but asserts that procedural safeguards can be employed to minimize or negate those problems. The Ninth Circuit had firmly established the general principle that the fact of hypnosis goes to the credibility of the testimony and not the admissibility, but in two cases the court had implied a qualification to the general rule: the testimony may be inadmissible if the procedures employed during the hypnotic session were improper. In *United States v. Adams*,[125] the court had expressed the concern "that investigatory use of hypnosis on persons who may later be called upon to testify in court carries a dangerous potential for abuse."[126] The court stated that "Great care must be exercised to insure that statements after hypnosis are the product of the subjects' own recollections, rather than of recall tainted by suggestions received while under hypnosis."[127] As minimum procedural insurance, the court suggested maintenance of a complete stenographic record of the hypnosis interview, and added that "an audio or video recording of the interview would be helpful."[128] "Only if the judge, jury, and the opponent know who was present, questions that were asked, and the witness' responses can the matter be dealt with effectively."[129] Lastly, the court implied that a "certified" hypnotist should conduct the interview.[130] Trial procedures that should be followed with respect to these safeguards were established the following year, in the case of *United States v. Awkard*:[131] "Objections to the subject testimony on the ground that such procedures were not followed should be heard by the district judge before trial, or out of the presence of the jury on voir dire of the witness. If the trial court overrules the objection and permits the subject to testify, the adverse party may, if it wishes, expose the details of the hypnosis to the jury."[132]

   In the same year as *Awkard*, a far more elaborate set of procedural guidelines was established by a Wisconsin trial judge in the case of *State v. White*.[133] The *White* court found that reliability of testimony free of undue suggestion and other potential hazards of hypnosis was dependent upon compliance with nine procedural safeguards.[134] The *White* court stressed that compliance with the guidelines did not guarantee admission of the testimony, nor did failure to comply require automatic exclusion. The guidelines were designed to assist the trial judge in assessing the reliability of the testimony of the previously hypnotized witness. "The central inquiry remains whether, as a result of events occurring during the hypnotic session, any subsequent statements made by the hypnotized subject should be considered so unreliable as not to be admissible [sic] at trial."[135] The *White* safeguards were based upon the four guidelines originally suggested by the psychiatrist, Martin Orne.[136] In 1980, the *White* guidelines were adopted by courts in New York[137] and, in modified form, by the New Jersey trial court[138] in *Hurd*.

In *Hurd*,[139] the sole prosecution witness, a victim of a night knife attack, was "unable or unwilling" to identify her assailant.[140] At the suggestion of the prosecutor's office, the victim underwent hypnosis by a psychiatrist to enhance her recollection. Through a process of hypnotic revivification, the victim was able to identify her assailant as the defendant, her former husband.[141] Although she subsequently expressed doubts about her identification, the police and the psychiatrist encouraged her to stick to it, explaining to her that unless she made an identification, the defendant would "remain free to attack her again, possibly leaving her children without a mother."[142] With this encouragement, the victim held to her identification and the defendant was indicted as a result. Prior to jury selection, the defense moved to suppress the proposed in-court identification, arguing that the testimony failed to meet the *Frye* test for admissibility of scientific evidence.[143] The trial court applied *Frye* but declined to hold that hypnotically refreshed testimony is per se inadmissible. It did, however, suppress the proposed identification because the state failed to meet the court's two-part test for admissibility.[144]

On appeal, the New Jersey Supreme Court accepted the trial court's test and reasoning. It agreed that hypnotically refreshed testimony must satisfy the *Frye* general acceptance standard of reliability in order to be admitted into evidence.[145] Unlike the court in *Mack,* however, it did not demand that hypnosis be generally accepted as a reliable means of "reviving truthful or historically accurate recall."[146] The *Hurd* court found that the purpose of using hypnosis "is not to obtain truth, as a polygraph...is supposed to do," but rather to overcome amnesia and restore the memory of a witness.[147] "In light of this purpose, hypnosis can be considered reasonably reliable if it is able to yield recollections as accurate as those of an ordinary witness, which likewise are often historically inaccurate."[148] The court examined the evidence submitted at trial and concluded that hypnosis was generally accepted as reliable for this purpose if it was conducted properly and used only in appropriate cases. Thus, the court formulated the rule that "hypnotically-induced testimony may be admissible if the proponent of the testimony can demonstrate that the use of hypnosis in the particular case was a reasonably reliable means of restoring memory comparable to normal recall...."[149]

Admissibility is not automatic, however, and the court proceeded to establish a two-step process for determining admissibility. First, after the proponent of hypnotically refreshed testimony has informed his opponent of his intention to introduce such testimony and has provided him with a record of the session, the trial court will conduct a hearing out of the jury's presence to determine whether the use of hypnosis was appropriate to overcome the particular type of memory loss involved.[150] The second step involves a determination as to whether the procedures used were reasonably reliable means of restoring the witness' memory. In order to provide an adequate record for evaluating reliability of procedures, and to ensure a minimum level of reliability, the court adopted the six procedural safeguards used by the trial court:

1. The hypnotic session should be conducted by a licensed psychiatrist or psychologist trained in the use of hypnosis.

2. The qualified professional conducting the hypnotic session should be independent of and not responsible to the prosecutor, investigator, or the defense.

3. Any information given to the hypnotist by law enforcement personnel prior to the hypnotic session must be in written form so that subsequently the extent of the information the subject received from the hypnotist may be determined.

4. Before induction of hypnosis, the hypnotist should obtain from the subject a detailed description of the facts as the subject remembers them, carefully avoiding adding any new elements to the witness' description of events.

5. All contacts between the hypnotist and the subject should be recorded so that a permanent record is available for comparison and study to establish that the witness has not received information or suggestion which might later be reported as having been first described by the subject during hypnosis. Videotape should be employed if possible, but should not be mandatory.

6. Only the hypnotist and the subject should be present during any phase of the hypnotic session, including the prehypnotic testing and posthypnotic interview.[151]

In demonstrating appropriate use of hypnosis and compliance with required procedures, the burden of proof is on the proponent of the evidence and the standard is that of clear and convincing evidence.[152] The court recognized that this standard is a "heavy burden" but one that is justified due to "the potential for abuse of hypnosis, the genuine likelihood of error, and the consequent risk of injustice."[153]

Hurd is arguably the best-known case in which a court has taken a guarded admissibility approach to hypnotically refreshed testimony by clearly articulating a list of guidelines designed to protect against undue suggestiveness and other risks of hypnosis and, thus, to assure the reliability of such testimony evidence. Numerous other courts have adopted a guarded admissibility approach to hypnotically refreshed testimony, but the variations in employing guidelines and tests are so great as to make generalizations extremely difficult.

The very term "procedural safeguards" has been treated differently among courts. To some, like *Hurd,* it has meant the establishment of predicate guidelines to ensure, and measure, reliability. To others, especially those courts which have rejected *Frye* as an appropriate test, procedural safeguards have meant the use of balancing tests, described and named in various ways by different courts, but essentially embodying the relevancy and probative/prejudicial principles of the Federal Rules of Evidence. Texas appellate courts, ignoring or rejecting *Frye,* have referred to the "totality of the circumstances" test.[154] The Fifth Circuit, similarly, in rejecting the *Frye* test as inappropriate, declined to formulate a list of guidelines, but used instead a test involving an assessment of relevancy and a balancing of probative versus prejudicial values.[155]

Considerable variance exists just among courts adopting a *Hurd*-type set of predicate guidelines. An Ohio appellate court has followed *Hurd,* using the *Frye* test to find that hypnosis is generally accepted as a reliable scientific means of refreshing memory, and adopting the *Hurd* guidelines.[156] The Wisconsin Supreme Court has rejected the *Frye* test as inappropriate, but has adopted *Hurd*-type guidelines (actually the nine guidelines of *White*).[157] Appellate courts in Illinois have also rejected *Frye* as inappropriate, and have adopted *Hurd* guidelines, although disagreement exists as to the application of the guidelines to similar fact patterns.[158] An appellate court in New Mexico largely ignored the *Frye* test in adopting the *Hurd* safeguards,[159] while the New Mexico Supreme Court, also ignoring *Frye* and citing the appellate court favorably, affirmed a conviction in which the established guidelines had not been followed, justifying its decision instead on the consonance of the pre and posthypnotic statements of the witness.[160] Oregon has adopted *Hurd*-type guidelines by statute, requiring, *inter alia,* that the hypnotic session must be recorded and made available to the adverse party as a pre-condition of admissibility.[161]

Elsewhere, Alabama has straddled the fence, holding that *Frye* is the appropriate test for hypnotically refreshed testimony, but refusing to apply either a per se rule of admissibility or one of inadmissibility, and failing to adopt procedural guidelines, while nevertheless cautioning proponents of such testimony to use safeguards to assure reliability.[162] Louisiana's Supreme Court has rejected a per se exclusion rule[163] but it has also refused to establish procedural guidelines, and instead has advised law enforcement authorities to follow "the guidelines and safeguards adopted in other jurisdictions."[164]

What almost all of these courts have in common is an aversion to the exclusion of relevant evidence, a recognition of the risks of hypnotically refreshed testimony, and a belief that procedural safeguards in the form of predicate guidelines and/or balancing tests can minimize or negate those risks. The guarded admissibility approach, then, rejects the unquestioning admissibility approach of *Harding* without automatically excluding relevant evidence by means of the per se inadmissibility approach of *Mack*.

The Approach of Per Se Exclusion: The Frye Test

While many courts responded to the potential hazards of hypnosis by employing balancing tests and procedural guidelines to ensure reliability, other courts, beginning with *State v. Mack*,[165] dealt with the problems of hypnotically refreshed testimony by simply excluding such testimony. These courts found hypnosis, and its products or results, to be scientifically unreliable and, therefore, excluded hypnotically refreshed testimony by means of a per se rule of inadmissibility. Such a rule is, of course, a Draconian device that effectively renders a previously hypnotized witness incompetent, at least with respect to the details of the hypnotic session and any memories recalled by means of hypnosis. Nonetheless, this approach to the problem has proved popular. In the five years following the *Mack* decision, a per se rule of inadmissibility has been adopted by the supreme courts in more than a dozen states,[166] and by lower appellate courts in several other states.

Among the courts taking this approach, "the most frequently employed rationale used to support a per se ban on the use of hypnotically refreshed testimony is that hypnosis as a memory enhancing technique fails...the general test for the admission of evidence resulting from the use of a new scientific technique originally articulated in *Frye*..."[167] In fact, these courts have invariably used the *Frye* test, or the "theory underlying *Frye*,"[168] or analogous reasoning.[169] The only variance among these courts has been in their enthusiasm for the *Frye* test, and in their interpretation of what the test is supposed to measure.

Within this approach, several cases seem especially noteworthy: *State v. Mack*,[170] *People v. Shirley*,[171] *State ex. rel. Collins v. Superior Court*,[172] and *State v. Collins*.[173] *Mack* is noteworthy because of its bold break from the *Harding* approach.[174] *Shirley* has attracted attention and criticism for its sweeping scope and for its polemical tone.[175] *State ex rel. Collins* attracted attention for its supplemental opinion modifying its original holding announced just four months previously. In *State v. Collins*, the Maryland Supreme Court undercut the foundation for the per se admissibility approach when it overruled its prior holding in *Harding*.

State v. Mack involved a prosecution for criminal sexual conduct and aggravated assault. The victim, apparently intoxicated and suffering from various "emotional problems" at the time of the incident, gave medical personnel and police conflicting versions as to how she acquired a serious injury to her vagina.[176] At the instigation of the police, the victim underwent hypnosis by a self-taught lay hypnotist. During the session, attended by two police officers, the victim recalled that her injury had been inflicted by the repeated plunging of a switchblade knife, wielded by the defendant.[177] The defendant was subsequently arrested, but moved to suppress the victim's testimony on the grounds that it was unreliable and that it would deny his right to confront the witness.[178] The trial court certified the issue of admissibility to the Minnesota Supreme Court after an extensive hearing on the motion to suppress.

The Minnesota Supreme Court considered legal and scientific authority[179] and determined that "although hypnotically-adduced memory is not strictly analogous to the results of mechanical testing, we are persuaded that the *Frye* rule is equally applicable in this context."[180] The court reviewed the expert testimony and found that although there was agreement that "historically valid memory can result from hypnotic recall,"[181] there were also indications of hypnotic hazards. The court noted the following problems: (1) the subject's increased susceptibility to suggestion; (2) the subject's tendency to creatively fill in gaps in memory; (3) the inability of the subject or of experts to determine which parts are fanciful, and which are lies; (4) the "hardening" of memory which makes the subject convinced of the truth of hypnotically recalled accounts and which would make it impossible to meaningfully cross-examine the witness.[182] For these reasons, the court concluded that hypnotically refreshed testimony was not scientifically reliable in being historically "accurate."[183] Thus, unlike the court in *State v. Hurd,* which found hypnosis reliable in yielding "recollections as accurate as those of an ordinary witness, which likewise are often historically inaccurate,"[184] the court in *Mack* found hypnosis to be unreliable by applying *Frye* to a higher standard of historical accuracy.

Within the next year and a half, the example set by the Minnesota Supreme Court in *Mack* was followed by the highest courts in Arizona,[185] California,[186] Michigan,[187] Nebraska,[188] and Pennsylvania.[189] In each case, the courts examined the issue of admissibility of testimony of a previously hypnotized witness, used some application of the *Frye* test to conclude that hypnosis was not generally accepted as a reliable scientific technique of restoring historically accurate memory, and, therefore, barred the admissibility of such testimony, effectively rendering the witness incompetent. In these cases, the question of whether testimony relating to pre-hypnotic memory was included in the ban was either unanswered or was answered in the affirmative. Belatedly recognizing the severe burdens that a total ban would place on police and prosecution, the courts in five of the six states mentioned above moved with surprising speed to clarify or to modify their decisions in order to allow witnesses to testify regarding those matters they were able to recall prior to hypnosis. By the end of 1983, only California's Supreme Court had retained, as it retains still, its sweeping rule that the testimony of previously hypnotized witnesses is "inadmissible as to all matters relating to those events [in issue], from the time of the hypnotic sessions forward."[190] No other supreme court has subsequently adopted California's approach.

The California decision of *People v. Shirley* is significant for reasons other than its singular sweeping rule of inadmissibility. The alternative procedural safeguard approach had been established by the time of the *Shirley* decision, and had gained authority and forward inertia as a result of the 1981 decision in *State v. Hurd*. Thus, the court in *Shirley* not only had the opportunity to reaffirm, and broaden, the approach established in *Mack*, but also to attack the procedural guidelines approach of *Hurd*.

The facts in *Shirley* represented a classic case of a rape prosecution in which the only two witnesses had conflicting versions of the same events, with the victim alleging rape and the defendant claiming voluntary participation. Due to discrepancies in the complainant's own version of events, she was hypnotized by a deputy district attorney three months after the events in question in order to "fill the gaps" in her stories.[191] The defense moved to suppress the complainant's testimony on the grounds that "this is an improper use of hypnosis" because "it is not in fact refreshing a witness's recollection" but "it is in fact manufactured evidence."[192] The trial court denied the motion on the ground that the fact of hypnosis went to the credibility of the witness, not the admissibility of her testimony. At trial, the defense produced only one expert witness, who testified that there is significant danger that hypnosis can result in inaccurate memory.[193]

Although the trial court did not address the issue of admissibility in terms of the *Frye* test, on appeal the California Supreme Court deemed it appropriate to decide the issue using the *Frye* test. It relied on the sole witness who testified at trial as well as various scientific and legal literature to conclude that it is not generally accepted that hypnosis produced reliable memory restoration.[194] The language of the opinion is somewhat muddled, but it appears that the majority considered reliable memory to be historically accurate memory. The majority considered hypnosis to be unreliable in restoring historically accurate memory because of the subject's increased susceptibility to suggestion, and the subject's tendency to confabulate and to lose critical judgment about his memory, becoming objectively unable to distinguish accurate memory from confabulation and yet becoming subjectively convinced of the accuracy of post- hypnotic memory.[195]

The majority addressed the subject of procedural safeguards by means of a three-paragraph criticism of the guidelines for failing to avoid the problems of confabulation, increased confidence in posthypnotic memory on the part of the subject, and loss of critical judgment.[196] Noting that the Attorney General proposed no safeguards to deal with those problems, the court added that even if guidelines had been proposed, the court doubted that such guidelines could be administered "without injecting undue delay and confusion into the judicial process."[197] The court referred to the *Hurd* guidelines as "pretense," and it rejected any attempt at formulating such guidelines, stating that "...the game is not worth the candle."[198]

Having found hypnotically refreshed testimony to be unreliable, and having rejected procedural safeguards to ensure and measure reliability, the court held that the testimony of a witness who has undergone hypnosis for the purpose of restoring his memory of the events in issue is inadmissible as to all matters relating to those events, "from the time of the hypnotic session forward."[199] The court stated that this rule did not foreclose the continued use of hypnosis for investigative purposes, although it proposed no guidelines for use in investigations, and it reiterated that anyone who has been hypnotized for such purposes "will not be allowed to testify as a witness to the events of the crime."[200]

The decision in *Shirley* has been sharply criticized for a variety of reasons, including its language and tone, its broad ban on pre and posthypnotic testimony, its application of the *Frye* test, and its practical foreclosure of investigative uses of hypnosis.[201] In an attempt to mitigate the harsher effects of a *Shirley*-type rule, the state supreme courts which had rendered similar or ambiguous decisions moved to clarify or modify their opinions. In short order, the supreme courts in Arizona,[202] Michigan,[203] Nebraska,[204] Pennsylvania,[205] and Minnesota[206] rendered decisions which retained a ban on posthypnotic memory but which allowed witnesses to testify as to matters they recalled prior to hypnosis.

In Arizona, in *State ex rel. Collins v. Superior Court,*[207] the Supreme Court had initially ruled, in January of 1982, that any person who had been hypnotized would "be incompetent to testify to *any* fact."[208] Justice O'Holohan filed a forceful dissent, pointing out some of the negative practical effects of such a holding.[209] The State's motion for a rehearing was granted and the Supreme Court delivered an extensive supplemental opinion in May, 1982, modifying its January opinion.[210]

The court's supplemental opinion noted that the month and a half old decision in *People v. Shirley* had found the *Frye* test useful in serving "the salutary purpose of preventing the jury from being misled by unproven and ultimately unsound scientific methods."[211] The court then offered its version of the *Frye* test, holding that it is satisfied when knowledgeable experts "have come to recognize the methodology as having sufficient scientific basis to produce reasonably uniform and reliable results that will contribute materially to the ascertainment of the truth."[212] Having said that, the court did not rely on expert testimony but upon a review of case law plus some scientific and legal commentary, finding that hypnosis was unreliable due to various factors.[213] Analyzing procedural safeguards, it found that they may increase reliability of hypnosis and allow it "to cross the *Frye* threshold,"[214] but it ultimately rejected the safeguard approach because that approach "will consume too much in the way of judicial resources, will produce conflicting results in different trial courts, and will produce few situations in which hypnotic recall is ever admitted."[215]

The court then recognized that hypnosis has value for investigative purposes, that the use of hypnosis for those purposes somehow entails less serious risks, and, therefore, the court modified its January opinion, holding that a previously hypnotized witness could testify "with regard to those matters which he or she was able to recall and relate prior to hypnosis."[216] The court ruled, however, that any investigating party is henceforth required to record a witness' prehypnotic recollections prior to placing the witness under hypnosis.[217] Admission of prehypnotic testimony absent such a procedure would be error. Further, the court suggested that parties intending to use hypnosis for investigative purposes follow some if not all, of the Orne procedural guidelines.[218]

In the next three years, the courts in a number of other states have followed the approach of per se exclusion of posthypnotic testimony. In addition to the states mentioned *supra,* the approach has been clearly adopted by courts in Colorado,[219] Massachusetts,[220] New York,[221] Maryland,[222] North Carolina,[223] Oklahoma,[224] Washington,[225] Delaware,[226] and most recently, Florida.[227] Of these, Maryland's adoption was especially notable, for in overruling *Harding,* the Supreme Court undercut the foundation for the admissibility approach.[228] While all of the states, except California, mentioned in this section allow prehypnotic testimony, most, like Arizona, have either required or suggested guidelines for investigative parties in order to avoid "tainting" prehypnotic memories with posthypnotic memories.

Analysis

There exist, now, three competing approaches to the issue of admissibility of previously hypnotized witnesses; the admissibility approach, the guarded admissibility approach, and the per se exclusion approach. While it is difficult to describe the last approach as the "majority" position, its adoption is at least currently a strong, if not dominant, trend among state courts. That this is so is unfortunate, for it is the approach of per se exclusion that contains the most significant analytical flaws and that produced the most serious negative practical effects.

Critique of the Per Se Exclusion Approach

Courts excluding hypnotically refreshed testimony have done so primarily because, applying some variation of the *Frye* test, they have found that hypnosis lacks general scientific acceptance as a means of restoring historically accurate memory. Hypnotically refreshed testimony is, therefore, unreliable as scientific evidence and must not be admitted lest it confuse or mislead the trier of fact. While this argument may seem superficially appealing, close scrutiny reveals a number of analytical flaws.

First, the *Frye* test is not appropriate to the issue of hypnotically refreshed testimony. As previously discussed, the *Frye* test explicitly applies in its terms to the admissibility of expert opinion deduced from a scientific test or principle. As it was originally applied, "the *Frye* test prevented an expert from vouching for the credibility of a witness and then supporting his (the expert's) testimony by reference to some scientific principle that purportedly proved that the initial witness was telling the truth."[229] Applying *Frye* in order to exclude eyewitness testimony is clearly an improper use of the test. In rejecting *Frye's* applicability to hypnosis, the Alaska Court of Appeals correctly noted that "strictly speaking, no expert is involved."[230] What is involved is eyewitness testimony which, whether refreshed by hypnosis or not, is simply not the same thing as expert opinion deduced from a scientific test. As the Fifth Circuit Court of Appeals recently stated: "The issue here is not the admissibility of a hypnotist's observations or statements made by the witness during hypnosis, but instead the admissibility of the testimony of a lay witness in a normal, waking state."[231] To use the *Frye* test to exclude such testimony is "to turn the. . .test on its head."[232]

Despite its inappropriate application, mere employment of the *Frye* test will not exclude hypnotically refreshed testimony if the court applies the standard correctly in framing the issue. If the court understands the true nature and purpose of hypnosis, it will frame the issue, as the court did in *State v. Hurd,* by inquiring whether hypnosis is generally accepted as a "reliable means of restoring memory comparable to normal recall."[233] Even critics of the use of hypnosis do not deny that the technique may enhance the memory of a witness.[234] Properly framing the issue according to the nature and purpose of hypnosis can easily enable a court to conclude, as the *Hurd* court did, that hypnosis is generally accepted as a reasonably reliable method of restoring a person's memory, at least "if it is conducted properly and used only in appropriate cases."[235]

A second analytical error of exclusionary-approach courts, then, lies in incorrectly framing the issue by asking whether hypnosis is generally accepted as reliable in producing historically accurate memory. Framing the issue in this fashion betrays a basic ignorance of the nature and purpose of hypnosis and sets up a standard which is discriminatory and unrealistic.[236] The *Frye* test is normally employed as a standard in assessing the reliability of expert opinion and experimental data commonly associated with technological devices capable of producing objectively measurable results.[237] Unlike the technological hardware with which some courts have forced it to associate, hypnosis has no dials to spin; it produces no hard results capable of precise and objective calibration or measurement. Most importantly, hypnosis is a technique which may prove helpful in refreshing the memory of a witness. It is not a guarantor of truth or of historical accuracy and should not be treated as such. Given popular misconceptions about hypnosis, it is understandable that some courts have equated hypnosis with techniques such as narcoanalysis and with machines such as polygraphs. But while this comparison may be understandable, it is nonetheless error, as two writers have stated:

> Requiring hypnosis to perform at truth-determinant function...distorts the scientific process and aborts its potential benefit to litigation. The value of hypnosis lies in its scientifically-established reliability as a device for retrieving relevant testimony previously forgotten or psychologically repressed, *regardless* of the factual truth or falsity of that testimony.[238]

A third error of exclusionary-approach courts is their assumption that hypnotically refreshed testimony is qualitatively different from, and inferior to, other memory. It is not. Courts which have refused to admit hypnotically refreshed testimony have recited the litany of potential hypnotic dangers: suggestibility, hypercompliance, confabulation, deliberate falsification, and an increased witness confidence in, and a "hardening" of, testimony. What these courts fail to realize, or at least to admit, is that these phenomena are not exclusive to memory enhanced by hypnosis. They are phenomena which may afflict, just as easily and in equal measure, the memory of non-hypnotized witnesses. Our minds selectively record and store information, and as new data is incrementally added, original perceptions become distorted and so intermixed with subsequent additions that it becomes impossible to distinguish original perceptions from sequential increments. As a noted authority on memory, Dr. E. F. Loftus, explains:

> Memory is imperfect. This is because we often do not see things accurately in the first place. But even if we take in a reasonably accurate picture of some experience, it does not necessarily stay perfectly intact in memory. . . .The memory traces can actually undergo motivation, with the introduction of special kinds of interfering facts, the memory traces seem sometimes to change or become transformed. These distortions can be quite frightening, for they can cause us to have memories of things that never happened.[239]

On a daily basis, we round out incomplete knowledge by confabulating, filling in gaps in our memory with our "biases, expectations, and past knowledges."[240]

Inaccuracies in normal memory may become magnified in the mind of an individual who has been a victim or witness of a crime.[241] Eyewitness testimony often is further distorted by the process of interrogation by police and lawyers.[242] One court recently observed that "the danger of confabulation, the danger that information supplied through suggestion will become a part of a witness's memory, and the danger that the witness will be as confident about the inaccurate recollections as the accurate recollections, are possible side effects of the interrogation process."[243] Increased confidence and hardening of testimony may occur in non-hypnotized witnesses simply as a result of cross-examination.[244] Because of the similarity of problems between hypnotically refreshed testimony and normal testimony, the exclusion of the former is completely unwarranted.[245] In fact, where a qualified hypnotist followed predicate guidelines designed to avoid these problems, hypnotically refreshed testimony should prove more reliable than testimony not subject to such safeguards.[246]

The exclusionary-approach not only contains serious analytical flaws, but it poses significant practical problems as well. The total exclusionary-approach of *Shirley* was criticized as effectively ending the investigatory use of hypnosis by law enforcement agencies[247] and as being unduly harsh on victims of crime.[248] To avoid the problems resulting from *Shirley's* total ban, other exclusionary-approach courts have adopted a modified rule which permits a witness to testify as to facts remembered prior to hypnosis. Unfortunately, this compromise rule only creates additional problems. It is illogical and unworkable. It presupposes that a witness had[249] a prehypnotic memory and that a record has been made of it. If both of those assumptions prove correct, then the witness may testify only with respect to what is on the record.[250] This may raise ethical problems for a witness who may be forced to violate his oath by testifying to prehypnotic memory he no longer accepts as true, as well as for a prosecutor who may be forced to violate disciplinary rules by instructing the witness to stick to the record the witness no longer accepts as true. The rule creates tactical problems for the defense whose cross examination is restricted by fear of bringing out recall tainted by hypnosis. The rule creates a procedural nightmare for the trial judge who must insure that the parties do not stray from the prehypnotic script.[251] Additionally, though the modified rule was adopted in part to encourage investigatory uses of hypnosis, it does not have that effect. Many of these courts have stated that even prehypnotic evidence would be barred unless proper procedural hypnotic safeguards were used, yet they have not specified what those safeguards are.[252] Guessing at procedures has to have a chilling effect on law enforcement authorities and others wishing to use hypnosis. Lastly, these exclusionary-approach courts seem to ignore the fact that if a witness had a good prehypnotic memory, it is unlikely that hypnosis would have been needed to refresh it. Ergo, the only memory that a previously hypnotized witness is allowed to testify to is a memory that was faulty and in need of refreshing.

A final criticism of the per se exclusion approach concerns both the *Frye* test and the reasons why some courts have applied it to hypnosis. One of the purported advantages of the *Frye* standard is that it "promotes uniformity of decision."[253] As has been seen, however, uniformity has not been produced. There have been inconsistencies in application and in results. Some courts have used the *Frye* standard, while others have rejected it as inappropriate. Among those courts which have employed the test, some have found hypnotically adduced evidence to be reliable, while others have not. McCormick has labelled the application of the test as "highly selective,"[254] and Giannelli has observed that "inconsistencies in application abound."[255] As to why this is the case, Professor Giannelli argues that instead of using *Frye* as a neutral analytical tool, "it appears that many courts apply it as a label to justify their own views about the reliability of particular forensic techniques."[256] Similarly,

Professor Weyrauch has observed that rules of evidence function as "legal masks" which hide the deep-seated value choices of judges.[257] One can only speculate as to the true reasons why some judges have chosen to exclude hypnotically refreshed testimony. It may be that they genuinely misunderstand the nature and purpose of hypnosis. It may be that they distrust the ability of jurors to properly weigh such testimony. It may be that they fear such testimony will excessively benefit the prosecution in criminal cases.[258] A better jurisprudence requires that judges cease to hide behind the mask of *Frye* reliability and openly expose and clearly articulate their true reasons in order that those concerns may be adequately debated and evaluated. Such debate is foreclosed and justice is impaired by the expedient employment of an inappropriate standard which may result in an automatic and overly board exclusion of relevant evidence.[259]

Critique of the Admissibility Approach

The admissibility approach has certain advantages to it. It does not automatically disqualify an entire class of witnesses. It encourages the use of hypnosis as an investigatory tool. Perhaps most importantly, it allows relevant testimony to reach the trier of fact. The approach has, however, several serious defects which render it unacceptable.

First, the approach fails to adequately recognize the potential for the abuse of hypnosis. While it is true that the possible negative effects of hypnosis may be produced in non-hypnotized witnesses, there is a difference between hypnosis and other techniques of investigation and interrogation. Hypnosis is inherently suggestive, and the subject must be willing to comply with suggestions if hypnosis is to have any value. The danger lies in the possibility that the hypnotist will, inadvertently or deliberately suggest the identity or culpability of a suspect. This danger is greatest when hypnosis is performed by unqualified personnel and/or by law enforcement authorities or their agents. In allowing the testimony of all previously hypnotized witnesses to reach the trier of fact, the court does not bar evidence made unreliable by undue suggestiveness.

Courts taking this approach answer that reliability is a component of credibility and is, as such, to be evaluated by the trier of fact. But this answer only betrays a second defect of this approach. Unlike most methods of refreshing the memory of a witness, hypnosis normally takes place prior to trial. Absent video tape recording, the jury is unable to observe the demeanor of the witness prior to hypnosis. Absent assurances that procedural guidelines were followed to prevent suggestiveness, the jury has no way of knowing whether, or how much, suggestiveness took place. The trier of fact, in short, has a markedly impaired ability to adequately evaluate either the reliability of the hypnotic procedures or the credibility of the witness' hypnotically refreshed memory.

A third, closely related, deficiency of this approach is that by placing such an unrealistic burden on the jury, the trial judge has abdicated some of his own responsibility. Under the Federal Rules of Evidence and analogous state evidentiary codes, a trial judge must subject even relevant evidence to a probative/prejudicial test. A per se admissibility approach effectively evades this obligation, shifting it to litigating counsel and the jury. In *United States v. Valdez*,[260] the Court of Appeals for the Fifth Circuit acknowledged the potential value of hypnotically adduced evidence, but it found reversible error in the decision of a United States district court which had admitted such evidence by means of a per se rule of admissibility, as opposed to an application of the probative/prejudicial test.

> Posthypnotic testimony can obviously be relevant...And we cannot say that it is always without probative value. In this case, however, the district court did not expressly weigh probative value against potential for prejudice. Admissibility was based instead on a rule-of-law decision that posthypnotic testimony was admissible and the jury might assess credibility.[261]

A final problem with this approach is that rule of per se admissibility of hypnotically adduced evidence does nothing to encourage law enforcement agencies and other investigators to employ qualified hypnotists and to follow procedures designed to avoid improper suggestions and to minimize other risks of hypnotic interrogation. Lacking any incentive to invest time, money, and effort in obtaining trained personnel and in using proper procedures, many agencies may use personnel and procedures that, however unintentionally, increase the probability of distorting the memory of a witness and, consequently, of prejudicing the rights of a defendant.[262]

Critique of the Guarded Admissibility Approach

The guarded admissibility approach has been subjected to various criticisms, especially by the courts which have rejected it in favor of a rule of per se exclusion. One of the more common criticisms is that the use of predicate guidelines only protect against suggestiveness and not against the other risks of hypnosis.[263] This argument is without merit for it betrays a misunderstanding of the nature and purpose of both hypnosis and of the guidelines. As has been previously stated, the purpose of hypnosis is to refresh memory and not to guarantee truth.[264] The purpose of the guidelines is to ensure that proper hypnotic procedures are used. As has been previously shown, if proper hypnotic procedures are used, restored memory should be at least as reliable as the memory of a nonhypnotized witness.[265]

The approach has also been criticized on the grounds that monitoring compliance with guidelines will prove difficult in practice, would be time consuming, and would not lead to uniform results.[266] These are ironic criticisms in view of the inconsistencies and practical problems of the per se exclusion approach.[267] They are also of little merit. A guarded admissibility approach provides a general standard in asserting that hypnotically refreshed testimony is reliable when hypnotic procedures were conducted properly. Guidelines provide uniformity of investigative practices within the jurisdiction. As investigative bodies and courts become familiar with the guidelines, monitoring compliance should be easier and inconsistent results should be fewer. In any event, any inconsistent results due to the peculiarities of a given case and any increased judicial expenditure of time in reviewing the facts of each case seem preferable to the intentional exclusion of relevant evidence and the disqualification of a class of witnesses.

Another criticism of the guarded admissibility approach is that it may admit evidence which could confuse the trier of fact since "hypnosis is cloaked in a veil of mysticism."[268] The same courts assert, however paradoxically, that because jurors find hypnosis to be confusing, they will give it added weight, placing "undue emphasis on what transpired during a hypnotic session."[269] This criticism exhibits an unfounded mistrust of jurors which, fortunately, is not shared by all courts.[270] Complex litigation, often involving expert testimony on subjects more esoteric than hypnosis, is a common feature of modern trial practice. There is no reason to single out hypnosis as confusing. Besides, as one judge commented in a recent decision involving hypnotism: "I am firmly of the belief that jurors are quite capable of seeing through flaky testimony and pseudo-scientific claptrap."[271] Vigorous cross examination by counsel and cautionary instructions from the bench should prove adequate in assisting juries in this task.

Given the previous discussions of the analytical and practical shortcomings of the approaches of per se exclusion and of per se admissibility, it is obvious that an alternative to both approaches is preferable. Although it too has suffered criticism, the guarded admissibility approach appears, on balance, to offer the best solution to the problems of hypnotically refreshed testimony.

Perhaps the central problem with this approach is that its component elements lack clear definition. Some courts have emphasized the probative/prejudicial test of the Federal Rules of Evidence or analogous state evidentiary codes.[272] Other courts have emphasized predicate guidelines.[273] Among the latter, some have referred to guidelines only vaguely, while most have articulated an explicit set of suggested or required guidelines. Among the courts requiring guidelines, there has not been complete agreement as to what the guidelines should require, although all of the guideline sets have their primordial genesis in the safeguards proposed by Martin Orne.[274]

In the authors' opinion, a guarded admissibility approach should contain three elements: (1) the establishment of predicate guidelines for hypnotic use, (2) the use of the probative/prejudicial analysis, and (3) the consideration of the existence and nature of corroborating evidence.

Establishing procedural guidelines is the best way to ensure that investigatory bodies will use hypnosis only in appropriate cases and that they will conduct hypnotic interviews only with qualified personnel utilizing procedures designed to protect against undue suggestiveness, confabulation and other hazards of the hypnotic interview-process. Appropriate use and procedural compliance should be determined by the court at a hearing out of the jury's presence. As the court in *Hurd* required, the burden of proof should be on the proponent of the evidence and the standard should be that of clear and convincing evidence.[275]

In deciding which guidelines to promulgate, the court has a variety of existing sets from which to choose. The guideline sets adopted by courts to date are understandably similar to one another, and all are adequate. Preferable to them, however, are the guidelines known as the "Federal Model,"[276] a standard used by the investigative departments of the Armed Services, the Secret Service, the Treasury Department and the Federal Bureau of Investigation.[277] The Federal Model is also similar to Orne's,[278] but it is an improvement on earlier models because it is richer in protective detail and because it expands "the concept of procedural safeguards beyond the hypnotic interview to the more basic considerations of circumstances for which such interviews are warranted."[279] By placing "appropriate use" within the guidelines, the Federal Model saves the court the task of a separate determination. If it finds compliance with the guidelines, appropriate use is guaranteed.[280]

After the court has determined that its hypnotic procedural guidelines have been followed, the court should apply the probative/prejudicial balancing test of the Federal Rules of Evidence or analogous state evidentiary codes.[281] Procedural guidelines, for all of their importance, are only suggested procedures to guide investigatory agencies and courts. Even if all of them are followed, the court may justifiably conclude that the hypnotically adduced evidence is not relevant because it is not probative, or that its probative value is substantially outweighed by its potentially prejudicial effect. Alternatively, the evidence could be admitted even if some of the guidelines were not followed if the court determines, under the totality of the circumstances, that the hypnotic process was not unduly suggestive and that the resulting evidence is sufficiently probative. The Federal Rules of Evidence create a presumption in favor of the admission of relevant evidence, and if the guidelines were followed it is likely that the trial judge will find the hypnotically refreshed memory of the witness to be as reliable as that of an ordinary witness, and, therefore, sufficiently probative and non-prejudicial to be put before the trier of fact. Nonetheless, guidelines cannot take away the sound discretion of the trial judge, nor can they remove his responsibility to exercise such judgment.

Lastly, in applying probative/prejudicial analysis, the court should consider the existence of corroborating evidence. This is not to say that corroborating evidence should be the only factor determining admissibility of hypnotically refreshed testimony. A judge may have sound reasons for admitting, or refusing to admit, such testimony apart from the issue of corroborating evidence. The existence of corroborating evidence is, however, a powerful guarantor of the reliability and probative value of hypnotically refreshed testimony.[282] If the Federal Model is used for procedural guidelines, corroborating evidence should always exist by the time of trial. The model precludes the use of hypnosis absent the likelihood of independent corroboration and states that information obtained through hypnosis may not form the basis of investigative conclusions without corroboration evidence.[283]

Conclusion

Hypnosis is a valuable techniques to assist a witnesses to recall previously forgotten or psychologically repressed memories. Its use, however, is not without some risk that a hypnotized subject will recall false memories. This risk is greatest when unqualified personnel induce hypnosis by using improper procedures. Many state courts have recently responded to this risk by excluding *per se* the testimony of previously hypnotized witnesses, holding that hypnosis is unreliable as a means of producing historically accurate recall. This approach is unwarranted—it distorts the nature and purpose of hypnosis, exaggerates hypnotic risks, and fails to adequately consider the ability of hypnotically refreshed testimony. Moreover, this approach is undesirable because it discourages the investigatory uses of hypnosis by law enforcement agencies and excludes relevant evidence by rendering virtually incompetent an entire class of witnesses.

On the other hand, almost equally unacceptable is the older judicial approach of *per se* admission of hypnotically refreshed testimony, which leaves to the jury the role of according proper weight to such evidence. This approach ignores the differences between hypnotism and other means of refreshing the memory of a witness and overlooks the possibility of undue suggestiveness during the hypnotic interview. It places an unrealistic burden on the factfinder and does nothing to encourage law enforcement authorities to us proper hypnotic procedures and qualified personnel.

Between these two extremes lies the approach of guarded admissibility. Under this approach, a court would, ideally, adopt hypnotic procedural guidelines, consider corroborating evidence or its absence, and employ standard probative/prejudicial analysis in determining the admissibility of hypnotically refreshed testimony in a given case. Procedural guidelines guarantee that undue suggestion did not occur during hypnosis and that the refreshed memory of the witness is as reliable as that of a non-hypnotized witness. Corroborating evidence further guarantees the reliability and probative value of hypnotically refreshed testimony. If, considering the totally of the circumstances, standard evidentiary analysis determines that the probative value of the testimony is high and that its prejudicial potential is low, the testimony should be admitted. Vigorous cross examination by counsel and cautionary instructions from the bench will assist the jury, the final determiner of truth, in properly weighing the credibility of hypnotically refreshed testimony.

References

¹For a useful and interesting early forensic history of hypnosis, see Laurence and Perry, *Forensic Hypnosis in the Late Nineteenth Century.* 31 J. of Clinical and Experimental Hypnosis 266 (1983). For a briefer discussion, see Diamond, *Inherent Problems in the Use of Pretrial Hypnosis on Prospective Witness,* 68 Cal. L. Rev. 313, 316-21 (1980).

²See *infra* notes 62-65 and accompanying text.

³*People v. Ebanks,* 117 Ca. 652, 655, 49 P. 1049, 1053 (1897).

⁴For a discussion of increased medical and investigative uses of hypnosis see *infra* notes 40-46 and accompanying text.

⁵The evidentiary problem at issue was that of admissibility of hypnotically refreshed testimony, i.e., of the testimony of a witness hypnotized prior to trial. Courts have been nearly unanimous in refusing to allow a witness to testify in court while under hypnosis and this article does not discuss that issue. For an interesting discussion of an exception to the general rule of inadmissibility of testimony of a witness hypnotized on the stand, see Teitelbaum, *Admissibility of Hypnotically Adduced Evidence and the Arthur Nebb Case,* 8 St. Louis U.L.J. 205 (1963).

⁶Dilloff, *The Admissibility of Hypnotically Influenced Testimony,* 4 Ohio N.L. Rev. 1, 22 (1977).

⁷Spector and Foster, *Admissibility of Hypnotic Statements: Is the Law of Evidence Susceptible?,* 38 Ohio St. L.J. 567, 613 (1977).

⁸For a discussion of the re-emergence of judicial skepticism and the development of alternative approaches to the issue of hypnotically refreshed testimony, see *infra* notes 109-122 and accompanying text.

⁹W. Wester and A. Smith, *Clinical Hypnosis: A Multidisciplinary Approach,* 19 (1984). Hypnosis has also been defined as "the act of inducing artifically a state of sleep or trance in a subject by means of verbal suggestion by the hypnotist or by the subject's concentration upon some object." Black's Law Dictionary 668 (5th ed. 1979). The American Medical Association has defined hypnosis as

> a temporary condition of altered attention in the subject which may be induced by another person and in which a variety of phenomena may appear spontaneously or in response to verbal or other stimuli. These phenomena include alterations in consciousness and memory, increased susceptibility to suggestion, and the production in the subject of responses and ideas unfamiliar to him in his usual state of mind.

Council on Mental Health, *Medical Use of Hypnosis,* 168 J.A.M.A. 186, 187 (1958). For other definitions, see "Hypnosis," Enclyclopedia Britannica 139 (15th ed., 174), and 9 New Enclyclopedia Britannica (Macropaedia) 133 (1979). Although most contemporary definitions have much in common with one another, there appears to be no consensus on a single, authoritative definition. "There are as many definitions as there are definers." W. Kroger, *Clinical and Experimental Hypnosis,* 113-18 (2d ed. 1977).

¹⁰Alderman and Barrette, *Hypnosis on Trial: A Practical Perspective on the Application of Forensic Hypnosis in Criminal Cases,* 18 Crim. L. Bull. 7 (Ja/F., 1982).

¹¹Kroger, *supra* note 9, at 36-37. Hypnotic states are commonplace occurences in daily life, and neither are they induced by a professional hypnotist nor is the subject aware of being hypnotized, as two commentators note:

> Hypnotic phenomena are common in everyday experiences, albeit rarely recognized as such. Examples include the lulling of an infant to sleep, advertising, and involvement with a spell-binding orator, a skillful advocate, or a good entertainer. Although each of these occurrences involves the superconcentrated state of mind that results in an increase susceptibility to suggestion that is typical of the hypnotic state, these occasions of indirect susceptibility are distin-

guishable from an induced hypnotic state. Under direct [sic] susceptibility, a person might respond fleetingly to a variety of suggestive stimuli, whereas in induced hypnosis, the suggestible state is purposefully created to permit the subject to be guided by the hypnotist. Under the influence of indirect suggestion, the subject is generally unaware of his usually responsive condition, and therefore may succumb to harmful suggestions. In induced hypnosis, however, the subject is aware of his vulnerability and remains capable of protecting himself from harmful suggestion. (footnotes omitted).
Spector and Foster, *supra* note 7, at 567.

[12]For a discussion of the various induction techniques, see Kroger, *supra* note 9, at 11-22.

[13]H. Arons, *Hypnosis in Criminal Investigation* 156-59 (1967); W. Hibbard and R. Worring *Forensic Hypnosis,* 64-90 (1981).

[14]Arons, *supra* note 13, at 137, Spector and Foster, *supra* note 7, at 571-72.

[15]Spector and Foster, *supra* note 7, at 570-71; E. Hilgard, *The Experience of Hypnosis* 6-10 (1968); G. Ulett and D. Peterson, *Applied Hypnosis and Positive Suggestion* 1-13 (1965)

[16]For a more detailed discussion of various techniques used to induce an hypnotic state, see Kroger, *supra* note 9, at 11-22.

[17]Davis and Husband, *A Study of Hypnotic Susceptibility in Relation to Personalty Traits,* 26 J. Abnormal Social Psychology, 175, 175-82 (1931). *See also* Spector and Foster, *supra* note 7, at 571-72.

[18]*See* R. Udolf, *Forensic Hypnosis* (1983)

[19]*See* R. Reif, *Hypnotic Age Regression* (1959); Kroger, *supra* note 9, at 11-22.

[20]Kroger, *supra* note 9, at 16-17.

[12]*Id. See also* White, Fox and Harris, *Hypnotic Hyperamnesia for Recently Learned Material,* 35 J. Abnormal Psychology 88 (1968).

[22]S. Krebs, *The Fundamental Principles of Hypnosis* 3-4 (rev. ed. 1957).

[23]Douce, *Hypnosis: A Scientific Aid in Crime Detection,* 46 Police Chief 60, 60 (May, 1979).

[24]*Id.*

[25]*Id.*, Krebs, *supra* note 22, at 3-4.

[26]Douce, *supra* note 23, at 60.

[27]K. Bowers, *Hypnosis for the Seriously Curious* 7-8 (1976).

[28]Ulett and Peterson, *supra* note 15, at 7-8.

[29]Bowers, *supra* note 27, at 7-8.

[30]Douce, *supra* note 23, at 60.

[31]Bowers, *supra* note 27, at 8-9.

[32]Douce, *supra* note 23, at 60. Braid was the individual who coined the word "hypnosis," naming it after *Hypnos,* the Greek god of sleep. Realizing later that the nature of hypnosis was not that of sleep, he tried to change the name, but the term had already become established. *Id.*

[33]D. Cheek and L. LeCron, *Clinical Hypnotherapy* 19 (1968).

[34]Council on Mental Health, *supra* note 9, at 187.

[35]E. Hilgard, *Hypnotic Susceptibility* 4 (1965).

[36]*The Admissibility of Hypnotically Induced Recollection,* 70 Ky. L.J. 187, 190 n. 18 (1981-82). Hypnosis is also utilized in certain investigations of various physiological systems, primarily the cardiovascular, the gastrointestinal, and the sensory, but also renal, respiratory and endocrine systems. . . Hypnosis is employed in the study of areas such as emotions, psychopathology, defense mechanisms, dreams, physiological processes, and test validation. Spector and Foster, *supra* note 7, at 579 n. 66.

[37]See generally Kroger and Douce, *Hypnosis in Criminal Investigation,* 27 Int'l J. Clinical and Experimental Hypnosis 358 (1979).

[38]Monrose, *Justice with Glazed Eyes: the Growing Use of Hypnotism in Law Enforcement,* 8 Juris Dr. 54, 54 (Oct.-Nov. 1978).

[39]For examples of such dangers and deficiencies, see notes 47-51 *infra,* and accompanying text.

[40]See generally Diamond, *supra* note 1.

[41]*Id.* at 313-14. This is not to say that local police invariably received the same training as federal agents. Generally, the training of federal agents is more extensive and, unlike many local police forces, federal agencies do not allow their own personnel to perform hypnosis. When hypnosis is used as an investigative tool by federal agencies, only medical professionals may induce hypnosis. See Ault, *FBI Guidelines for Use of Hypnosis,* 27 Int'l J. Clinical and Experimental Hypnosis 449, 449-51 (1979).

[42]Graham, *Should Our Courts Reject Hypnosis?* St. Louis Post Dispatch (October 25, 1981) cited in Margolin and Coliver, *Forensic Uses of Hypnosis: An Update,* Trial, Oct. 1983, at 45, 105 n.2; Feldman, *Hypnosis: Look Me in the Eyes and Tell Me That's Admissible,* Barrister, Spring 1981, at 5.

[43]See *e.g.,* resolutions passed by the Society for Clinical and Experimental Hypnosis in October 1978 and by the International Society of Hypnosis in August 1979, reported in 27 Int'l J. Clin. & Exp. Hypnosis 452, 453 (1979).

[44]For examples of judicial concern, see *infra* notes 182-215 and accompanying text.

[45]*E.g.,* the Michigan Society for Investigative and Forensic Hypnosis was founded in 1981 to address the concerns of competency in the application of hypnosis for investigative purposes. Powell, *Law Enforcement Hypnosis in Michigan,* 32 Law and Order 52 (Feb. 1984). "The organization consists of law enforcement officers as well as health care professionals. Proof of successful completion of an approved course of study, as well as demonstrated proficiency, are prerequisites for membership in this organization." *Id.* at 52.

[46]Douce, *supra* note 23, at 60. "The use of hypnosis often helps an eyewitness more accurately recall the incident, including many important details that would not have been remembered otherwise,. . . it is possible that the relationship with the hypnotist provides a comfortable setting which makes it easier for the person to remember. . . ." Schafer and Rubio, *Hypnosis to Aid the Recall of Witnesses,* 26 Int'l J. Clin. & Exp. Hypnosis 81, 81 (1978). In one recent study, a hypnotized group of subjects recalled twice as much information as did a non-hypnotized control group. Unfortunately, the hypnotized group also made three times as many errors. Dockasi, *Validity of Hypnosis-Enhanced Testimony Questioned,* Trial, Dec. 1983, at 6 citing findings of a study published in Science, Oct. 14, 1983, at 184-185.

[47]Kroger and Douce, *supra* note 37, at 366; Spector and Foster, *supra* note 7, at 591.

[48]Dilloff, *supra* note 6, at 4.

[49]See generally Kroger and Douce, *Forensic Uses of Hypnosis,* 23 American J. of Clinical Hypnosis 86-93 (1980).

[50]*Id.*

[51]Dilloff, *supra* note 6, at 5. It is for this reason that a suspect in a crime is never an appropriate subject for hypnosis.

[52]See *infra* notes 239-46 and accompanying text.

[53]Hibler, *Forensic Hypnosis: To Hypnotize, or Not to Hypnotize, That Is The Question!,* 27 Am. J. Clinical Hypnosis 52, 55 (1984).

[54]The investigative departments of the Armed Forces, the Secret Service, the Treasury Department, and the Federal Bureau of Investigation have established a single standard for the use of hypnosis. *Id.* These guidelines, known as the Federal Model, ensure the proper use of hypnosis with appropriate subjects. For these reasons, the authors recommend the model as the ideal standard for investigative uses of hypnosis. The model is discussed at greater length *infra* notes 276-80 and accompanying text.

[55]See Dilloff, *supra* note 6, at 7.

[56]Timm, *The Factors Theoretically Affecting the Impact of Forensic Hypnosis Techniques on Eyewitness Recall,* 11 J. of Police Science & Adm. 442, 448 (1984).

[57]Orne, *The Use and Misuse of Hypnosis in Court,* 27 International J. of Clinical & Experimental Hypnosis 311, 335 (1979); accord, Council on Scientific Affairs, *Scientific Status of Refreshing Recollection by the Use of Hypnosis,* 253 J.A.M.A. 1918, 1923 (1985). All states now require licensure for psychologists. Typical state legislation establishes administrative boards with the authority to reprimand, suspend, or revoke the license of a psychologist for practicing in an area for which he is untrained. Hypnosis is a recognized area of specialization of psychology and stringent training standards are set by the American Society of Clinical Hypnosis. The Federal Model incorporates these standards by reference. See Hibler, *Investigative Aspects of Forensic Hypnosis,* in W. Wester and A. Smith, *Clinical Hypnosis: A Multidisciplinary Approach* 555-57 (1984).

[58]See *e.g.,* Mutter, *The Use of Hypnosis with Defendants,* 27 Am. J. of Clinical Hypnosis 42, 44-47 (1984).

[59]*Id.*

[60]For examples of proposed safeguards, see *infra* notes 133-55 and accompanying text. See also Timm, *Suggested Guidelines for the Use of Hypnosis Techniques in Police Investigations,* 29 J. of Forensic Sciences 865 (1984).

[61]See generally Laurence and Perry, *supra* note 1.

[62]*People v. Worthington,* 105 Cal. 166, 38 P. 689 (1895). In this case, a young woman was given a revolver by her husband, along with instruction that she should use the revolver to murder the paramour she had acquired while her husband was abroad. She complied. Found guilty of second-degree murder, and sentenced to 25 years in prison, she appealed using the defense of innocence by reasons of insanity and hypnotism. On the defense of hypnotic influence, the appellate court held:

> The [trial] court ruled out the evidence, and I think rightly. There was no evidence which tended to show defendant was subject to the disease (hypnosis), if it be as such. Merely showing that she was told to kill the deceased, and that she did it, does not prove hypnotism, or, at least, does not tend to establish a defense to a charge of murder.

Id. at 167, 38 P. at 691.

[63]*People v. Ebanks,* 117 Cal. 652, 49 P. 1049 (1847).

[64]*Tyrone v. State,* 77 Tex. Crim. 493, 180 S.W. 125 (1915) (seduction asserted as provocation for homicide); *State v. Donovan,* 128 Iowa 44, 102 N.W. 791 (1905); *Austin v. Baker,* 110 App. Div. 510, 96 N.Y. Supp. 814 (1906). The latter two cases were civil actions for seduction. In *Donovan,* the plaintiff was successful, the court holding that a combination of flattery, love-making, and hypnotism was sufficient to prosecute for seduction. In *Austin,* however, the defendant prevailed. The plaintiff had not only allegedly been seduced as a result of hypnotic suggestion, but she had been given a suggestion that she would forget the incident later. The defendant produced testimony by two medical doctors who were skeptical that the plaintiff could have been made to forget her acts of intercourse with the defendant, especially since she was allegedly a virgin prior to the incidents.

[65]Herman, *The Use of Hypno-Induced Statements in Criminal Cases,* 25 Ohio St. L.J. 1, 2 (1964). The "one reported case" referred to by Professor Herman was the 1930 case of *Louis v. State,* 24 Ala. 120, 130 So. 904 (1930). In *Louis,* the defendant allegedly used hypnosis to obtain money from his victim. His conviction for robbery was reversed on appeal, the court accepting the defense argument that mere hypnotism of the victim was insufficient to establish the necessary element of force or fear required for the crime of robbery. Apparently, it did not occur to the prosecution to charge the defendant with larceny by trick nor did it occur to the court to apply the doctrine of constructive force.

In the year following Professor Herman's time reference (1915-1950), a New York court held an inculpatory statement by a defendant under hypnosis to be inadmissible on the grounds that it was an involuntary confession. *People v. Leyra,* 302 N.Y. 353, 98 N.E2nd 553 (1951).

[66]See *e.g.,* the unreported case of *State v. Nebb,* No. 39, 540 (Ohio Com. Pl., Franklin Co., May 28, 1962). By stipulation of counsel, the defendant was hypnotized before the jury and testified while under hypnosis. After questioning by both the prosecutor and the defense counsel, the state reduced the charge of first degree murder to that of manslaughter, to which the defendant eventually pled guilty. The case is the focal point of the article by Herman, *supra* note 65.

[67]Dilloff, *supra* note 6, at 11-12.

[68]*Id.* at 12.

[69]*Id.* (footnotes omitted). Dilloff observes that just because testimony from hypnotized witnesses is not generally admissible there is no reason for the courts to prohibit the use of hypnosis to assist the defense where defense counsel believes such assistance may be helpful. Indeed, Dilloff cites *Cornell v. Superior Court,* 52 Cal.2d 99, 338 P.2d 447 (1959), in which the refusal to allow the defendant's attorney to employ a hypnotist in an effort to enable the accused to recall crucial events was held to be an abuse of discretion by the trial court. *Id.* at 14.

[70]Alderman and Barrette, *supra* note 10, at 6.

[71]The Fifth and, especially, the Ninth.

[72]5 Md. App. 230, 246 A.2d 302 (1968), *cert. denied,* 395 U.S. 949 (1969).

[73]*Id.* at 234, 246 A.2d at 305.

[74]*Id.* at 234, 241-42, 246 A.2d at 305, 309.

[75]*Id.* at 236, 246 A.2d at 306.

[76]*Id.* at 230, 246 A.2d at 303.

[77]*Id.* at 244, 246 A.2d at 310.

[78]81 Am. Jur.2d *Witnesses* Sec. 438 (1976).

[79]See generally 3 J. Wigmore, *Evidence* Secs. 758-63 (Chadbourn rev.ed. 1970); C. McCormick, *The Law of Evidence* Sec. 9 at 14-19 (2d ed. 1972).

[80]*United States v. Rappy,* 157 F.2d 964, 967 (2d Cir.), *cert. denied,* 324 U.S. 806 (1946).

[81]*Fanelli v. United States Gypsum Co.,* 141 F.2d 216, 217 (2d. Cir. 1944). While the courts have been liberal regarding what may be used to refresh the memory of a witness, it is within the discretion of the court to determine if the memory of the witness is indeed impaired and in need of such aid. McCormick, *supra* note 79, at Sec. 9.

[82]*State v. Collins,* 296 Md. 670, 464 A.2d 1028 (1983).

[83]See *e.g., State v. Jorgensen,* 8 Or. App 1, 492 P.2d 312 (1971) (credibility was issue for jury and cross-examination was effective safeguard); *Creamer v. State,* 232 Ga. 136, 205 S.E.2d 240 (1974) (evidence not tainted by pretrial hypnosis); *State v. McQueen,* 295 N.C. 96, 244 S.E.2d 414 (1978) (credibility of testimony was a matter for the jury); *People v. Smrekar,* 68 Ill. App.3d 379, 385 N.E.2d 848 (1979) (hypnosis not unduly suggestive); *State v. Greer,* 609 S.W.2d 423 (Mo. Appl. W.D. 1980, *vacated on other grounds),* 450 U.S. 1027 (1981) (hypnosis evidence not inadmissible as a matter of law); *Chapman v. State,* 638 P.2d 1280 (Wyo. 1982) (appellant's attack on credibility of witness was an issue for the jury).

[84]*People v. Hughes,* 59 N.Y.2d 523, 538, 466 N.Y.S.2d 255, 262, 453 N.E.2d 484, 491 (1983).

[85]In overruling *Harding,* the Maryland Court of Appeals reviewed a number of cases that followed *Harding* and "found little discussion. . .other than reliance upon *Harding.*" *State v. Collins,* 296 Md. 670,   , 464 A.2d 1028, 1035 (1983). The "lack of careful judicial scrutiny" and "the dearth of helpful precedent" in the cases following *Harding* is also noted in Margolin and Coliver, *supra* note 42, at 45. See also *State v. Mena,* 128 Ariz. 226, 229-30, 624 P.2d 1274, 1277-78 (1981) (*Harding* handled admissibility cursorily

and subsequent cases failed to analyze effects of hypnosis); *State v. Mack,* 292 N.W.2d 764, 770-71 (Minn. 1980) (assumptions of *Harding* unwarranted).

[86]See *e.g., State v. McQueen,* 295 N.C., 96, 120-121, 244 S.E.2d 414, 427-28 (1978); *State v. Jorgensen,* 8 Or. Appl. 1, 9, 492 P.2d 312, 315 (1971).

[87]See *e.g., State v. Brown,* 337 N.W.2d 138 (N.D. 1983) (an attack on credibility is proper method of determining value of hypnotically induced testimony); *State v. Little,* 34 Crim. L. Rptr. 2330 (Mo. App. E.D. 1984) (state has burden of proving absence of impermissibly suggestive hypnotic session); *Pote v. State,* 695 P.2d. 617 (Wyo. 1985) (an attack on credibility, not on competency, is the proper method for determining value of testimony; testimony of previously hypnotized witness did not violate defendant's right of confrontation).

[88]Perhaps this is the case because most trials involving the use of hypnotically enhanced testimony are criminal and often involve violent crimes. There is, of course, relatively little federal criminal statutory law, especially with respect to the most common crimes of violence.

[89]*Rucker v. Wabash Railroad Company,* 418 F.2d 146 (7th Cir. 1969) (no error in exclusion of plaintiff's taped statement made under hypnosis because tape did not clarify or explain, but merely corroborated and restated testimony on direct); *United States v. Dailey,* 759 F.2d 192, 200 (1st Cir. 1985) ("We find nothing in the facts of this case to suggest a degree of unreliability comparable to that associated with witnesses who have undergone hypnosis.").

[90]*United States v. Harvey,* 756 F.2d 636, (8th Cir. 1985).
Whether hypnotically enhanced testimony is admissible is a question of first impression for this court....However, it is unnecessary...to rule on the admissibility of hypnotically refreshed testimony. . . .We hold that, because of the overwhelming evidence of guilt in the present case, substantial rights of appellants were not affected and thus, even if this testimony was erroneously admitted, the error was harmless.
Id. at 644-45.

[91]503 F.2d 506 (9th Cir. 1974).

[92]*Id.* at 508-09.

[93]*Id.* at 509.

[94]*Id.*

[95]*Id.*

[96]*Id.*

[97]523 F.2d 1067 (9th Cir. 1975).

[98]*Id.* at 1069.

[99]*Id.* at 1068-70.

[100]581 F.2d 193 (9th Cir. 1978).

[101]*Id.* at 198-99.

[102]*Id.* at 198.

[103]484 F.2d 456 (5th Cir. 1973).

[104]*Id.* at 457.

[105]722 F.2d 1196 (5th Cir. 1984).

[106]*Id.* at 1203.

[107]See *e.g., U.S. v. Harrelson,* 754 F.2d 1153 (5th Cir. 1985); *U.S. v.* Solomon 753 F.2d 1522 (9th Cir. 1985) (rationale for admitting hypnotically refreshed testimony extended by analogy to testimony refreshed by prior narcoanalysis).

[108]See, *e.g., United States v. Narcisco,* 446 F. Supp. 252, 282 (D. Mich. 1977) ("The relation of events...depends on many factors, e.g., the ability to observe, memory, interest, mental condition, probability and corroboration. Consequently, the resolution of that type of factual situation has traditionally been the function of the jury and relies on the strength of the adversarial process."); *United States v. Waksal,* 539 F.Supp. 834 (S.D. Fla. 1982).

[109]See, *e.g.,* Fed. R. Evid. 402.

[110]Fed. R. Evid. 401.

[111]See McCormick, *supra* note 79, 491.

[112]*Frye v. the United States,* 293 F. 1013 (D.C. Cir. 1923).

[113]*Id.* at 1014.

[114]See, *e.g., Bundy v. State,* 471 So.2d 9, 13 (Fla. 1985). "Some jurisdictions have held that the testimony of witnesses who have undergone hypnotic memory enhancement is inadmissible per se, either because the technique has not been established as reliable under *Frye* or because the scientifically recognized danger of unreliability of such testimony outweighs its probative value as a matter of law, or for a combination of such reasons."

[115]See Fed. R. Evid. 401-03.

[116]Giannelli, *The Admissibility of Novel Scientific Evidence: Frye v. United States, a Half-Century Later,* 80 Colum. L. Rev. 1197, 1204 (1980).

[117]*Id.* at 1205.

[118]Alderman and Barrette, *supra* note 10, at 28 (footnotes omitted).

[119]*State v. Weston,* 16 Ohio App.3d 279, 283, 475 N.E.2d 809, 810 (1984). This typical quotation not only implies that hypnosis is a "novel scientific method," but it equates science with things which are "mysterious and unfamiliar" and which have a "significant potential for abuse." (citations and footnotes omitted).

[120]See, *e.g., United States v. Awkard,* 597 F.2d 667, 669 (9th Cir. 1979) ("But admissibility of such evidence has not been an issue in the federal courts of this circuit since *Wyller.* . . . Because there is no issue about the admission of hypnotically refreshed evidence, there is no need for a foundation concerning the nature and effects of hypnosis.") (citations and footnotes omitted).

[121]See, *e.g., United States v. Valdez,* 722 F.2d 1196 (5th Cir. 1984).

[122]292 N.W.2d 764 (Minn., 1980).

[123]86 N.J. 525, 432 A.2d 86 (1981).

[124]292 N.W.2d 764 (Minn., 1980).

[125]581 F.2d 1983 (9th Cir. 1978).

[126]*Id.* at 198.

[127]*Id.* at 198, 199.

[128]*Id.* at 199, n.12.

[129]*Id.*

[130]*Id.* at 199, n.13.

[131]597 F.2d 667 (9th Cir. 1979).

[132]*Id.* at 699, n.2. It is interesting to note that this procedure is analogous, albeit less detailed and stringent, to the procedures required by the Federal Rules of Evidence to determine the admissibility of writings which are sought to be used in refreshing a witness' recollection. The Rules provide:

> An adverse party is entitled to have the writing produced at the hearing, to cross-examine the witness thereon, and to introduce in evidence those portions which relate to the testimony of the witness. If it is claimed the writing contains matters not related to the subject matter of the testimony, the court shall examine in camera, excise any portions not so related and order delivery of the remainder to the party entitled thereto. Any portions withheld over objections shall be preserved and made available to the appellate court in the event of an appeal. If a writing is not produced or delivered pursuant to order under this rule, the court shall make any order justice requires, except that in criminal cases when the prosecution elects not to comply, the order will be one striking the testimony or, if the court in its discretion determines that the interests of justice so require, declaring a mistrial.
>
> *Fed. R. Evid.* 612(2).

[133]26 Crim. L. Rep. 2168 (Milwaukee County Cir. Ct. Mar. 27, 1979).

[134]*Id.* The nine guidelines are:

1. The person administering the hypnotic session ought to be a mental health person with special training in the uses of hypnosis, preferably a psychiatrist or psychologist.

2. This specially trained person should not be informed about the case verbally. Rather, such person should receive a written memorandum outlining whatever facts are necessary to know. Care should be exercised to avoid any communication that might influence the person's opinion.

3. Said specially trained person should be an independent professional not responsible to the prosecution, investigators, or the defense.

4. All contact between the specially trained person and the subject should be videotaped from beginning to end.

5. Nobody representing the police or the prosecutor or the defendant should be in the same room with the specially trained person while he is working with the subject.

6. Prior to induction a mental health professional should examine the subject to exclude the possibility that the subject is physically or mentally ill and to confirm that the subject possesses sufficient judgment, intelligence, and reason to comprehend what is happening.

7. The specially trained person should elicit a detailed description of the facts as the subject believes them to be prior to hypnosis.

8. The specially trained person should strive to avoid adding any new elements to the subject's description of her/his experience, including any implicit or explicit cues during the pre-session contact, the actual hypnosis and the post-session contact.

9. Consideration should be given to any other evidence tending to corroborate or challenge the information garnered during the trance or as a result of posthypnotic suggestion.

[135]*Id.* The *White* guidelines were adopted by the Wisconsin Supreme Court in *State v. Armstrong,* 110 Wis.2d 555, 571 n.23, 329 N.W.2d 386, 394-95 (1983).

[136]Orne's four guidelines were first proposed in his 1979 article. See Orne, *supra* note 57.

[137]See *People v. Lewis,* 103 Misc.2d 881, 883, 427 N.Y.S. 2d 177, 179 (1980) (*White* guidelines used as prerequisite to admission of expert testimony on an hypnotic interview to insure reliability of statements); *People v. McDowell,* 103 Misc.2d 831, 834-37, 427 N.Y.S.2d 181, 182-84 (1980). *McDowell* is a useful illustration of the discretionary nature of the *White* guidelines. The New York court found compliance with the *White* safeguards even though the hypnotist had not conducted a prehypnotic interview and had been in contact with the local sheriff's department. Moreover, there had been no transcription or recording of contacts between the hypnotist and the subject beyond the actual hypnotic session, and the video recording of that session was poor. *Id.*

[138]*State v. Hurd,* 173 (N.J.Super. 333, 363, 414 A.2d 291 (1980).

[139]*State v. Hurd,* 86 N.J. 525, 432 A.2d 86 (1981).

[140]*Id.* at 530, 432 A.2d at 88. The chief suspects were the husband the ex-husband of the victim. *Id.*

[141]*Id.* at 531, 432 A.2d at 88, 89. Besides the victim and the psychiatrist, a medical student and two police officers were present at the session. *Id.*

[142]*Id.* at 531-32, 432 A.2d at 89.

[143]*Id.* at 532, 432 A.2d at 89.

[144]*Id.* The test required first that the state prove, by clear and convincing evidence, that it complied with six procedural safeguards (essentially the same as *White's* guidelines, though consolidated) suggested by Martin Orne, an expert witness for the defense. Secondly, if these procedures had been followed, the state would then have to show, again by clear and convincing evidence, that "there had been no impermissibly suggestive or coercive conduct by the hypnotist and law enforcement personnel connected with the hypnotic exercise." *Id.; State v. Hurd,* 173 N.J. Super. 333, 363, 414 A.2d 291, 306 (1980). Since the New Jersey Supreme Court adopted the trial court's procedural safeguards, an itemization of those safeguards may be found in the text *infra.*

[145]*State v. Hurd,* 86 N.J. 525, 536, 432 A.2d 86, 91 (1981).

[146]*Id.* at 538, 432 A.2d at 92.

[147]*Id.*

[148]*Id.*

[149]*Id.*

[150]*Id.* at 544, 432 A.2d at 95.

[151]*Id.* at 545-46, 432 A.2d at 96-97. It is ironic that Dr. Orne, an opponent of the use of hypnotically refreshed testimony, was the individual who recommended these safeguards originally. Orne did also say, however, that as long as hypnotically refreshed testimony is subject to independent verification, "its utility is considerable and the risk attached to the procedure minimal." Orne *supra* note 57, at 318. Orne's recommendations are, of course, also the basis for the guidelines in *White, Lewis,* and McDowell. See notes 134 and 137 *supra.*

[152]*Id.* at 546-47, 432 A.2d at 97. The court applied this standard to criminal proceedings. It left unanswered the question of whether the proponent in a civil proceeding also had to establish the reliability of hypnotically refreshed testimony by means of the clear and convincing standard. Also unanswered was whether a proponent in a civil proceeding would need to comply with all six safeguards. The court did suggest, however, that it deemed a recording of the hypnotic session to be an essential minimum requirement. *Id.*

[153]*Id.* at 547, 432 A.2d at 97-98. The court noted that the imposition of the clear and convincing standard may relate in an interesting fashion to due process challenges regarding suggestive indentification procedures. The United States Supreme Court has held that "reliability" is the key in determining the admissibility of identification testimony. *Mason v. Braithwaite,* 432 U.S. 98, 114, 97 S.Ct. 2243, 2253 (1977). Since the defendant normally bears the burden of demonstrating the unreliability of identification procedure by preponderance of the evidence, any such due process challenge will be closely related to the threshold question of admissibility of hypnotically refreshed testimony.

> If the hypnotically refreshed testimony is inadmissible because of its unreliability, there will be no need to consider the due process issue. Conversely, it is difficult to imagine that an identification would violate due process once the court has determined that the testimony meets the more stringent standard for reliability we have established today.

Id. at 548, 432 A.2d at 98.

[154]See *e.g., Walters v. State,* 680 S.W.2d 60 (Tex. App. 7 Dist. 1984):

> . . .This Court rejected mechanistic approaches and emotional overreactions to the problem of hypnotically refreshed testimony, preferring instead to evaluate such testimony just as all other evidence is evaluated: Is it reliable?. . .Posthypnotic testimony is admissible where the totality of the circumstances surrounding the hypnotic session shows that the session was not so impermissibly suggestive as to give rise to a substantial likelihood of. . .mis-identification.

Id. at 63; *Zani v. State,* 679 S.W.2d 144, 150 (Tex. App. 6 Dist. 1984) ("Posthypnotic identification testimony by a nondefendant witness is admissible when the totality of the circumstances surrounding the hypnotic session shows the session was not so impermissibly suggestive to give rise to a substantial likelihood of an unreliable. . .identification.").

[155]*United States v. Valdez,* 722 F.2d 1196 (1984).

> Our evaluation. . .considers three basic evidentiary precepts: first, the principle embodied in Federal Rules 402 and 601 that "all relevant evidence is admissible" and "every person is competent to be a witness," subject only to certain explicit exceptions; second, the jurisprudential rule that, in determining admissibility, the trial judge's discretion is wide. . .; and finally, the limiting rule that even relevant evidence may be excluded if its probative value is substantially outweighed by such factors as "the danger of unfair prejudice, confusion of the

issues, or misleading the jury."
Id. at 1201.

[156]*State v. Weston,* 16 Ohio App.3d 279, 286-87, 475 N.E.2d 805, 813 (1984).

[157]*State v. Armstrong,* 110 Wis. 2d 555, 56772, 329 N.W.2d 836 (1983).

[158]The guidelines used in Illinois differ from those adopted by *Hurd.* Although the purposes of assuring, and measuring, reliability are the same, the guidelines are less stringent in determining the threshold question of admissibility since emphasis is placed on the trier-of-fact's evaluation of reliability as a component of witness credibility. The guidelines, established in *People v. Smrekar,* 68 Ill. App.3d 379, 385 N.E.2d 848 (1979), involve an examination of the qualifications and independence of the hypnotist, the presence or absence of suggestiveness in the hypnotic session, the existence of independent corroboration of witness testimony, the opportunity of the witness to observe the events which he or she purported to recall during hypnosis, and the similarity of the witness' pre- and posthypnotic statements.

The application of these guidelines to similar fact patterns has, however, led to different emphases and conclusions. In *People v. Gibson,* 117 Ill. App.3d 270, 452 N.E.2d 1368 (1983), the court held that it was error (albeit harmless) to admit the testimony of a previously hypnotized witness because the hypnotic session had been conducted by an unqualified hypnotist, a police officer with one week of hypnosis training at police school. In *People v. Cohoon,* 120 Ill. App. 3d 62, 457 N.E.2d 263 (1984), however, the court rejected the *Gibson* court's application of the *Smrekar* guidelines, holding that a police officer with 30 hours of training was a qualified hypnotist. (Concerning the guidelines of consonance of pre- and posthypnotic statements, the Cohoon court seemed impressed that the only difference between the victim's original description of her attacker and the description given under hypnosis was that during the latter she remembered that the rapist had very large ears.)

[159]*State v. Beachum,* 97 N.M. 682, 643 P.2d 246 (App. Ct. 1981).

[160]*State v. Hutchinson,* 99 N.M. 616, 661 P.2d 1315 (1983).

[161]*Or. Rev. Stat.* Secs 136.675, 136.685, 136.695 (1977). For a judicial application of the statute, see *State v. Luther,* 663 P.2d 1261 (1983).

[162]*Prewitt v. State,* 460 So.2d 296, 304 (Ala. Cr. App. 1984) ("We caution those who so use it to properly document pre-hypnosis evidence to insure its admissibility in appropriate cases and refute claims that it is somewhat 'tainted' by hypnosis. We also caution the proponents of hypnotic evidence to take every possible precaution to assure its reliability.").

[163]*State v. Wren,* 425 So.2d 756 (La. 1983).

[164]*State v. Goutro,* 444 So.2d 615, 618 (La. 1984).

[165]292 N.W.2d 764 (Minn. 1980).

[166]These cases are mentioned and discussed in the text and notes *infra* in this section. A list of such decisions may also be found in *State v. Peoples,* 311 N.C. 515, 319 S.E.2d 177 (1984).

[167]*State v. Armstrong,* 110 Wis.2d 555, 567, 329 N.W.2d 386, 392 (1982).

[168]*State v. Peoples,* 311 N.C. 515, 319 S.E.2d, 177, 187 (1984).

[169]See, *e.g.,* *State v. Davis,* 490 A.2d 601 (Del. Super. 1985) (holding hypnosis scientifically unreliable.)

[170]292 N.W.2d 764 (Minn. 1980).

[171]31 Cal.3d 18, 181 Cal. Reptr. 243, 641 P.2d 775 (1982).

[172]132 Ariz. 180, 644 P.2d 1266 (1982).

[173]296 Md. 670, 464 A.2d 1028 (1983).

[174]Prior to *Mack,* courts followed *Harding* and admitted hypnotically refreshed testimony. Courts refused to admit hypnotic evidence only if such evidence consisted of prior out of court statements made by the witness while actually under hypnosis. See, *e.g.,* *State v. Pierce* followed 263 S.C. 23, 207 S.E.2nd 414 (1974); *Jones v. State,* 542 P.2d 1316 (Okla. Crim. App. 1975).

[175]*People v. Williams*, 132 Cal. App.3d 920, 926, 1983 Cal. Rptr. 498, 500-01 (1982) (Gardner, J., concurring) ("*Shirley* is really more of a polemic than an opinion. As a polemic it makes interesting reading.").

[176]292 N.W.2d 764, 765-66.

[177]*Id.* at 766.

[178]*Id.* at 767. The court did not rule on the confrontation right argument because it found for the defendant on the issue of admissibility. *Id.* at 772.

[179]*Amicus curiae* briefs were filed by the Minnesota State Public Defender and the California Attorneys for Criminal Justice. Five experts on hypnosis testified at the trial hearing. *Id.* at 765-66.

[180]*Id.* at 768.

[181]*Id.*

[182]*Id.* at 768-69.

[183]*Id.* at 768.

[184]86 N.J. 525, 538 432 A.2d 86, 92 (1981).

[185]*State v. Mena*, 128 Ariz. 226, 624 P.2d 1274 (1981) (posthypnotic testimony excluded until hypnosis gains general acceptance as reliable tool to restore memory accurately).

[186]*People v. Shirley*, 31 Cal.3d 18, 181 Cal. Rptr. 243, 641 P.2d 775 (1982) (lack of reliability of statements following hypnosis renders testimony inadmissible).

[187]*People v. Gonzales*, 415 Mich. 615, 329 N.W.2d 743 (1982) (hypnosis to enhance memory not yet proven reliable).

[188]*State v. Palmer*, 210 Neb. 206, 313 N.W.2d 648 (1981) (hypnotic evidence inadmissible until hypnosis gains wide acceptance as accurately improving memory).

[189]*Commonwealth v. Nazarovitch*, 496 Pa. 97, 436 A.2d 170 (1981) (hypnosis has gained sufficient acceptance as means of accurate restoration of memory).

[190]31 Cal.3d at 47, 181 Cal. Rptr. at 272, 641 P.2d at 804.

[191]31 Cal.3d 18 at 25-29, 181 Cal. Rptr. 248 at 245-48, 641 P.2d 775 at 777-80. The complainant's refreshed testimony was not only in sharp contrast to her statements made prior to hypnosis, but she continued to contradict her own testimony during the trial. "Her testimony was vague, changeable, self-contradictory, or prone to unexplained lapses in memory. Indeed, on occasion she professed to be unable to remember assertions that she herself made on the witness stand only the previous day." *Id.* at 24, 131 Cal. Reptr. at 245, 641 P.2d at 777. Her inconsistent and self-contradictory testimony may be partly attributed to the fact that she was intoxicated during a portion of the period in question and had shortly thereafter consumed 100 milligrams of Mellaril, a major tranquilizer used for treatment of psychotic states, schizophrenia, and manic-depressive cases. *Id.* at 24-29, 181 Cal. Reptr. at 245-48, 641 P.2d at 777-780. One may question the suitability of hypnosis to refresh the memory of a woman who "was having problems," "couldn't be emotionally turned on by men" yet had seven children in the "Knightstown Home for Children," and who used "Mellaril and alcohol frequently." *Id.* One may wonder how much memory she had to be "refreshed" by hypnosis, yet, curiously, the majority did not address this question. Only Justice Kaus, concurring and dissenting, noted that "it is by no means clear to me that the facts of this case are typical of hypnosis cases in general." *Id.* at 74, 181 Cal. Rptr. at 277, 641 P.2d at 809. The majority did, however, hold that complainant's intoxication had not rendered her incompetent as a witness. *Id.* at 72, 181 Cal. Rptr. at 276, 641 P.2d at 807. In other words, the majority believed the jury was capable of weighing the possible effects of alcohol and tranquilizers on the memory of a witness, but the jury was not capable of weighing the possible effects of hypnosis on the memory of a witness.

[192]*Id.* at 29, 181 Cal. Reptr. at 248, 641 P.2d at 780.

[193]*Id.* at 31-32, 181 Cal. Reptr. at 250, 641 P.2d at 781-82.

[194]*Id.* at 53-59, 181 Cal. Reptr. at 263-66, 641 P.2d at 795-98.

[195]*Id.* at 64-66, 181 Ca. Reptr. at 271-72, 641 P.2d at 802-04.

[196]*Id.* at 39, 181 Cal. Reptr. at 255, 641 P.2d at 787.

[197]*Id.*

[198]*Id.*

[199]*Id.* at 47, 181 Cal. Retpr. at 272, 641 P.2d at 804.

[200]*Id.* at 67-68, 181 Cal. Rptr. 273-74, 641 P.2d at 805.

[201]See, *e.g.*, *State v. Contreras,* 674 P.2d 792 (Alaska Ct. App. 1983); Comment, *People v. Shirley: An Unwarranted Per Se Exclusion of Hypnotically Enhanced Testimony?,* 14 Sw. U.L. Rev. 777 (1984). What is perhaps the strongest criticism of the language and tone of *Shirley* may be Justice Gardner's concurring opinion in *People v. Williams,* 132 Cal. App.3d 923-34, 183 Cal. Rptr. 498, 500-01 (1982):

> *Shirley* is more of a polemic than an opinion. As a polemic it makes interesting reading. The protagonists are so clearly defined.
>
> The pro-hypnosis expert is a lowly police psychologist, wretchedly educated ("Ed. E."), who is, of all things, a director of a "proprietary school"...(Just what that has to do with this case escapes me.)
>
> On the other hand, the anti-hypnosis experts are "highly experienced," "nationally known," "pioneers," and "respected authorities" who present the "generally accepted view" which is set forth in "scholarly articles" and "leading scientific studies." Thus, the guys in the white hats and those in the black hats are clearly defined and appropriately labeled.
>
> Somehow, lost in the shuffle, is the fact that the majority rule in this country is that hypnotically induced testimony is admissible.
>
> According to *Shirley,* cases following that rule rely on an authority which "summarily disposed" of this issue with "little or no analysis." The part I really like is the classification of all contra authorities as "moribund."
>
> Of course the cases to the contrary [to the *Harding* and *Hurd* approaches] are "well reasoned" and "leading." Certainly.

[202]*State ex rel. Collins v. Superior Court,* 132 Ariz. 180, 644 P.2d 1266 (1982).

[203]*People v. Gonzales,* 417 Mich. 968, 336 N.W.2d 451 (1982). The Michigan Supreme Court modified its earlier ruling (*People v. Gonzales,* 415 Mich. 615, 329 N.W.2d 743), stating that it had not announced a per se prohibition on the testimony of a previously hypnotized witness. On remand, the court of appeals decided that a witness was not disqualified from testifying regarding prehypnotic information. *People v. Perry* 126 Mich. App. 86, 337 N.W.3d 324 (1983) (on remand). The Michigan Supreme Court later approved of the appellate court's approach by adopting that position in *People v. Nixon,* 364 N.W.3d 593 (Mich. 1984) (a witness may testify at trial to facts which the witness recalled and related prior to hypnosis).

[204]*State v. Patterson,* 213 Neb. 686, 331 N.W.2d 500 (1983).

[205]*Commonwealth v. Taylor,* 249 Pa. Super. 171, 439 A.2d 803 (1982); *Commonwealth v. Smoyer,* 476 A.2d 1304 (Pa. 1984).

[206]*State v. Koehler,* 312 N.W.2d 108 (Minn. 1981).

[207]321 Ariz. 180, 644 P.2d 1266 (1982).

[208]*Id.* at 193, 644 P.2d at 1279 (Feldman, J., supplemental opinion). The court had also, in January, extended its rule of total incompetency to civil cases in *Lemieux v. Superior Court,* 131 Ariz. 214, 644 P.2d 1300 (1982). *Id.*

[209]"It is indeed a sorry result when the victim of a rape cannot even take the stand to say she was raped." *Id.* at 192, 644 P.2d at 1279.

[210]"A decent respect for the doctrine of *stare decisis* [is overcome]...where issues

of important public policy are involved . . . [and] . . . where the rule in question is not of long-standing duration." *Id.* at 194, 644 P.2d at 1280 (Feldman, J., supplemental opinion).

[211]*Id.* at, _____, 644 P.2d at 1285.

[212]*Id.*

[213]The court enumerated the various familiar problems: Hypersuggestibility, hyper-compliance, confabulation, increased subject confidence in recalled memories, and inability to distinguish between true memories and pseudo memories. The latter two problems impair effective cross-examination and effectively deny the defendant the right to confront his accusors. *Id.* at, 644 P.2d at 1286-1292.

[214]*Id.* at _____, 644 P.2d at 1288-93.

[215]*Id.* at _____, 644 P.2d at 1294.

[216]*Id.* at _____, 644 P.2d at 1295.

[217]*Id.* at _____, 644 P.2d at 1296.

[218]*Id.*

[219]*People v. Quintanar,* 659 P.2d 710 (Colo. App. 1982).

[220]*Commonwealth v. Kater,* 388 Mass. 519, 447 N.E.2d 1190.

[221]*People v. Hughes,* 59 N.Y.2d 523, 452 N.Y.S.2d 408, 453 N.E.2d 484 (1983).

[222]*State v. Collins,* 296 Md. 670, 464 A.2d 1028 (1983).

[223]*State v. Peoples,* 311 N.C. 515, 319 S.E.2d 177 (1984).

[224]*Robinson v. State,* 677 P.2d 1080 (Okl. Cr. 1984).

[225]*State v. Martin,* 101 Wash.2d 713, 684 P.2d 651 (1984).

[226]*State v. Davis,* 490 A.2d 601 (Del. Super Ct. 1985).

[227]*Bundy v. State,* 471 So.2d 9 (Fla. 1985).

[228]The influence of the recent Maryland decision in *State v. Collins, supra* note 222, can be seen in the North Carolina decision of *State v. Peoples, supra* note 223: "We followed *Harding* in *McQueen* and the recent overflowing of *Harding* . . . erases the cornerstone of the credibility approach to hypnotically refreshed testimony and, hence, the basic premise of *McQueen.* 311 N.C. at _____, 319 S.E.2d at 187.

[229]*State v. Contreras,* 674 P.2d 792, 817 (Alaska Ct. App. 1983).

[230]*Id.* at 816.

[231]*United States v. Valdez,* 722 F.2d 1196, 1201 (5th Cir. 1984).

[232]*Contreras,* 674 P.2d at 817. The Alaska Court of Appeals was harshly critical of the California Supreme Court's use of the *Frye* test in its *Shirley decision.*

> In *Shirley* the California Supreme Court permitted an expert, Dr. Diamond, to attack the credibility of a class of witnesses, i.e., those who had been hypnotized prior to trial, based on scientific principles derived from the results of studies of the impact of improper interrogation techniques on the memory of hypnotized subjects. Based on this testimony, the California Supreme Court disqualified previously hypnotized witnesses as a class [footnote omitted]. Curiously, the court did not examine whether Dr. Diamond's views had received general scientific acceptance. Dr. Diamond readily concedes that his view regarding the effects of memory distortion in eyewitnesses is a minority view among experts familiar with the subject.

Id.

[233]*State v. Hurd,* 86 N.J. 525, 528, 432 A.2d 86, 93 (1981).

[234]See, e.g., Diamond, *supra* note 1 at 340; Orne, *supra* note 57 at 317-18.

[235]*Hurd,* 86 N.J. 535 at 528, 432 A.2d 86 at 92 (1981).

[236]The standard of historical accuracy is discriminatory because it is selectively applied. Courts do not demand that the memories of non-hypnotized witnesses be historically accurate. The standard is unrealistic because by requiring historical accuracy, the courts have equated reliability with infallibility, for one cannot be "a little" historically accurate any

more than one could be "a little" pregnant. McCormick has noted the tendency of courts using the *Frye* test to require that scientific techniques produce infallible results. He has criticized that tendency by pointing out that a scientific community whether a device produces results generally accepted as reliable. "In the case of matters labeled 'lie detector,' 'truth serum,' 'voiceprint,'. . .the courts seem to conclude that the jury will consider the tests infallible, and so require that they be shown to be infallible before they are submitted." McCormick, *supra* note 79 at 490 n.32.

[237]The *Frye* test has been applied, *inter alia,* to neutron activation analysis, ion microprobic analysis, atomic absorption, remote electro-magnetic sensing, bitemark comparisons, sound spectrometry, gaschrome-biographic analysis, chromotograhic analysis, and forward looking infrared systems. See Giannelli, *supra* note 116, at 1198-1201 for a listing of cases applying *Frye* to these and other types of novel scientific evidence. Amidst this array of evidence from the natural sciences, hypnosis appears, and is, incongruously placed.

[238]Spector and Foster, *supra* note 7, at 584.

[239]E. Loftus, *Memory* at 37 (1980).

[240]*Id.* at 40.

[241]See E. Loftus, *Eyewitness Testimony* (1979): P. Wall, *Eyewitness Identification in Criminal Cases* (1965); Loftus, *Eyewitness: Essential But Unreliable,* 18 Psychology Today 22 (Feb. 1984); Note, *Did Your Eyes Deceive You? Expert Psychological Testimony on the Unreliability of Eyewitness Identification,* 29 Stan. L. Rev. 969 (1977).

[242]See Marshall, Marquis and Oskamp, *Effects of Kind of Question and Atmosphere of Interrogation on Accuracy and Completeness of Testimony,* 84 Harv. L. Rev. 1620 (1971).

[243]*Contreras,* 674 P.2d at 817. The court concluded that, because of the variables of witness motivation and the interrogation process, any effect of the hypnotic process could be produced in a non-hypnotized witness.

> Further,. . .any hypnotic effect will be duplicated with a subject who has not
> been hypnotized, so long as the subject has sufficient interest in the success
> of the experiment and rapport with the experimentor. . . . It would be inappro-
> priate to say that a previously hypnotized witness' trial testimony was any more
> the produce of the hypnotic session than a nonhypnotized witness' trial testimony
> is the produce of the interviews she previously had with police and prosecutors.

Id. The Alaska Court of Appeals relied heavily on the work of psychologist T. Barber, who explains hypnotic behavior as a function of the subject's attitudes, motivations, and expectations of a given experiment and who argues that any effect of hypnosis can be duplicated without a formal hypnotic induction process. See T. Barber, *Hypnosis: A Scientific Approach* (1969); Barber and Calverley, *Empirical Evidence for a Theory of Hypnotic Behavior: Effects on Suggestibility of Five Variables Typically Included in Hypnotic Induction Procedures,* 29 J. Consulting Psych. 98 (1965). The New Jersey Supreme Court, in *State v. Hurd,* 86 N.J. 535, 543, 432 A.2d 86, 94 (1981) did not refer to Barber but did recognize other psychological research that demonstrates the similarity of problems common to both normal and hypnotically enhanced memory, and its decision reflects that recognition. The California Supreme Court, in *People v. Shirley,* 31 Cal.3d 18, 181 Cal. Reptr. 243, 641 P.2d 775 (1982), did not adequately take into account this similarity, and Justice Kaus, concurring and dissenting, was sharply critical of the majority for its failure to do so. *Id.* at 76, 181 Cal. Rptr. at 279, 641 P.2d at 810 (Kaus, J., concurring and dissenting).

[244]Spector and Foster, *supra* note 7, at 584, note that cross-examination may cause the witness to feel attacked and abused. ("This kind of interrogation may force the witness to defend his perception and memory of the event and elicit defense mechanisms that make the witness appear more assertive and confident than the accuracy of his testimony may warrant." *Id.*

[245]The argument that previously hypnotized witnesses should be disqualified from tes-

tifying gains force only if hypnotism creates a risk of distorting memory that is substantially greater than, or qualitatively distinct from, the risk ordinarily posed by interrogating a victim who has rapport with her questioner and who has a vital interest in the identification of her assailant. In contrast, if improper interrogative techniques and the normal experience encountered by eyewitnesses account for virtually all instances of memory distortion, then no special rule for hypnotism would appear warranted.
Contreras, 674 P.2d at 802.

[246]The array of complexities inherent in the attempt to glean accurate information, while relying upon the functioning of errant human faculties, encourages support for the courts' responsiveness to testimony retrieved through pretrial hypnotic induction. A witness whose memory has been refreshed through hypnosis may be able to recount an observed event more fully and accurately than any other witness.
Spector and Foster, *supra* note 7, at 590.

[247]See, *e.g., State ex rel. Collins v. Superior Court* 132 Ariz. 180, 1983, 644 P.2d 1266, 1277 (1982) (Holohan, C. J. dissenting from original opinion). ("No law enforcement agency can risk using hypnosis because the person subjected to hypnosis cannot thereafter be used as a witness.")

[248]See, *e.g., People v. Williams,* 132 Cal. App.2d 920, 928, 183 Cal. Rptr. 498, 502 (1982) (Garnder, J., concurring) ("The idea that the predator may testify and yet his victim may not offends my sense of justice. It appears to me that the scales of justice are tilted—dangerously.") *Williams* is one of several decisions in which California appellate courts have, by distinguishing facts or by an interpretation of *Shirley,* evaded the precedent of their own state's highest court. See, *e.g., People v. Parrison,* 137 Cal. App.3d 529, 187 Cal. Rptr. 123 (1982) (using test of relevancy, not *Frye,* to admit hypnotic testimony); *People v. Adams,* 137 Ca. App.3d 346, 187 Cal. Rptr. 505 (1982) (hypnotic testimony uncontaminated, unlike *Shirley*); *People v. Glaude,* 141 Cal. App. 3d 633, 190 Cal. Rptr. 479 (1983) (admission of testimony not prejudicial to defendant).

[249]The past tense is used because, by the reasoning of these courts, it is impossible for a person to "have" a prehypnotic memory. Exclusionary-approach courts asset that the act of hypnosis terminates prehypnotic memory and substitutes a new, inaccurate, and unreliable memory.

[250]In this situation there is no real need for the witness to testify, for the record itself could be admitted either under the recorded recollection hearsay exception of Fed. R. Evid. 803(5) or, if the requisite conditions were met, under the former testimony hearsay exception of Fed. R. Evid. 804(B) (1).

[25]Most of the problems of the modified rule discussed in the text to this point are treated in greater detail in *State ex rel. Collins v. Superior Court,* 132 Ariz. 180, 201, 644 P.2d 1266, 1297-98 (1982) (Gordon, V. C. J., concurring and dissenting from the supplemental opinion).

[252]The *Collins* court is one of several courts that did not specify what hypnotic standards were necessary, and Vice Chief Justice Gordon, concurring and dissenting, criticized that omission: "I would not have litigants guess at which or how many standards would be enough to satisfy this Court that prehypnotic testimony was properly admitted." *Id.* at 202, 644 P.2d at 1299.

[253]Margolin and Coliver, *supra* note 42, at 47.

[254]McCormick, *supra* note 79, at 490.

[255]Giannelli, *supra* note 116, at 1219.

[256]*Id.*

[257]Weyrauch, *Law as Mask—Leqal Ritual and Relevance,* 66 Calif. L. Rev. 699, 710-77 (1978).

[258]See, *e.g., People v. Hughes,* 59 N.Y.2d 523, 530, 452 N.Y.S.2d 408, 415, 453 N.E.2d 484, 491 (1983) ("And like the present case, evidence is usually offered by the prose-

cutor. . . ."); *State v. Mack*, 292 N.W.2d 764, 770 ("It is significant, however, that this. . . clearly favors only the prosecution. . . .").

²⁵⁹In declaring previously hypnotized witnesses competent to testify, the *Contreras* court was critical of courts that seemed more concerned with developing general evidentiary rules than with the interests of justice in the particular case before them.

> We recognize that a number of the cases addressing these issues approach them from a slightly different perspective. They view the case *sub judice* purely as a vehicle for announcement of a broad prophylactic rule of general application. To reach a conclusion these cases ask whether pretrial hypnotism is a good or bad practice as a general rule. . . .These conclusions motivate these courts to establish a "per se" rule barring testimony by witnesses hypnotized prior to trial. . . .The cases before us are not solely vehicles for the announcement of general rules of evidence. They are equally concerned with whether Contreras sexually assaulted S. J. and E. L. and whether Grumbles burglarized Hall's residence and assaulted her.

674 P.2d 792, 795-96 (Alaska Ct. App. 1983).

²⁶⁰722 F. 2d 1196, 1203 (Fifth Cir. 1984) (concluding that prejudicial effect outweighs probative value where a hypnotized subject identifies for the first time a person he has reason to know is already under suspicion).

²⁶¹*Id.* at 1201.

²⁶²One of the better known recent decisions taking a general admissibility approach is *Chapman v. State*, 638 P.2d 1280 (Wyo. 1982). The facts represent a near-perfect antithesis of the Orne safeguards. The hypnotist was a police officer with little training in hypnosis. There was no record made of the witness' recollection prior to hypnosis. Several other people, including police officers, were present at the hypnotic sessions. No written transcript of the sessions was made nor did anyone take notes. The sessions were videotaped but one video tape was lost and the other two were mostly inaudible. In his dissent, Justice Brown took note of these facts in commenting: "Stripped of its veneer, this case holds that a police officer who occasionally plays around with hypnotism can manipulate the recall of a witness and receive the blessing of this court. . . .The admission of hypnotically enhanced testimony, developed by a rank amateur absent any scientific procedure is totally unreliable." *Id.* at 1286-87 (Brown, J., disenting).

²⁶³See, *e.g.*, *People v. Shirley*, 31 Cal.3d 18, 39, 181 Cal. Rptr, 243, 255, 641 P.2d 775, 786-87 (1982); *People v. Hughes*, 59 N.Y.2d 523, 543-44, 466 N.Y.S.2d 255, 265-66, 453 N.E.2d 484, 494-95 (1983).

²⁶⁴See *supra* notes 233-38 and accompanying text.

²⁶⁵See *supra* notes 239-46 and accompanying text. As the *Contreras* court noted, the Orne safeguards specifically protect against confabulation as well as suggestion. Confabulation occurs when someone with no memory of an event is placed under pressure to recall a memory by someone he wishes to please. The Orne safeguards attempt to minimize the pressure on the witness to have memories. *State v. Contreras*, 674 P.2d 792, 809 (Alaska Ct. App. 1983).

²⁶⁶Such a "time consuming and expensive course is precisely what the [*Frye*] tests seeks to avoid." *Commonwealth v. Kater*, 388 Mass. 519, 526, 447 N.E.2d 1190, 1196 (1983); see also *People v. Shirley*, 31 Cal.3d 18, 30, P.2d 710, 712-13 (Colo. Ct. App. 1982).

²⁶⁷See *supra* notes 249-59 and accompanying text.

²⁶⁸State ex. rel. Collins v. Superior Court, 132 Ariz. 180, 186, 644 P.2d 1266, 1272 (1983).

²⁶⁹*Id.*

²⁷⁰"We are content to rely upon the good sense and judgment of American juries, for evidence with some element of untrustworthiness is customary grist for the jury mill. Juries are not so susceptible that they cannot measure intelligently the weight of identification

testimony that has some questionable feature." *Manson v. Braithwaite,* 432 U.S. 98, 116 (1977).

[271]*People v. Williams,* 132 Cal. App.3d 920, 928, 183 Cal. Rptr. 498, 502 (1982) (Garnder, J., concurring).

[272]See, *e.g., Zani v. State,* 679 S.W.2d 144, 150 (Tex. App. 6 Dist. 1984); *Walters v. State,* 680 S.W.2d 60, 63 (Tex. Appl. 7 Dist. 1984); *United States v. Valdez,* 722 F.3d 1196, 1201 (Fifth Cir. 1984).

[273]See, *e.g., State v. Hurd,* 86 N.J. 535, 432 A.2d 86 (1981); *State v. Weston,* 16 Ohio App.3d 279, 475 N.E.2d 805 (1984); *State v. Armstrong,* 110 Wis. 2d 55, 329 N.W.2d 836 (1983); *People v. Smrekar,* 68 Ill. App.3d 379, 385 N.E.2d 848 (1979).

[274]See *supra* notes 128-51 and accompanying text.

[275]*State v. Hurd,* 86 N.J. 525, 547, 432 Ap.2d. 86, 97-98 (1981).

[276]See Ault, *FBI Guidelines for Use of Hypnosis,* 27 International J. Clinical & Experimental Hypnosis 449-51 (1979); Hibler, *supra* note 57 at 555-57.

[277]In the Federal Model, in contrast to Orne's recommendations, an investigator is present during the hypnotic session. In the FBI version, the investigator is known as the "coordinating agent," an individual who has been trained, not as a hypnotist, but in the theory, techniques, and hazards of hypnosis. In the FBI version, the required guidelines are contained in a checklist used by the coordinating Agent. The checklist is partially reprinted below:

Preliminary:

1) Only witnesses and victims should be hypnotized and only after other methods of investigation have been exhausted.

2) Refer to and follow existing FBI policy.

3) Video tape requirements will be planned in advance of the first interview and should include:

—Location.

—Equipment.

—Properly cleared personnel to operate equipment.

—A proper briefing for camera crew.

4) Choice of professional—only a psychiatrist, psychologist, physician, or dentist.

5) Items to be discussed with professionals:

—FBI requirements.

—Dangers for cueing.

—Desire for coordinator to do the interviewing. [This is not an inflexible rule. At this time, many psychiatrists and psychologists have done enough work with FBI Agents that the professional himself can and does conduct much of the interview.]

—Agreement on payment.

—Long-term arrangements, such as the possibility of obtaining security clearance for the doctor and the doctor's future participation in FBI cases.

—Comfort of witness.

The Hypnosis Session:

1) The preinduction interview, that portion conducted on tape prior to the hypnosis session, should include:

—Discussion of hypnotist's background.

—Voluntary participation of witness. Signing consent form.

—Brief description of procedures.

—Removal of misconceptions.

—Discussion of basic health of witness. Any health problems must be resolved prior to interview.

2) Prior to taped interview, coordinating agent will confer with others who may be present to advise them of the need for keeping quiet and unobtrusive.

3) Prior to hypnotic induction, the witness will be allowed to relax and recount all the details he/she can recall of the incident in question. Do not lead or question. Merely allow the witness to recount details in any order he desires.

4) The induction will be done by the professional. The coordinator should note for his records the doctor's opinion of the depth of the trance and by what method the doctor estimates that depth.

5) The doctor may then transfer rapport to the coordinator for questioning about the incident. The coordinator will again simply let the witness recall the incident without prompting. After the witness has recalled the incident, the coordinator may go back and "zero in" on specific details.

6) Rapport will be transferred back to the doctor who will dehypnotize the witness. The doctor is in charge of the session.

7) The original video tapes obtained from the interview are evidence and are treated accordingly. The chain of custody is maintained, and the tapes are provided to the Behavioral Science Unit of the Training Division at the FBI Academy for assessment and research.

Ault, *Hypnosis—The FBI's Team Approach,* 49 FBI Law Enforcement Bull. 5, 5-8 (1980); Hibler, *supra* note 57 at 555-57.

[278]The Federal Model is similar to Orne's safeguards except that the federal guidelines are more detailed, indicate appropriate uses of hypnosis and proscribe inappropriate ones, and provide for the presence of an investigator at the hypnotic interview. By providing that both a qualified hypnotist and a trained criminal investigator be present at the interview, "there is confidence that the well-being of the interviewee, the stipulated use of hypnosis, and the proper forensic exploration of the event in question are maintained. Thus, investigators do not function as doctors, and doctors do not function as investigators." Hibler, *supra* note 53, at 55.

[279]*Id.* at 53.

[280]Under the Federal Model, hypnosis is appropriately used when *all* of the following conditions apply: (1) As a last resort in an attempt to provide information obtainable by no other means, (2) Where a felony offense is involved, (3) Where the witness or victim was able to perceive details which may have the potential for further enhancement, (4) Where there is the likelihood of independent corroboration. Hypnosis should not be used in known-subjects cases and may not be used where the credibility of the interviewee is in question, or where the witness has a medical or psychological history that indicates that hypnosis could exacerbate that condition. *Id.* at 54-55.

[281]Evidence is relevant if it is probative. All relevant evidence should be admitted unless its probative value is substantially outweighed by the dangers of unfair prejudice, confusion of the issues, or misleading the jury. See *Federal R. Evid.* 401-03.

[282]It is interesting to observe that in many of the cases using a guarded admissibility approach, corroborating evidence existed, and the courts noted this fact in their decisions. On the other hand, in a number of cases (*e.g., Mack, Shirley*) using a *per se* exclusion approach, corroborating evidence was absent, yet the courts seemed to ignore this fact, as the *Contreras* court noted: "Since the cases adopting *per se* rules are frequently cases in which eyewitness testimony was not corroborated, it is strange that the courts do not even consider limiting the *per se* rule to cases in which no corroboration exists." *State v. Contreras,* 674 P.2d 792, 816 (Alaska Ct. App. 1983).

[283]Hibler, *supra* note 53, at 54. Even in the absence of the Federal Model, the percentage of corroboration may be quite high. "A police study of the Los Angeles Police Department demonstrated that 91% of all testimony from 500 witnesses under hypnosis was verified by independent corroboration." Comment, *Hypnosis: A Primer for Admissibility,* 5 Glendale L. Rev. 51, 61 (1983).

19 HYPNOSIS IN ASSERTIVENESS AND SOCIAL SKILLS TRAINING

CAROLYN KOWATSCH, Ph.D.

This chapter is basically a description of an assertiveness group which combined both hypnotic and psychodrama techniques.* Combining these approaches proved beneficial to clients who wished to improve their assertiveness and social skills.

The assertive individual respects his rights and gets his needs met, but not at the expense of others. The theoretical approach for the group was that self-esteem is positively correlated with the effectiveness of assertive behavior and social skills. As self-esteem increases, social skills improve. As social skills improve, self-esteem frequently increases. The literature supports these hypotheses (Lorrim and More, 1980; Percell, Berwick and Beigel, 1974; Zuker, 1983).

Psychodrama and role playing have frequently been used to improve both social skills and self-esteem. Psychodrama fine-tunes the more general role-playing techniques (Moreno, 1946, Wolberg, 1977; Yablonsky, 1975). Systematic approaches for improving social behavior go as far back as 1949, with Salter's *Conditioned Reflex Therapy.* Wolpe, in 1958, suggested that assertive responses can inhibit anxious feelings. Lazarus (1966) used the term "behavioral rehearsal" to combine modeling and role-playing techniques. Bandura (1971) used modeling with guided participation to reduce fears. Currently, there are many excellent guides for training programs utilizing these techniques, for example, Liberman, King, DeRisi and McCann, *Personal Effectiveness* (1975); Wilkinson and Center, *Social Skills Training Manual* (1982); and Zuker, *Mastering Assertiveness Skills* (1983).

Hypnosis has also been used for many years to enhance self-esteem and improve social skills. The *Syllabus on Hypnosis and a Handbook of Therapeutic Suggestions,* published by the American Society of Clinical Hypnosis (1973), has some excellent ego-strengthening suggestions. Araoz (1979) used ego-strengthening suggestions in group hypnosis and found them successful. Hypnosis has frequently been used in groups to improve social skills (DeVoge, 1975; Hartman, 1969; Sanders, 1976; Klauber, 1984).

---

* The group was run by a colleague, Elizabeth R. Miller, Ph.D., and this author. Dr. Miller has had much training and experience in psychodrama; my expertise lies in the area of hypnosis.

A variety of hypnotic techniques have been used to improve social skills. Most employ guided visual imagery, that is, mental rehearsal (DeVoge, 1975; Kazdin, 1975, 1976; Sanders, 1976). The client sees himself feeling or behaving the way he would like to. Often age progression is added, since he visualizes himself performing well in the future (Astor, 1973). Many hypnotherapists will also train the client in self-hypnosis, so that he can relax himself as he approaches the anxiety-provoking social situation (Hartman, 1967; DeVoge, 1975). Some use age regression. Gardner (1981) age-regressed children to a happy feeling experience which they could keep with them as they approached anxious situations. Barnett (1982) age-regressed clients to the critical experiences holding them back; they resolved their problems so that they could be free to change their behavior. Some therapists prefer to give more direct, confidence-building suggestions. Once clients are hypnotized they are told, "People will like you," etc. (Cooke and Vogt, 1965). Other therapists like to have clients role play the new behavior under hypnosis with the therapist or in a group (DeVoge, 1975; Kroger, 1977). Ericksonian techniques can also be utilized. Guerra and Taylor (1977) present four assertiveness myths, in fable form, that can be told to clients under hypnosis. The actual number of useful techniques is determined only by the therapist's creativity.

Treatment Program

General Format

In our assertiveness groups, we limited group size to between four and 12 participants. Since our initial group was somewhat experimental, we kept it small. Four clients were referred to the group by their individual therapists. We assessed with their therapists their appropriateness for the group. All clients were diagnosed as *not* having a psychosis or a borderline personality disorder. There were three females and one male, ranging in age from early 20's to mid 30's. Two of the women worked outside the home and the other was a homemaker; the male was a college student. In subsequent groups, some self-referred clients were assessed by one or the other group leader.

The format was six one-and-a-half hour sessions. In subsequent groups there were eight sessions because participants felt they needed more time than the six sessions permitted.

The group was titled, "Assertiveness and Problem-Solving Group." The goal for the group was to differentiate and better deal with non-assertive, assertive, and aggressive behavior in both the self and others, so that group participants could increase self-esteem and become more self-confident, comfortable, and successful in handling such interpersonal situations as the following:

Giving and receiving compliments
Requesting help, assistance, favors
Expressing liking, loving, and affection
Initiating and maintaining conversations
Standing up for legitimate rights
Refusing requests when appropriate
Expressing personal opinions even if in disagreement with others
Expressing justified annoyance and displeasure
Expressing justified anger and resolving conflicts

We divided each session into both didactic and experiential parts. We felt that many individuals need to be informed about their right to be assertive, what assertiveness actually means, and how our perceptions affect this and other concepts. Participants were given a folder for keeping various handouts. Recommended readings were *Your Perfect Right* by Alberti and Emmons (1982) and "The Four Assertive Myths: A Fable" by Guerra and Taylor (1977). A more extensive bibliography was given to subsequent groups. As the sessions progressed, the didactic portion decreased and the role-playing increased.

Session One: Introduction

1. Self-assessment was to be an integral part of the program. Consequently, participants were asked to come early for the first session. They were administered the Sixteen Personality Factors Test (16PF) and the Edward's Personal Preference Schedule (EPPS) by our psychology assistant.

2. A brief break was given to participants.

3. Initial introductions were made.

4. Two brief self-assessment inventories were given: Self-Esteem Index (Barksdale, 1972) and Assertion Inventory (Rathus, 1973).

5. The basic plan for the sessions was explained.

6. The "No" exercise was practiced. Participants were divided into groups of two. One partner was to make a request of the second one. The second partner was instructed to continue saying "no" whatever the request. The task was then discussed.

7. Participants chose a task from the Assertion Inventory for role-playing.

Session Two: Basic Concepts

1. The Self-Assessment Assertiveness Inventory was given (Galassi and Galassi, 1977).

2. Didactic information and handouts were given on the meanings of and differences between assertive, non-assertive, and aggressive behavior. *Your Perfect Right,* mentioned earlier, was the main reference for this part of the session. Further attention was given to passive-aggressive behavior. Focus was also placed on basic human rights (Jakubowski-Spector, 1977).

3. Role-playing suggestions were taken from the inventories and the personal experiences of the participants and then utilized.

4. During the last half hour, feedback was given on the Edward's Personal Preference Schedule. Each participant was given his or her profile to take home and examine.

Session Three: Hypnosis

1. Questions were answered from the EPPS.

2. A general introduction to hypnosis was provided. Attention was given to the standard concerns, like expectations, myths, dangers, etc.

3. Participants helped construct a script. Their specific needs and suggestions were integrated with the general plan of the leader. Several relaxing fantasy images were suggested, and participants settled on one that was acceptable to all (beach).

4. The hypnosis session was held. (See Appendix 19-1 for the specific procedures and suggestions given.) Participants tape recorded this session. They were instructed to listen to it daily initially, and as often as they felt it would be beneficial thereafter.

5. The computer printout of the 16PF (minus the final clinical page) was given to the participants to take home and read. Some orientation to it was provided.

Session Four: Emotions and Assertiveness

1. General questions from the 16PF were answered.

2. Information was provided on how emotions can affect behavior, particularly assertive behavior; Bower and Bower (1976) provide an excellent discussion here. Also, Jones and Banet (1976) present useful information on dealing with anger. Two other handouts were distributed, one on the perceptual act, the other clarifying psychodynamics and the effects of anxiety. These are placing "shoulds" on feelings. You feel what you feel. It is what you do with that feeling, the behavior, that needs to be controlled or directed.

3. Role-playing suggestions were taken from the participants and utilized.

4. One half hour was provided at the end for questions the participants had about their test results; this consultation was on an individual basis.

Session Five: Positive Self-Assertions

1. A large poster board was placed in the front of the group. Participants were asked to stand, one at a time, and make positive statements about changes in their behavior, which were then printed on the poster for all to see. Participants were also asked to discuss any successes with assertiveness they felt they had achieved.

2. Questions regarding the hypnosis were answered.

3. Role-playing suggestions were requested and utilized.

Session Six: Conflict Resolution, Reassessment and Evaluation

1. Participants took the Self-Esteem Index and the Assertion Inventory again.

2. They were given a handout on the Ten Commandments for Conflict Resolution (Dreikurs, 1964). This general topic was discussed, with particular attention paid to anger.

3. Role-playing suggestions from the participants were utilized.

4. Time was provided at the end for the participants to evaluate the program, provide suggestions for improving it, and give constructive criticism to the leaders. The biggest criticism was that six weeks was too short a time; consequently, future groups lasted eight sessions.

Assessment of Effectiveness

The participants all reported improvement when they retook their self-assessment inventories and reported their general feelings about themselves. Since they indicated that they would like more sessions and they would be interested in an advanced group, we concluded that they felt the group was useful.

Future Trends

A combination of hypnosis with a well-defined assertiveness training program gives the client the benefits of two very useful techniques. Some therapists will probably prefer to have the participants hypnotized during the role-playing part of the session. Hypnotherapists will continue to use a variety of tactics to improve social skills and self-esteem since hypnosis is frequently helpful.

APPENDIX 19-1

Exerpt of Session

A variety of induction techniques can be used. I began with Speigel's (1978) eye-roll technique. Since I was interested in the participants' learning to use self-hypnosis, I wanted to teach them this quick method. I followed with deep muscle relaxation. Since so many clients coming to an assertiveness group are dealing with anxiety in interpersonal situations, I prefer to use a relaxation technique as part of the induction techniques. For deepening, I went to a fantasy image (beach) that all participants said was relaxing. I suggested that they enhance that image in their minds as I counted from one to five. I then gave them suggestions regarding their ability to move into hypnosis quickly and easily whenever it would be useful. I also reinforced their desire to do the self-hypnosis and/or listen to the tape. Finally, I moved into the more specific self-esteem, assertiveness, and social skills suggestions.

Verbalization	Comment
You already have in your mind's eye a videotape of yourself and how you see yourself performing, and on that videotape there are many negative images. You see yourself not performing successfully. Perhaps you see the times in the past that you have tried to do things and they have not gone well. Maybe you see yourself failing. You see yourself not being the way you want to be. You hear yourself saying to yourself, "It's not the right time. I'm afraid of this other person's response. Maybe they won't like me. Maybe they'll get angry with me. I might lose something. I might risk too much, and get hurt. Maybe they'll think I'm too bold or too shy. Maybe they just won't like me. Is this the wrong decision? I can't do this. I always do this wrong. I don't know how to talk in groups. I look self-conscious. I don't know how to be comfortable in social situations."	The goal is to clarify the self-messages that need to be changed. Some of these come from Satir (1972).
You are now going to take out that negative-thinking videotape. You will take out that tape and put in a brand new one. You are going to program this one differently. I want you to see yourself looking and feeling the way you would like to look and feel. See yourself behaving the way you	Guided visual imagery, with age progression implications, is provided to model how the person wants to behave.

want to behave. See yourself going through the motions, saying the things that you should say, being assertive when that's important, standing up for yourself, being able to take compliments, to take risks, to be spontaneous. See yourself being yourself in the fullest sense of the word, the person you have always wanted to be and would like to be. Now see yourself becoming. . . more and more. The more real you make that image, the more it will draw you toward it like a magnet, modifying your thoughts about yourself, your attitudes, your behavior. . .until you and that image can merge into one. So you will make that positive image as clear as you can, and it will continue to get clearer with each day that passes.

There will be a new voice track on this videotape, new mind-talk. You will say to yourself, "I am no longer so worried about timing. This is the right time. The moment that it's needed is the right time. It doesn't have to be the perfect time, the perfect moment." You will say to yourself, "I am capable of handling things well. I have a number of competencies and capabilities that *I* have kept myself from using effectively. I have held myself back in the past, but this is no longer true. I am very capable, and I am going to act on those capabilities. I have the good feeling that I can be in control. I can handle things and I am O.K. Especially, I can *trust* myself. I can be more sure of myself. I can trust my feelings, and I can trust my responses and assume that they will be good most of the time. I am free to behave more spontaneously, knowing that I will behave in ways that make me feel good about me."

You will see yourself as the attractive individual that you are. Every individual has an attractiveness within, and you are going to see that within yourself, beginning to move toward the surface and becoming more real. With this comes a certain confidence that you can talk comfortably, be relaxed, and think clearly. Even if the per-

Positive self-messages are given to replace the previous negative ones.

Participants are given positive images regarding their feelings toward themselves. They need to feel attractive in some way. Attention is paid to behavior with the opposite sex, as requested by some group members.

son is very attractive, you will be able to think clearly, to feel good about yourself, and to behave appropriately. If it is appropriate, you will find yourself feeling comfortable asking someone a question, even asking someone for a date or a favor. Because you are relaxed, you will find yourself able to do this effectively. You will trust your own opinions more and feel more comfortable acting or reacting on the basis of those opinions.

You are going to treat your body well. Because you are going to value yourself more as a person, you are also going to value your body. You will have a respect for your body and see it as a thing of dignity and worth. Your habits with regard to your body will reflect this basic respect for yourself, giving you a disciplined attitude toward eating and drinking and exercise and the things that are good for your body. You will treat it well because it is an extension and a very integral part of yourself. It allows you to experience a variety of positive sensations. It allows you to live. So you owe your body genuine respect and protection.

They are encouraged to take good care of themselves to help them be more attractive. Self-esteem is also enhanced when they treat themselves with respect.

You are also going to see yourself being more assertive, more self-expressive, more honest, more direct and firm. You will be respectful of the rights of others, but you will also be respectful of your own rights . . . respectful of your own rights and giving them their proper place. You will not go overboard and become inconsiderate and overbearing. You will respect others *and* yourself. You will see yourself as having the kinds of skills, the appropriate social skills that you need to function comfortably and effectively with other people, whether it is in a social situation, work situation, or home situation. You will be able to behave appropriately, in a way that says I respect myself but I also respect you. You have rights. I have rights.

They are given specific assertive suggestions, using the concepts they have learned from the didactic part of the sessions.

You are going to find that relaxing yourself regularly you will become more relaxed in your life in general. With every

Adapted from Hartland (1966). These are excellent ego-strengthening suggestions. Emphasis here is placed on self-single day that passes, you are going to feel more comfortable. Your body will feel physically stronger and fitter. You will be more alert, energetic during the day, much less easily tired or discouraged or fatigued.

You will find that you will be able to sleep more soundly at night and awake refreshed in the morning, as you create this tension-free environment for your body. . . and that is what you do when you relax yourself deeply with regularity. . .you create a tension-free environment for your body for a few minutes. . .and it will reward you with increasing feelings of relaxation and inner peace. Your nerves will feel stronger and steadier, and you will be so deeply interested in whatever you are doing, so deeply interested in whatever is going on that your mind will be much less preoccupied with yourself in any negative, self-conscious or self-critical way. So that if you are talking with someone, you will be thinking so much about what you are saying, what you want to communicate to them that you will not be thinking about how they are perceiving you or worried about how you are coming across. You will allow your own spontaneous and appropriate behavior to come forth. You will be free to be yourself.

Your mind will be calmer and clearer. You will think clearly, concentrate better . . .and you are going to see problems in their true perspective without magnifying them or allowing them to get out of proportion. With every day that passes you are going to feel emotionally much calmer and more settled. More able to take things in stride. Like water rolling off a duck's back, things will not bother you as much. You will have a greater feeling of personal well-being. . .a greater feeling of personal safety and security than you have had in a very long time. Every day you will become and remain more and more completely relaxed, both mentally and physically, through your own resources, by calling on your own inner strengths.

esteem, assertiveness and self-confidence.

As you become and you remain more relaxed and less tense each day, you will develop much more confidence in yourself, much more confidence in your ability to do not only what you have to do each day but also what you *ought* to or would *like* to be able to do, without fear of failure, without fear of bad consequences, without unnecessary anxiety, without uneasiness. Every day you will feel more independent, more able to stick up for yourself, to stand on your own feet and to hold your own, no matter how difficult and trying things may be. But the key to your success is your confidence, your confidence in yourself and your ability to do whatever you truly want to do, confidence that you can and will accomplish your own goals through the power of your own mind, the power of your own thoughts. You have already been using that power. . . but negatively. You have been using that power against yourself by imaging the things you do wrong, mentally rehearsing your errors, and stamping in the likelihood of their recurring. But you are now going to use this ability to create images positively, to help you encourage the behaviors you now want to use, mentally rehearsing doing things right. What you tell yourself has the greatest of power over your life. What you tell yourself determines whether you feel cheerful or worried. What you tell yourself ultimately determines what you are or are not able to do.

Adapted from the ego-strengthening suggestions of Wilson and Barber (1971).

In this relaxed state, you tell yourself, I really know, deep down, that I am truly valuable in many ways, that I have many good qualities that for various reasons others have not seen, probably because I have not shared them or even permitted others to see them. Sometimes, I blame those others for not seeing and knowing the good qualities I really have. Maybe if I want to be and reflect my real self, so that others can experience and better enjoy who I really am, I have to be like the sculptor who was asked how he sculpted a beau-

These comments, added by the co-therapist, provide a more metaphorical approach.

tiful elephant. He explained, "I just chipped away all the marble that did not look like an elephant." To find and share my real self, maybe I need to chip away and eliminate what is not truly me, become more aware and loving toward my own wonderful, complex, and potential self, take full charge of my life and accept full responsibility for my own well-being and my own actions.

Now I would like to strengthen your ability to help yourself...

I want you to think for a moment about the power of your mind...that just by thinking of something heavy you were able to create such a feeling of heaviness in your hand that it actually moved...and just as you can use images to create a feeling of relaxation and confidence in your body, even in situations that used to upset you or make you anxious. You need only think of the right images, and you can allow your body to have that kind of experience, and the behavior will follow. You are going to get very good at using images to create useful feelings within yourself.

Any ideomotor technique can be used to raise their confidence level and to result in deepening; I used a "heavy bucket." The verbalization is not provided since it will vary based on the technique used. The confidence gained from the ideomotor technique is reinforced. The "feeling of heaviness" should be replaced with whatever sensation was created.

Any standard closing suggestions can follow this verbalization.

References

Alberti RE, Emmons ME: Your Perfect Right: A Guide to Assertive Behavior. San Luis Obisopo, CA, Impact Publishers, 1982

Araoz DL: Hypnosis in group therapy. Int J Clin Exp Hypn 27:1, 1979

Astor MH: Hypnosis and behavior modification combined with psychoanalytic psychotherapy. Int J Clin Exp Hypn 21:8, 1973

Bandura A: Psychotherapy based upon modeling principles. In Bergin AE, Garfield SL (eds): Handbook of Psychotherapy Change: An Empirical Analysis. New York, Wiley & Sons, 1971

Barksdale LS: Building Self-Esteem. Los Angeles, Barksdale Foundation for the Future of Human Understanding, 1972

Barnett EA: Unlock Your Mind and Be Free. Kingston, Ontario, Canada, Publishing Co. Limited, 1982

Bower SA, Bower G: Asserting Yourself: A Practical Guide to Positive Change. Reading, MASS, Addison-Wesley Publishing Co., Inc., 1976

Cooke CE, Vogt AE Van: The Hypnotism Handbook. Alhambra, CA, Borden Publishing Co., 1965

DeVoge S: A behavioral analysis of a group hypnosis treatment method. Am J Clin Hypn 18:127, 1975

Dreikurs R: Children: The Challenge. New York, Hawthron/Dutton, 1964

Galassi JP, Galassi MD: Assessment procedures for assertive behavior. In Alberti RE (ed): Assertiveness: Innovations, Applications, Issues. San Luis Obispo, CA, Impact Publishers, Inc., 1977

Gardner G, Olness K: Hypnosis and Hypnotherapy with Children. New York, Grune & Stratton, 1981

Guerra JJ, Taylor PA: The four assertiveness myths: a fable. In Alberti RE (ed): Assertiveness: Innovations, Applications, Issues. San Luis Obispo, CA, Impact Publishers, Inc., 1977

Hartman BJ: Group hypnotherapy in a university counseling center. Am J Clin Hypn 12:16, 1969

Jakubowski-Spector P: Self-assertive training procedures for women. In Carter DK, Rawlings ET (eds): Psychotherapy With Women. Springfield, ILL, C. Thomas Co., 1977

Jones JE, Banet AG: Dealing with anger. In Pfeiffer JW, Jones JE (eds): La Jolla, CA, University Asso., 1976

Kazdin AE: Assessment of imagery during covert modeling of assertive behavior. J Behav Ther Exp Psychia 7:213, 1976

Kazdin AE: Covert modeling, imagery assessment, and assertive behavior. J Consult Clin Psych 43:716, 1975

Klauber RW: Hypnosis in educational and social psychology. In Wester WC, Smith AH (eds): Clinical Hypnosis: A Multidisciplinary Approach. New York, JB Lippincott Co., 1984

Kroger WS: Clinical and Experimental Hypnosis. Philadelphia, JB Lippincott Co., 1977

Lazarus AA: Behavior rehearsal vs. non-directive therapy vs. advice in effecting behavior change. Behav Res Ther 4:209, 1966

Liberman RP, King LW, DeRisi WJ, McCann M: Personal Effectiveness. Champaign, ILL, Research Press, 1975

Lorrim M, More WW: Four dimensions of assertiveness. Multivariate Behavioral Research 15:127, 1980

Moreno JL: Psychodrama and group psychotherapy. Sociometry 9:249, 1946

Percell L, Berwick P, Bergil A: The effect of assertive training on self-concept and anxiety. Archives of General Psychiatry 31:502, 1974

Rathus SA: A 30-item schedule for assessing assertive behavior. Behav Ther 4:398, 1973

Salter A: Conditioned Reflex Therapy. New York, Farrar, Straus and Giroux, 1949

Sanders S: Mutual group hypnosis as a catalyst in fostering creative problem solving. Am J Clin Hypn 19:62, 1976

Satir V: Peoplemaking. Palo Alto, CA, Science & Behavior Books, Inc., 1972

Spiegel H, Spiegel D: Trance and Treatment. New York, Basic Books, 1978 A Syllabus on Hypnosis and a Handbook of Therapeutic Suggestions. Chicago, ASCH-Education and Research Foundation, 1973

Wilkinson J, Canter S: Social Skills Training Manual. New York, John Wiley & Sons, 1982

Wilson SC, Barber TX: An example of positive suggestions for well-being. In Hartland J: Medical and Dental Hypnosis. Baltimore, Williams & Williams Co., 1971

Wolberg LR: The Technique of Psychotherapy. New York, Grune & Stratton, 1977

Wolpe J: Psychotherapy by Reciprocal Inhibition. Stanford, CA, Stanford University Press, 1958

Yablonsky L: Psychodrama lives. Human Behavior 4:25, 1975 Zuker E: Mastering Assertiveness Skills. New York, AMACOM, 1983

APPENDIX 19-2

Handouts on Emotions
Elizabeth R. Miller, Ph.D.

PSYCHO-DYNAMICS

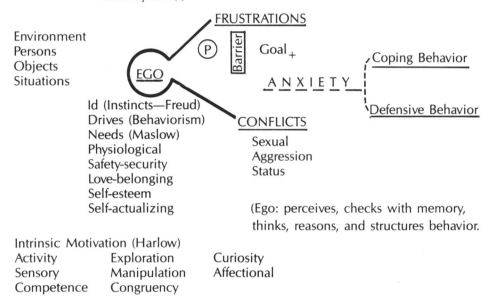

Super Ego (Freud)
Child's conscience
Conscience
Value System(s)

Environment
Persons
Objects
Situations

FRUSTRATIONS

EGO (P) Barrier Goal +

ANXIETY

Coping Behavior

Defensive Behavior

Id (Instincts—Freud)
Drives (Behaviorism)
Needs (Maslow)
Physiological
Safety-security
Love-belonging
Self-esteem
Self-actualizing

CONFLICTS
Sexual
Aggression
Status

(Ego: perceives, checks with memory,
thinks, reasons, and structures behavior.

Intrinsic Motivation (Harlow)

Activity	Exploration	Curiosity
Sensory	Manipulation	Affectional
Competence	Congruency	

EFFECTS OF ANXIETY

Slight Anxiety	Moderate Anxiety	Severe Anxiety
General Alerting	Less spontaneity	Behavior organization breaks down
Increased sensitivity to outside events	Rigidity, reliance on old, "safe" ways of doing	Inability to recognize difference between safe and harmful stimuli
Body preparation for action	Reduced ability to tackle new problems	Rigid, unadaptive, random-appearing behavior patterns
Effective integration of behavior	Increasing effort to maintain adequate behavior	Irritability, distractability
Increased ability for learning, thinking	Narrowing and distortion of perception	Impaired learning and thinking

PERCEPTUAL ACT:

Perception is a process requiring time from point of stimulation of Receiver to behavior which reflects the meaning of the stimulation to the Receiver.

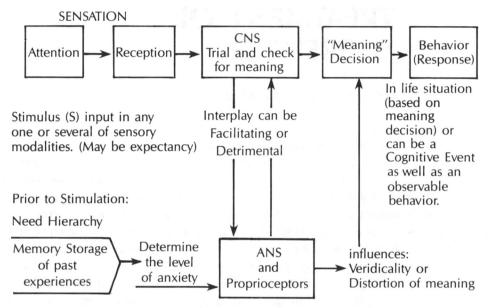

SENSATION

| Attention | → | Reception | → | CNS Trial and check for meaning | → | "Meaning" Decision | → | Behavior (Response) |

Stimulus (S) input in any one or several of sensory modalities. (May be expectancy)

Interplay can be Facilitating or Detrimental

In life situation (based on meaning decision) or can be a Cognitive Event as well as an observable behavior.

Prior to Stimulation:

Need Hierarchy

Memory Storage of past experiences

Determine the level of anxiety

ANS and Proprioceptors

influences:
Veridicality or
Distortion of meaning

Proprioceptors: Muscles, tendons, nerves in deeper structures of body.

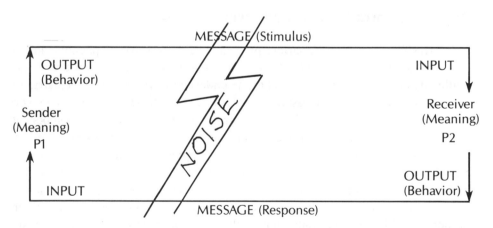

MESSAGE (Stimulus)

OUTPUT (Behavior)

INPUT

Sender (Meaning) P1

Receiver (Meaning) P2

NOISE

INPUT

OUTPUT (Behavior)

MESSAGE (Response)

Adapted by Elizabeth R. Miller, Ph.D. from Charles M. Salley and Gardner Murphy *Development of the Perceptual World*, New York: Basic Books, Inc., 1960.

20 HYPNOSIS IN THE TREATMENT OF DEPRESSION

MOSHE S. TOREM, M.D.

Depression, manifested in many medical and psychiatric conditions, is one of the most common symptoms. However, clinicians often disagree on the meaning of depression. In using the term "depression," we sometimes mean sadness, such as that observed in a state of normal grief and mourning, and other times we refer to a psychopathological condition associated with self-derogatory and self-deprecatory thoughts, feelings of guilt, and suicidal ideations. In a previous publication (Torem, 1983), I indicated the need for a distinction between depression as illness, that is, an affective disorder or as a symptom of an underlying illness, medical or psychiatric. In this chapter, I plan to clarify the types of depression in which hypnosis can be useful and to explain the technique of using hypnosis as an explorative and therapeutic tool in a special subgroup of patients with depression.

Types of Depression and Underlying Causes

DSM-III (1980) classifies the various psychiatric disorders using a phenomenological approach based on behavioral observations and natural history of the illness. Little attention, however, is devoted to the underlying dynamics of psychiatric illness. Research studies in the past 20 years have consistently shown that certain types of depression have a strong biological, perhaps even genetic etiological component. These were named major affective disorders of the unipolar and bipolar type. The patients with this condition cycle in and out of depression or mania, regardless of what happens in their environment. They recover from a depressed state regardless of whether they had psychotherapy or other treatments, providing there is no suicide. These people usually respond well to antidepressant medication and lithium carbonate, which may not only shorten the cycle but even decrease the intensity of symtpoms, frequency of relapses, and sometimes totally prevent the cycles of depression. If the patient has an underlying stable and healthy personality, the positive results of biological treatments can be very dramatic. However, if the patient has an affective disorder superimposed on a borderline personality structure or any other type of character disorder, the biological treatments will result in less dramatic responses, since the remaining psychopathology will still be manifested due to the patient's underlying character or order disorder.

There is, however, another group of depressions in which the symptoms represent an interesting constellation of dynamics. The complex of depression may be manifested in the form of a variety of symptoms and behaviors stemming from underlying intrapsychic dynamics.

The Symptom Complex of Depression: Variability in Manifestation

The symptoms may manifest in the form of depressed mood, excessive sadness, crying spells, or aches and pains in various parts of the body. Headaches, abdominal pain, chest pains, and backaches are the most common pain symptoms. G. Engel (1959) referred to this group of patients, especially when they take on a chronic pattern, as "pain-prone patients." Depression may also be manifested by a sleep disorder, insomnia or hypersomnia, poor appetite, binge-eating episodes associated with excessive weight-gain, or reduced intake of food and liquids associated with weight-loss, self-neglect in physical appearance and personal hygiene, difficulties in making decisions concerning activities of daily living, and the inability to experience joy (anhedonia).

The patient's thoughts are dominated by excessive pessimism, gloom and doom, failure, low regard for oneself, and ideas of being undeserving of love, respect, or success. Moreover, self-derogatory and self-deprecatory thoughts are not uncommon.

Some cases, where the depressed mood is not that conspicuous and instead the clinical picture is dominted by aches, pains, and other physical symptoms, have been referred to as cases with "masked depression" or "depressive equivalents"; that is, the patient has a depressive illness but it is manifested mostly by other symptoms (Lopez-Ibor, 1973; Pichot and Hassam, 1973). Another way in which depressive psychopathology may manifest itself is in the patient's lifestyle and object relations. These patients may not be able to tolerate success, and subconsciously may be motivated to sabotage any success in their careers or other areas of their lives. They have been referred to in the literature as having a masochistic character (Berliner, 1958; Torem, 1979), and their behavior may also be manifested by their repeated associations in close relationships in which they are being exploited or even abused. They appear unhappy and miserable, and their actions continue to perpetuate that pattern.

The Psychodynamics of Depression Patterns

I refer here to those cases where biological elements play a rather small role in the etiology of depression. In exploring the psychodynamics of depression patterns, the clinician will find hypnosis to be a very valuable tool, and its skillful use may facilitate a rapid uncovering of the major underlying conflicts and set the road to resolution and recovery. What are these major underlying dynamics?

1. An Unconscious Sense of Guilt:

   The self-inflicted pain and suffering serve as a way to expiate for the guilt feelings. Thus the pain, although unpleasant, becomes the lesser of two evils. The patient's attempts to atone for his guilt may be manifested in repeated patterns of psychogenic pain, as described eloquently by G. Engel (1959) in his classic paper "Psychogenic Pain and the Pain-Prone Patient."

   The following case vignette illustrates this dynamic. A 42-year-old man was admitted to the hospital complaining of chest pain and shortness of breath. After a thorough examination, it became clear that he had no organic disease. An intensive interview revealed a man with a long history of pain and suffering associated with accidents, injuries, and repeated operations. He had felt miserable all his life, and even when the occasion called for it he could not experience happiness or joy. A further interview, using the hypnoanalytic technique of affect bridge, revealed an interesting story of the patient having lost a twin brother at the age of five due to an accident in which the brother was struck in the head by a heavy swing as the two were playing. This accident had a major impact on the patient's life, and he survived living with an intense subconscious sense of guilt which was partially alleviated through self-inflicted suffering, unhappiness, and depression.

2. Masochism

   The patient engages in behavior which is characterized by the repetition of misery and suffering associated with interpersonal relationships. B. Berliner, who devoted many years to the study of the phenomena of masochism, had described this condition in a number of his writings (1942; 1947; 1958). In his article from 1966, titled "The Psychodynamics of the Depressive Character," Berliner (former president and training analyst of the San Francisco Psychoanalytic Institute) states: "The depressive character is immensely frequent, at least in western civilization." He later stated that the depressive personality is what makes masochism possible and that masochism is a symptom, not a nosological entity. Masochistic suffering is seen as a bid for affection from a parent figure who hates, rejects, and depreciates. This is not a "lust for pain."

3. Re-enactment of Childhood Traumata

   Every depressive character has its roots in a very unhappy childhood filled with traumatic experiences. This mechanism forces the patient to re-enact the original childhood trauma by living in misery, sorrow, pain, and sadness, subconsciously inflicted on himself or herself without the conscious awareness of it. Consciously, the patient complains and begs for help. However, if this mechanism is not identified and uncovered (hypnosis is a very useful tool to uncover it), the patient will be locked into a vicious cycle of suffering, misery, and pain, and may even show a "negative therapeutic reaction" in the face of some symptom relief and act out in self-destructive behavior (Sandler, Holder, and Dare, 1970).

4. Identification With the Aggressor

In this mechanism, which was first described by Anna Freud (1947), the patient subconsciously identifies with the introjected, hateful, rejecting and abusing parent. The trauma lives on, through self-inflicted sadness and suffering. The patient in a way turns against himself, not his own aggression, but the hate and abuse of an incorporated love-object that may have become part of the patient's self.

5. Persecuting Hidden Ego States

Here, again, the patient had suffered repeated traumata in childhood, but the hateful, abusing parent was not only introjected, but later split off from conscious awareness through the mechanism of dissociation. Dissociation was followed by amnesia to the traumatic events of the past. The use of hypnosis can save much time in uncovering these hateful ego states that are responsible for the patient's self-derogatory and self-deprecatory thoughts.

6. Unresolved Grief and Anniversary Reactions

The patient's depression represents an underlying, unresolved grief or a form of pathological, prolonged, incomplete mourning reaction. When this is set off by a specific date, such as the patient reaching the age of the lost love-object at the time of death, or the patient's child reaching the age of the patient when the loss occurred, or the arrival of the calender date of the loss, there may follow a set of depressed feelings, accompanied by low self-esteem, insomnia, aches and pains, difficulties with concentration, a sense of worthlessness, and sometimes suicidal thoughts. This phenomenon has been described by many authors (Pollock, 1970; Engel, 1975), and hypnosis can be helpful for a rather quick identification of the underlying dynamics. The following case is illustrative of such a mechanism.

A 39-year-old Caucasian married woman and mother of three children was admitted to the hospital due to severe depression, insomnia, and suicidal thoughts. She had a poor appetite and had been neglectful of her personal hygiene. The clinical interview elicited wishes to die so that she could be in peace. A more detailed interview, under hypnosis, revealed that this patient had an older sister to whom she had been very close, who had died at the age of 39 in a car accident. The patient had never fully completed the process of mourning her sister's sudden death, and she reported having no memory of the funeral or the viewing.

When the patient turned 39, the age of her sister at the time of her death, she became increasingly sad and depressed. The depression culminated with strong suicidal ideations on the date of the tenth anniversary of her sister's death. The use of hypnosis not only helped to uncover these dynamics, but also allowed the patient to begin the long overdue task of mourning to finally resolve the loss in a healthy way.

Hypnosis as an Explorative Tool in Depression

Hypnosis can be a very useful tool in facilitating the exploration of the various underlying dynamics responsible for a patient's depression. The following is a list of the various techniques in which hypnosis can be used as an explorative tool.

1. The Affect Bridge

In 1971, J. G. Watkins described a technique whereby a patient, under hypnosis, is moved experientially from the present to a past incident over an affect common to the two events. In fact, it is a technique used to explore the roots of past events which are responsible for the patient's depression. In the clinical setting, the hypnotherapist guides the patient into hypnosis and instructs the patient to focus on a feeling which typifies his depressed state. This feeling is then enhanced and intensified. When it reaches its peak strength, the therapist leads to the patient back in time to the origin of this feeling. Thus, the patient is "bridged" from the present to the past, to the event responsible for the patient's original emotions of depression and hopelessness. It is not uncommon for dramatic abreactions to accompany this technique, and therapists using it must be trained in handling abreactions. The uncovering of the original trauma allows the therapist to set the stage for the next phase, in which hypnosis is used as a tool to facilitate therapeutic change and promote recovery from depression.

2. Movie/TV Screen Imaging

The patient is guided into a hypnotic trance and is instructed to imagine a movie or television screen. He is then instructed to imagine himself watching a movie of his life, going through various events and situations that may have originated in hopelessness, helplessness, and the present-day depression. This method has the advantage of keeping the patient dissociated from the emotions and feelings associated with the original trauma. He can focus on a simple, logical reporting of the facts in a detached manner, thus avoiding the intense, sometimes premature, abreactions which may lead to the patient leaving therapy before resolution is accomplished.

3. The Crystal Ball Technique

In 1964, Wolberg described the use of a crystal ball with a patient who was first led into hypnosis with his eyes closed, and, while in a trance, was given the suggestion to let his eyes open. The patient was then instructed to gaze into the crystal ball and identify significant events from the past which were related to the depression in the present. M. Erickson (1954) described a variant of this technique in which the crystal ball could be imagined or hallucinated by the patient who remained with his eyes closed.

4. Age Regression

The patient is led, under hypnosis, to a younger age at which he re-experiences, and, in a way, relives the original trauma that led to the depression of the present. Age regression can be accomplished with greater ease in patients who are highly hypnotizable. A variety of techniques have been used such as counting backwards from the present age to a previous age in which the depression or feelings of helplessness/hopelessness first started. Once this is accomplished, the patient is further instructed to continue the age regression to a previous time in which these depressive feelings and symptoms had not existed. The patient is then instructed to move forward so that the memory of the forgotten event can be shared, explored in greater detail; thus, the patient is ready for therapy.

5. Ideomotor Signaling

This technique is one of the major ones used in analytical hypnotherapy. The patient is guided into hypnosis. Then the signals for "yes," and "no," "I don't know," and "I don't want to answer" are established and agreed upon. The questions used in the interview must be constructed in a special close-ended way to avoid confusion and allow for one of the above choices to be signaled as an answer. The best signals are finger-lifting signals, all on one hand. Although this variation was first recommended by Cheek in 1968, ideomotor phenomena are not new and were described before by Erickson (1954) and LeCron (1954). The whole idea of communicating with the subconscious mind through ideomotor signaling is still controversial regarding its reliability and validity, but it is the most widely used uncovering technique.

6. Indirect Methods of Uncovering

These methods offer an alternative mode of hypnotic exploration which is especially useful when the direct methods have not worked.

(a) Automatic Writing

The patient is guided into hypnosis and later, with his eyes open, is trained to communicate important unconscious information. Naturally, a writing note pad and pen must be at hand. Some patients respond very well when a suggestion is given that the writing hand will be dissociated and is no longer under the patient's conscious control or awareness. Thus, the questions directed at the unconscious mind will be answered in writing by the dissociated hand.

(b) The Personal Diary Technique

The patient is taught self-hypnosis and, after some practice, is given the suggestion to write in the personal diary an answer to a question that is posed. The suggestion is made that the answer may come later, even during sleep or in a dream. The patient is to keep the personal diary at hand and to sign his name at the end of each entry. The patient brings the personal diary to each session and the writings are looked at and examined. Some patients make it a habit to write daily and reflect upon the events of the day, their thoughts and feelings, future plans, and internal conflicts. Not infrequently, hidden, subconscious ego states emerge to report about tramatic events from the past or internal conflicts of the present. Clues to such emerging ego states include a change in handwriting, a change in the style and vocabulary, and a change in the patient's signature at the end of the diary entry.

(c) Dream Induction

Wolberg (1964) recommended giving the patient a suggestion that he will have a significant dream that night which will have an answer and sometimes the solution to the problem. The patient will report this dream in the following session. Naturally, the therapist must be skilled in dream interpretation. Some patients can be trained to produce the dream right there in hypnosis and come out of hypnosis to report the dream relevant to the problem the patient is facing.

(d) The Unconscious Body Image

This technique was described by Freytag (1961), who postulated that the hallucinated, unconscious body image is the picture that the individual forms of himself in his unconscious mind. Freytag reported that she asked the patient, under hypnosis, to halluncinate a full-length mirror and see his reflection in it. After he described it, he was told that this was just a reflection of his body as it existed in space. The patient was then told that each person has another picture of himself in his unconscious mind which symbolically expresses significant emotional problems and conflicts. The patient was told to wait for the appearance of this unconscious body image and to describe in detail what he saw. According to Freytag, this technique is not only useful for exploration and uncovering, but also in doing hypnoanalytic therapy by suggesting changes in the unconscious body image that will effect the true mirror image of the patient.

Hypnosis as a Therapeutic Tool in Depression

In using hypnotherapy for the patient with depression, the clinician must carefully avoid a direct symptom removal approach, especially before the explorative phase has been completed and the underlying dynamics are fully understood. Such avoidance will lessen the risk of suicide attempts or other self-destructive acts, motivated by a powerful need for self-punishment and suffering. However, general ego-strengthening techniques, focusing on calmness, relaxation, and inner peace, are safe when they are associated with permissive suggestions in which the patient is allowed to keep his sadness if he still needs it or if it serves an important function. The use of hypnosis in patients with depression is best done by therapists who are well-trained in psychodynamics and in the care of suicidal patients. Hypnosis should always be used with caution and only after the doctor-patient relationship has been well established with a stable working and therapeutic alliance.

1. Therapeutic Abreaction

Abreaction as a therapeutic tool was first discovered by Freud and Breuer in their studies of hysterical patients. They explained that the effectiveness of abreaction was due to a discharge of what they called "strangulated affects" attached to the supressed mental acts. "Language," these two authors said, "serves as a substitute for action." Today, we see abreaction as a process in which pent-up emotions, previously unconscious to the patient, are discharged through verbal and non-verbal expression. Abreactions may occur spontaneously with the use of hypnosis and are most effective in the crisis-intervention of patients with post-traumatic disorders. The sooner the abreaction, the most likely it is to avoid the development of a chronic post-traumatic stress disorder associated with depressive symptoms. Many depressed patients have a variety of underlying dynamics associated with traumatic events from the past. In these patients, it is not uncommon to observe spontaneous abreactions during the hypnotic explorative phase. The therapist's handling of the patient's abreaction is very important in making this a therapeutic experience rather than just reliving the traumatic event. The therapist must be supportive and continuously provide the patient with a grounding in the present reality so that the patient is not lost in an uncontrolled regression. The following is an illustrative case example.

A. S. was a 28-year-old married woman who suffered from depression, insomnia, phobias, and low self-esteem. After two initial diagnostic interviews, the patient was instructed in the use of hypnosis, and she agreed to cooperate in further exploration of her symptoms under hypnosis. During the first hypnotic session, she spontaneously regressed to the age of eight and abreacted emotionally to an experience in which she was raped by her uncle. She was shaking in fear, and while crying profusely she described in a quivering voice the helplessness and hopelessness she felt and her fear and humiliation. The therapist, listening in a supportive way, asked gently that the patient continue describing the events that took place using such statements as: "And then what happened?" or "Go on. I am listening," or "You are safe here. It is O.K. to cry." These facilitating statements encouraged the patient to continue describing the entire event in detail.

She was told that when she came out of hypnosis she would remember only what she needed to remember and was ready to safely handle in order to accept consciously the disturbing event. If she was not ready, she did not have to remember. When the patient came out of hypnosis, she was fully alert and remembered all the details of her abreaction. She apologized for her intense crying, but reported feeling a great relief, as if "a heavy weight has·been lifted off my chest." She spontaneously started to talk about how she now understood the reason for feeling dirty and unclean around the Easter holiday, which was when the rape occurred. Therapy continued with working through the guilt and other feelings regarding the rape.

2. Working Through

This concept was first developed by Freud (1958), who pointed out that in psychotherapy one cannot expect an immediate cure following an abreaction. The patient often shows resistance to giving up old notions and assimilating new insight. Therefore, the material that the patient becomes consciously aware of has to be be examined and re-examined repeatedly, each time from a different slant, allowing the patient time to assimilate and incorporate the new insight, thus letting go of distortions and misconceptions regarding past traumatic events. In the case of the woman who was raped by her uncle, she felt considerable guilt about the event, and the guilt contributed to her depression. In the working through process, the patient gradually accepted the notion that this happened not because she was a bad girl but because her uncle was drunk; she was simply a helpless, innocent victim. This new insight allowed her to let go of the guilt and accept what happened as an unfortunate event for which she had no responsibility.

3. Ego-Strengthening and Therapeutic Suggestions

Hartland (1965; 1971) stated that only a few patients will let go of their symptoms before they feel strong enough to do without them. He pointed out that the effectiveness of symptom-removal is enhanced by intensive psychotherapy in which hypnosis plays a facilitating role. Hartland's "ego-strengthening" techniques are comprised of positive suggestions of self-worth and personal effectiveness. The following is an example of "ego-strengthening" under hypnosis as used in a depressed patient.

Mrs. R. D. was a 28-year-old married woman, who had been referred for the evaluation and treatment of chronic depression. In the initial interview, it became evident that she suffered from a chronic state of depression which involved poor self-esteem dating back to her childhood. The emphasis, in the first few interviews, was on establishing good rapport with the patient by meeting the patient on her level and attending to her immediate needs. This method inaugurated a good working and therapeutic alliance with the patient. She complained of much tension and a sense of restlessness. She was asked if she wanted to learn self-hypnosis to help reduce her tension and create a sense of internal calmness. She agreed and turned out to be a good subject for learning self-hypnosis. After mastering the technique of self-hypnosis, she was guided into hypnosis and the following ego-strengthening suggestions were made.

> As you are sitting here in this chair, you may allow yourself to be calm and experience a state of internal harmony, whereby your subconscious mind continues to pay attention to my voice and accepts whatever is needed so that you can go on with your life in a healthy, mature way. Whatever it was that happened in the past belongs to the past, and you can simply let go of it, even if you don't fully remember or understand all that actually happened. Living goes on in the present. Every day, you become physically stronger and more alert, more wide awake, more energetic, and more helpful. Yes, you deserve to live your life with hope and optimism. You have suffered enough. Every day, your nerves become stronger and more stable, your mood more pleasant and hopeful. You will become interested in what you do and in whatever goes on around you, and as this happens, your mind becomes more calm, serene, and peaceful, more clear and composed, more tranquil, more in harmony with your body. Your thinking will be clearer, and your concentration easier. You will accept yourself with grace and ease, viewing yourself in a positive light, developing greater confidence in your talents and gifts, and greater confidence in your abilities, with faith in your future. Now, all these things may not happen that quickly. They may take some time, but only as much time as you need for all of this to take place. Therefore, they can happen as rapidly as you want, and it is O.K. if you don't want them to happen that fast. Now, you may want to take a moment to reflect privately on what your life will be like with all these positive changes occurring, and then, whenever you are ready, simply count back from three to one. When you get to one, your eyes will open and you will be fully alert and awake, calm and relaxed. Even though you may not remember everything, your subconscious mind will continue to retain all those positive suggestions. It will continue to guide you to a full recovery. Ready, three...two...and one. Eyes open, fully alert and awake. That's right.

In reviewing the wording of the ego-strengthening and therapeutic suggestion technique, the reader should remember the following points:

(a) All suggestions are phrased in the affirmative, emphasizing the positive.

(b) The patient is told of her own internal strengths, that the cure and healing will continue even after the session.

(c) Self-hypnosis is taught to avoid dependency.

(d) The patient is given the choice regarding the speed of her recovery.

(e) The patient is encouraged to reflect on the future consequences of her recovery and to get ready by using guided imagery.

There are many variations to this technique, and each therapist needs to find the technique that is tailored to the patient's needs, incorporating the five points mentioned above.

4. Reframing and Relabeling

Watzlawick, Weakland, and Fisch (1974), defined "reframing" as changing the individual's conceptual viewpoint in relation to the situation in which it is being experienced and placing it in another frame where the "fact" still fits, but the meaning is entirely changed. In other words, the meaning attributed to the situation is entirely changed.

"Relabeling" refers simply to changing the label attached to the person's problem or symptom, without necessarily changing the frame of reference or conceptual model.

In the case of depression, the symptoms of guilt, self-accusation, and depression are relabeled to responsibility, reliability, courage and willingness to explore, through self-examination, strong feelings and thoughts. Depression is viewed as a process of self-examination, internal review, and a willingness to re-evaluate a situation and consider new options. The following case illustrates the use of hypnosis to facilitate change, through refaming and relabeling, in a patient with depression.

D. J. was a 32-year-old man, who was seen for the evaluation and treatment of depression. After an extensive set of interviews in which an organic basis for his depression was ruled out, it was recommended that he be seen for brief psychotherapy for six sessions. The patient's symptoms included low self-esteem and a set of derogatory thoughts in which he was criticized for agreeing to work for his father and allowing himself to be dominated by him. The patient revealed that he was planning to leave his father's business and look for a new job, but his father's illness complicated the situation and he could not leave him. Thus, he felt that he had no backbone. The patient's father was diagnosed as suffering from an advanced stage of cancer and was given less than one year to live. Further investigation, under hypnosis, revealed that the patient had a competitive father who needed to be admired, respected, and looked-up to by others in order to maintain his own self-worth.

The patient was then given a new definition of his symptoms using the techniques of reframing and relabeling. This was first done under hypnosis, and was later reinforced with discussions when the patient was out of the hypnotic trance. While under hypnosis, the patient was told that he should continue to behave

in a submissive way toward his father and continue to act helpless since this behavior gave his father a chance to show how strong and wise he was allowing
him to instruct his son on how to run the business. Moreover, the patient was
told that he was a good and loving son to his father, and that by acting in a helpless way he was, in fact, showing his great and deep love for his father, who
had a limited time to live. In the discussion following the hypnotic session, the
patient said he never thought of it that way, and that maybe his subconscious
found a mysterious way to communicate his love for his father.

These techniques of reframing and relabeling were reinforced by telling
the patient that he showed a great deal of courage in wanting to search for the
truth. The patient's depressed mood and self-criticism were thus reframed into
a positive mode regarding his relationship with his father. The patient's symptoms disappeared within two weeks, and in a follow-up visit, seven months later,
he reported that on his father's death he resolved the loss by mourning his loss
in a healthy way, without any signs of guilt.

5. Redirecting

This technique can be especially effective for dealing with feelings of guilt
and remorse. The patient is told, under hypnosis, that he made a mistake and
that all humans make mistakes at times. Remorse shows a high degree of hu-
manness, and it is a true element of courage to reflect internally in order to move
forward. The technique here follows the concept mentioned by Arthur Keostler
in his book *Act of Creation.* He referred to psychotherapy as an artificially-induced
regeneration, relying on the basic process of "reculer pour mieux sauter"—to
take a step backward in order to make a better leap forward. In hypnosis, the
patient is told that his subconscious mind will find new ways to guide him into
good deeds to expiate for his mistake. The following case illustrates the use of
this technique.

A. K. was a 35-year-old man, who was involved in a car accident in which
he lost control of his car, ran into another car, causing an accident in which two
people were killed. Later, it was learned that he had been drinking too much
at a party earlier that evening. The patient was very depressed and suffered from
insomnia, feelings of guilt and remorse, and he could not forgive himself, although
more than three years had passed and he had not touched a drop of alcohol in
that time. During an interview, under hypnosis, an ego-state of this patient emerged
spontaneously and called itself "The Superego of A. K." This ego state reported
that the patient, A. K., will get some emotional peace only if he joins Alcoholics Anonymous and then becomes active in the movement of Citizens Against
Drunk Driving. This ego state further communicated that A. K. is to be instructed
to share his experience with young, teen-age drivers so that his mistake will serve
as a lesson for others. When he emerged from hypnosis, the patient had only
a vague memory of what was discussed. He was then instructed to join in the

above-mentioned activities. Follow-up with this patient a year later revealed that he was very actively involved in activities to prevent drunk driving. Further, he was energetic and had no symptoms of depression.

6. Ego-State Therapy

This form of therapy involves the utilization of family and group treatment techniques for the resolution of conflicts between different ego states, which constitute a "family of self" within a single individual. According to J. and H. Watkins (1979-80; 1981), who have written prolifically on this subject, an ego state is defined as an organized system of behaviors and experiences, whose elements are bound together by some common principle, but are more or less permeable. In some patients with depression, the underlying dynamics may involve the persecution and expression of hostility from a hidden ego state that represents the introject of a hostile, unloving parent. When such underlying dynamics are uncovered by the use of hypnosis, ego-state therapy is the most useful technique in alleviating the patient's depression. Each ego state involved in the patient's depression is individually activated through the use of hypnosis, followed by a thorough study of each ego-state to determine its origin, its needs, its objectives, and its significance in affecting the patient's mood and thinking. The therapist becomes a diplomat, who negotiates with the persecuting ego state to change its behavior while keeping its original aim.

For example, W. D. was a 33-year-old married woman, who was evaluated for depression associated with insomnia, inability to experience pleasure, poor appetite, and crying spells. She reported thoughts of being a bad mother to her newborn baby and was afraid she might hurt her baby. A further hypnoanalytic interview revealed that this woman had suffered great neglect and physical abuse from her own mother. She later made a vow to herself not to be like her mother when she has her own children. The hypnoanalytic technique identified an ego state that represented the introjected image of the patient's mother. This ego state attempted to influence the patient's behavior towards her baby by making her do to the baby what had been done to her. These impulses were experienced as bad thoughts and impulses in the patient's adult ego state, resulting in symptoms of anxiety and depression. In treatment, using ego-state therapy, the persecuting ego state was activated and it was found that it felt unloved and unappreciated by the patient. The therapist negotiated an agreement between this ego-state and the patient, whereby this ego-state would keep its influence on the patient, but instead of instilling thoughts of neglecting the baby it would influence the patient to pay more attention to her looks, makeup, body shape, and clothes. The patient's adult ego state, in turn, agreed to recognize the hidden child ego state and include it as part of the patient's makeup.

This chapter discussed the utilization of hypnosis as a tool used to uncover the various dynamics involved in a patient's depression. Moreover, it also demonstrated the efficacy of hypnosis as a facilitating tool in the psychotherapy of depression by enhancing such techniques as abreaction, working through, therapeutic suggestion and ego-strengthening, reframing and relabeling, redirecting, and ego-state therapy. The need to rule out organic, biologic elements in depression before hypnotic techniques are employed was emphasized.

References

American Psychiatric Association. Diagnostic and Statistical Manual III, Washington, D.C., American Psychiatric Association, 1980

Berliner B: The concept of masochism. Psychonanal Rev 29:386-400, 1947

Berliner B: On some psychodynamics of masochism. Psychoanal Quart 16:459-471, 1947

Berliner B: The role of object relations in moral masochism. Psychoanal Quart 27:38-56, 1958

Berliner B: Psychodynamics of the depressive character. Psychoanal Forum 1:243-251, 1966

Cheek DB, LeCron LM: Clinical Hypnotherapy. New York, Grune and Stratton, 1968

Engel GL: Psychogenic pain and the pain-prone patient. Am J Med 26-899-918, 1959

Engel GL: The death of a twin: Mourning and Anniversary Reactions. Fragments of ten years of self-analysis. Int J Psychoanal 56:23-40, 1975

Erickson, MH: Special techniques of brief hypnotherapy. J Clin Exp Hypn 2:109-129, 1954

Freud A: The Ego and the Mechanism of Defense. New York, Int. Universities Press, 1946

Freud S (1914): Remembering, repeating and working-through. The Collected Writings of S. Freud, Standard Edition. London, Hogarth Press, 12:155, 1958

Freud S, Breuer J (1893): Studies in Hysteria. The Collected Writings of S. Freud, Standard Edition. London, Hogarth Press, 2:8, 1955

Freytag FK: Hypnosis and the Unconscious Body Image. New York, Julian Press, Inc., 1961

Hartland J: Further Observations on the use of ego-strengthening techniques. Am J Clin Hypn 14:1-8, 1971

Hartland J: The value of ego-strengthening procedures prior to direct symptom removal under hypnosis. Am J Clin Hypn 8:89-93, 1965

LeCron LM: A hypnotic technique for uncovering unconscious material. J Clin Exp Hypn 1:76-79, 1954

Lopez-Ibor JJ: Depressive equivalents. In Kielholz P (ed): Masked Depression. Bern, Switzerland, Hans Huber Publishers, 1973

Pichot P, Hassan J: Masked depression and depressive equivalents: Problems of definition and diagnosis. In Kielholz P (ed): Masked Depression. Bern, Switzerland, Hans Huber Publishers, 1973

Pollock GH: Anniversary reactions, trauma, and mourning. Psychoanal Quart 39:347-371, 1970

Sandler J, Holder A, Dare C: Basic psychoanalytic concepts VII: The negative therapeutic reaction. Brit J Psychiat 117:413-435, 1970

Torem M: Pseudomasochism: A clinical report. Hillside J Clin Psych 1:161-192, 1979

Torem M: Depression as illness and mood: The implications for diagnosis and treatment. Ohio State Med J 79:792-795, 1983

Watkins JG: The affect bridge: A hypnoanalytic technique. Int J Clin Exp Hypn 19:21-27, 1971

Watkins JG, Watkins HH: Ego states and hidden observers. J Altered States Consciousness, 5:3-18, 1979-1980

Watkins JG: Ego-state therapy. In Corsini RJ (ed): Handbook of Innovative Psychotherapies. New York, John Wiley and Sons, 1981

Watzlawick P, Weakland J, Fisch R: Change: Principles of Problem Formation and Problem Resolution. New York, W. W. Norton, 1974

Wolberg LR: Hypnoanalysis. New York, Grune and Stratton, 1964

21 HYPNOSIS IN SEXUAL DYSFUNCTION

HERBERT MANN, M.D.

More than two thousand years ago,the unknown author of the Book of Proverbs poetically proclaimed:

There are three things too wonderful for me,
Yea, four which I understand not:
The way of an eagle in the air,
The way of a serpent upon the rock,
The way of a ship in the middle of the sea,
The way of a man with a maid.

Of all the world's mysteries, none is more baffling than human sexuality. Our sexual nature is startlingly primitive, disturbingly anthropoid, yet distinctly human. While our atavistic, animalistic nature demands sexual gratification, our spiritual conditioning inhibits and restrains us from satisfying those demands. We are, therefore, continually at war with ourselves. Conflict between our animal origins and spiritual aspirations frequently leads to a kind of neuroticism and torment manifested by overt sexual disorder or covert sexual dysfunction encrusted with a potpourri of somatic symptoms. Hypnotherapy, which is often recommended as a last resort, is especially well-suited to the treatment of sexual disorders, including impotence, premature ejaculation, frigidity and anorgasmia, and dyspareunia.

No one is beyond the influence of sex. Sex is a fundamental process that gives us our most powerfully experienced moments of being alive. Sex is far more than a physical expression; it is a deep and pervasive aspect of personality. A power of splendid potential, it is the most intimate mode of communication. The very nakedness of the sexual act is symbolic of the fact that sex pierces through the disguises, games and fictions which ordinarily obscure human relationships (Calderone, 1966).

The present era may be described as an erotic renaissance, a time of hedonism and orgasmic preoccupation. Our society is sex-oriented, sex-centered, sex-exploited, and sex-saturated. Never in history has there been such freedom to experiment with new modes of sexual expression and to explore such a diversity of sexual lifestyles. Sexual liberalism has become the order of the day.

Stress inherent in adapting to the demands of rapidly-changing sexual mores exacts its toll. In the everyday practice of medicine, increasing numbers of patients are seen with overt problems such as premature ejaculation, impotence, anorgasmia, dyspareunia, or an infinite variety of somatic complaints masking inner turmoil of sexual conflict. At least 60 percent of patients seen in family practice suffer from self-related problems (Hawkins, 1966). Many patients are totally unaware of the relationship between their somatic complaints and unconscious sexual conflicts. Others have some idea that their problems are sex-related but are inhibited in divulging intimate details. It is our responsibility as therapists to create an atmosphere of trust and confidence that permits and invites free and open discussion of sexual problems.

Hypnosis is well-suited to the treatment of sexual disorders because it encourages a therapeutic alliance. In an aura of relaxation and contemplation, patients are more receptive to ideas and understandings that can effect alterations in psychophysiologic processes and behavior. Hypnosis lends itself to the type of psychotherapy envisioned by Dr. Jules Masserman, professor of psychiatry at Northwestern University. He defines the indivisibility of psychiatry and general medicine as "humanitarian psychiatry," a comprehensive behavioral science that fosters a deeper understanding of man's uniquely human pursuits (Masserman, 1971). Hypnosis encourages an empathetic, collaborative relationship within which more profound alterations of sexual attitudes and behavior may be achieved in a limited time than with more traditional methods.

There are no effective standardized methods of dealing with sexual dysfunction. Each patient is unique. Treatment strategy should be customized to meet the particular needs of each patient and his or her distinctive symptom complex.

Therapeutic goals should be oriented toward the making of realistic, reasonably mature adjustments to sexual feelings, attitudes, and behavior. Patients should be helped to understand and manage their sexual power without repressing or distorting it. They should be encouraged to express their sexuality creatively and constructively, and to reevaluate old concepts and new learnings toward the promotion of healthy intrapsychic and interpersonal relationships.

Trance Induction

Trance induction should not be treated as an isolated process that precedes therapy. Induction is an integral part of the therapeutic process, teaching control of behavior, feelings, and sensations. Varied and extensive hypnotic experience not only leads to deeper trance states but increases the patient's ability to function effectively in therapy. Optimal levels of trance can be maintained by reminding patients to enjoy the trance state, to let nothing disturb them, and to have confidence that they can meet well any problem or task presented.

Impotence

Impotence is defined as the inability to attain or maintain an erection of sufficient quality for effective sexual functioning either in autoerotic activity or heterosexual or homosexual relationships. Only if there has never been a successful erection should the term "primary impotence" be applied. "Secondary impotence" refers to varying degrees of erectile dysfunction following at least one successful sexual performance. Most men experience occasional erectile problems due to fatigue, excessive use of alcohol, boredom, an unattractive partner, and so forth. The term "secondary impotence" should be reserved for frequent erectile failure occurring without obvious reason and usually associated with a high level of anxiety that intensifies the problem.

An estimated 70 to 90 percent of impotence is psychogenic. It is rarely necessary to spend much time and money on extensive work-ups to differentiate between psychogenic and organic impotence. Although psychogenic impotence is a diagnosis of exclusion, several factors readily differentiate it from organic impotence. There is little likelihood of organic dysfunction if a man has frequent and sustained early morning erections, nocturnal erections, orgasmic dreams, auto-erotic erections, or if impotence is selective to partners. Psychogenic impotence usually has a relatively rapid onset, while organic impotence is characterized by insidious development as in the aging process, where there may be lowered testosterone levels due to defects in the hypothalmic-pituitary-gonadal axis. Although the indications for the use of hypnotherapy in psychogenic impotence is self-evident, hypnosis may also be very helpful in coping with the emotional components of organic impotence.

Premature Ejaculation

Premature ejaculation is a term describing ejaculation that occurs relatively soon after the attaining of erection. The time between arousal and ejaculation varies considerably from one male to another, varies in different situations, varies with different sexual partners and with different types of sexual activity. Practically, premature ejaculation may be defined as the inability to exercise control until the male's sexual partner has been afforded a reasonable time for arousal and gratification.

Occasional premature ejaculation rarely prompts the male to seek professional help. Habitual premature ejaculation is a serious problem that can be devastating in its effect on the male ego and on female partners, who are frustrated with early termination of sexual activity. Theories to account for premature ejaculation include anxiety over sexual performance, sadistic feelings toward women, and the desire to frustrate sexual partners. Masters and Johnson, after interviewing a large number of patients, concluded that premature ejaculation probably has its roots in a conditioned response resulting from haste in early sexual experiences (Masters and Johnson, 1970).

Frigidity and Anorgasmia

Unfortunately, the terms "frigidity" and "anorgasmia" are often used interchangeably. More accurately, "frigidity" implies disinterest in sexual activity while "anorgasmia" describes the absence of orgasmic response. A totally frigid woman lacks any desire for sexual expression and may go so far as to denounce such activity as repugnant. Partial frigidity may be characterized by varying degrees of mild interest in sexual stimulation (McCary, 1967). Many women who are anorgasmic nevertheless enjoy sexual activity and should not be labeled as "frigid." Sexual dysfunction in women is further confused by the fact that orgasm in females is frequently difficult or impossible to recognize, subjectively or objectively, in contradistinction to males whose orgasms are associated with definite psychological and physiological activity.

Dyspareunia

Dyspareunia is defined as pain on intromission and/or during coitus and is usually associated with vaginismus, an involuntary spasm of vaginal musculature. Occasionally, it is caused by a rigid hymenal ring, urogenital inflammation, endometriosis, or other pelvic pathology. Far more frequently, dyspareunia is psychogenic in origin. Dyspareunia may reflect unconscious rejection of coital activity because of hostility, fear of pregnancy, punishment of male partners, anxiety, a belief that sex is sinful, resentment of the inferior, passive role of women in our androcentric society, or a host of other psychogenic factors.

Case Reports

Hypnotherapy is an art, not a science. It would be foolhardy to assume that a clinically significant change in one patient can be replicated in another patient by following an identical treatment plan. Therefore, the following case reports are offered only as a guide in developing treatment strategies that meet the needs of individual patients and their distinctive overt or covert sexual disorders.

Case of Overt Impotence in an
"Unhypnotizable" Patient

A 26-year-old male was referred for treatment of relative impotence, a problem that had begun two years prior to his referral. Physical examination and endocrinological studies were normal. Once or twice a week, he experienced penile tumescence upon awakening in the morning but attempts at masturbation failed as his penis rapidly became flaccid. He had been active sexually since his mid-teen years, participating in many and varied sexual experiences with a procession of female acquaintances. The relationships were essential physical; emotional involvements were avoided. Anti-depressants had been prescribed to help him cope with the emotional impact of the threat to his manhood. Although his internist and a consulting urologist gave him a clean bill of health, the patient felt that his problem had to be organic. He consented to see me to rule out the possibility of a psychogenic factor responsible for his impotence.

The patient was a post-graduate student in psychology. As a volunteer subject in experimental work with hypnosis, he was considered unhypnotizable because of his low score on standard responsivity tests. In accord with Milton Erickson's methodology in accepting the patient's belief system and behavior, the patient and I agreed that it would be futile to attempt hypnosis inasmuch as he was unhypnotizable. He was assured that there were other methods effective in well-motivated patients to aid in differentiating between psychogenic and organic impotence. The patient listened attentively to the statement that the subconscious might be imprinted with a memory of some event or series of events that could have an effect on optimal sexual functioning. He agreed with me that psyche and soma were closely interrelated and that the subconscious controls much of our behavior.

While we were discussing psychosensory and psychomotor activity, the patient was encouraged to concentrate on feelings of warmth by visualizing himself exposed to hot desert sun. Within 10 minutes, he was able to produce an appropriate skin response. His focusing attention on an image of himself lying wet and naked in a snow storm resulted in shivering that was relieved by his returning to the mental picture of desert heat. An image of his hand encased in an iron glove that was being lifted by a powerful electromagnet produced arm levitation. During a two-hour session, the patient learned that he was capable of experiencing a wealth of sensory and motor activities.

Encouraged to go back in time to an occasion that might have influenced his sexual problem, the patient described a sexual liaison with a casual girl friend who was helping herself to chocolate candy from a bedside table while slipping out of her clothes. Coitus ensued with the patient apparently enjoying the act even though his female partner assumed an entirely passive and unresponsive role. As he continued his thrusting activity, she reached over to the box of candy and put a piece of chocolate in her mouth, apparently unconcerned with the coital act. The patient reacted with a feeling of astonishment, rejection, and, as he described it, "unrealness." His erection receded, he disengaged himself, got dressed and walked out on his ill-behaved partner. He phoned another girl friend, arranged to see her later that evening and enjoyed a successful sexual liaison with her. However, as time went on, he began to have difficulty attaining and maintaining an erection. Within a few weeks, he became totally impotent.

The patient was encouraged to remember everything that he had experienced and discussed during our lengthy hypnotic session. At a conscious level of awareness, the patient asked whether or not he had been in hypnosis, but that was something he had to decide for himself. He concluded that, inasmuch as he was successful in experiencing so many phenomena of hypnosis, he must have been in a trance even though he had been unresponsive and unhypnotizable in a university setting.

At our second session, the patient used the trance state to relive, in slow motion, the details of his unfortunate sexual experience with the chocolate-loving partner and to analyze the depth of his emotional response to her behavior. In and out of trance, he learned to accept the fact that one sexual performance failure, especially under such bizarre circumstances, need not have a permanent effect on his sexual functioning. The patient was encouraged to use imagery in recalling two or three past sexual experiences that were especially stimulating and satisfying, and to anticipate a full recovery within a reasonable time.

The third session was held one week later, at which time the patient reported a successful sexual performance. He decided to continue treatment to discuss in depth a subject that we had casually introduced at our first session—his enhancement of sexual pleasure by integrating physical sex with an appreciation of emotional fulfillment for himself and his sexual partner or partners. His compulsive, hedonistic behavior gradually underwent a transformation as he learned to conceptualize sex not only as a physical expression, but as a major aspect of personality.

Case of Anorgasmia

A 19-year-old married woman had lost excess weight by modifying her eating habits with the help of hypnosis. Her success prompted her to ask about the use of hypnosis in a sexual problem. Although she and her husband enjoyed an intimate relationship, they were both frustrated by her inability to experience a recognizable orgasm. They were influenced by the profusion of articles encouraging women to enhance sexual gratification through orgasm as the ultimately satisfying physical and emotional response. They had followed instructions in several "how to" books on sexual performance, used manual, oral, and vibrator clitoral stimulation, but the woman failed to reach orgasm. She began to have doubts about her ability to ever experience the liberated woman's sexual goal.

In trance, we discussed orgasm as a sensory and physiologic response under control of the subconscious, not the conscious mind. Paradoxically, the harder one tries the more difficult it becomes to reach orgasm. Hypnosis can be used as a pathway to the subconscious mind to imprint new ideas, learnings, and experiences that automatically stimulate the sex organs to make appropriate responses. In and out of trance, we discussed reducing the focus on mechanical clitoral stimulation while developing a relaxed aura for enriching life with an appreciation of human sexuality's delicate beauty and ecstatic joy.

The second session was devoted to a discussion with the patient and her husband, who fortunately was cooperative and understanding. Since he spontaneously developed a light trance while observing his wife in hypnosis, they both benefited from the trance experience and new focus on the totality of love-making and mutual pleasure.

Five more weekly sessions, with both husband and wife, were devoted to reinforcing the idea that sex is far more than a physical expression; it is a process that encompasses the totality of mutal caring, love, and the deep, pervasive desire to give of oneself. Orgasm is an expression of an enhanced appreciation of a loving relationship.

As husband and wife responded with a relaxed attitude and increased pleasure in sharing sexual feelings, the patient experienced very powerful sensations that she began to intrepret as orgasm. As time went on, she reported an increase in clitoral sensations, then experienced a definite peak of sexual feelings combined with flushing and vaginal spasm followed by resolution and relaxation. Since then, she has experienced orgasm of varying degrees of intensity with a fair degree of frequency. Both husband and wife are delighted with the enriched sexual relationship.

Case of Relative Importance with an
Unrealistic Goal

A 42-year-old male, married 15 years, had been having coitus with his wife about once or twice a week. After being introduced to swinging, which he and his wife found pleasurable recreation, the patient wanted to be hypnotized to improve upon his sexual performance. He complained about his inability to have more than three or four firm erections leading to ejaculation during a weekend party even though there was no limit to the number of available sexual partners. This is a common complaint among swingers, not unlike the frustration experienced by gluttons in "all you can eat" restaurants when food is still available but the stomach rebels. The patient who looks upon hypnosis as some magical formula to reach unrealistic goals needs guidance in learning to accept limitations.

This patient was encouraged to use hypnosis as a modality for reducing performance anxiety, to stop focusing on numbers of erections, and to thoroughly enjoy the quality of his interpersonal relationships, especially his relationship with his wife. After several sessions, he reported an increase in frequency in marital coitus and arranged to have a joint session with his wife who wanted guidance in improving her sexual response. Hypnosis helped immeasurably in having husband and wife communicate with each other, express their needs and desires, and discuss methods for attaining sexual gratification. Within a few weeks they reported not only a remarkable improvement in their sexual relationship but also in their total life relationship. As they developed closer ties to each other, their interest in swinging decreased. Hypnosis served as a catalyst in replacing extramarital unemotional sex with authentic intimacy. In a follow-up phone call three months after their final session, they reported no further interest in swinging and a much more satisfying marital and social relationship.

This case illustrates the therapist's responsibility in guiding patients away from unrealistic goals and toward modes of behavior that are realistic, achievable, and emotionally satisfying.

Case of Relative Impotence in Marriage

A 56-year-old recently divorced man married a 23-year-old former employee. For two years prior to his divorce, he had been having a clandestine affair with the woman and frequently engaged in exciting sexual interludes. However, soon after marriage, he found it increasingly difficult to attain an erection of sufficient firmness for intromission. On one occasion, when his homecoming was delayed because of a business appointment, his wife accused him of infidelity. Apparently, his sexual inadequacy prompted her to suspect an extramarital liaison. Her attitude put further pressure on him to perform adequately. Anxiety and tension increased, with a further reduction in erectile response. When antidepressant medication failed to afford any relief, he was referred for hypnosis in the hope that sexual performance could be improved and his marriage saved.

The patient seemed distraught over his relative impotence and his deteriorating marital relationship. He was a well-motivated, intelligent person, who easily responded to an informal, naturalistic induction procedure while discussing his feelings and attitudes about himself, his wife, and their sexual and social relationship. The patient was taught to use imagery seeing himself in alternative situations. One alternative was to observe his behavior within his present marital situation as time went by and he attempted to improve the total relationship. Another alternative was to free himself through a separation or divorce, to see himself as a simple man with an option of engaging in another relationship. A further alternative was a reconciliation with his former wife. He readily learned to use self-hypnosis to review his alternatives.

Within three weeks, he concluded that he had made a grave mistake in confusing an infatuation with a young, attractive woman with the kind of love necessary to develop a lasting, profound marital relationship. He realized that during their clandestine relationship her physical attractiveness readily accounted for his sexual responsiveness. But as they settled into a more mundane, routine lifestyle, the former excitement wore off and he realized that they had little or nothing on which to build a mutually satisfying relationship. Fortunately, the woman, too, recognized her own disappointment with their marriage and an amicable divorce was arranged. Several months later, the patient was able to convince his former wife that he had made a grievous error and that he wanted to return to her. I counseled the couple over many months, watching as their love was renewed and their differences resolved. A repentant husband and a forgiving wife remarried. There was no further problem with impotence.

Case of Impotence Related to
Early Teen Experience

A 24-year-old dental student was referred for treatment of impotence. For over a year, he and a young woman had been sharing an apartment and planning on marriage. They enjoyed prolonged foreplay, but attempts at intromission failed because of his inability to attain an erection firm enough to consummate the act. They spent several weeks practicing sensate focus as recommended by Masters and Johnson, but had no success in resolving the erectile dysfunction. They finally decided to seek professional help.

Following a brief discussion of hypnosis, naturalistic induction techniques were interspersed with questions concerning the patient's early sex life. He drifted into trance while recalling past experiences and the feelings and emotions that were an integral part of those events. He described his early sexual awakenings, nocturnal emissions, erections and ejaculation during petting and masturbation.

His first attempt at coitus was as a high school junior when he attended a beer party at which a girl permitted several boys in succession to have sex with her. While waiting for his turn, he felt nauseated, perhaps as a result of the beer he had consumed and/or revulsion at the public, animalistic sexual display. He would have preferred passing up his turn at coitus but was reluctant to risk peer criticism. He had difficulty inserting his semi-erect penis into the vaginal introitus, but finally succeeded with manual assistance of his sexual partner. Soon after he began thrusting movements, his friends insisted that he hurry because they were leaving for another party. Under that kind of pressure, his erection subsided, his penis slipped out of the vagina, and he left without having ejaculated.

Subsequent occasional attempts at coitus with casual dates during his senior high school and college years followed a pattern of erectile dysfunction, with either inability to penetrate the introitus or loss of erection almost immediately following intromission. There appeared to be no loss of libido. Masturbation three or four times a month, with full erection, gave him pleasurable relief from sexual tension.

While relating his sexual history, he was given assurance that his trance state would spontaneously deepen, that nothing would disturb his concentration on the work that had to be done, that he could enjoy the hypnotic experience with complete confidence in his ability to adequately resolve his sexual problem.

The first session was terminated with instructions in self-hypnosis. To re-experience the trance state, the patient need only recall his feelings, sensations, and thoughts during our office session. If he wanted to implement that technique, he could silently count from one to 20 as a signal or symbol to go into deeper and deeper levels of trance. Whenever he was ready to return to a conscious level of awareness, he could do so either by letting himself "awaken" or by letting the numbers from 20 to one come to mind as a signal for terminating the trance state.

Prior to ending the first trance session, the patient was told that during his self-hypnosis sessions the subconscious mind, the seat of all memories, habit patterns, and automatic body functions, would be free to focus attention on his problem and bring into conscious awareness probable underlying emotional conflict.

At our second visit one week later, the patient arrived with his fiancee. They were both ecstatically happy with the dramatic change in his sexual performance and his relief of anxiety. On the fourth day following his office visit, while practicing self-hypnosis, he recalled in vivid detail the high school beer party, the raucous remarks of his friends, his nausea and disgust, and his embarrassment at hearing the girl's derogatory remarks about his manhood as she manipulated his semi-erect penis into her vagina. The thought came to him that if he could wipe that experience from his mind his problem would disappear. On the following day, during a self-hypnosis session, the thought came to him that amnesia for the traumatic event was not a practical solution. A more rational approach might be to put that day's events into proper perspective, to accept his behavior as an emotionally immature, stupid mistake that need not have a lasting, debilitating effect. That evening, the couple went to bed and indulged in kissing, petting, and genital manipulation. To their amazement, the patient attained a full erection sufficient for coital activity. Since then, there has been no erectile problem.

Case of Intense Pruritis Masking
Sexual Conflict

An unmarried male computer programmer, 32 years of age, was referred by a dermatologist for hypnosis to help relieve intense pruritis and depression. For two years, he had been treated unsuccessfully for eczema of undetermined origin. His dermatitis was limited to the upper and lower extremities. He wore "long johns" to prevent his outer clothing from being soiled by blood produced from scratching.

The patient seemed reluctant to spend time on history-taking, saying that he had gone through "all that" with his internist and dermatologist. When questioned about his perception of the problem, he seemed uneasy and expressed a desire to get started with hypnosis. He was very cooperative in learning to develop a trance state by narrowing his attention and focusing on a limited area of pruritis. His trance deepened as he concentrated on various hypnotic phenomena including increasing the intensity of pruritis, then decreasing the discomfort by experiencing a soothing coolness, followed by numbness, then lightness associated with arm levitation. He was then told to "awaken" with confidence in his ability to reexperience the learned sensory and motor phenomena. He was given time to go through the learned sequence of events by himself. When his arm levitated, he was encouraged to practice self-hypnosis whenever it was appropriate and convenient.

At our next session a week later, the patient reported success in controlling the intensity of pruritis while in self-hypnosis but no improvement outside of the trance state. In and out of trance, we discussed the skin as a mirror of our emotions, exemplified by blushing in response to embarrassment or pallor as a result of fright. The patient was taught to develop analgesia and anaesthesia to enhance control over pruritis and as a deepening technique. Prior to terminating the trance, a suggestion was offered to encourage introspection and the freedom of the patient to seek help with any conflict he was experiencing.

Although we had made an appointment for the following week, the patient phoned two days after our last session asking to see me the following day. He immediately volunteered the information that he was a homosexual. In his early teens, he knew that he was different from his peer group in sexual preference. He gradually accepted his lifestyle while concealing his homosexuality from family, co-workers, and casual acquaintances. However, his secrecy, fear of exposure, and pressure from family to settle down and get married caused increasing anxiety. Invitations to parties obviously arranged to have him meet eligible females added to his discomfiture and distress. He now realized that his dermatitis probably reflected inner turmoil, but was at a loss to find a solution.

In and out of trance, we discussed various alternatives available to him. Using imagery, he visualized himself continuing in his present situation with increasing distress and discomfort. Then he observed his behavior and emotional reaction if he were to "come out of the closet" and let it be known that he was a homosexual. Another alternative was to keep his secret while building an emotional fence against people who insisted on arranging dates for him. He could secretly enjoy the thought that he was an inevitable winner in any struggle to marry him off. Eventually, his friends would give up and he could concentrate on the pleasure of being a healthy, productive, creative person with a lifestyle that satisfied his needs.

The patient was seen once a week for two months, with follow-up visits at monthly intervals for three more months. Two weeks from the time he started to use imagery seeing his alternatives, the dermatitis began to clear. It took five more weeks for the skin to become totally free from eczema. As the dermatitis cleared up, the patient's anxiety and depression dissipated. Ego enhancement was evident in his decision to let his internist and dermatologist know the whole story of his sexual conflict.

Case of Sexual Conflict Underlying
Headache and Pelvic Pain

A 27-year-old married woman, mother of two children, spent many months in a futile search for the cause and relief of severe headaches and pelvic pain. An extensive work-up at a university hospital failed to establish any definite etiology or satisfactory treatment. As is so often the case when conventional diagnostic and therapeutic methods fail, hypnosis was recommended as a last resort.

During the first few sessions good rapport was established and various phenomena of hypnosis were taught. The patient attained a fair degree of pain relief by experiencing time distortion and analgesia. During each session, a casual suggestion was made that in the near future she would want to explore meaningful events in her life that might be related to her distress.

During our sixth session, while I was teaching automatic writing as a dissociative phenomenon that can help control pain, the patient seemed preoccupied. After a silence, she asked if guilt feelings could be causing her problem. She was assured that many somatic symptoms are based on psychogenic factors and that pain is frequently caused by underlying conflicts. She then hesitantly revealed her participation in an extramarital relationship that started several months prior to the onset of her headaches and pelvic pain. Her guilt feelings and fear of discovery led her to terminate the relationship, but headaches and pelvic pain continued.

At subsequent sessions, the patient found it easier to talk about her extramarital episode, both in and out of trance, and to cope with her guilt feelings. As she learned to accept the extramarital episode as a foolish adventure that should be put in proper perspective, her headaches and pelvic pain slowly lessened in intensity and frequency. Hypnotic sessions were continued every two weeks for five more sessions. The patient fully recovered and has remained free from pain during a follow-up program of four monthly visits. She enjoys using self-hypnosis as a daily relaxing experience.

Impotence Following a Premature
Ejaculatory Experience

A 41-year-old married man became impotent three months prior to our first meeting. Although his wife assured him that it was probably a temporary condition due to fatigue and overwork, he became increasingly depressed. His failure to attain an erection with his wife's cooperation utilizing manual and oral stimulation reinforced his fears that his impotence was irreversible. Because of the rapid onset of impotence in an otherwise healthy man, his internist believed the condition was psychogenic in origin and referred him for hypnotherapy.

At our first session, the patient emphasized the fact that his libido was intact, that his wife was a very attractive woman, and that he was trying desperately to regain his sexual potency. We discussed erection as an unconscious response that cannot be experienced by conscious effort. Mention of the possibility that some past experience might have had an inhibiting effect on his sexual responsiveness met with the patient's reluctance to talk about anything in the past. He was anxious to proceed with hypnosis in the belief that he could be persuaded to regain his sexual potency.

He attained and maintained a fairly deep trance level by experiencing a wealth of hypnotic phenomena. He learned to reproduce the trance state by himself and was dismissed with instructions to spend time each day enjoying a relaxing trance experience and perhaps discovering something important that we could discuss at our next session.

Several days later, at our second session, the patient reported that daily self-hypnosis was helpful in reducing the level of anxiety, but had no effect on his erectile dysfunction. However, each time he used self-hypnosis, he found himself reliving an event that disturbed him. After entering hypnosis, he hesitantly described an incident that occurred two weeks prior to the onset of impotence, while he was on a business trip to the Orient.

At a dinner party, an attractive young woman, who had been assigned as his companion, indicated that they could spend the night together. He had conflicting feelings about having an extramarital affair, but he took the woman to his hotel room. Unfortunately, his attempt at coitus ended precipitously with premature ejaculation. He recalled being terribly embarrassed and was relieved when the woman left. He spent a restless night disturbed by mixed feelings of disgust over his sexual performance and guilt over his infidelity. Several days later he returned home, had an erection when in bed with his wife, but immediately upon intromission his penis became flaccid and slipped out of the vagina. Since that time, repeated attempts to attain an erection ended in failure.

At a conscious level of awareness, the patient rejected the idea that one illicit relationship with an embarrassing premature ejaculatory experience could have caused him to become impotent. In trance, finger signal responses revealed a deep feeling of guilt over his extramarital experience and an unconscious desire to punish himself for his transgression. He was asked to evaluate how much guilt he should experience over one illicit incident and how long a time his punishment should last. A suggestion was made that perhaps he would discover, within a short time, that his guilt feelings could dissipate and that his punishment had been sufficiently long and severe. The patient was dismissed with instructions to think over the matter during his self-hypnosis sessions.

The following week, the patient entered the office with a sheepish grin. He reported that, although he rarely attended church services, during the night of his previous office visit he dreamed that he was confessing his sins to a compassionate minister, who relieved him of guilt feelings and as penance extracted a promise from him to be a devoted husband. In the early hours of the morning, he awakened with an erection and a desire to enjoy a sexual interlude with his wife. He and his wife were delighted with his recovery and indulged in coitus on two more occasions during the week. A follow-up phone call one month later confirmed the fact that impotence was no longer a problem.

Case of Hyperhydrosis as a Symptom of Sexual Conflict

A 36-year-old woman was referred for help in controlling hyperhydrosis so severe that it interfered with her work and social life. She had been married 17 years, had two teenage daughters, and had no family or financial problems. During the past year, axillary perspiration had become so profuse that protective absorbent pads had to be changed several times a day to prevent her outer clothing from becoming moist. A thorough medical work-up shed no light on possible causes for this embarrassing symptom. Plastic surgery on the axillae, removing sections of gland-bearing skin, failed to make any appreciable change in the condition. Her family physician recommended a trial of hypnotherapy to help her cope with a feeling of helplessness and frustration.

At our first session, the patient wanted reassurance that in the hypnotic state she would not be made to reveal anything that might be embarrassing or that had no relationship to her hyperhydrosis. She was assured that hypnosis was a very special state of awareness, that it was not unconsciousness, and that she would be in full control of her behavior and responses. My role was that of a teacher, who would offer her a variety of interesting experiences that she could use in controlling her excessive perspiration.

The patient responded well to a naturalistic induction technique that focused on her feelings of increasing axillary perspiration, as she imagined herself in an anxiety-provoking situation, followed by an image of herself in a relaxed mood enjoying axillary coolness and dryness. I discussed the autonomic nervous system and its control over various body functions while teaching her to experience arm levitation and glove anesthesia. In that way, trance deepening techniques were integrated with therapeutic suggestions. Self-hypnosis was practiced and the patient was encouraged to spend time each day developing a trance state at home in preparation for more extensive work in the office.

During our second session, automatic writing was taught as a dissociative phenomenon. A suggestion was made that the patient could use automatic writing to communicate an idea or thought that she might like to share with me either at present or in the near future. In a barely decipherable script, she wrote, "I want to talk to you about something, but not now." She was told that she had the freedom to choose the appropriate time, that perhaps during our next session she would be comfortable sharing her thoughts with me.

At the next office visit, the patient told me that she now felt more secure about herself and about her relationship with me. While practicing self-hypnosis at home, she recalled very vividly what she had automatically written at our previous session. She became aware that it might be related to her hyperhydrosis and, as the days went by, decided to discuss her problem with me.

The patient told of her initiation into wife-swapping with a neighboring couple about two years prior to the onset of hyperhydrosis. Wife-swapping led to involvement with swinging groups. For variety, she occasionally indulged in love-making with other women and found homosexuality increasingly pleasurable. Gradually, she became anorgasmic with men and increasingly orgasmic with women. As it dawned on her that her sexual orientation was changing, she began to experience mild symptoms of anxiety and profuse axillary perspiration. The fact that her internist, two dermatologists, and the plastic surgeon neglected to question her about her sex life reinforced her feelings that her hyperhydrosis was not related to her sexual behavior.

Therapy was directed toward giving her the freedom, in and out of trance, to discuss her feelings and attitudes toward heterosexuality and homosexuality. During the next few weeks she used self-hypnosis to recall and relive orgasmic experiences with her husband and other men with whom she was intimate as a swinger. She focused attention on erotic heterosexual phantasies and reinforced the concept that situational homosexuality was not uncommon as a transient phenomenon that could be relinquished.

At our seventh session, the patient reported that she was again enjoying heterosexual activities, was orgasmic with men, and decided to give up lesbian relationships. Almost as an afterthought, she mentioned that she no longer suffered the inconvenience and embarrassment of hyperhydrosis even though we had done nothing to directly influence it. The patient returned several months later with a daughter who wanted to use hypnosis to improve concentration in a competitive sport. There had been no recurrence of hyperhydrosis.

Case of Dyspareunia and Vaginismus

A 21-year-old woman, married two and a half months, was referred for treatment of severe dyspareunia and vaginismus. The slightest contact of the penis with the introitus caused pain and muscle spasm. There was nothing in her social, sexual, or religious background to account for her problem. For several years prior to her marriage she had at times indulged in "heavy petting" and in masturbation with orgasm. Her marriage followed a courtship of several months during which the couple enjoyed intimate sex play but stopped short of attempting coitus. One month prior to their marriage, the patient had a pelvic examination which she described as uncomfortable but not painful. At that time, she was started on birth control pills.

On their wedding night, when dyspareunia became apparent, the couple passed it off as a temporary condition that would correct itself. During the succeeding two months, love-making was limited to mutual masturbation, oral sex, and occasional attempts at intromission that failed because of pain.

A second visit to the gynecologist again revealed no organic reason for dyspareunia. Vaginal examination was performed without pain or spasm. The gynecologist suggested a psychiatric consultation, but the patient refused. At the suggestion of a close friend, the patient visited a lay hypnotist who guaranteed results in treating a vast array of behavioral problems including sexual disorders. The lay hypnotist had the woman focus on a swinging pendulum while telling her that she would go into a deep sleep and would follow his suggestions. As she began to feel relaxed, he told her that she would automatically go into a trance and not feel any pain when her husband made love to her. At that moment, she became very nervous and felt her heart pounding. She refused to continue the session. However, she was intrigued with the possibility that a more qualified hypnotist might help solve her problem.

At our first meeting, the patient was given the opportunity to ask questions about medical hypnosis, to learn about the difference between authoritarian, direct symptom removal commands of lay hypnotists and the cooperative therapeutic relationships between patients and qualified therapists. The patient learned that she would be in control of her behavior and that hypnosis was a form of communication that could be utilized in determining and discussing underlying subconscious reasons for her problem.

A naturalistic induction process was set in motion while I took her history and discussed dyspareunia as a subconscious defense mechanism. Althought he conscious part of the mind wanted to consummate the sexual act, the subconscious mind set up obstacles in the form of dyspareunia. Our goal was to cooperate in a therapeutic alliance to determine the cause of her symptom and to develop a strategy to resolve the problem. Interspersed in this discussion were suggestions for putting the patient at ease and developing a satisfactory trance. As the patient learned to develop hand levitation, glove anesthesia, and automatic writing, trance deepened and increased her ability to function at a subconscious level of awareness. Because of her unfortunate experience with the lay hypnotist, I deemed it prudent to give her sufficient time to recognize that she was in control of the trance process. She was taught self-hypnosis and encouraged to practice at home.

At our second session, the patient reported that she felt comfortable with me and had no reservations about continuing to use hypnosis. She readily learned to regress and talk about her late teen years. She recalled vividly discussions with her mother about the terrible time her mother had during labor and delivery when the patient was born. The patient abruptly ended her recital, remained silent, then asked if I thought that had anything to do with her pain. She was encouraged to think about the question herself and to give her subconscious mind the opportunity to reveal the answer. By using finger signals, the patient recognized that a fear of pregnancy, labor, and delivery was the foundation upon which she developed dyspareunia and vaginismus. Taking birth control pills apparently was not sufficient assurance that she would not become pregnant.

As a supplement in easing her fear of becoming pregnant while proceeding with hypnotherapy, her gynecologist agreed to instruct her in the use of a vaginal diaphragm in addition to birth control pills. The patient was seen twice a week for six weeks to discuss, in and out of trance, her reaction to her mother's story of painful labor and delivery. She came to the conclusion that her mother demonstrated in many ways a need for self-punishment and sympathy and that her mother's experience, real or imaginary, should be no deterrent to her own desire to have children. We discussed the modern trend toward recognition of childbirth as a natural process, the excellent care available to pregnant women, and the joy of motherhood.

As her fear of pregnancy diminished, the patient began to painlessly accept intromission, at first very cautiously and only as coitus interruptus, then after two weeks fully participating in the coital act without the diaphragm. Ten months from the time of the patient's first visit, she stopped using birth control pills, became pregnant, attended classes given by her obstetrician, and had three hypnosis sessions to reinforce her use of self-hypnosis during labor and an uneventful delivery.

In the treatment of sexual dysfunction, hypnosis offers a realistic, humanistic, comprehensive approach to the total person. Hypnosis is predicated upon a unitary, holistic view of health and disease, an appreciation of man as an integrated being with psyche and soma beautifully coordinated and synchronized. Hypnotherapy is an art of medicine that can be employed to restore and maintain a state of physical, emotional, social, and sexual well-being.

References

Calderone MS: An Analysis of Sexual Response. New York, New American Library, 1966

Erickson MH: Medical Clinics of North America, Vol. 28, No. 3, May 1944

Hawkins D: AMA Panel Discussion on Sex Education, 1966

Masserman JH: A Psychiatric Odyssey. New York, Science House, 1971

Masters WH, Johnson VE: Human Sexual Inadequacy. Boston, Little, Brown and Co., 1970

McCary L: Human Sexuality. New Jersey, Van Nostrand Co., 1967

22 HYPNOSIS IN THE TREATMENT OF TOURETTE SYNDROME

DAVID N. ZAHM, Ph.D.

Giles de la Tourette syndrome was first clearly delineated by Georges de la Tourette. Tourette's syndrome (T.S.) is thought to result from an alteration of catecholamine neurotransmitter releases with hyperactive brain dopaminergic functioning. Tourette's syndrome involves: 1) multiple, rapid and stereotypic muscular and verbal tics; 2) early onset between the ages of two and fifteen years; 3) a fluctuating clinical course; and 4) symptoms that disappear during sleep and moments of increased relaxation and decreased internal and/or external stress (Shapiro, Shapiro, Bruun, and Sweet, 1978). Vocalizations and movements such as coprolalia, copropraxia, echolalia, and echopraxia are often associated with the disorder. Although the primary treatment for T.S. is pharmacological, hypnosis has proved successful as an alternative to medication and as an adjunct to drug treatment.

In regard to pharmacological treatment, since Seignot (1961) first reported the successful use of the antipsychotic butyrophenone haloperidol in a patient with T.S., haloperidol has been the prescribed drug in reducing symptomatology of patients with T.S. Another drug most often used for treatment of hypertension, clonidine, has more recently been described as beneficial and an effective alternative to haloperidol (Cohen, Detlor, Young, and Shaywitz, 1980). The published accounts are equivocal with other reports of minimal or no additional benefit with clonidine (Shapiro, Eisenkraft, and Shapiro, 1983). Haloperidol remains the most common treatment strategy (Gillies and Forsythe, 1984). Treatment with haloperidol, however, involves continual balancing between beneficial clinical dosage and resultant negative side effects.

The mediating effect of anxiety and environmental stress upon T.S. tics has been clearly documented. Surwillo, Shafii, and Barrett (1978) reported a 20-month longitudinal study of the relationship between stressful life events and the frequency of tics in a 10-year-old boy diagnosed with Tourette's syndrome. Surwillo et al. noted that stressful life events were related to an increase in tic frequency, actually overcoming beneficial medication effects in the patient they studied. Lieh-Mak, Luk, and Leung (1979) also suggested that psychological influences or environmental events were a factor in the frequency of tics in the five cases of Gilles de la Tourette syndrome they reported occurring in the Chinese, providing cross cultural evidence *319* of the effect of anxiety and stress upon the tics. Given these environmental influences, nonpharmacological treatment approaches focus upon developing coping mechanisms for dealing with stressful events and their impact upon symptoms such as tics. As a treatment approach, hypnosis can be of benefit either as an alternative to haloperidol or, more likely, as adjuct to drug treatment, possibly permitting dosage reduction and thereby decreasing and/or eliminating negative drug side effects.

Successful Non-pharmacological Treatment

There is a body of literature describing the successful reduction and/or elimination of symptoms associated with T.S. utilizing non-pharmacological treatment approaches. Successful outcomes have been reported with behavior therapy (Clark, 1970; Cohen and Marks, 1977; Rosen and Wesner, 1973), relaxation training (Friedman, 1980; Thomas, Abrams, and Johnson, 1971; Turpin and Powell, 1984), and hypnosis (Kohen and Botts, 1983; Zahm, 1982; Zahm, Foreman, O'Grady, and Ricks, 1983).

There have been an increasing number of clinical reports of hypnosis treatment of the tics associated with Gilles de la Tourette syndrome. Erickson (1964) described the successful use of hypnosis in two patients diagnosed as having T.S. Eisenberg, Ascher, and Kauner (1959) reported success with a child who was treated by hypnosis. Fernando (1967) noted the use of hypnosis with one of the four cases he initially reported. Hypnosis was described by Lindner and Stevens (1967) as being of principal benefit in the decreasing of tics in a 19-year-old Tourette patient. Lindner and Stevens described a high stress home environment in their patient and reported successful diminution of tics with hypnosis. Treatment was prematurely discontinued by the family; however, the tics were reported to have remained minimal at a nine-year follow-up.

One case report of particular interest is provided by Clements (1972). Clements described the treatment of a child diagnosed with Tourette syndrome since the age of four. This boy was followed by Clements for approximately 12 years, with the active use of hypnosis introduced after three years of psychotherapy and haloperidol (1 mgm, t.i.d.) proved unsuccessful at significant reduction of coprolalia and muscular tics. With hypnotherapy, the coprolalia and movements decreased and were completely controlled after nine weeks. Although the boy remained on haloperidol during the period of hypnotherapy, the dosage was gradually decreased and eventually discontinued. At periodic follow-up sessions, the boy remained tic and drug free. This is a noteworthy clinical case study as it represents the more typical clinical situation with the client being on medication, usually haloperidol, and hypnosis initially provided as adjunct to the haloperidol. Efficacious use of hypnosis has more recently been reported by Kohen and Bates (1983) in treating four children with T.S. Zahm, Foreman, O'Grady, and Ricks (1983) also reported upon the beneficial use of hypnotherapy with four children diagnosed with Tourette's syndrome.

Clinical Process

Assessment

Gilles de la Tourette syndrome is most often diagnosed in childhood with a three to one ratio of boys to girls (Shapiro et al., 1978). Therefore, the typical T.S. patient is a male child. To be effective, the clinician must first have a solid understanding of pediatric hypnosis. Although the subject is beyond the scope of this chapter, the reader is referred to a particularly comprehensive review in Gardner and Olness' (1981) book on the subject of hypnosis and hypnotherapy with children.

The Tourette patient and his parents usually seek symptom reduction but are skeptical of hypnotherapy. The patient and his parents have often endured a long period of frustration and failure in previous efforts to control the tics. Prior to diagnosis of T.S., many patients have been described as nervous, attention-seeking, hyperactive, emotionally disturbed, or mentally retarded by teachers, pediatricians, and/or other diagnosticians. With the T.S. diagnosis, there is a paradoxical relief in that patients and parents are informed of the organic basis to the disorder and of the fact that the tics are involuntary in nature. The child is told that he is not accountable for the often socially inappropriate tics and that voluntary efforts at control are transitory at best. Despite such negative prognosticating, such information is often initially perceived as anxiety reducing and consoling in view of previous failure at symptom reduction. The child feels relieved to learn that he is not responsible for the tics. The parents are also pleased to learn that they share no responsibility. This approach often underscores the need for medication while minimizing the mediating effect of anxiety or stressful life events upon tic frequency.

Typically, the Tourette patient and/or his parents seek hypnotherapy after medication has either not proved beneficial or, most often, when negative side effects to medication require dosage reduction to less effective levels. As such, most T.S. patients come to hypnotherapy on medication and do so seeking adjunct or additional treatment to obtain further symptom reduction. Given the patient's and parents' understanding of T.S. and emphasis upon organicity, preparation for hypnosis is crucially important.

Preparation for Hypnosis

During the preparation stage the neurotransmitter dysfunction hypothesis to T.S. is reinforced. But the mediating effect of anxiety and stressful life events upon tic frequency is also stressed. The patient is taught that, while he is not responsible for having contracted T.S. nor for symptom expression in general, the total emphasis upon external, that is, organic locus of control may well be inappropriate and excessively negative prognostically.

Hypnosis is described as a natural phenomenon, with emphasis on the relaxation and focused concentration components to hypnosis. The benefit of these hypnotic components is then related to the assumption of the mediating effect of anxiety to tic frequency. In addition, there is the need to deal with common myths and misunderstandings of hypnosis as well as to engage in frank discussion of the limitations of hypnotherapy.

While children typically approach hypnosis with interest and a willingness to cooperate, parents may be resistant due to myths and misconceptions about hypnosis. When he is treating the child with hypnosis, it is imperative for the therapist to involve the parents in the process to offset parental obstacles or possible treatment sabotage due to parental anxieties regarding hypnosis. Gardner (1974) suggests the use of one or more educational, observational, or experiential approaches with parents. Frequent didactic discussions are held with the parents regarding hypnosis with the aim of reducing misconceptions and gaining parental support for the hypnotic procedure. In addition, the parents are invited to observe the hypnotic procedure at least on one occasion to further diminish misunderstanding and reduce anxiety.

Self-Hypnosis

The distinction between hetero-hypnosis and self-hypnosis is also presented during the preparation phase. Hetero-hypnosis is a descriptive term referring to the hypnotic experience resulting from the aid or guidance of another person, a hypnotist. Self-hypnosis refers to unaided hypnosis that has been typically preceded by hetero-hypnosis. Self-hypnosis emphasizes the subject's motivation and talent with hypnosis while underscoring the hypnotist as a facilitator rather than one who imposes upon or controls the subject. Nevertheless, there is a distinction between the more typical clinical hetero-hypnosis event and the patient employing self-hypnosis in practice away from the office.

Gardner (1981) notes that children are generally quite able and willing to learn hypnosis and are equally adept with self-hypnosis. Emphasizing self-hypnosis places the responsibility upon the child for achieving the hypnotic experience and for potential benefits. This is of particular importance as self-hypnosis provides the child with a means by which he can exercise some control and have direct, active involvement in treatment. As Gardner (1981) notes, with hypnotherapy the child learns to focus on solving problems rather than having merely to experience them.

Self-hypnosis is a major component of treatment. The children are encouraged to practice self-hypnosis at home and record practice times. Additionally, the patient and his parents are informed that the practice of self-hypnosis is solely the responsibility of the patient in order to reduce the possibility for such practice becoming a power struggle between patient and parents as well as to underscore the patient's control.

Case Presentation-Background Material

The following case example illustrates the treatment process and gains possible. B. was an 11-year-old white male at initiation of treatment. Functionally an only child as his nearest sibling was 18 and out of the home, B. was a planned child. Pregnancy was described as unremarkable resulting in a full-term birth after one hour of easy active labor. The baby presented head first with a birth weight of 8 pounds 10 ounces and a birth length of 18 inches. Although the process was un-complicated, B. was jaundiced at birth, and mucous was noted in the lungs. He readily cried, but it was necessary to place him in an incubator and provide oxygen as a precaution. He remained in the incubator for two days and was kept in the hospital nursery for another seven days for observation. B. came home to his par-ents from the hospital at nine days of life. After the initial concern during his ne-onatal period, his infancy was described as unremarkable. The developmental and medical history was also unremarkable.

At the start of treatment, B. was enrolled in the sixth grade at a public elementary school. His academic record was excellent, with a good relationship with teacher and peers. He had never been retained in a grade and was functioning at or above grade level.

At eight years of age, B. had begun to evidence eye(s) blinking. His parents took him to an ophthalmologist who found no optical difficulties. Later visits to the pediatrician resulted in the blinking being dismissed as a habit. In time, the blinking led to a facial grimace of severe nose twitch, where the upper lip and nose were pulled upward, often causing the eyes to close. The parents noted that B.'s tics increased in frequency during times of stress or when he was upset.

At age nine, he was diagnosed as having Gilles de la Tourette syndrome. Haloperidol was administered, slowly titrating to an existing dose of three milli-grams daily, one and a half milligrams twice a day. This dosage remained consis-tent throughout treatment. The patient's tics were poorly controlled by this relatively low dosage of medication. Weight gain was the primary negative side effect.

B. was described interpersonally as a generally well-balanced child who en-joyed peer relationships. He had many friends, was a member of a baseball team, and adept at drawing and receiving praise and encouragement for this activity. The parents reported no major problem behaviors at home and were generally proud of and pleased with their son.

Intervention Process

As it is known that the tics associated with Gilles de la Tourette syndrome can vary considerably over time (Shapiro et al., 1978), obtaining a stable baseline is crucial. Obtaining baseline measures is important as the clinician may not observe true tic frequency at first encounter of the T.S. patient. It is commonly reported that T.S. patients attempt to actively restrain symptom expression when first meeting a new person, particularly a professional (Shapiro et al., 1978). In office tic frequency baseline measures, best obtained through videotaping, are recommended over at least a two-week period and at best a four-week period. The optimum would be for the patient to be videotaped twice a week for four weeks. Training the parents to observe and measure tic frequency in home baseline measures can also be useful. However, home measures do not provide the same objective observations and measurement as that obtained through careful viewing of videotape.

The treatment process is fairly intensive as the preferred method of scheduling is to see the patient for outpatient hypnotherapy twice weekly. While patients have been seen on the more usual weekly basis, the twice-weekly schedule affords earlier mastery of hypnosis, permits greater encouragement of self-hypnosis practice, enhances commitment to the treatment process, strengthens suggestions given, and yields a more rapid awareness of treatment gains. This latter point is particularly important as initial response to treatment is often gradual, a factor to be discussed later.

Hypnosis is induced after careful inquiry with the patient. Younger patients, ages three to six years, typically require more active involvement on the part of the hypnotherapist and enjoy inductions involving imagination. It is not uncommon for young children to remain active during hypnosis and to keep their eyes open throughout the procedure. This does not mean that they are not participating or benefiting since they can remain quite focused on the imaginative material. Older children, ages seven to adolescence, are often able to identify a favorite television program to "watch" or a favorite special place to hypnotically visit. Children vary in their ability to use imagery, remain focused, utilize eye fixation, and/or evidence deep muscle relaxation. Through pre-induction inquiry, the hypnotherapist gathers crucial material relating to the patient's individual skills and abilities while developing a model of induction based upon the information gained.

An extensive induction procedure is rarely necessary once the patient has mastered self-hypnosis. Merely instructing the patient to "go to your special place" can soon be sufficient to bring about a moderate to deep hypnotic trance. Other patients may utilize an agreed upon physical cue such as touching thumb to index finger or placing their hands in their lap.

Once hypnosis is evident and deepened, specific suggestions are given focusing upon relaxation and anxiety reduction. In addition, the suggestions emphasize mastery and developing control, with the intent of diminishing the patient's sense of being a helpless victim. The suggestions specifically note the patient's tics in relation to suggestions of control and mastery. As the patients are typically children, the suggestions are rather direct and somewhat more autocratic than would be used with an adult. Children often respond well to a direct approach that might offend adults.

The patient, encouraged to practice self-hypnosis at home, is provided with a self-hypnosis monitoring sheet to record frequency of self-hypnosis practice. In addition to yielding a self-reported log of home practice, this monitoring sheet also serves to provide both a reminder and subtle pressure to practice self-hypnosis. Self-hypnosis is seen as reinforcing hetero-hypnosis and suggestions offered during hetero-hypnosis. The primary benefit to self-hypnosis, however, is the patient's eventual realization of mastery and perceived shift in both locus of control and attribution of improvement. Through self-hypnosis, the T.S. patient is offered the opportunity to achieve an enhanced awareness of his body within the context of relaxation and subsequent tic frequency reduction. The beauty of self-hypnosis for the T.S. patient lies in the self-control component of self-hypnosis, as it is practiced away from the office and removed from the performance of treatment upon the patient.

Case Study Continued—Treatment

B. entered active treatment after a four-week baseline period. In the office, tic frequency measures were obtained by videotaping. He was seen for 12 hypnotherapy sessions over six weeks, with a one-month follow-up after the last hypnotherapy session. Baseline procedures provided a clear initial frequency pattern to B.'s tics, a pattern which was then incorporated into the hypnotic suggestions during hetero-hypnosis and instructions for self-hypnosis. With the baseline data, it became evident that a severe eye(s) blink tic was the most frequent. This tic occurred with a mean frequency of 136 times per 10 minutes on videotape. Treatment planning focused upon this troublesome eye(s) blink tic.

B. was a developing artist. He enjoyed imagery and was readily able to describe a detailed pleasant scene identified as his special place. Induction employed a progressive relaxation procedure combined with the imagery of his special place. Deepening was obtained through utilization of staircase imagery with suggestions for deepening as descending. At the bottom of the "stairs" was a "door" through which B. would find himself wholly involved in his "special place." The extent of imagery used was based upon this patient's enjoyment of such imagery and ready skill for such hypnotic visualization.

B. was quite adept with hypnosis and found the procedure intriguing. Induction eventually involved suggesting to B. to "go to your special place" with additional deepening as needed. He was proud of his new-found skill and was interested in teaching his parents hypnosis so they could share his experience. His parents were supportive and reinforcing of his hypnotic experiences and frequently expressed their pleasure with B. and treatment outcome.

Treatment Outcome

In a consideration of treatment outcome, it is important to keep in mind that Tourette syndrome is a chronic neurological disorder. While there have been case reports of hypnotherapy resulting in symptom cessation (Clements, 1972), the more common outcome is a clinically significant reduction in tic frequency and severity (Zahm, 1982). While no treatment is successful in all cases, positive outcome in tic frequency and severity has been observed across in office measures and home frequency measures. Symptom reduction has been observed with T.S. patients receiving haloperidol and with T.S. patients receiving no medication. Reduced tic frequency and severity is typically stable over time, with reports of treatment gains being maintained after one-month follow-up (Zahm et al., 1983), six-month follow-up (Clements, 1972), and nine-year follow-up (Lindner and Stevens, 1967). It may be unreasonable to anticipate total symptom cessation. The patient and his parents are best aided by frank discussion of the chronicity of T.S. and the limits of hypnotherapy outcome to avoid excessive expectations or unrealistic expectations of cure. In the author's experience, discussion of the limitations of hypnotherapy enhances credibility while also enabling the patient and parents to better recognize and appreciate treatment gains.

Assessment of treatment effectiveness is threefold. The patient's and his parents' perceptions of tic frequency reduction is of principal importance. In addition to the patient's self-report, tic frequency measures are examined across baseline and treatment. To rule out chance fluctuation, statistical analyses can be performed. If analyses are performed, interrupted time series analyses are recommended. Lastly, a planned follow-up or sequence of follow-ups is needed to indicate stability of treatment gains. Follow-up is particularly crucial as symptom waxing and waning is characteristic with the T.S. patient (Shapiro et al., 1978).

The general pattern during hypnotherapy is an initial gradual reduction in tic frequency leading to a more rapid decline. The clinician is wise to note this initial gradual process because hynotherapy may be prematurely abandoned if only initial gains are considered. This gradual process may reflect both the patient's growing mastery of hypnosis and his growing confidence in the procedure.

Case Study Continued—Outcome

B. enjoyed considerable success with hypnotherapy. As indicated in Table 22-1, tic frequency was significantly reduced from baseline to treatment, with treatment gains remaining stable at follow-up. Figure 22-1 provides a graph of the videotaped tic frequency, including both raw data and a computer generated model of the data with the autoregressive characteristic of the data statistically removed. The initial gradual treatment effect noted above is observed.

Both B. and his parents perceived symptom reduction. B. remained committed to treatment and actively practiced self-hypnosis at home, both during treatment and during the period of time between treatment and follow-up. Parenthetically, a potentially disruptive event occurred during B.'s treatment. For financial reasons, his parents felt it imperative to move from the neighborhood B. had known all his life to a new neighborhood, necessitating B.'s adjustment to a new school and a new peer group. This move occurred during the fourth week of treatment. The effect of this stressful life event upon tic frequency is strikingly evident as presented in Figure 22-1. On observation 16, his eye(s) blink frequency increased. B.'s tics were clearly affected by stressful life events and mediated by anxiety. To his credit, he was able to employ the treatment procedures learned to better cope with this stress.

Table 22-1. B.: Videotape Frequency Data for Eye(s)

Blink Tic in Order of Observation

Baseline	Treatment	Follow-up
127.0	144.5	7.5
126.0	125.5	9.5
203.0	149.0	0.0
119.0	119.5	5.0
114.0	50.5	
106.0	41.5	
140.0	29.5	
152.5	46.0	
	2.0	
	4.0	
	2.5	
	2.0	
$\overline{X}$	$\overline{X}$	$\overline{X}$
136.06	59.67	5.35

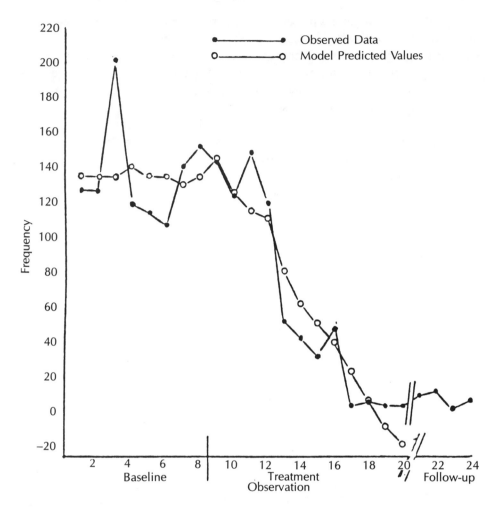

Figure 22-1: Observed Data and Model Predicted Values for B.'s Primary Tic—Videotape Frequency Data

Future Trends

The case presented a practical example of the mediating effect of anxiety and stressful life events upon the tics associated with Gilles de la Tourette syndrome. There is a growing body of literature on the efficacious use of hypnotherapy with T.S. and an increase in practitioners employing hypnosis to aid T.S. symptom reduction. Published accounts, however, typically involve clinical case reports with minimal attempts at controlling threats to internal or external validity. Recent reports do reflect a trend toward more systematic study (Zahm et al., 1983), but fall short of the need for better research design including larger samples, use of control groups, and systematic longitudinal follow-up. With the increase in utilization of hypnosis with T.S., it is likely that such research will be forthcoming.

For the present, there appears to be sufficient reason not only to support the use of hypnotherapy in treating Tourette syndrome but also to maintain an optimistic appraisal of the Tourette patient's ability to gain significant control over his tics. Rather than being condemned to a life as an innocent victim of his neurological system, a Tourette patient may regain a sense of mastery with successful hypnotherapy.

Description of a Session—Suggestions Given

Patients are typically seen individually, away from their parents. In the author's experience, most patients are very self-conscious of the tics and even the presence of parents may inhibit self-disclosure. Parents are seen, however, throughout treatment for treatment description as well as elicitation of parents' perceptions of progress. Parents are invited to observe at least one hypnotherapy session to further therapeutic alliance.

A hypnotherapy session is characterized by three phases. If the patient is videotaped, videotaping is done prior to the actual treatment session and can be administered by a technician. The first phase of treatment is devoted to discussion of home practice, self-hypnosis. Home practice sheets are collected and discussed. The patient is reinforced and encouraged to maintain home practice.

The second phase is hetero-hypnosis, with induction and deepening provided through individualized mechanisms most beneficial to the patient. After the patient has entered a light to medium trance, the suggestions are provided. The following are generalized suggestions emphasizing mastery, anxiety reduction, relaxation, and control:

> On each word that I say, you may let all other thoughts—all other feelings—all other sounds fade, fade away into the distance so that everything that I tell you you may take to help you with your tics. As I talk to you, you may let yourself relax more and more completely, and without even thinking about it, your mind automatically makes each suggestion a part of your everyday life, helping to solve your problems. As you drift along, you feel yourself relax, deeper and deeper relaxed—way down—so that more and more you know that you are the boss of your body. You can control your tics—all your tics (list specific tics). Now, right now, you can begin to control your body and relax and be rid of your tics. You have control, you have the say. You are relaxed and very very comfortable now and are able to control your tics. Now, very good, you can and will be able to control your tics and relax other times, whenever you wish. You are the boss, you can make your body do what you want it to. You can relax your muscles and make your body stop ticcing—stop (list specific tics).
>
> Now, as you drift along deeper, deeper relaxed, deeper, deeper relaxed—way down, you feel very very sure that you are able to relax and control your own

muscles. These suggestions may sink down, down into your memory and you will be able to completely remember. You know that you are the boss of your own body, and that you can relax and stop your tics—all your tics (list specific tics).

You can use this very nice calm relaxed feeling to help you throughout the week. Whenever you are tense or uptight, you can relax, just like now, and feel the tension leave your body. Each time you practice at home, you will be better able, better and better all the time, to relax and control your tics. You are getting better and better—relaxing and able to control your tics. You know what to do whenever you are upset or tense, just relax and calm yourself—you're the boss of your own body, you have the ability to control your muscles and stop your tics. Each time you practice, you get better and better, more and more relaxed and able to control your body.

Now that you fully understand and are able to enjoy and use this pleasant relaxation, I want you to begin to become more alert, beginning to wake up, feeling very very good—refreshed and very comfortable. You remember that each time you practice, either at home or here, you will be able to better relax and enjoy this calm sense of relaxation. Soon it will be time to be fully alert, fully awake. Feeling fresh, feeling fine. And as you awake, now awake, you remember and feel fine, feel very good.

Phase three consists of discussion of the hypnotic experience, setting expectations for continued improvement, providing home practice sheet(s) for the time period between sessions, and praising the patient for his efforts.

References

Clark DF: Behavioral approaches to treatment of Gilles de la Tourette's syndrome. New York State J Med 90:2205-2210, 1970

Clements RO: Gilles de la Tourette's syndrome—an overview of development and treatment of a case using hypnotherapy, haloperidol, and psychotherapy. Am J Clin Hypn 14:167-172, 1972

Cohen DJ, Detlor J, Young JG, Shaywitz BA: Clonidine ameliorates Gilles de la Tourette syndrome. Arch Gen Psych 37:1350-1357, 1980

Cohen DJ, Marks FM: Gilles de la Tourette's syndrome treated by operant conditioning. Brit J Psychiatry 130:315, 1977

Eisenberg L, Ascher E, Kanner L: A clinical study of Gilles de la Tourette's disease. Am J Psychiatry 115:715-723, 1959

Erickson MH: Experimental hypnotherapy in Tourette's disease. Am J Clin Hypn 7:325-331, 1964

Fernando SJM: Gilles de la Tourette's syndrome. Brit J Psychiatry 113:606-617, 1967

Gardner GG: Parents: Obstacles or allies in child hypnotherapy. Am J Clin Hypn 17:44-49, 1974

Gardner GG: Teaching self-hypnosis to children. Int J Clin Exp Hypn 29:300-312, 1981

Gardner GG, Olness K: Hypnosis and Hypnotheraphy With Children. New York, Grune & Stratton, 1981

Gillies DR, Forsythe WI: Treatment of multiple tics and the Tourette syndrome. Developmental Medicine and Child Neurology 26(6):830-833, 1984

Kohen DP, Botts PJ: Applications of relaxation/mental imagery (self-hypnosis) to the management of Gilles de la Tourette's syndrome: Experience with four children. Paper presented at the annual scientific meeting of the American Society of Clinical Hypnosis, Dallas, TX, 1983

Lieh-mak F, Luk SL, Leung L: Gilles de la Tourette's syndrome: Report of five cases in Chinese. Brit J Psychiatry 134:630-634, 1979

Lindner H, Steven H: Hypnotherapy and psychodynamics in the syndrome of Gilles de la Tourette. Int J Clin Exp Hypn 15:151-155, 1967

Rosen M, Wesner C: A behavioral approach to Tourette's syndrome. J Consul Clin Psych 41:308-312, 1973

Seignot MJN: Un cas de maladie des tics de Gilles de la Tourette queri par le R-1635. Annuals Med Psych 22:523-524, 1961

Shapiro AK, Eisenkraft GJ, Shapiro E: Treatment of Gilles de la Tourette's syndrome with clonidine and neuroleptics. Arch Gen Psych 4:1235-1240, 1983

Shapiro AK, Shapiro ES, Bruun RD, Sweet RD: Gilles de la Tourette Syndrome. New York, Raven Press, 1978

Surwillo WW, Shafii M, Barrett CL: A 20-month study of the effects of stressful life events and haloperidol on symptom frequency. J Nervous Mental Disease 166:812-816, 1978

Thomas EJ, Abrams KS, Johnson JB: Self-monitoring and reciprocal inhibition in the modification of multiple tics of Gilles de la Tourette's syndrome. J Behav Therapy Exper Psychiatry 2:159-171, 1971

Turpin G, Powell GE: Effects of massed practice and controlled relaxation on tic frequency in Gilles de la Tourette's syndrome. Behaviour Research and Therapy 22(2):165-178, 1984

Zahm DN: A clinical outcome study of hypnosis treatment upon the tics associated with Gilles de la Tourette syndrome. (Doctoral dissertation, University of Cincinnati, 1982). Dissertation Abstracts International 4:1635B, 1982

Zahm DN, Foreman ME, O'Grady D, Ricks DR: A clinical outcome study of hypnosis treatment upon the tics associated with Gilles de la Tourette syndrome. Paper presented at annual scientific meeting of the American Society of Clinical Hypnosis, Dallas, TX, 1983

23 HYPNOSIS AND ONCOLOGY

ALEXANDER A. LEVITAN, M.D.

The role of hypnosis in oncology is varied and constantly evolving. There is a large body of literature supporting the use of hypnosis to control the symptoms of cancer and the side effects of therapy. Hypnosis has proven effective in controlling pain (Finer, 1979; Spiegel and Bloom, 1983; Zeltzer and LeBaron, 1982; Ament, 1982), anticipatory vomiting (Reed et al., 1982; Morrow et al., 1982), chemotherapy-related vomiting (Zeltzer, LeBaron, Zelter, 1984), learned food avoidance (Fotopoulos et al., 1980), and in dealing with the stress of cancer diagnosis and treatment (Kellerman et al., 1983).

There are additionally numerous studies which suggest a relationship between stress and the development of malignancy (Bahnson, 1980, 1981; Matje, 1984). Similarly, another area of burgeoning interest is the field of psychoneuroimmunology, which specifically addresses the issue of the mind-body interaction as it applies to the immune system (Solomon, 1981; Loche, 1982; Kiecolt-Glaser et al., 1984).

Certain researchers have attempted to employ hypnosis or "behavior modification" to favorably effect the outcome of cancer therapy (Olness, 1981). Others have attempted to employ self-hypnosis to reduce the incidence of malignancy (Finkelstein, 1984). This chapter will describe some of the literature noted above and outline how it has been applied to the clinical management of cancer patients in practice.

Stress and Cancer

Bahnson in 1980 wrote an excellent, well-referenced review on the subject of stress and cancer. He pointed out that as early as 200 A.D. Galen observed that "melancholic women" were more prone to develop breast cancer than those of a more normal mental state. Schmale and Iker in 1966 developed a predictive technique based on manifestations of loss and hopelessness, which was accurate in predicting which women having abnormal pap smears would develop cervical cancer.

Numerous other, principally retrospective, studies have confirmed a relationship between depression and disintegration of the family and the development of cancer within six months to two years after the stressful event (Kowal, 1955; Meerloo, 1954). In a retrospective study by Neumann (1959), eight percent of her clients with cancer had lost a significant "other" in the two years prior to the malignancy becoming clinically manifest. Similarly, Greene and Swisher (1969) studied monozygotic twins, one of whom developed leukemia while the other did not. They found an increased incidence of loss or frustration in the twin who developed the leukemia as opposed to the sibling who did not.

Numerous researchers have sought to explain the increased incidence between stress and the subsequent development of malignancy in terms of a diminished responsiveness of the immune system. It is theorized that all of us are exposed to a variety of factors including viruses, radiation and carcinogens, which are modulated by genetic predisposition and which interact with the normal biologic process of cell division to cause the development of malignant cells within our bodies. In most of us, these malignant cells are detected and eliminated by our ever-vigilant immune system before they are able to replicate sufficiently to establish a permanent existence. If the functioning of the immune system were diminished by stress through other mechanisms, then an increased incidence of clinical malignancy might result.

Animal studies have established that mice raised in a stressful environment developed 13 times the incidence of mammary tumors as those raised in a protected environment (Riley, 1975). Similarly, animals exposed to aversive stimuli had a more rapid progression of implanted tumors and/or diminished survival as contrasted to control animals, who did not experience the aversive stimuli (Sklar, 1981).

Human research has established a reduction in the natural killer activity of mononeuclear cells from medical students obtained during the final exam week as opposed to one month prior to the exam week (Kiecolt-Glaser, 1984). Similar studies have confirmed a diminished lymphocyte immune capability following the loss of a spouse or loved one, although the numerosity of the lymphocytes did not change (Scheilser et al., 1984).

In 1978, Carl O. and Stephanie Simonton wrote a book entitled *Getting Well Again,* in which they postulated that psychotherapeutic intervention directed at the cancer patient could interrupt stress-caused compromise of the immune system. They felt that such intervention might then have a beneficial effect on the course of malignant disease and could explain some of the great individual variation in outcome in apparently similar cases of cancer. They published a paper in 1980 purporting to show a prolongation in cancer survival based on retrospective controls (Simonton et al., 1980). The results of this paper have not been confirmed, and the Simonton approach was classified as an "unproven method of cancer management" by the American Cancer Society (Ca, 1982).

More recently, two studies have been published addressing the issue of "behavioral intervention" for cancer patients and both have failed to demonstrate a positive effect on survival (Cassileth, 1985; Aaroz, 1983) although improvement in the quality of life has been well established (Newton, 1982).

Despite the inconclusive studies alluded to above, the use of hypnotherapy for oncology patients has proved highly valuable.

Preliminary Steps to Hypnotherapy

Oncology patients may present for hypnotherapy as a consequence of self-referral or referral from family practitioners, surgeons, internists, oncologists, oncology nurse practitioners, former patients, or friends or relatives of former patients. The nature of the referral will have significant impact on both the patient's expectations and the eventual outcome.

The initiation of the hypnotic trance usually begins well before the patient presents to the office. The very fact that the patient has been diagnosed as having cancer serves to alter the patient's usual state of consciousness. This knowledge not infrequently renders patients more susceptible to a variety of both direct and indirect suggestions. If a satisfied patient or relative is the principal source of referral, not infrequently the patient will present with a positive but realistic expectancy as to potential therapeutic outcome. Similarly, if the patient is referred because "nothing else has worked—you might as well try hypnosis," then the negative mind-set which results must be overcome before a satisfactory response to hypnotherapy can ensue. In a similar fashion, patients can present with unrealistic expectations based on misconceptions promulgated by the media or well-meaning lay people.

In order to adequately assess patients for hypnotherapy, it is often useful to ask them to define the current status of their illness and their expectations from hypnotherapy. Simple questions are: "What is your understanding of the state of your illness and its present treatment? Why are you here? What do you know about hypnosis? What do you expect will be the outcome of our working together?" These questions may be phrased in a sympathetic fashion and should be designed to facilitate a mutual understanding of the patient's current disease state and the role for hypnotherapy in the patient's overall treatment program. Patients may tend to deny or appear ignorant of the advanced nature of their disease. Not infrequently, this denial may be combined with thinking in terms of unrealistic expectations of hypnotherapy. On a rare occasion, communication between the patient and the medical treatment team may be so limited that the patient may not have been fully informed as to the severity of his or her illness. Sometimes, relatives have intervened requesting that the patient not be informed of the true status of the illness. Despite such well-meaning interventions on the part of relatives, most patients are clearly aware of ongoing deterioration in their health.

If there is any doubt on the part of the hypnotherapist as to whether he or she has a full appreciation of the current status of the patient, it is always appropriate to call the physician primarily in charge of the patient's care. Not only does this contact confirm concern on the part of the therapist, but it allows him or her more effectively to interface with the current treatment program. It also enables the therapist to respond with sympathetic candor to any inquiries which the patient may make. After the therapist has an understanding as to the status of the patient's disease, it is appropriate for him or her to understand the patient's knowledge of hypnosis and the role it may play. It is useful to stress to the patient the fact that all hypnosis is self-hypnosis and to diminish the role of the operator in the eventual outcome. Thus, a dependency relationship with the therapist is avoided, and the patient reestablishes a sense of self-worth and becomes an active participant in the treatment program. This approach is in sharp contrast to the contemporary concept that once an individual is tainted with cancer he or she should be disposed of as quickly and mercifully as possible. Patients frequently express the feeling that beginning with diagnosis and extending through the therapeutic process they are treated as specimens rather than as individuals, and they object to the dehumanization process.

While not all patients have equal capacity to employ self-hypnosis to maximal advantage, it is worthwhile to initiate instruction in self-hypnosis with all patients. The assessment of the patient begins with the initial contact between the hypnotherapist and the patient. Careful observation of the patient's body language, tone of voice, and verbalization enable the operator to develop a therapeutic course of action. Experienced therapists learn to rely on their intuitive sense as to what approach might prove most effective in a particular case. Novice practitioners are encouraged to "Let the Force be with you."

Although the knowledge of a variety of therapeutic techniques is highly useful, the selection of the specific approach must often be based partially on intuition and partially on past experience. Few experienced or even novice practitioners of the healing arts have not had the experience of coming into the presence of a patient and immediately sensing that they could or could not help that patient. Often one has the desire to tell the patient after he or she has uttered a few sentences, "Don't bother telling me anymore—I know I can help you." Conversely, when in the presence of a professional "scalp-hunter," one knows that despite the patient's protestations that all other therapists contacted were "quacks" and that he or she is absolutely certain that a cure will result if the present therapist will only help, failure is assured unless the patient's resistance can be utilized to therapeutic advantage.

In dealing with such patients, I have found it advantageous to utilize the orientation expressed by J. Halcy in *Strategies in Psychotherapy* (1963). Haley describes all human contact as falling into three categories of relationships: symmetrical, complementary and metacomplementary. The symmetrical relationship is that between two equals such as between two colleagues in a practice, neither of whom is senior to the other and both of whom merit equal respect and salaries. They are, in essence, identical in all psychological respects.

The complementary relationship is such that one individual excels in a certain area but depends on the other individual in the relationship to complement him or her in those areas in which a deficiency exists. The concept is rather like that of the "ying" and the "yang" coming together to form a whole. An example might be that of a married couple in which the father assumes the role of disciplinarian and the mother that of the giver of unconditional love. Both are equally necessary and one cannot function effectively without the other.

The metacomplementary relationship is one in which the individual appears totally at the mercy of either circumstances or the will of another, but by utilizing that symptom he or she is experiencing mastery over the actions of another. An example here is the wife who is so incapacitated by her fear of flying that her husband has to pay great attention to her in order for them to travel together at all. It is the latter type of relationship that many resistant patients endeavor to establish with their therapists. Typically, the patients may say, "The pain is so severe I can barely stand it. You must take my pain away." If the therapist is successful in diminishing the pain, the patient has gained control by directing the actions of the therapist. If the therapist is unsuccessful in relieving the pain, the patient has gained control by proving that the therapist is a failure. In either case, the patient wins and the therapist loses.

Some Case Histories and Suggestions for Therapy

An appropriate response to the patient's request that the therapist take the patient's pain away is "I can't take your pain away, but I can show you how *you* can make it better." A characteristic case is that of Lester H., a 56-year-old male who had undergone extensive radiotherapy. He developed severe radiation osteonecrosis of the mandible and was unable to open his mouth more than a few millimeters, barely sufficient space for him to insert either a cigarette or a Percodan tablet, both of which he used liberally. By virtue of his persistent smoking, despite his progressive weight loss and requests to the contrary from his wife, it was apparent that some component of self-destructive thinking was operative if only on a subconscious basis. A great deal of hostility was enunciated by the patient with regard to his past therapy and its adverse consequences.

He initially presented on referral from his otolaryngologist because of recurrent carcinoma in his posterior pharynx and because of his severe pain. Combination chemotherapy was initiated to control his metastatic disease. The subject of the use of hypnotherapy for pain control was repeatedly avoided by the therapist and strategically delayed until both the patient and his wife had requested for him instruction in self-hypnosis for this purpose. Because of the patient's inability to open his mouth, it was impossible for him to undergo adequate oral examination as to the status of his tumor. The previous attempt at a direct examination under inhalation anesthesia had been extremely painful for the patient since it necessitated insertion of a nasotracheotube and multiple attempts at blind intubation with the patient still semi-conscious.

At the recommendation of his otolaryngologist, the patient was scheduled for a semimandibulectomy following a tracheostomy to gain command of the patient's airway and exclude the endotracheal tube from the operative field. Because of the impending surgical procedure, the patient was well motivated to learn self-hypnosis for pain control, and during the course of two 15-minute sessions he learned to perform regional hypnoanesthesia so that he was able to undergo a tracheostomy without any local or systemic chemical anesthesia and with a minimum amount of concern or bleeding. After the tracheostomy tube was in place, inhalation anesthesia was administered and the hemimandibulectomy and examination under anesthesia was completed.

The patient had a satisfactory result from the surgery and survived for a significant period of time before succumbing to his malignancy. He continued to use self-hypnosis for pain and symptom control with good success. An additional benefit for this patient was an increased respect on the part of his wife for his accomplishments. The relationship was thereby strengthened, and they remained mutually supportive until the time of his death. The patient maintained some degree of hostility toward the medical profession as evidenced by the fact that he continued to smoke as soon as his tracheostomy healed over despite his therapist's urging that he discontinue the practice.

Cancer patients may present for hypnotherapy with a variety of problems other than pain. These involve chemotherapy symptom control including anticipatory emesis, imagery therapy designed to promote mobilization of inner resources and self-healing, anxiety related to fear of death, and even more mundane matters such as a desire to stop smoking.

In regard to the latter, personal experience indicates that most persons who continue to smoke despite the diagnosis of cancer, particularly lung cancer, do very poorly in terms of duration of survival. It is as if these patients have accepted the progressive deterioration of their bodies and are unwilling to expend effort or experience discomfort in order to delay their demise. Often, they will agree to participate in radiotherapy or chemotherapy programs but in a half-hearted way. These patients often utilize their illness in order to manipulate the behavior of others and to maximize any secondary gain therefrom. Conversely, patients who sincerely want to stop smoking and are willing to undertake whatever is necessary in order to maximally assist their bodies in healing themselves often exceed the customary median survival for their disease. The technique used for smoking cessation is covered in an earlier chapter of this text and will not be elaborated upon here, but cancer patients who continue to smoke should be made aware of the paradox in their actions, particularly if a desire to live is consciously expressed. Where appropriate, psychotherapy, including the use of hypnotic uncovering techniques, may be employed to resolve this conflict.

It is important to adhere to the contract requested by the patient despite a belief on the part of the therapist that additional therapeutic approaches might be helpful. A typical example is Margaret M., a 73-year-old female with diffuse intraabdominal spread of an adenocarcinoma of the ovary. The patient was referred by an oncology nurse practitioner because of marked anxiety and anticipatory emesis occurring in conjunction with the administration of Cis-platinum and Adriamycin chemotherapy. The patient was scheduled to receive her chemotherapy on an every-three-weeks basis. For one to two days immediately prior to her receiving chemotherapy, she would experience repeated episodes of vomiting in association with a sense of increasing anxiety. The patient was seen on two occasions, then expressed an interest in learning to use hypnosis to facilitate the starting of her intravenous infusion and to prevent pre- and post-chemotherapy vomiting. A verbatim transcript of her hypnotherapy sessions is recorded at the end of this chapter. Since the patient was not interested in utilizing hypnosis for either self-healing or generalized pain control, her goals were respected by the therapist.

The patient's anticipatory emesis was controlled with self-hypnosis and her post-therapy vomiting was reduced to a tolerable minimum. The patient visualized engorgement of the veins of her hands and arms in order to facilitate venipuncture and the administration of therapy. In this regard, she was reasonably successful as attested to by the chemotherapy nurse who was also instrumental in encouraging the patient to use self-hypnosis for symptom control. The patient experienced nasocongestion as a consequence of the receipt of Cis-platinum, and the chemotherapy nurse suggested that the patient visualize inhaling dry desert air as a therapeutic approach to that problem, an approach which proved quite successful.

Eventually, after three years without evidence of disease, the patient experienced a relapse for which she elected not to receive any systemic chemotherapy. Ultimately, the patient presented at the hospital and announced that she had arranged to have her three elderly dogs put to sleep and that she was now prepared to die herself. This she proceeded to do a few days after admission. Hypnotherapy allowed the above patient to remain fully in control of her disease and its treatment and enabled her to experience a comfortable death.

Patients who present for imagery therapy are generally familiar with some of the work of Carl and Stephanie Simonton (1978). These patients may be actively involved in conventional therapy or may have been advised that therapy for their malignancy has little to offer. It is important for the therapist to reframe the patient's expectations in accordance with reality. It is also useful to take into account the patient's frame of reference and belief structure. An interesting case is that of Sister Mary Teresa, a 42-year-old teaching sister, who presented with recurrent oral cancer. She had had extensive previous radiotherapy and as a result had markedly diminished ability of her jaw. She was able to open her mouth only sufficiently to admit a tongue depressor sideways. In addition she had a foul-smelling growth in the back of her throat resulting in a continuous bad taste and breath odor. This constellation of symptoms was particularly troublesome for this woman, who had devoted her entire life to the service of God through her voice as a teacher. She requested instruction in the use of self-hypnosis for the mobilization of self-healing in order to reverse a rapid deterioration in her clinical condition. In addition, she was experiencing appreciable oral pain and a progressive weight loss secondary to advancing anorexia.

A variety of issues were met during the course of her therapy including her belief that the development of her cancer was God's will. It was difficult for her to develop an aggressive posture with regard to mobilizing her host defense mechanisms against her cancer. Her entire life had been spent meekly accepting the direction of others as they helped her understand God's will. In order for the therapist to interface with her efforts at imagery, an imagery drawing technique as described by Jean Ackterberg-Lawliss (1976) was employed. Fortunately, Sister Mary Teresa was an excellent artist and produced the drawings in Figures 23-1 through 23-4. Figure 23-1, her first attempt at drawing her malignancy, shows an amorphous mass of black cancer with very little evidence of anything else.

Fig. 23-1. Sister Mary Teresa's first attempt at drawing her malignancy.

The patient was eventually educated to the fact that cancer cells are really very weak, foolish cells that serve no real function other than the destruction of their host which results in turn in their own extermination. They serve no useful purpose such as production of nerve impulses, transportation of oxygen or the purification of bodily fluids. The number of cancer cells present in her body was infinitely less than the number of healthy cells which could be utilized to achieve their destruction. If it indeed was God's will that she experience her cancer it was also God's will that the hypnotherapist be available to help her. These concepts she accepted gradually as is evident in the altered configuration of her drawings. Her drawings eventually began to diminish the numerosity of the cancer cells and to increase the number of host defense cells. She additionally began to localize the tumor to a distant part of her body and to isolate it from the bulk of her healthy tissues. Throughout this treatment, she continued to express her religious orientation as evidenced by Figure 23-2, which shows a tiara of cancer cells.

Fig. 23-2. A tiara of cancer cells.

In order to assist the patient in visualizing a population of aggressive, hostile host defense cells, she was asked to describe the most powerful, aggressive image possible. Because agression was at first an entirely foreign concept to her, her initial description was that of a storm pounding on a shoreline of rocks. This image was utilized to help her visualize her own white cells and antibodies attacking her cancer cells and washing them away. Her drawings, however, continued to reflect a very passive approach on behalf of her immune system, which was described as gentle, soothing, caressing and healing. This fact is evident in her drawing of her imune system in Figure 23-3, which shows a pair of praying hands raised upward toward God. Figure 23-4 shows her immune system in the shape of a hand raised upward to the wind, with her cancer cells gently being allowed to blow away with the breeze.

For the orientation of the patient's imagery to a more aggressive stance, she was asked under hypnosis to describe an animal which might reflect such characteristics. She chose a tiger. She was asked to bring to her next therapy session some pictures of the tiger which she had visualized. She returned the next week with pictures of the most adorable tiger, with large, soulful eyes and a contented expression. After seeing these pictures, the therapist asked Sister Mary Teresa what might make her tiger angry. She responded that her tiger was a female tigress and that should any danger threaten her cubs she would defend them to the death. It was this image of a tigress fiercely defending her cubs, even at the expense of her own life, that was eventually employed as the analogy of her immune system. After much theological discussion, the patient agreed that she was indeed one of God's children, as are we all, and that it was appropriate for both the therapist and the patient's immune system to fight together as fiercely as possible to prolong her survival. Sister Mary Teresa was reminded that all her life she had served as one of God's spokeswomen and that she had no right to allow her disease to silence Him now.

The matter of death and dying was also addressed during the therapy sessions. Sister Mary Teresa admitted that although she was fully prepared to accept death she was afraid of the experience and was disappointed that her religious training had not enabled her to avoid this feeling. On a deeper level, she questioned whether her fear of death might not reflect a lack of true belief on her part. She was assured that everyone is afraid of an unknown experience, and she was told a metaphor dealing with the first time the therapist experienced a venapuncture as a requirement for applying to medical school. The therapist nearly fainted and at that point questioned whether he should undertake the profession of medicine. But the therapist was reassured when he subsequently spoke to several of his college classmates, who reluctantly admitted experiencing the identical sensation during their own venapuncture.

The hypnotic death rehearsal technique was then described for Sister Mary Teresa (Levitan, 1985). This is a technique of hypnotic future projection, during which the patient can visualize his or her own death. Sister Mary Teresa visualized

Fig. 23-3. Praying hands raised upward toward God

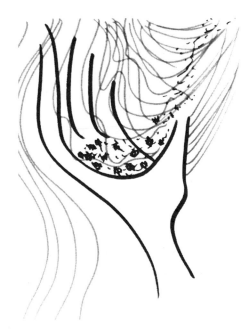

Fig. 23-4. Represents Sister Mary Teresa's immune system in the shape of a hand raised upward to the wind

herself as dying painlessly, surrounded by her concerned and attentive colleagues who had passed on before her. The therapist's familiarity with the nursing order of the Little Sisters of the Poor proved to be of great benefit here since he had been an attending physician at their local nursing home and could attest to the superlative caliber of nursing and patient care provided there. Sister Mary Teresa, having once experienced her own death, found it much more comfortable to face her actual demise whenever it might occur. She then left therapy with the understanding that she could return whenever she wished.

As long as the therapist remains comfortable with his or her own mortality, it is easy to discuss death with cancer patients. Helping someone to die is entirely different from causing someone to die. Death is merely a final stage of life and as such should be as natural and welcome as birth. As Henry David Thoreau so aptly phrased it, "Every blade in the field, Every leaf in the forest, Lays down its life in its season as beautifully as it was taken up."

The medical team caring for the patient may also need therapy. Certain oncologists and oncology nurses interpret the death of a patient as a failure on their part. This is true only if they have not done their job honestly and faithfully. Almost every good practicing oncologist receives cards of thanks from the family following the demise of a patient. In addition, every oncologist has a personal inner barometer as to the realistic expected survival of each patient who presents for care. It is only when this expectation is not met that there should be cause to question the treatment given.

When a patient does better than expected, it is useful for the therapist to confirm this fact for the patient and to congratulate the treating team as well. In many communities, these long-term survivors of cancer are utilized as a resource for newly-diagnosed patients in the form of contact through the CanSurmount Program. This program involves long-term survivors of specific types of cancer who visit newly-diagnosed patients with the same type of cancer in the hospital to provide both emotional and experiential support. Similar support programs, usually hospital based, include the hospital chaplaincy program, I Can Cope, and a support group for relatives of cancer patients. The I Can Cope program is an education program providing information about anatomy and physiology as well as pharmacology as it relates to the cancer patient. It is important that the hypnotherapist familiarize himself with all of these programs so that his therapy can most effectively interface with them.

It is also important for the hypnotherapist to become familiar with the various types of cancer experienced by patients whom he is treating. An excellent inexpensive resource text in this regard is *Clinical Oncology for Medical Students and Physicians,* edited by Philip Rubin and available from any branch of the American Cancer Society. This 536-page text, covering a basic description of and customary treatment and current survival data for most forms of cancer, is updated periodically, with the most recent revision in 1983.

Other resources which are extremely useful for the hypnotherapist include a sense of humor and an ability to accept cancer patients into their own lives. As an example of the former, a metaphor which has proven useful in helping ostomy patients adjust to their external appliances is "the popcorn story." When a resident, with the responsibility of teaching a medical school microbiology course, the author, interested in devising a diet which would simultaneously combat obesity and make the author wealthy, devised the popcorn diet. This was before the days of hot air popcorn poppers, and the author reasoned that if popcorn could be prepared with a non-absorbable oil, such as mineral oil, the resultant product would be not only filling but low in calories. One evening, the author's wife, having obtained some mineral oil, made a potful of popcorn, which tasted delicious. The next day while delivering a lecture to the entire second year medical school class, the author experienced a need to relieve himself of some gas. Since he was wearing a long white lab coat and there was considerable background noise in the auditorium, he took the liberty of doing so. Instantly, his pants were filled with a large volume of liquid stool, which dripped down both his legs. He then abridged his lecture, dismissed the class, and waddled off the auditorium stage. Patients find the above true anecdote amusing, and it establishes the fact that all of us are subject to embarrassment. By sharing such confidences with cancer patients, hypnotherapists can induce them to share some of their own deep felt concerns and secrets.

In a similar fashion, it is useful to give patients a reason for living in contrast to the reason for dying provided by the diagnosis of cancer. Many cancer patients are highly responsible individuals, who find it difficult not to fulfill the expectations of family and friends by dying promptly as expected. Similarly, the concept of disposables prevalent in our society extends to the cancer patient as well. Just as disposable napkins, forks, spoons and glasses are intended to be discarded shortly after use, so patients tainted with cancer are frequently deemed disposable by society. It is useful for the hypnotherapist to understand operant family dynamics in order to select appropriate reasons for the cancer patient to live. Paradoxical as it may seem, it is often valuable to point out that the cancer patient's spouse might not be able to function in his or her absence. Wives are reminded that their husbands are totally helpless in matters of cooking and self-care. No responsible parent, it is suggested, would leave children without adequate supervision, and similarly the cancer patient has no right to die and leave a spouse without resources. It is usually not difficult even in the case of the most self-sufficient spouse to discover some area of need that would be unmet in the event of the death of the other spouse. With older patients who have already lost their spouses, reasons for living can range from matters as simple as the continued care of household pets to the responsibilities of a grandparent to convey the culture and family heritage to the grandchildren.

It is often useful for the hypnotherapist and the office staff to become directly involved in the lives of the patients. A helpful way to strengthen the therapeutic relationship is to make personal demands upon the patient, thereby suggesting that the patient has something which is desirable to the therapist and by extrapolation to society in general. Requests may be as simple as a stated desire for Christmas cookies during the Christmas season or a request for a sample of fresh produce from a highly-prized garden. Under appropriate circumstances, it is also useful to involve patients in literature searches or in the editing and preparation of professional papers. The author keeps pictures of his family on his desk and has encouraged his office personnel to do so. Patients appreciate the opportunity to share in the personal lives of those rendering them care.

Physical contact in the form of a comforting touch or an arm around the shoulder when mutual congratulations relative to success are indicated can be very helpful. It is important for cancer patients to realize that they are not untouchables and that the therapist always has enough time for them to voice their concerns. For further discussion of the role of touch in hypnotherapy, the reader is referred to the author's recent paper in the *American Journal of Clinical Hypnosis* (Levitan and Johnson, 1986).

A combination of the above techniques can often be highly successful in contributing to long-term survival. An example is the case of Dorothy C., a 54-year-old female with metastatic inflammatory breast cancer. The patient initially presented with extensive edema of her breast and arm secondary to her infiltrating carcinoma. At the time of the development of her cancer, she was involved in significant marital conflict as a result of her husband's chronic low back syndrome, which had proven unresponsive to five surgeries and multiple other attempted interactions, including treatment by pain clinics for drug habituation.

It may be theorized that Dorothy C. developed her cancer in order to obtain appropriate family attention for herself. Indeed the status of her marriage improved significantly as a consequence of an increased attentiveness on the part of her husband and family.

When first discovered by the patient, the cancer was ignored until it had progressed to the point where the disease could only be palliated. When she was first seen, her oncologist anticipated a survival of no more than one year. The patient dutifully accepted all therapeutic recommendations including the use of both radiotherapy and chemotherapy. The patient would show up for each treatment with her husband, and they both experienced the side effects which resulted.

Dorothy C. sought hypnotherapy after having read *Getting Well Again* (Simonton OC et al., 1978) on the recommendation of a friend. She proved to be an enthusiastic hypnotic subject and eagerly sought additional information as it related to the field of imagery and self-healing. She was an active participant in a group designed to provide hypnotherapy for cancer patients and families and eventually took leadership of the group. She arranged to have the group meet at her house or local restaurants rather than at the hypnotherapist's office adjacent to the hospital where the patients received their chemotherapy. All members of the group agreed that such a setting was far more pleasant than the therapist's office.

A variety of self-education aids were made available to the group by the author. Included among these were *Managing the Stress of Cancer: A Handbook for Patients and Their Friends and Families* by Ronna Jevne and Karen Kebarle, developed by the Cross Cancer Institute in Edmonton, Alberta, for use with their patients, and *Saying "No"* (Jevne, 1976), a manual designed to teach patients how to say "no" to inappropriate requests and expectations without feeling guilty. In addition, Dorothy C. obtained a variety of audio tapes, from which she selected the best to present to the group. Among these were tapes of presentations by Bernard Siegal, M.D. (1983), Gerald Jampolsky, M.D. (1983), and Lawrence LeShan, Ph.D. (1984). Books found useful and recommended to the group included *We the Victors: Inspiring Stories of People Who Conquered Cancer and How They Did It* by Curtis Bill Pepper (1984) and *The Cancer Survivors—And How They Did It* by Judith Glassman (1983).

Touching and hugging was especially important to both Dorothy C. and other members of the group. Each session included an imagery session designed to enable the participants to reduce stress and visualize their own self-healing. Imagery drawings were made by the group individuals and shared for mutual discussion and evaluation. Dorothy C.'s drawings initially showed her as incomplete, tentative and not in touch with her surroundings. Through the group interaction process, her drawings and those of her fellow patients became more positive and assertive.

As the various members of the group succumbed to their disease, Dorothy C. and the remaining members participated in the grieving process with the bereaved families. By so doing, they were also grieving for their own potential deaths. Many of the group members survived significantly longer than might be expected on the basis of the status of their disease at the time of their initially joining the group. All patients experienced a greater degree of comfort with their disease and its therapy.

All the original members of the group are dead except Dorothy C. Her disease remains under control, and she continues to counsel fellow cancer patients and their relatives, usually by telephone. Dorothy C. does not regard the deaths of the patients in her group as a failure, but rather deems the unexpected duration and quality of their survival a success. At present, Dorothy C. has lived for two years after the diagnosis of her widespread inflammatory breast cancer.

The role of the hypnotherapist in dealing with patients like Dorothy C. is like that of teaching someone to ride a bicycle and then allowing him or her to take it at will. The hypnotherapist provides a sturdy bicycle, appropriate maps of the terrain, and is available in the event that unexpected problems, breakdowns, or the need for repairs arise. Many patients can go unexpectedly long distances utilizing their newly-acquired vehicle skills.

Important Current Research

Exciting innovations that bear on hypnotherapy for cancer patients are being developed through the burgeoning field of psychoneuroimmunology. This discipline, which seeks to define the role of the mind in influencing the immune system, is based in part on the pioneering work of Robert Ader (1975). Dr. Ader, a psychologist working in the Behavioral Medicine Department of the University of Rochester School of Medicine and Dentistry, was interested in studying aversive conditioning in rats.

The rats were offered drinking water sweetened with saccharin, which was paired with an intraperitoneal injection of cyclophosphamide (CTX, trade name Cytoxan) as the aversive conditioning. The intraabdominal injection of CTX was painful, and the rats quickly learned to avoid drinking the saccharinated water lest they experience severe abdominal pain. Extinction experiments were then performed, during which the rats were offered saccharinated water but were not simultaneously given intraabdominal injections of CTX, in order to determine how much time need elapse before the animals would again begin to drink the sweetened water. During the extinction experiments, there was an increased mortality in these rats as contrasted to the control population after both groups of rats were given only saccharinated water to drink. The hypothesis was that these rats were experiencing a learned suppression of their immune system and thus were rendered more vulnerable to latent pathogens in their environment. This hypothesis was advanced since CTX is an agent commonly used in chemotherapy to reduce or destroy circulating lymphocytes and other antibody-forming cells. When the hypothesis was tested by the administration of an agent that normally works an appreciable immune response in all rats, the CTX-saccharin trained rats demonstrated a reduced immune response when only saccharin, and no CTX, was administered. Dr. Ader reasoned that conditioning of the animals' immune response had occurred.

In a subsequent study designed to determine whether the above discovery had any therapeutic application, the utilization of conditioned immunosuppression in an animal model involving systemic lupus erythematosus (SLE) was demonstrated (Ader, 1982). New Zealand mice spontaneously developed SLE, the onset of which can be delayed by the administration of CTX. It was demonstrated that animals trained via the saccharin-CTX model and given only one-half of the customary therapeutic dose of CTX have the same survival as control animals given the full therapeutic dose.

If a similar accomplishment could be achieved in humans, it would be theoretically possible to treat cancer with only one-half of the currently administered doses of chemotherapy, thereby dramatically reducing the incidence of side effects. Alternatively, it might also be possible to achieve twice the therapeutic effect of currently-administered standard doses.

Just as it has been possible to demonstrate a conditioned suppression of the immune response, other animal studies have demonstrated the capacity to condition an increased immune response. Skin grafting studies in nonidentical strains of rats have demonstrated an augmentation of the immune response as a consequence of the rats' pairing the administration of an anesthetic with the receipt of a nonidentical skin graft, which was eventually rejected. Administration of the anesthetic alone to conditioned rats resulted in an increase in antibodies and white count similar to that seen during the rejection of a foreign skin graft (Ader, 1975).

This same principle if applied to humans would permit the development of a conditioned antibody response which might be of material benefit in combating an existing cancer. A variety of research studies are underway aimed at a determination of how hypnosis can interface with the above objective. The author believes that there may be some dramatic breakthroughs in the near future.

Excerpt of Therapy Session with Margarget M.

Verbalization	Comments
Therapist: Suppose you tell me a little bit about the problems you are having with the chemotherapy and what has happened since you have learned hypnosis. When you were having the chemotherapy, what problems did you run into?	
Margaret M.: I was nauseated even a day before I knew I was coming for my treatment. I would get sick.	Anticipatory emesis is very amenable to hypnotherapy (Redd, 1982).
Therapist: Why do you suppose that was?	
Margaret M.: I really can't say.	
Therapist: Did you try to talk yourself out of it, saying that there was no reason to be nauseated or anything of the kind?	
Margaret M.: No!	Patients expect nausea to be an inherent part of treatment.
Therapist: So you would become nauseated. Did you actually vomit on occasion on the days before?	
Margaret M.: No! I just felt an upset stomach, that's all.	Increasing anxiety approaching panic prior to chemotherapy.

Therapist: You must, therefore have really looked forward to coming into the hospital!

Margaret M.: I felt like running in the other direction.

Therapist: Did you become very nervous? Was it very stressful to you to come to the hospital?

Margaret M.: Yes. The day before I just couldn't sit still.

Therapist: What led to this? What was the cause for this? Would the drugs as they were administered to you cause the nausea? Would the vomiting occur later? What happened?

Margaret M.: Right after I got through with the injections or whatever they are called.

Therapist: You would vomit almost immediately after receiving the drug?

Margaret M.: I would have to go into the bathroom and vomit.

Aversion conditioning in classive Pavlovian fashion. This is often reinforced by the mistaken impression nausea must ensue or the chemotherapeutic agents are not working.

Therapist: Then what would happen over the next period of time?

Margaret M.: In the car on the way home I would be sick. One day I vomited all over myself.

Destruction of a sense of self-worth. Humiliation.

Therapist: In the car?

Lack of control.

Margaret M.: Yes.

Therapist: And then what would happen after that. When would the vomiting stop? How long would it go on?

Margaret M.: All day up until 11:00 at night.

Therapist: Even though you had taken nausea medication and tried a variety of medication? Did anything prove effective at all? Any of the anti-nausea medications?

Margaret M.: No.

Therapist: All right, Margaret. Tell us what has happened since the last time we met when you learned a little about hypnosis.

Margaret M.: I felt a lot more comfortable this last time and I didn't have that sick feeling in my stomach.

Return of a sense of control.

Therapist: OK, even before coming, you mean.

Margaret M.: Yes.

Therapist: After you received the chemotherapy, did you become nauseated or not? Did you vomit at all after therapy?

Margaret M.: Oh, yes.

Therapist: You did vomit. Was that any better than it had been previously or was it about the same?

Margaret M.: It was better. I wasn't going to turn inside out. It wasn't that way.

Therapist: Fair enough. And have you practiced the relaxation that I taught you?

Patients should be encouraged to practice relaxation frequently, even if only for a moment.

Margaret M.: Once this morning already.

Therapist: On the average, how many times each day do you practice?

Margaret M.: Yesterday, twice.

Therapist: I think the more times you practice, the better. Perhaps you could practice relaxing whenever the hour on the clock changes. Just let a lovely wave of relaxation descend over your body. Give yourself your own personal signal . . . perhaps taking an extra deep breath and then letting everything go. . . perhaps by putting your thumb and index finger on the same hand together to make an O.K. sign. Each time you do this it will be as if a magic switch has closed and a sudden rush of relaxation will enter your body. You can do this whenever you wish, with your eyes open or closed. No one else need know what you are doing. It can be your secret. By doing this every waking hour, you are putting another coin in a parking meter, you might say, and obtaining another several hours of comfort and peace.

As a point of information, we only spent 20 minutes together that one time. So I think that you will become even more successful. Things will get even better for you. When you do relax, what do you like to think about?

Margaret M.: Oh, pleasant places!

Therapist: Such as?

Margaret M.: Sunshine!

Therapist: All right, that's fine. Let's take a moment and work on that now. Why don't you get yourself good and comfortable in the chair? It is a nice comfortable chair, as you know. And why don't you let your eyes close and let yourself relax? Let yourself relax totally, completely, deeply, quickly, soundly relaxed. That's fine. It's nice to be able to be at peace. That's good! Let yourself relax totally. It's nice to be able to just let go and find the place that you like to think about. The place with the lovely sunshine. Notice the lovely colors, the greens and the blues. . .the sky and the clouds and the movements of the trees in the breeze. Perhaps even the water and the waves. Smell the smells, the flowers, the fresh salt air. . .the colors so deep. . .even the tastes, all of those things making *you* relaxed, helping you to feel ever so much more comfortable. That's good. Just notice

Inducing a positive expectancy.

Involve all sense in the visualization: color, movement, smell, taste, hearing, touch.

the colors, the movements, the sounds, the smells, the tastes. And while you are relaxing, it is nice to know that *you* are in control, that *you* are in charge, and that *you* have accomplished what you have. *You* will become even more successful knowing that from now on you can be at peace and not concerned. Knowing that if it is comfortable to do so, you can just put the previous treatments to the back of your mind and pull the shades. Any previous experiences can be allowed to go to the back of your mind where you do not have to worry about them, not have to remember them. Just be at peace, knowing that the treatment you are to receive is to help you recover your health, to help you return to work, to help you feel good in every way. It is you that are doing these things for yourself. You're in control. You're in charge. And your success will make you even more successful at all the other things you choose to do. You will be more self-confident, more self-reliant, more self-assured. All of these good things will come to you.

In a similar fashion, if ever anyone says anything negative to you about hypnosis or if ever you have any self-doubts, it will have no effect. It will be as if a foreign language was spoken, one that you don't understand. Those negative thoughts and comments will have no effect. If anything, they will intensify your desire to succeed. They will prove to you that you can win. You can be a winner! Know now within the deepest part of your being that you will win!

And I want you to take a moment to see the drugs helping you. You know that we are all here working together for your benefit. You're on the team, too. You are a member of our group. Feel the medicines going into your system. See them searching out any remaining cancer cells that might be anywhere in the body, anywhere in your abdomen. See them attacking those cells and destroying them. See the cancer cells dying. See the battle raging as one

Returning focus of control to the patient.

Suggestion for amnesia of previous negative experiences. This avoids anticipatory dread of the next chemotherapy session.

The patient is part of the team working to return him or her to good health.

Ego support. Patient can never get enough of this!

Reframing negative comments to the benefit of the patient.

blow is delivered from one drug, then another blow from the other drug. Knocking out the cancer cells, destroying them totally. Then see your own defense mechanisms, your own white cells, your own antibodies going in there administering the final blows, cleaning up the breakdown products, the trash, the residue. See it being taken up by the blood stream and excreted from your body, expelled from your body in your urine and your stool. See the inside of your abdomen, healthy, clean, free of any hints of cancer cells. All of this is within your power. All of this you can do for yourself. It is a good feeling to be in control. It's nice to be in charge. It's nice to be the captain of the ship.

Holistic imagery.

Now, while you are relaxing and enjoying the peaceful place you have chosen, I want you also to know that you can control the other feelings you have. Just as you have learned to turn the pain switch off to your hand so that you need not have any discomfort when the IV is set, you can turn off the switch that controls any unpleasant feelings in your stomach. Any hint of nausea can be turned off. Find the switch on the switchboard which controls that and turn that switch off. Let the light go out over the switch, let that feeling extinguish itself. Some people even like to think about a house, a house with all the rooms lighted. Find the room in the house that controls the stomach, and turn the light off. Let that feeling leave you totally and completely. Replace it instead with a comfortable, peaceful, pleasant feeling. Almost as if that part of the body didn't belong to you any longer. Almost as if you didn't even have to think about it. That's good. Enjoy that feeling and keep it there as long as you want. Know that it is available for you whenever you wish. You are in control, you can turn that switch off anytime you wish, and you can set the timer to leave it off as long as you like.

Isolation and dissociation from negative feelings.

And if there ever should be any little hint of discomfort, any little hint that something isn't quite right, all you have to do is take in a deep breath, let yourself relax and it will disappear. It will be replaced with the same feeling of peace and contentment you have now. And now, why don't you decide which hand you would like to numb up and when you have fully numbed it up, that's fine, just let it become heavy, free of discomfort, free of painful sensations. Let the veins in the back of the hand dilate up. Let them become like swollen, full rivers. Let the needle go in properly into the vein when the IV is set. Let the vein and the skin wrap themselves tightly around the needle so that there will be no chance of any leakage, there will be no black and blue marks, no bleeding and certainly no discomfort. That's fine. Just let that happen. OK. And when you're ready, let us know by raising the finger and we will set the IV.

Anchoring patient to good feelings. Providing an instant source of comfort whenever it is required.

No need to confine suggestions to anatomically or physiologically known functions. The mind has influence far beyond what we can accurately describe and explain. Glove anesthesia does not correlate with neuroanatomy, and neither need these suggestions.

References

Aaroz DL: Use of hypnotic techniques with oncology patients. J Psychosocial Oncology 1(4):47-54, 1983

Achterberg J, Lawlis GF: Imagery of Disease: An Evaluation Tool for Behavioral Medicine. Institute for Personality and Ability Testing, Inc., P.O. Box 188, Champaign, IL 61820, 1976

Ader R, Cohen N: Behaviorally conditioned immunosuppression. Psychosom Med 37(4):333-340, 1975

Ader R, Cohen N: Behaviorally conditioned immunosupression and murine systemic lupus erythematosus. Psychosom Med 44:127-128, 1982

Ament P: Concepts in the use of hypnosis for pain relief in cancer. J Medicine 13(3):233-240, 1982

Bahnson CB: Stress and cancer: The state of the art, part I. Psychosomatics 21(12):975-981, 1980

Bahnson CB: Stress and cancer: The state of the art, part II. Psychosomatics 22(13):207-220, 1981

Cassileth BR, Lush EJ, Miller DS, Brown LL, Miller C: Psychosocial correlates of survival in advanced malignant disease? NEJM 312(24):1551-1555, 1985

Finer B: Hypnotherapy in pain of advanced cancer. In Bonica JJ, Ventafridda V (eds): Advances in Pain Research and Therapy. New York, Raven Press, 1979

Finkelstein S, Greenleaf-Howard M: Cancer prevention—a three year pilot study. Am J Clin Hypn 25(2-3):177-183, 1982

Fotopoulos SS, Teel LS, Botts PJ, Knapp TM: Psychophysiological aspects of cancer anorexia. Presented at annual meeting Am. Coll of Nutrit. In Von Eys J, Seelig MS (eds): Nutrition and Cancer. New York, Medical and Scientific Books, 1979

Glassman J: The Cancer Survivors—And How They Did It. Garden City, NY, The Dial Press-Doubleday, 1983

Greene WA, Swisher SN: Psychological and somatic variables associated with the development and course of monozygotic twins discordant for leukemia. Ann NY Acad Sci 164:394-408, 1969

Haley J: Strategies in Psychotherapy. New York, Grune & Stratton, 1983

Jampolsky G: Coping with Illness Through Love. Audio Cassette, Effective Learning Systems, Inc., 5221 Edina Ind. Blvd., Edina, MN 55435, 1983

Jevne R, Kebarle K: Managing the Stress of Cancer: A Handbook for Patients and Their Friends and Families. Edmonton, Alberta, Cross Cancer Institute, 1984

Jevne R: Saying "No." Alberta Rural Development Studies Series D: For People Power . . . .Edmonton, Alberta, Rural Education and Development Association, 1976

Kellerman J, Zeltzer L, Ellenberg L, Dash J: Hypnosis for the reduction of the acute pain and anxiety associated with medical procedures. J Adoles Health Care 4(2):85-90, 1983

Kiecolt-Glaser JK, Garner W, Speicher C, Penn GM, Holliday J, Glaser R: Psychosocial modifiers of immuno-competence in medical students. Psychosomatic Med 46(1):7-14, 1984

Kowal SJ: Emotions as a cause of cancer: Eighteenth and nineteenth century contributions. Psychoanal Rev 42:217-227, 1955

LeShan L: Meditation and Psychic Healing. Audio Cassette, Effective Learning Systems, Inc., 5221 Edina Ind. Blvd., Edina, MN 55435, 1984

Levitan AA: Hypnotic death rehearsal. Am J Clin Hypn 27(4):211-215, 1985

Levitan AA, Johnson J: The role of touch in hypnotherapy. Am J CLin Hypn 28(4):218-223, 1986

Locke SE: Stress, adaptation and immunity: Studies in humans. General Hospital Psychiatry 4:49-58, 1982

Matje SD: Stress and cancer: A review of the literature. Cancer Nursing 7(5):399-404, 1984

Meerlo JA, Psychological implications of cancer. Geriatrics 9:154-156, 1954

Morrow GR, Morrell C: Behavioral treatment for the anticipatory nausea and vomiting induced by cancer chemotherapy. NEJM 307(24):1476-1480, 1982

Neuman C: Psychische besonderheiten bei krebs patienten. Z Psychosom Med 5:91-101, 1959

Newton BW: The use of hypnosis in the treatment of cancer patients. Am J Clin Hypn 25(2):104-113, 1982

Olness K: Imagery (self-hypnosis) as adjunct therapy in childhood cancer. Am J Ped Hem/Onc 1(3):313-321, 1981

Pepper CB: We The Victors: Inspiring Stories of People Who Conquered Cancer and How They Did It. Garden City, NY, Doubleday, 1984

Redd Wh, Andersen GV, Minagawa RY: Hypnotic control of anticipatory emesis in patients receiving cancer chemotherapy. J Consult Clin Psych 50(1):14-19, 1982

Riley V: Mouse mammary tumors: Alteration of incidence as apparent function of stress. Science 189:465-467, 1975

Rubin P, Bakemeier RF, Krackov S: Clinical Oncology for Medical Students and Physicians: A Multidisciplinary Approach. American Cancer Society, 1983

Schleifer SJ, Keller SE, Camerino M, Thornton JC, Stein M: Suppression of lymphocyte stimulation following bereavement. JAMA 250:374-377, 1984

Schmale AH, Iker HP: The affect of hopelessness in the development of cancer. Part I: The prediction of uterine cervical cancer in women with atypical cytology. Psychosom Med 28:714-721, 1966

Siegal BS: Love, Medicine and Miracles. Audio Cassette, Effective Learning Systems, Inc., 5221 Edina Ind. Blvd., Edina, MN 55435, 1983

Simonton OC, Matthews-Simonton S, Creighton J: Getting Well Again. Los Angeles, JP Tarcher, 1978

Simonton OC, Matthews-Simonton S, Sparks TF: Psychosomatics 21(3):226-233, 1980

Simonton OC: Unproven methods of cancer management. Ca—A Cancer J for Clinicians 32(1):58-61, 1982

Solomon GF, Amkraut AA: Psychoneuroendocrinological effects on the immune response. Ann Rev Microbiol 35:155-185, 1981

Spiegel D, Bloom JR: Group therapy and hypnosis reduce metastatic breast carcinoma pina. Psychosomatic Med 45(4):333-339, 1983

Zeltzer L, LeBaron S, Zeltzer PM: The effectiveness of behavioral intervention for reduction of nausea and vomiting in children and adolescents receiving chemotherapy. J Clin Onc 2(6):683-690, 1984

Zeltzer L, LeBaron S: Hypnosis and nonhypnotic techniques for reduction of pain and anxiety during painful procedures in children and adolescents with cancer. J Pediatrics 101(6):1032-1035, 1982

24 HYPNOTHERAPY IN BULIMIA

ARUNA THAKUR, M.B.
KRIPA THAKUR, M.B.

In the last decade, the incidence of the eating disorders anorexia and bulimia has increased to nearly epidemic proportions. Most health professionals are involved in dealing with these disorders. The treatment of the bulimic "eating and purging" syndrome is as difficult if not more difficult than that of anorexia. Hypnotherapy has proved successful both as an adjunct to the treatment of bulimia and as the main treatment modality.

The clinical features of the disorder called bulimia are delineated in DSM III:

Table II. Diagnostic criteria for bulimia (DSM III)

A	Recurrent episodes of binge-eating (rapid consumption of a large amount of food in a discrete period of time, usually less than 2h)
B	At least three of the following
	(l) Consumption of high-caloric, easily ingested food during a binge
	(2) Inconspicuous eating during a binge
	(3) Termination of such eating episodes by abdominal pain, sleep, social interruption, or self-induced vomiting
	(4) Repeated attempts to lose weight by severely restrictive diets, self-induced vomiting, or use of cathartics or diuretics
	(5) Frequent weight fluctuations greater than l0 lb (4.5 kg) due to altering binges and fasts
C	Awareness that the eating pattern is abnormal and fear of not being able to stop eating voluntarily
D	Depressed mood and self-depreciating thoughts following eating binges
E	The bulimic episodes are not due to anorexia nervosa or any known physical disorder

Bulimia, a complex condition with a multi-factorial origin, can be only a symptom of behavior which is the tip of the iceberg of some gross psychopathology. It is also a culture-bound symptom, as it seems to be developing at an increasing rate in affluent countries.

Some bulimics share common elements with smokers, alcoholics, chemical addicts, and obese people. Others have various concurrent emotional and characterological problems, such as anxiety, depression, phobias, impulsiveness, rejection, sensitivity, anger towards authority, which may result in petty criminal behavior, prostitution, and family problems. Thus, a custom-made approach to the treatment of patients with bulimia must be considered, one recognizing the fact that individual patients are unique.

Review of published literature indicates that various treatment modalities have been tried to achieve the above goal. The following are popular approaches: psychodynamic psychotherapy, family therapy, cognitive psychotherapy, classical behavioral psychotherapies, group psychotherapy, combined group and individual treatment, and pharmacotherapy. There is evidence of some success with all these methods.

The Use of Hypnosis

The use of hypnosis in the treatment of bulimia, however, has not been reported. As of 1984, the Medline Research Library did not list any publications on the use of hypnotherapy for bulimia. This chapter discusses the various therapeutic approaches that have been tried under the non-traditional methods of hypnotherapy, such as self-hypnosis, autogenic training, biofeedback techniques, hypnosis, and hypnoanalysis.

Because hypnotherapy is non-traditional, we see bulimic patients in a relatively advanced condition with various complications. Bulimics are referred for hypnotherapy when other forms of treatment have failed or when progress has been unsatisfactory.

In the last 10 years, we have treated 300 cases of bulimia and bulimarexia. Almost all these patients chose us to treat them with hypnotherapy. Prior to arriving at our clinic (Thakur Clinic), most patients had been briefed by a general practitioner, ex-patients, relatives, or self-help groups and were encouraged to attend our clinic.

The patients who presented themselves for treatment of bulimia were almost exclusively women in their mid-twenties or early thirties. They had often developed the illness in their late teens.

All patients required physical and dental checkups, including ECG's and electrolyte assessment. Those who indulged in purgative abuse were asked to have a sigmoidoscopy done. In addition, they filled out an Anorexia Nervosa and Bulimia

Self-Report Questionnaire, EAT, EDI, Zung depression rating scale, and Eysenck Personality Inventory.

Seriously ill patients, such as those with suicide risk, electrolyte imbalance, colonic complications and kidney complications, were hospitalized in the general psychiatric ward. These patients were thoroughly assessed by medical internists and were seen every day for one or two-hour sessions in order to balance the physiological functioning and to break through their resistance, increase their motivation, and make them more aware of the use of hypnotherapy.

Patients treated only as out-patients were seen once or twice a week for a half hour or a one-hour session. These sessions were recorded on a cassette tape, and patients were encouraged to listen to the session at home at least once or twice a day. They were also asked to keep a diary and communicate with us either through writing or calling the clinic.

Unstructured group therapy at various levels between acutely ill patients and recovering patients was encouraged. Periodically, the family was seen, alone or with the patient, mainly as a supportive tool, not as formal family therapy.

Four to six months of intensive treatment was carried out for both out-patients and patients who had originally been seen in the hospital. They were subsequently followed up at one or two-month intervals for at least two years.

Long-standing cases, having had the illness for more than four years, took longer to respond. There was overall improvement in bulimic symptoms in 85 percent of the cases in four to six months. Binge eating and vomiting, however, were brought under control in four to six weeks of treatment. Binge eating with laxative combination took about nine to 12 months. Bulimics with exercise compulsion were somewhat difficult to manage. During the treatment, a few cases relapsed temporarily for one to two weeks once or twice a year.

Fifteen percent of the cases did not improve satisfactorily. They had greater emotional dependence on the therapist or other professionals who tried to help them, or they could not take the responsibility of growing up; or they did not attend our clinic regularly and did not follow the recommendations.

The few male patients responded just as well as female patients to hypnotherapeutic interventions.

Hypnosis is an art of interpersonal relationships. It is a communication of ideas in such a manner as to encourage patients to explore their potential for modifying psychophysiological responses and behavior. Hypnotherapy is not an entity unto itself, but a psychotherapy applied in an altered state of awareness.

Steps in Treatment with Hypnosis

In the beginning, the patient is educated about hypnosis. Misconceptions are removed, both initially and throughout the treatment if they are causing resistance. The patient is reassured that it is safe to learn and to use hypnosis.

Since the patient is already apprehensive about losing control on the bulimic symptoms, due to misconceptions and ignorance about hypnosis it is common for a patient to resist hypnosis. The patient feels she will lose further control of herself, that the therapist will be controlling her. She is reassured that she will not do anything which she would not like to do. The paradox is that the patient wants the therapist to control her bulimia, but does not want the therapist to control her in hypnosis.

The new patient receives a demonstration of induction techniques on a patient who is already in therapy. Thus, the new patient is reassured that hypnosis is a safe procedure to learn and use on herself. All patients are taught various ego-strengthening techniques to reduce their anxiety and to enhance their confidence.

Most cases are taught autogenic training and self-hypnosis techniques while being closely monitored on various biofeedback equipment, such as GSR biofeedback, thermal biofeedback, pulse watch, and EMG biofeedback. The most common techniques that these patients learn are hand warming, warmth of solar plexus, forehead cooling, and several breathing exercises.

Once the patient has learned self-hypnosis and autogenic training techniques, the patient is taught to experience various hypnotic phenomenon, such as hypnotic analgesia and anesthesia, temperature alteration, amnesia, catalepsy, ideomotor and ideosensory activities, dissociation, time distortion, automatic writing, relaxation, age regression, and age progression.

When the patient is ready and feels confidence in applying various induction techniques, the patient is further taught to relax the abdominal muscles (rectus abdominus) and to relax intercostal muscles and breathe out through the epigastrium.

Guided Imagery Techniques

Various guided imagery techniques are taught to enhance the normal physiology of the swallowing reflex.

Some examples of guided imagery technique are as follows: coolness in the throat; imagining a waterfall, that the food goes in only one direction, from the mouth to the stomach; peristalsis in the esophagus goes downwards only; passive breathing is encouraged by imagining that the chest is being expanded and contracted by someone else. Similar imageries are used to increase the mass peristalsis to open the bowel without using any laxatives and enemas.

Depending upon the frequency of vomiting, the patient is given the suggestion to vomit at a certain time and on certain days of the week. In a typical case, the patient is asked to binge eat and vomit between 5 p.m. and 7 p.m. on Wednesday and Sundays. After initial skepticism and hesitation, patients often accept this contract.

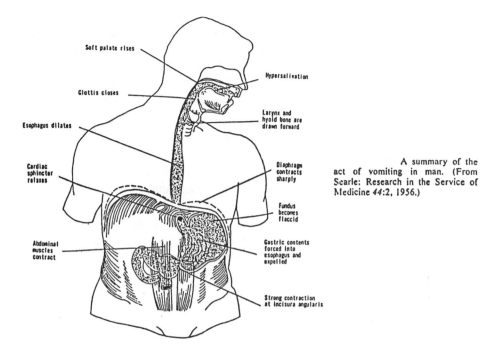

Soft palate rises

Hypersalivation

Glottis closes

Larynx and hyoid bone are drawn forward

Esophagus dilates

Cardiac sphincter relaxes

Diaphragm contracts sharply

A summary of the act of vomiting in man. (From Searle: Research in the Service of Medicine 44:2, 1956.)

Fundus becomes flaccid

Abdominal muscles contract

Gastric contents forced into esophagus and expelled

Strong contraction at incisura angularis

Figure 24-1. Vomiting

Now, at least in theory, the patient has some control over vomiting. Instead of vomiting occurring at any time, it is now restricted to certain time periods. If the patient cannot vomit, she is unlikely to binge. As there is reduction in the number of binges and vomits, she starts losing weight.

This is a turning point in the treatment of bulimia. Now, the patient has more confidence in the therapy. Her anxiety is reduced as her weight comes under control. Electrolytes are soon restored. As the patient spends less time with bulimic rituals and body chemistry returns to normal, psychological changes take place. The patient's mood becomes more stable, depressive moods occur less often, self-worth improves, and the patient starts socializing with more confidence and looks forward to economic independence.

The patient is repeatedly told that bulimia was a faulty adaptation to allay anxiety and insecurity. By permitting the patient to practice bulimia in a structured manner, the therapist offers the patient insight as to how ridiculous and useless it is to vomit according to a plan or contract. As she can vomit, she is now not afraid of gaining an enormous amount of weight. She also realizes that vomiting by itself does not reduce weight. As she is not binge eating in the first place, there is no need to vomit afterwards.

The patient's weight, binge eating, vomiting, electrolyte imbalance, depression, social isolation, and poor finances all seem to be interrelated in a vicious circle. Hypnobehavioral methods can successfully alter the reactions in this circle. The patient has more options to act upon, and finally she gains mastery over her pernicious compulsion of bulimia.

With guided imagery techniques, the patient is asked to visualize binging alternating with vomiting for at least five to ten minutes per day. This procedure eventually produces strong aversion in the patient. In severe cases, more drastic measures have been suggested to patients in order to develop in them deep disgust; such measures include storing vomit in their bathrooms or living rooms, carrying a small bottle of vomit in their purses, keeping a vomit bowl on the dinner table, or listening to prerecorded vomiting and toilet flushing sounds.

We have borrowed a concept from R. D. Lang's book *The Knots*. According to this concept, a bulimic patient reasons that she binge eats, therefore she vomits; she vomits because she binge eats. She is advised to alter her position and reason that she cannot vomit, therefore she cannot binge eat; she cannot binge eat because she cannot vomit. This concept is illustrated with the two circle diagrams.

The patient is afraid of gaining more weight if she does stop vomiting. She forgets that when she is not vomiting her eating is also under control. Actually, she loses some weight when she controls her vomiting. She develops more confidence in herself and the therapeutic maneuvers.

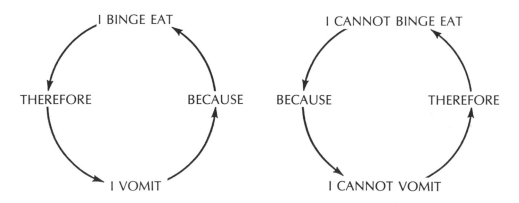

Dynamic Interpretation

Without dynamic interpretation, therapy remains incomplete. Sometimes a traumatic event is the source of a bulimic pattern. Early trauma not discussed during regular sessions might be revealed during the hypnotic age regression. Recognition of such a childhood event and working through the abreacted feelings may lead to successful resolution of bulimia. Once the resolution has taken place, then the patient is

Picture drawn by former client regarding her distorted body image.

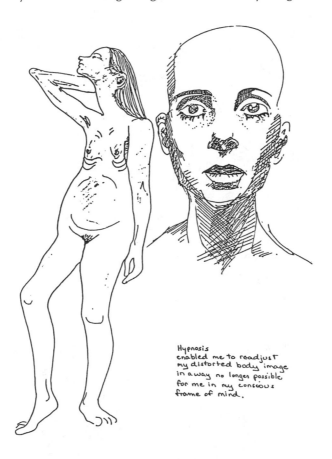

Hypnosis enabled me to readjust my distorted body image in a way no longer possible for me in my conscious frame of mind.

allowed to rewrite her script in age progression techniques under hypnosis, identifying some of their future goals along with building up her ego-strength.

The suggestions given were: "Now, I want you to consider that your life is written in a book. The pages of the book you can turn forward and backward. This book is not yet complete. There are plenty of blank pages left for the future. Imagine you are turing the pages backward, and whenever you find a significant event you can stop and tell me what is written on that page. If the event is too painful to deal with, you can always turn the pages further back or close the book temporarily. Now that we have gone through the past, dealt with various emotional events, and learned from the experience about how to cope with life, we can move forward. Imagine what the future would be like—I mean what will be written on the blank pages. See if you can identify yourself living a successful and fulfilling life. See if you are actualizing yourself—reaching higher purpose and meaning in your life."

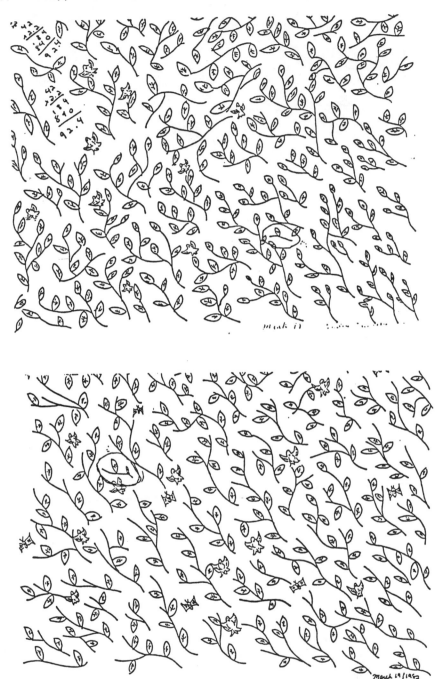

Figure 24-2. *(Top)* These are leaves, and I am somewhere here (circled) and *(Bottom)* 1 week after therapy, same picture, this time, however, she draws herself as a bud (circled)

Under hypnosis I felt an unknown freedom as if all that
existed were the voice that spoke to me and my
own being who listened.
What it did was calm me down enough so that
I was receptive to positive suggestions.
Only then was I able to allow myself to gain
enough weight to get myself out of physical
danger.

Fig. 24-3. Patient gaining self-confidence to allow change to occur

Some of our patients described having distorted body image. To realize this distortion, under hypnosis the patient is given the suggestion that she will draw pictures of herself the way she sees herself. Sometimes she is asked to stand in front of the mirror and describe how she visualizes herself.

The patient is given suggestions to make her perceptions more sensitive. All of her senses—touch, pain, temperature, vibrations, position of the body, limbs, and head, body movements, sight, and sound—are utilized to heighten the awareness about the self.

I was able to look honestly at myself.

Fig. 24-4. Patient gaining insight

Indirectly the patient is given messages that she can perceive the correct size, shape, and weight of other objects. Without a confrontation, she is told that the distortion in her body image is satisfying some need in her. As she feels totally helpless in controlling her world, she instead controls her body. Distorted perception of her body further justifies her acts of bulimia to correct the distortion which does not really exist.

Suggestions are also given to the patient to draw, write, and make clay models. Then interpretations are given to increase her awareness.

Sometimes an investigative technique like automatic writing has been useful. The suggestion is given, "Let your right hand write the traumatic event while you enjoy the tranquility and relaxation of hypnosis."

If the patient's weight is low, even though not meeting the formal criteria for anorexia nervosa, dietary caloric content should be adjusted to bring weight into the goal range. The opposite is also true—weight may need to be lowered if the patient is truly overweight.

Fig. 24-5. Patient recognizes the smothering love of her mother

The key concept is for the patient to begin eating for the acceptable maintenance range with well-balanced meals. Regular meal intake often reduces the possibility of binging. In initial therapy, potassium, Vitamins B6 and Bl, and zinc are given to the patients. Almost all patients are advised to see a nutritionist.

Out-patients are required to weigh themselves regularly throughout their therapy. They are also advised to contact a self-help group called The Anorexia Nervosa and Bulimia Foundation of Saskatchewan, Inc.

All these patients voluntarily tried hypnotherapy over other treatment modalities. That fact itself indicates their motivation to try hypnosis. Our case studies show an overall success rate of 85 percent.

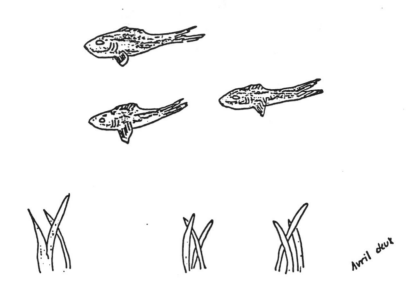

Fig. 24-6. Patient demonstrates the sibling rivalry—she draws herself as the last fish

Certain selected cases seem to fare better with hypnotherapy in conjunction with other behavior modification and psychodynamic methods. But it is our experience that hypnosis can be used not only as an adjunct to treatment but also as the main treatment modality for bulimia. For the treatment of bulimia, hypnosis certainly should be considered as an alternate therapy.

References

Erickson MH: Control of physiological functions by hypnosis. Am J Clin Hypn 20(1):8-19, 1977

Freytag F: The Body Image in Gender Orientation Disturbances. New York, Vantage Press, 1977

Garfinkel PE, Garner DM, Kennedy S: Special problems of inpatient management. In Garner DM, Garfinkel PE(eds): Handbook of Psychotherapy for Anorexia Nervosa and Bulimia. New York, The Guilford Press, 1985

Gross M: Correcting perceptual abnormalities, anorexia nervosa and obesity by use of hypnosis. J Am Soc Psychosomatic Dentistry and Medicine 30(4):142-150

Gross M: Hypnosis in the therapy of anorexia nervosa. Am J Clin Hypn 26(3):175-181, 1984

Fig. 24-7. Patient removes the "mask" of bulimia

Jencks B: Your Body: Biofeedback at its Best. Chicago, Nelson Hall, 1977
Menninger K: Man Against Himself. New York, Harcourt, Brace & World, Inc., 1938
Schultz JH, Luthe W: Autogenic Training. New York, Grune & Stratton, 1959
Thakur KS: Hypnotherapy for anorexia nervosa and accompanying somatic disorders. In Wester WC, Smith AH (eds): Clinical Hypnosis: A Multidisciplinary Approach. Philadelphia, JB Lippincott, 1984
Yager J: The treatment of bulimia: An overview. In Powers, Fernandez (eds): Current Treatment of Anorexia Nervosa and Bulimia. New York, Karger, 1984

BEFORE I GO

Please God..Don't let me go just yet..
Forgive me first..I pray!
  I've ended up in so much debt..
  With sin along the way!

I have not lived..only..for You..
But for the world..For me!
  Forgive me..Help me pay my due..
  Please hear my heart..My plea!

You bore the cross for all of sin!..
But oft' I didn't pray..
  Don't close the door..Please let me in!
  Please take my debt away!

Have mercy..Lord..left for me yet..
My heart..my soul..You know!
  Forgive me first..my sins in debt..
  Forgive..Before I go!!

Fig. 24-8. After writing this poem, a critically ill patient decides to get better

Index